Active
Alpha

Founded in 1807, John Wiley & Sons is the oldest independent publishing company in the United States. With offices in North America, Europe, Australia, and Asia, Wiley is globally committed to developing and marketing print and electronic products and services for our customers' professional and personal knowledge and understanding.

The Wiley Finance series contains books written specifically for finance and investment professionals as well as sophisticated individual investors and their financial advisors. Book topics range from portfolio management to e-commerce, risk management, financial engineering, valuation and financial instrument analysis, as well as much more.

For a list of available titles, visit our Web site at www.WileyFinance.com.

Active Alpha

A Portfolio Approach to Selecting and Managing Alternative Investments

ALAN H. DORSEY

John Wiley & Sons, Inc.

Published by John Wiley & Sons, Inc., Hoboken, New Jersey.
Published simultaneously in Canada.

Wiley Bicentennial logo: Richard J. Pacifico.

For general information on our other products and services or for technical support, please contact our Customer Care Department within the United States at (800) 762-2974, outside the United States at (317) 572-3993 or fax (317) 572-4002.

Wiley also publishes its books in a variety of electronic formats. Some content that appears in print may not be available in electronic books. For more information about Wiley products, visit our Web site at www.wiley.com.

Library of Congress Cataloging-in-Publication Data

Dorsey, Alan H.
Active alpha : a portfolio approach to selecting and managing alternative investments / Alan H. Dorsey.
   p. cm.
Includes bibliographical references and index.
ISBN-13 978-0-471-79132-4 (cloth)
1. Portfolio management. 2. Investments. 3. Factor analysis. I. Title.
HG4529.5.D675 2007
332.63—dc22

2007007058

Printed in the United States of America.

10   9   8   7   6   5   4   3   2   1

I dedicate this book to my wife, Missy, who is the center and warmth of my life; my daughter Ellie, who is the style and grace in my life; my daughter Emily, who is the inspiration and creativity in my life; and my youngest daughter Greta, who is the compassion and joy in my life.

Contents

PART ONE

Alternative Investments and Investors

Preface

This book was written to solve a dilemma for institutional and high-net-worth investors. How should an investor move beyond token allocations to alternative investments in an integrative fashion with traditional asset classes that is grounded in sound portfolio construction methodology? Once initial allocations have been made to hedge funds, private equity, real estate, and other types of alternative assets, a large number of investors find themselves at a loss as to how to proceed.

Many investors have added alternative investments to their portfolios in a haphazard fashion, because alternative investments are not well suited to traditional portfolio construction approaches. Investors frequently cap the use of alternative investments in their portfolios, but do so using artificial constraints. Establishing constraints is done for a combination of reasons that often are qualitative in nature, rather than derived from objective quantitative analysis. Although the return enhancement and diversification attributes of these investments are readily observable, all but the largest investors lack a legitimate quantitative process and organizational capacity to integrate them into vastly larger allocations that exist for traditional asset classes. The utilization of factor analysis can foster a more integrated approach to the use of alternative investments in conjunction with traditional asset classes. With the help of regressions, multiple betas can be identified across a diverse portfolio. Efficient portfolios can be considered in terms of optimizations of factors rather than asset classes, which often provide no definitional inclusion of many types of alternative investment strategies. Investors then are free to focus their attentions on the identification of managers who can generate unique sources of return, the evaluation of investments on an equal footing across numerous alternative investment types, the comparison and negotiation of terms and fees across investments, the creation of synthetic portfolios of passive benchmarks, and the isolation of alpha and its active component.

This book's introduction, contained in Chapter 1, states its thesis, which is that all alternative investments can be evaluated using factor analysis. This approach provides for a more efficient construction of portfolios and more readily identifies potential factor redundancies and deficiencies. It presents a quantitative road map for investors seeking a pathway to emulate the experience of successful endowments in using alternative investments.

A benefit from this methodology is enabling the greater use of alternative investments in portfolios that seek their benefits but may have a limited ability to increase allocations to them beyond placeholder amounts. Through this, multiple factor betas can be used in portfolio construction and alpha can be more precisely measured.

Chapter 2, "Investors in Alternative Investments and the Necessary Ingredients for a Successful Program," compares different types of investors and their use of alternative investments. High-net-worth investors, endowments, foundations, pension plans, and insurance companies each have different considerations when utilizing alternative investments. This chapter reviews the necessary ingredients for creating and managing a successful alternative investment program. This includes organizational management, strong governance, the proper setting and management of expectations, and division of duties among participants to the process. The role of portfolio management is described in its component features, including: adhering to an investment policy statement, maintaining diversification and a growth orientation, having fidelity to rebalancing the portfolio, being aware of most-favored-nation issues, and making careful moves when changing strategic target allocations.

Implementation issues are described as they pertain to asset allocation and manager selection, assessment, due diligence, and monitoring. In some cases, these skills can be augmented with assistance from investment management and consulting firms, which can provide fiduciary support, expertise, experience, consolidated reporting, risk management, and economies of scale as it pertains to investing in alternative investments. Nevertheless, not all investors are well suited to broadening their alternative investment programs. Such instances are identified as it pertains to investor skill, manager access, staff depth for handling alternative investment mechanics, and a lack of quantitative methodology. Moreover, the perception of risk and organizational discomfort can define investor suitability. Some investors have a structural mismatch with alternative investments, because of the investor's size and portfolio reliance. Others may have difficulty integrating with the liquidity, lockups, and duration of alternative investments.

Chapters 3 through 6 provide a detailed overview of hedge funds, private equity, real estate, currencies, commodities, timber, and oil and gas. The discussion of these alternative investments entails a description of underlying strategies, their basic attributes, and their qualitative return drivers. The attraction for investors to each strategy as well as the investment risks are identified. Also provided are illustrations of portfolios constructed solely using the alternative investment strategies described in each of these chapters. An application for portfolios using isolated alternative investment strategies is provided through a description of funds of funds and investors considering the construction of their own internal portfolios of hedge funds, private equity, or real estate. This approach is focused on strategy-specific combinations through optimization, rather than the factor analysis approach detailed in Chapter 11.

A trend for hedge funds to invest across asset classes makes an analysis of hedge funds difficult by historical methods. Chapter 7, "The Migration of Hedge Funds into the Private Equity Realm," discusses this issue. Hedge funds may be gaining market share from private equity funds. The infiltration by hedge funds into private equity is changing the shape of the private equity industry. Elements of change that hedge funds may be causing or contributing to private equity include potentially reducing expected returns, increasing competition for deals, impelling a migration to larger-sized buyout deals, and lengthening duration of investments. Although there are certain inefficiencies for hedge funds to make this transformation, their robust fee structures increasingly provide them with the financial wherewithal to add resources to do so. Hedge funds tend to have greater expertise at making secured private equity investments than equity-driven investments that require a great deal of company building. Furthermore, from an investor's perspective, there are certain inefficiencies in hedge fund fee structures versus private equity fee structures. This chapter details an analysis of this fee comparison, noting the valuable clawback feature that is present for many private equity funds.

Chapter 8, "Cash Flow Forecasting and Its Implications for Rebalancing," provides a detailed review of the cash flow aspect of alternative investments and the implication it can have for rebalancing portfolio allocations to hedge funds, private equity, real estate, and other alternative investments. Also discussed is the requirement for an overcommitment to private equity in order to achieve invested amounts that approximate portfolio allocations. Two additional areas examined in detail are cash flow models and the utilization of proxies to emulate certain alternative investments. In its totality, this chapter focuses on the following three topics: (1) the forecasting of cash flows to manage alternative investment liquidity, (2) the ability of an investor to meet strategic asset allocations for alternative investments and effectively rebalance these allocations, and (3) quantitative tools to help with these tasks, including cash flow models and the use of alternative investment proxies during periods of mismatched cash flows.

Chapter 9, "Leverage and Portable Alpha," considers leverage as a potential source of risk and identifies the portable alpha strategy as a form of leverage. When mixed with illiquidity and directionality, leverage can be more combustible than expected. If alpha generators in portable alpha become correlated to the asset classes to which they are ported, an investor must possess staying power in order to ride out mark-to-market losses. There are approaches other than portable alpha to capture beta and alpha in an efficient manner. One of those approaches is alpha core, which uses uncorrelated, alpha-producing strategies at the core of a portfolio and augments these holdings with allocations to increasingly risky but higher-returning assets. Leverage also is depicted as a structural component of some strategies, where it is not an accurate measure of risk.

Furthermore, leverage is described in terms of notional leverage through derivatives contracts and organizational leverage. Leverage provides risks and opportunities for investors, depending on how it is defined and applied. The returns that an investor experiences from alternative investments may be more attributable to leverage than to either discrete sources of alpha or factor betas. It is difficult to separate the degree to which index returns for alternative investments are proportioned between leveraged and unleveraged sources. An explicit understanding of the leverage used in an alternative investment and its perceived versus real risks must be determined by an investor.

Factor analysis is evaluated both in Chapters 10 and 11. Chapter 10, "Factor Analysis: The Rationale," reviews of the basic supporting methodologies and quantitative building blocks that underpin factor analysis when applied to investment management. This chapter identifies quantitative factors as components of alternative investments through regression analysis. It also describes the definitional qualities of asset classes and the limiting effect that asset-class definitions can have on portfolio construction. Qualitative factors, such as illiquidity and counterparty risks, also are defined as characteristics that affect many alternative investments regardless of their type. This chapter reviews the marketplace changes that warrant factor analysis as a technique for the construction of portfolios using alternative investments. Processes are described for risk budgeting using investment factors, organizational considerations, systemic views, and managers.

Chapter 11, "Factor Analysis: The Findings and Discovering Active Alpha," is a quantitative illustration of factor analysis applied to the major strategies for hedge funds, private equity, real estate, currencies, commodities, timber, and oil and gas. It supplies the reader with a methodology for conducting factor analysis on a blended portfolio of alternative investments and traditional asset classes, such that factor diversification and efficient exposures can be attained. A benefit of this approach is the consideration of alternative investments on an equal factor basis. This provides an objective footing for judging investment vehicles by their terms and fees. It also enables an investor to more clearly measure alpha that is unaffiliated with factor betas as well as identify the active and passive components of alpha. A further by-product is the ability to create passive beta benchmarks for disparate factors and therefore offer the possibility to create synthetic alternative investment portfolios. This chapter concludes with a discussion of ongoing factor measurement through investment manager portfolio transparency for risk monitoring and portfolio rebalancing.

Acknowledgments

Foremost, I wish to thank my wife, Missy, and daughters Ellie, Emily, and Greta for their patience and sacrifices in enabling me to write this book. The support and foundation they have given has enabled me to realize my dreams. My thanks also go to Tim Barron, who gave me the latitude to pursue intellectual creativity. I also would like to thank George Walker for his wisdom and guidance. My sincerest appreciation extends to those who were helpful in commenting on aspects of this book or were instrumental in the creation of figures and tables, including: Steve Case, Srivatsa Kilambi, Adam Kimball, Alan Kosan, Linda McDonald, Soonyong Park, Donna Rosequist, John Ross, Cynthia Steer, Brooke Stiver, Kenneth Voon Keat Sui, Andrew Taylor, Michael Crook, Juliana Davydov, and Rafael Aussie Haryono Putro. I also would like to thank Bill Falloon, my editor at John Wiley & Sons, for his care and advice from start to finish of this project. Finally, I would like to extend my thanks to the following individuals for their comments on the drafts of this work: John Aiello, Stephen Grobman, Aaron Gurwitz, Brian Hayes, Brian Kriftcher, Dan Murphy, Marc Nuccitelli, Doug Hepworth, and Sharon Robinson.

About the Author

A lan H. Dorsey is a managing director and alternative investment strategist at Lehman Brothers. He is co-head of portfolio advisory for the Private Investment Management group that serves Lehman's high-net-worth clients and head of portfolio strategy for multiasset-class institutional portfolios with a focus on alternative investments. Alan also serves as a trustee of the Lehman Brothers defined benefit pension plan. Prior to joining Lehman Brothers, he was managing director and director of nontraditional investments and research at RogersCasey, a leading consultant to pension funds and other institutional investors. In this role, Alan had responsibility for managing research and investment teams pertaining to hedge funds, private equity, real estate, and hard-asset investing. Previously, he was managing director, director of research, at Bryant Park Capital, Inc. Alan began his career as a securities analyst. Alan holds a BA in economics from Wesleyan University and is a Chartered Financial Analyst. Since 1997, he has served as a member of the investment committee for Wesleyan University, where he is a past trustee.

Alan is the author of numerous publications on selecting, implementing, and managing investments. His recent book, *How to Select a Hedge Fund of Funds: Pick the Winners and Avoid the Losers*, was published by Institutional Investor Books in 2004. Other published works include: "Examining the Increasing Institutionalisation of an Industry: What Are Institutional Investors' Expectations of Hedge Funds?" in Euromoney Books' *Hedge Funds: Crossing the Institutional Frontier*, 2006; "Implementation Considerations when Using Absolute-Return Strategies for Traditional Portfolio Risk Reduction" in Risk Books' *Managing Hedge Fund Risk*, 2005; and "The Perspective of Consultants on Hedge Fund and Private Equity Risk" in Euromoney's *The New Generation of Risk Management for Hedge Funds and Private Equity*, 2003.

One

Alternative Investments and Investors

A lternative investments do not belong in every investor's portfolio. Some investors are not well suited to these assets, despite their attractive features. This potential misfit tends to center either on an investor's inability to manage these assets or the irregular characteristics of the investments. Part One discusses both of these considerations as well as the investor ingredients that are necessary for a successful alternative investment program, which can be augmented by full-service investment management firms or consultants. The suitability of alternative investments for investors depends on the characteristics of the investors. One qualitative artificial constraint to employing alternative investments is a general lack of experience or level of comfort in their use by some investors. Clearly, many investors have gained comfort in some level of use of these investments, but not to the degree that they have in their traditional assets. These issues will be examined more carefully in this section.

Furthermore, investors are required to have a certain size of assets to be able to qualify as an investor in various private placement vehicles. Alternative investments generally are seen as diversifiers in portfolios of traditional asset classes. This diversification benefit and the performance enhancement that alternative investments can provide may be less valued at the margin by investors with smaller-sized assets. Furthermore, alternative investments can be complex in their traits. This complexity is seen in difficult benchmarking, illiquidity, and nontraditional sources of return. Some alternative investments can be volatile. In the context of a diversified portfolio with low correlation among assets, incidental volatility is tolerable. However, volatility in an asset about which an investor has only partial understanding can lead to misgivings.

Topics in Part One comprise the organizational and implementation issues for investors adopting alternative investments, including capabilities, staffing, governance, due diligence, and access to funds. Chapters are devoted to hedge funds, private equity, real estate, and other alternative investments such as currencies, commodities, timber, and oil and gas. Sections that pertain to a type of alternative investment detail the basic attraction of each as well as the qualitative return drivers that tend to affect them. Alternative investment strategies are fully described along with their various tactics, substrategies, and forms of fund. Each chapter on individual alternative investments concludes with considerations for the construction of portfolios dedicated solely to each type of alternative investment.

CHAPTER 1

Introduction

There is a developing trend among investors to consider alternative investments (hedge funds, private equity, real estate, currencies, commodities, timber, and oil and gas) as a group of assets driven by a series of measurable return and risk factors. Heretofore, many investors have added these alternative investments purely on the initial merits of diversification and return potential, without a sophisticated approach to integrating them into a portfolio construction process. However, there is a more elegant way to conduct this implementation using factor and cash flow analysis, in order to identify common investment and structural factors and more accurately depict the correlations among these investments. This approach leads to improved veracity of portfolio construction with fewer redundancies and greater efficiency.

Potential benefits include more precise answers to the quantity of each type of alternative investment to use during the construction of a portfolio, in what combinations, and how rebalancing should occur based on forward-looking factor views for each alternative investment. Resolution of these issues provides a road map with quantitative and qualitative underpinnings for the migration of investors to the promise that they recognize in alternative investments but many have yet organizationally to achieve. In this fashion, the effectiveness exemplified by sophisticated endowments that have ample allocations to alternative investments is attainable by a much broader range of investors.

INTEGRATION OF ALTERNATIVE INVESTMENTS AND TRADITIONAL ASSET CLASSES THROUGH FACTOR ANALYSIS

Alternative investments keep creeping into many portfolios with little more portfolio cognition than for the sake of diversification. As these token allocations to nontraditional investments mature across a broader range of investor portfolios, a deeper contemplation of their merits and risks is being sought by investors, trustees, and other fiduciaries. The turning point for most traditional investors in considering an increase in allocations to these investments often results from a desire for improved investment performance or from the persuasion of a trustee or adviser. Then, the desire for a quantitative understanding of the portfolio role for individual alternative investments is brought into the bright light of day. A problem many investors face is how to move beyond initial allocations to alternative investments in a holistic way that integrates these investments into traditional asset-class exposures and enables efficient portfolio construction. The thesis of this book is that this dilemma can be resolved through the practical application of factor analysis. Factor analysis can be applied both to alternative investments and to traditional asset classes when constructing efficient portfolios. This approach reveals the unique factors that drive returns, volatility, and correlation for alternative investments and their overlap with traditional asset classes.

Traditional style analysis, such as small versus large capitalization or growth versus value investing, is fairly limited in its explanation of investment choices within asset classes. Given the efficient nature of traditional asset classes, such as equity and fixed income, it perhaps is surprising that there is a litany of descriptors for styles. If styles are members of the same asset class, then they likely have high correlations to one another. In contrast, alternative investments not only have a range of types (such as private equity, real estate, and commodities) and a range of strategies (such as leverage buyouts, mezzanine debt, and venture capital), but also an entire genus of factors (such as credit spreads, volatility, and liquidity) that determine their outcome. However, the traditional investment world tends not to think about alternative investments in these terms. Investors have been slow to broaden their understanding of the unique drivers of return and risk for alternative investments. This stonewalling seems to be on the precipice of change.

APPROACHES TO PORTFOLIO CONSTRUCTION

A yearning for how alternative investments truly fit in the context of portfolio construction initially has led to the recognition that they do not fit well into traditional methodologies. For instance, when considering alternative investments in the framework of mean variance optimization, many practitioners realize that this tool is not completely accurate and assumes the expectation for a normal distribution of returns for each asset class, which often is not the case for alternative investments. A user of mean variance optimization also often is forced to constrain allocations to various asset classes, in order to artificially maintain diversification. While mean variance analysis may continue to be used as an informative tool, it can be augmented by regressions that identify factor sensitivities of alternative investments. This tactic provides a better understanding of the sources of return and risk that underlie alternative investments.

There are winners and losers from the use of this methodology and the knowledge that it provides. Winners include investment managers who really do generate their returns from unique sources of returns. Losers are investors who may be slow to recognize an alternative investment manager that generates a majority of its returns from multiple beta exposures to traditional asset classes. Some factors that drive returns for alternative investments can be associated with traditional asset classes. A hedge fund that derives its returns from volatility, credit spreads, and some equity beta is not necessarily deceptive. It is only that those are the key factors from which that fund generates profits and losses. It should be relieving once those factors are established, so that they can be monitored and estimates for their direction can be determined by the fund manager and its investors. Conversely, a large-capitalization equity fund ostensibly derives the vast majority of its returns from a beta to only one factor—the equity market. The separation of alpha from beta should be no different for alternative investment managers, except they may have exposures to a larger number of factor betas. Alpha can become quite small once a more careful analysis is conducted and multiple factor betas are used to explain returns.

Nevertheless, an investor may be likely to find a greater opportunity for alpha in less efficient alternative investment areas than traditional asset classes. The smaller alpha becomes, it may begin to be rivaled in size by the error term in a regression calculation, which seeks to divine factor betas and alpha for an investment.

THE IDENTIFICATION OF ALPHA AND BETA IN NEW INVESTMENT STRATEGIES

Discussing alternative investments in terms of two simple subcomponents— alpha and beta to the equity market—is woefully inadequate. Alpha often is a virtual catchall for the return generated by an alternative investment that is not considered to be related to equity beta. However, there are many types of betas to various factors that can be present in alternative investments. The ability to identify a greater number of factor betas provides a better explanation of a new investment strategy and renders its alpha less mysterious. Whether it is unique factor betas or unique alpha that a new investment strategy provides, both are of value to an investor. Still, the process of identifying the unique sources of returns for new strategies is helpful when combining a range of investments in an effort to ensure that a portfolio is optimized.

Beta is the amount of return for a security or fund that is explained by its benchmark or component benchmarks. A high beta for a fund is a measure of its directional movement with its benchmarks. In a traditional sense, nondirectional hedge funds should have betas near zero and generate returns that are unrelated to the returns of traditional market benchmarks, and alpha is a measure of a fund's return that is independently generated from the beta return that is influenced by the fund's benchmark. However, this rationale presumes single independent variable regressions where there is only one beta, presumably to the equity market. Many investors in low-beta hedge funds seek an independent alpha return that these investments are capable of generating. When added to a diversified portfolio, these uncorrelated returns may improve overall returns and reduce volatility. Nevertheless, the alpha from these funds can be deconstructed into numerous additional factor betas.

Alpha is the value added by an investment manager. It is the component of return that is unrelated to the manager's association with any market or beta. The importance of identifying alpha and multiple betas from new investment strategies is twofold. First, idiosyncratic alpha represents a new source of absolute return relative to a new investment strategy and is different from alpha generated by other investment strategies in an investor's portfolio. Second, new betas often are uncorrelated with betas generated by other asset classes. However, the identification of alpha is never as easy as it appears. This is particularly true as more independent factors are added to a multivariable regression analysis. As independent variables are identified, they represent new unique sources of return and risk with low correlation to other independent variables.

For example, consider the financing of imported goods as a new hedge fund strategy. Assume that this strategy is based on a lack of effective local banking support in an emerging country to pay local exporters for their goods while in transit to a developed nation. The developed country importer of the goods does not wish to pay until receipt, and then on a 60- or 90-day-payable basis. Therefore, an opportunity exists for financing the period of shipment. In this instance, a benefit for the financial firm filling this void is financing a strong credit from a developed country importer. A key to such a strategy is the velocity of transactions, or having multiple turnovers of these transactions annually. Another benefit should be repeat transactions with importers that have strong credit ratings and are located in developed countries. The risk-free rate might be the base price above which the facilitator prices its service, thereby creating a spread equaling a risk premium.

In this example, one might ask: What is alpha and what is beta for this strategy? If there is only one player in this scenario, it is tempting to say that there is no beta and that the entirety of net returns above the risk-free rate is alpha. Beta requires more than one player in a unique investment strategy in order to measure returns that may deviate from the mean experience. Furthermore, beta to mean index returns potentially presumes that the index is investable and offers a passive investment alternative to selecting an active manager. The beta of a manager's performance in this example might be associated with the strategy's average return, which equals the risk-free rate plus a risk premium. Manager returns that fall above or below this can be attributed to the manager's positive or negative alpha, respectively. However, the unique return drivers associated with this strategy and the strategy's low correlation to other strategies may be more important than determining beta and alpha for a manager operating in the strategy. Simply identifying the attributes of a new strategy will result in new beta through the selection of any manager to execute the strategy. Incremental alpha may be negligible relative to the benefit of adding the new independent drivers of returns to an investor's portfolio. Over time, the absolute-return margin above the risk-free rate may decline as more participants enter a new strategy and push down returns through their competitive pressures. Not only can alpha be converted to beta over time for new absolute-return strategies, total returns can evaporate. This concept is quite different than considering a manager's beta to the S&P 500, which has return characteristics in its own right.

Another area of examination when accepting a new investment factor is sustainability. This analysis can identify some faulty assumptions about alpha and beta as they relate to a new unique investment factor. This is not an issue of the sustainability of alpha for a manager. Nor is it an issue of alpha becoming beta for managers in a strategy over time. Certain return drivers, or independent factors, disappear over time. The lack of sustainability of return may result from increased competition, changes in marketplaces, or regulation. Using the example of export receivables financing, this market opportunity could evaporate over time as local banks offer credit to the exporters, the costs of growing crops in one country make it less competitive with another country, or new duties by developed nations cause a reduction in imports.

Historically, diversification has been considered in the light of adding as many unique asset classes as possible. The archetypal return features of asset classes are generalized by their benchmark returns. An investor has the choice of passively replicating these asset classes through investable indexes or employing active management of asset classes to attempt to generate positive returns above the asset-class benchmarks, net of fees. The appropriate measure of success for active management is generating positive incremental returns above a benchmark, otherwise known as positive alpha. Within the context of active management, diversification can be rendered through exposure to multiple-asset-class or independent factor betas, as well as to multiple sources of manager alphas. The greater the number of discrete alphas that can be added to a diversified portfolio, the better. When evaluating discrete returns that are separate from a benchmark's beta (independent investable factors), more idiosyncratic return (alpha) is desirable. In light of the fact that asset-class and factor betas can be passively replicated, it behooves investors to focus their attentions on ways to generate independent alphas from an array of asset-class managers. Accumulated alphas minus the risk-free rate, which is a form of passive alpha, may then be depicted as active alpha. Successful investors increasingly are taking a portfolio approach to selecting and managing alternative investments through attention to generating active alpha.

WHAT THE FUTURE HOLDS

The future for success in the alternative investment realm may increasingly rely on methodologies for the accurate estimation of the future direction for these factors, their volatilities, and their correlations to each other. A full appreciation of alternative investment characteristics may ultimately lead to a renaissance for classical economists. Indeed, portfolio managers of the future may likely find their success measured by an ability to forecast the factors that are chief drivers of return and risk in their portfolios. Successful forecasting of these factors and applying accurate weightings for the optimization of these factors in a diversified portfolio should be at the heart of portfolio construction using alternative investments. Furthermore, investors should focus on identifying investment managers who are creative and capable enough to identify new investment opportunities.

SUMMARY

The use of factor analysis in determining the drivers of return and risk for alternative investments should enable a more accurate appraisal of these investments and lead to their broader use. The quantitative pathway exists through factor analysis to give investors a more explicit risk and return interpretation of their portfolios when alternative investments are employed. This approach moves beyond traditional methods such as mean variance optimization and style analysis. The description of investment returns by their factor betas provides better delineation in portfolio construction. The identification of returns that are unaffiliated with traditional or exotic beta factors leads to a more accurate depiction of alpha generation by individual investment managers who operate in each asset class. This also enables a deciphering of the active component of alpha in total returns. Factor analysis also provides investors with a framework to include and measure new alternative investment strategies, rather than avoiding them because they do not fit within the context of historical analytical techniques. This process should liberate investors to focus their attentions on identifying investment managers who truly have access to unique sources of returns, which are ever more valued in an increasingly competitive investment landscape.

CHAPTER 2

Investors in Alternative Investments and the Necessary Ingredients for a Successful Program

S uccessful investment in alternative investments can be attained by many different types of investors, as long as they are willing to set parameters and live by them. Virtually all successful investment programs utilizing alternative investments have a unified culture that enables them to create and support an organizational management structure, a portfolio construction methodology, and a system for implementation. Often, the linchpin in keeping such a program on track is the existence and maintenance of a well-designed investment policy statement. This governing document should contain well-defined policies and procedures that delineate division of duties and enable the utilization of alternative investments. Once the organizational management structure is in place, including education of constituents and the appropriate setting of expectations, it frees the investment staff or agents to execute their primary tasks of portfolio construction and implementation. The key elements of portfolio construction are accomplishing diversification, maintaining a growth orientation, and ensuring fidelity to rebalancing.[1] Implementation of an alternative investment program entails asset allocation and investment manager selection based on due diligence. Monitoring of the program and investment managers is an ongoing commitment to ensuring that investment goals are met and guidelines are maintained. Some investors find themselves unable to attain a level of expertise in each of the tasks required to implement alternative investments. For these investors, outside resources from investment management and consulting firms can be employed to augment required capabilities. Nevertheless, investors must conduct a candid appraisal of their suitability for a meaningful allocation to

11

alternative investments. Limitations to moving beyond token allocations to alternative investments are found in an organization's or an investor's perception of its own capabilities, risk tolerance, and structural fit with the terms and illiquidity of alternative investments.

TYPES OF INVESTORS AND THEIR APPROACHES TO ALTERNATIVE INVESTMENTS

Investors who use alternative investments in their portfolios can be defined both by their categorization and their organizational capabilities. These investors may be endowments, foundations, pension plans, insurance companies, family offices, or high-net-worth individuals. However, regardless of investor type, some have common characteristics in length of duration of liabilities, taxable or nontaxable status, and a need to conform to certain regulatory oversight. Most investors who consider the use of alternative investments do so in hopes of accomplishing one or all of the following potential benefits from these investments: diversification brought to a portfolio that is populated with traditional investments, by virtue of the low correlation of alternative investments to traditional investments; reduction in volatility for a portfolio of traditional investments, because of the diversification benefits of the alternative investments; and enhancement of performance in a diversified portfolio that is populated by both alternative and traditional investments.

High-Net-Worth Investors

Any addition of new alternative investments must be considered within the existing asset framework of a high-net-worth individual or family. A principal consideration for most high-net-worth investors is taxation. Some alternative investments, such as higher-turnover hedge funds or trading strategies, can be tax inefficient for tax-paying investors. These strategies generate the majority of their profits through short-term gains. In contrast, other types of alternative investments can be very tax efficient and pass through tax-deductible operating expenses to the limited unit holders in investment trusts and master limited partnership structures, which is the case for certain oil and gas, timber, and real estate investments. Furthermore, private equity investments in venture capital and leveraged buyouts can have favorable tax treatment through generating the majority of their profits in the form of long-term gains.

Wealthy individuals and families may have concentrated positions in either private or public equity holdings and, possibly, direct real estate investments. These assets, many of which represent the core wealth of these groups, must be considered when assembling a diversified portfolio. This is particularly true with the use of alternative investments, which may have characteristics that overlap these holdings, such as illiquidity and return, risk, and correlation attributes. For instance, an important portion of the alternative investment universe is comprised of real estate and private equity, which may directly overlap large real estate holdings or private equity in a family business. Another type of core investment that may be overweight in a high-net-worth portfolio is municipal bonds that have attractive tax features. For high-net-worth portfolios that have concentrated positions in one type of asset, there often is a need for diversification. For United States investors in this position, there usually is a significant concentration of currency risk. For example, U.S. high-net-worth investors often not only have highly concentrated assets but also enormous U.S. dollar–centric portfolios. The use of international equities and foreign sovereign bonds for currency diversification, either in a long-only strategy or an alternative investment format, can provide a benefit in these instances.

Endowments and Foundations

The process used by endowments and foundations for implementing alternative investments tends to be idiosyncratic. These investors often rely heavily on either their trustees or a group of investment staff members with strong skills in alternative investments. In either the case of heavy trustee or staff reliance, one common theme tends to be strong decision making in the hands of a focused group of individuals with experience in alternative investments. Many times, the decisions that these groups make in selecting alternative investment managers rely on direct firsthand knowledge of the managers, either through prior mutual employment or investment. For example, a trustee may have worked with a hedge fund manager at an investment bank, or a trustee or investment staff member may have invested with the manager personally or through another endowment or foundation. It is through this prior close association with the investment decision makers that comfort and trust is established and often the way in which these types of institutions place funds in care of alternative investment managers.

Pension Plans

Although clearly endowments have led the way in the utilization of alternative investments, other investors are following in their footsteps, but often with a greater emphasis on process. Endowments and foundations tend to have less direct linkage of their assets with their liabilities. Endowment and foundation liabilities are the budgetary or predetermined levels of grants or benevolent expenditures that they are required to make. In contrast, other investors such as pension plans have more exact liabilities in the form of pension and medical benefit payments to retirees. Pensions also have more regulation in some cases, such as by the U.S. Labor Department under the Employee Retirement Income Security Act of 1974 (ERISA). This difference explains the rate of adoption of alternative investments as well as the approach that each of these investors has taken to this process.

Both corporate and public defined benefit pension plans are well suited to the use of alternative investments. Although these organizations are variably suited to the administrative burden of alternative investments, many of these tasks can be outsourced to or facilitated by financial services companies, such as investment management firms, consultants, risk evaluators, fund administrators, and custodians. The real suitability of pension plans to alternative investments is the long-dated liabilities that pension plans possess and their ability to accept greater illiquidity in their assets. Pensions are well suited to more sophisticated portfolio construction with greater diversification.

The decision-making process for pension plans can be far more onerous than for many other investors. For these institutions, the trustees and investment staff members make investment decisions on behalf of pensioners. Not only are pension plans in some cases regulated, such as corporate plans in the United States by the Department of Labor under ERISA law, they also may face high levels of scrutiny by their constituents. Therefore, the due diligence in which they engage tends to be far more robust than what one might see at an endowment or foundation. In this instance, due diligence not only includes acquiring references from investors on alternative investment managers, but also some or all of the following: background checks; portfolio analysis; performance attribution analysis; evaluation of deal pipelines; and counterparty reference checks from banks, brokers, fund administrators, law firms, and auditors.

Insurance Companies

Insurance companies investing in alternative investments have their own set of requirements. Certain restrictions may apply regarding the use of alternative investments. Nevertheless, diversification and investment performance are important goals for these entities. However, one of the main benefits from an insurance company perspective in using alternative investments is the compatibility they may have with long-duration liabilities. Although short-term cash needs for insurance companies may require them to have liquidity in an area of their portfolios, a vast section of long-duration actuarial liabilities are well suited to some use of less liquid alternative investments where regulatory capital restrictions allow. From this vantage point, insurance companies can utilize their position to be a prime beneficiary of the illiquidity risk premiums that certain alternative investments offer. Private real estate, private equity, and hedge funds all are areas that can offer this opportunity to insurance companies. Additionally, for the less liquid portion of their assets, insurance companies can withstand assets with higher volatility. As long as volatility is accompanied by higher expected returns, this type of exposure can be attractive.

Nevertheless, a risk pertaining to insurance company investment in alternative investments is a hidden-factor exposure in these assets that may coincide with insured liabilities. As hedge funds migrate into more esoteric fields, such as property and casualty reinsurance, there may be a greater incidence of correlation between alternative investments and insurance company liabilities. Increasingly, hedge funds are creating reinsurance companies and dealing in catastrophe bonds, weather derivatives, and life insurance policies. These investments may be either opposed to or coincident with risk exposures and hedges taken by insurance companies. The risk of overlap extends into the credit derivatives market, where hedge funds are significant purchasers and some insurance companies are sellers as well as buyers. In some cases, the exposure to hedge funds dealing in these areas will act as a hedge for the liabilities entered into by the insurance companies. In other cases, they will provide redundant risk exposures. Accordingly, the use of factor analysis and security transparency are becoming vital for insurance companies seeking to evaluate their alternative investment exposures.

Penetration and Rate of Adoption of Alternative Investments by Investors

Aggregate information on alternative asset investing by pension plans and endowments and foundations is readily available through surveys conducted by research firms. This information, when considered over a length of time, has created some interesting trends. Although similar information might be garnered for high-net-worth investors, many of these investors operate independently from one another. It may be that more definitive conclusions can be drawn from fund flows that result from institutions. Peer comparison of performance, style, structure, and methodology is closely tracked in the endowment, foundation, and pension worlds. Indeed, these investors have a greater incidence of unified decision making regarding portfolio allocations to the point where over a period of time a critical mass or direction of investment into an investment area can induce other investors in similar peer groups to take similar actions, thereby creating a self-perpetuating trend.

There has been a trend of positive capital inflows to alternative investment managers from the broad institutional investor universe since 2000. As depicted in Figure 2.1, a fairly broad sample of U.S. institutional investors (1,950 in 2006) had an allocation to all alternative investments

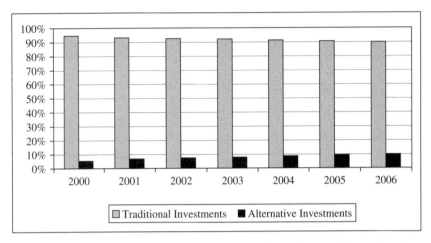

FIGURE 2.1   U.S. Pensions and Endowments: Traditional versus Alternative Asset Allocation
Note: Alternative investments are real estate, private equity, and hedge funds. Traditional investments are all other investments, primarily comprised of equity and fixed income.
Source: Greenwich Associates survey data, dollar weighted.

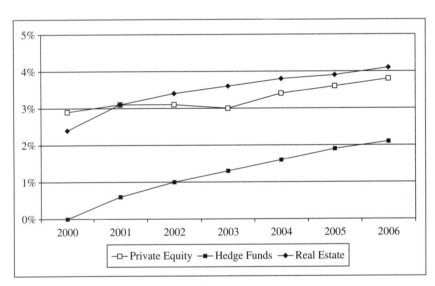

FIGURE 2.2   U.S. Pension and Endowment Alternative Investment Asset Allocation
Source: Greenwich Associates survey data, dollar weighted.

of 10.0 percent in 2006 compared with 5.3 percent in 2000. Within this allocation for 2006, private equity accounted for 3.8 percent, real estate was 4.1 percent, and hedge funds were 2.1 percent. Figure 2.2 shows a comparison of the allocations to these three alternative investment areas. Although the allocation to hedge funds is lower than either real estate or private equity allocations, its rate of increase appears to be much greater. As illustrated in Figures 2.3 and 2.4, a trend remains for further investment in alternative investments, with increasing prospective allocations likely to hedge funds, private equity, and real estate by institutional investors. Corporate pensions, public pensions, and endowments and foundations indicated likely significant increases when queried by Greenwich Associates, a research firm, as to their intentions regarding further allocations to alternative investments. In total, 22 percent, 20 percent, and 34 percent of these investors indicated an expectation for making a future increase in allocations to hedge funds, real estate, and private equity, respectively. By contrast, 24 percent and 13 percent of these same investors indicated likely significant future decreases in their allocations to active U.S. equity and total fixed income, respectively. In brief, these investors appear to be using their traditional long-only U.S. equity and fixed-income investments as a source of capital to fund new and growing allocations to alternative investments.

THE NECESSARY INGREDIENTS FOR A SUCCESSFUL ALTERNATIVE INVESTMENT PROGRAM

The ingredients for a successful alternative investment program essentially are focused in three areas: organizational management, portfolio management, and implementation. Organizational management issues include strong governance through installation of appropriate policy and procedures, the setting of expectations, and creation of a well-defined division of duties. In portfolio management, important elements for long-term success include diversification, maintaining a growth orientation, and fidelity to rebalancing.[2] In implementing a successful program, the critical pathways include asset allocation and the selection, assessment, due diligence, and monitoring of investment managers.

Organizational Management

Organizational management among investors in alternative investments is an area not to be underestimated in its importance. As an investor adopts and manages alternative investments, there is a life cycle to the partnerships and funds that has many features new to most investors. These characteristics become apparent over time, and in some cases can take the length of

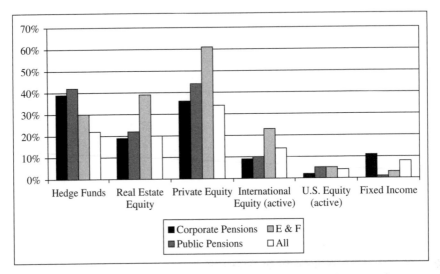

FIGURE 2.3 Percentage of Survey Respondents Expected to Make "Significant Increase" in Allocation Through 2009
Source: Greenwich Associates, based on 1,023 respondents.

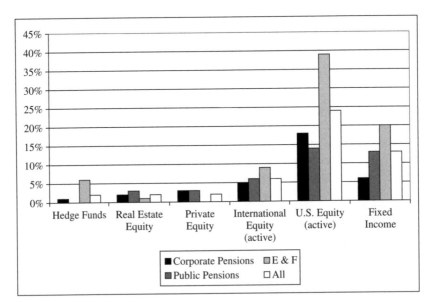

FIGURE 2.4 Percentage of Survey Respondents Expected to Make "Significant Decrease" in Allocation Through 2009
Source: Greenwich Associates, based on 1,023 respondents.

investment cycles to reveal themselves. Strong governance is one of the most importance aspects of effective organizational management for investors dealing with alternative investments. Governance is evidenced in the form of leadership and committee personnel who provide oversight for the assets as well as having a well-conceived investment policy statement. Investment policies should have guidelines that pertain to the features of alternative investments, which are different in many respects from traditional asset class structures, risks, and documentation. A benefit of strong governance is that it usually provides a clear setting of expectations for the risks and rewards associated with alternative investments as well as their illiquidity and cash flow features. Furthermore, governance structures provide a clear delineation of duties for internal staff and external service providers.

Strong Governance   The cornerstone of a functional alternative investment program is an effective decision-making body that governs the program. Typically, small committees with strong leadership are winning combinations in this area. Alternative investments tend to be out of the ordinary for most fiduciaries, even among some knowledgeable professionals who have investment experience. The decision to embark on a path of incorporating alternative investments into a portfolio requires strong leadership to initiate and maintain involvement in such a program, especially in its early years. Furthermore, a small-sized committee that is comprised of trustees or beneficiary representatives is imperative. As this group becomes large, the ability for strong leadership to be effective diminishes. Each member of the governing body is not required to have explicit experience in alternative investments, some of which can be achieved through the knowledge possessed by the group's leadership as well as attained by consultative and investment manager assistance. A main benefit associated with having a small committee is its ability to make decisions and to do so in a timely fashion. Furthermore, small committees are less likely to become disengaged in the process of alternative investments as they unfold over time.

Strong governance structures through sound and documented policies and procedures also will ensure institutional memory. Indeed, an important benefit from institutional memory, generated through documentation and continuity of personnel, is the avoidance of making the same mistakes twice. An investment policy statement in most cases will be rewritten or heavily changed as alternative investments are added to an investor's portfolio mix. Changes to investment policy statements should be included in regular review materials for investment committee members. Such a facility offers a trail of organizational decisions that were made as the foundation for the ultimate implementation of alternative investments. Furthermore, it is helpful not to make policies and procedures pertaining to an alternative investment program too complex and lengthy. The more complex the procedures are, the more likely that they will not be adhered to or that they will be unintentionally violated. The alternative investment marketplace is in its infancy. Therefore, concrete boundaries in investment policy statements must be made with an understanding of the possible limitations that they create for taking advantage of the flexibilities that make alternative investments attractive. A key goal in this regard is to make an investment policy statement flexible enough to capture investment opportunities, but rigorous enough to ensure that fiduciary responsibility is executed with efficacy.

Setting Expectations Setting expectations for an alternative investment program entails thorough education in this area of investment provided to the investor and its constituents. Constituents may include representatives of the beneficiaries of the pool of assets being invested, trustees, investment committee members, and executives. These constituents may have a strong understanding of investments in general, but less of an in-depth knowledge of alternative investments. Although an investment staff may have a strong understanding of the benefits and pitfalls associated with alternative investments, all too often there is not enough time spent on the task of educating constituents. Problems that arise from not doing so include having to sidetrack an alternative investment program during its initiation because of a lack of understanding of the benefits and risks involved or the manifestation of a risk that is unexpected by a member of the constituents, which also can lead to a retrenchment of the program. Time is required to understand and place into perspective expectations for the nominal and real risks associated with topics such as hedge fund fraud, volatility in performance, high correlation of hedge fund returns to traditional asset classes during periods of crisis, and lack of liquidity in alternative investments. A program's temporary cessation due to insufficient education is counterproductive, and it could generate redundant consultative, legal, and staff expense. Keeping the group of constituent representatives small facilitates reasonable communication and accomplishes initial and ongoing education.

One way in which education can be accomplished is through consultative, agent, or staff-led educational sessions with constituents. These discussions should occur on regular basis. It is a mistake to consider one brief session enough to sustain knowledge on the various complex topics associated with an alternative investment program. Indeed, following initial overall education, ongoing education is best conducted on an iterative basis and focused on the relevant topics pertaining to investments under implementation.

Division of Duties   Division of duties in the execution of an alternative investment program is another area that seems simple, but can be a source of failure. Typically, the most effective division includes the creation of a small board of trustees or committee of representatives to oversee and approve decisions made by an investment representative or staff that works for an investor. Problems arise when there is insufficient delineation of responsibilities as they it pertain to oversight or the investment decision-making task. For example, at times boards of directors of corporate ERISA pension plans will become fully engaged in the oversight of an alternative investment program, rather than selecting ongoing members of a subcommittee to participate in oversight. Such a subcommittee might include the company's chief investment officer, head of personnel, and the chief investment officer of the pension plan. Another example is an endowment whose board members force the inclusion of certain alternative investment managers, in spite of insufficient due diligence and investment staff involvement. Alternatively, from a bottom-up perspective, too much delegation of the alternative investment program to agents or consultants can lead to decisions being made too quickly or beyond the educational readiness of an investor or its staff or oversight board. If agents have not been given authority to make discretionary decisions, they should not be given virtually all tasks in the process. Most investors who retain discretion have done so for a set of rational reasons. To abdicate all decisions to agents without granting them discretion often will lead to late-stage second-guessing by the investor. In all of these cases, it should be noted that the role of a strong chief investment officer in the case of an institutional investor or high-net-worth family office is paramount. Such an effective leader will be able to identify either hyperinvolvement of boards or runaway agents or consultants. With such leadership, an alternative investment program stands a much better chance of staying on course over the long term. Continuity of leadership further facilitates institutional memory throughout the inevitable turnover of oversight committee members and organizational regime change.

The Role of Portfolio Management

The management of multiasset-class portfolios that utilize alternative investments requires fidelity to process, yet flexibility to alter course through the use of tactical measures. Commitment to process occurs through adherence to an investor's policy statement, in which goals, restrictions, and methodologies for investment are described. Typically, investment policy statements describe the expected diversification of and strategic asset ranges for various types of assets to be used in a portfolio. An important role for portfolio management is the maintenance of diversification among assets that are approved for use in a portfolio. Furthermore, persistent rebalancing of these asset classes is an important element to manage. Nevertheless, preservation of a growth orientation in capturing investment opportunities helps to position a portfolio for maintenance of purchasing power over the long term. Ensuring that an investor receives fair and equal treatment by investment managers who are employed is another important element of overall portfolio management. Although investment policy statements may be altered to include alternative investments, making gradual tactical moves when incorporating new strategic directions is another skill to be relied upon by an effective portfolio manager and steward of an investor's assets.

Modification of and Adherence to the Investment Policy Statement   Portfolio management involves the implementation of alternative investments often in a portfolio with preexisting traditional investments. There are a number of steps required to facilitate a transition that incorporates the use of alternative investments. The first is an adjustment to an investor's strategic investment policy. Investment policy statements often restrict the use of alternative investments, because of provisions that disallow the use of illiquid assets, leverage, derivatives, and unregistered private partnerships. These restrictions must be softened to allow the inclusion of alternative investments that are viewed as assisting an investor in attaining investment goals and meeting liabilities. Nevertheless, a softening of restrictions must always be accompanied by restrictive guidelines that place certain limits on items that theretofore may have been restricted on an absolute basis. For example, limits may pertain to the magnitude of leverage that is allowable, or the notional leverage involved in any strategy that is employed. In conjunction with program restrictions, guidelines pertaining to alternative investment managers must be explicit. These guidelines usually have considerations that are different from traditional asset manager guidelines. Alternative investment manager guidelines may involve manager limits on the amount and use of leverage, security concentration, minimum requirements for managers to provide certain levels of risk transparency, and maintenance of regulatory registration. The following items summarize some of the investment policy statement areas that are of importance during the implementation of alternative investments:

- **Strategic policy.** Set agreed-upon investment goals for asset growth, income, and protection.
- **Portfolio guidelines.** Delineate expectations for investment returns, volatility, risk management, liquidity, duration, leverage, and benchmarks.
- **Tactical implementation.** Manage the magnitude and rate of migration toward policy targets from a current portfolio that may not include alternative investments.

Asset class allocation ranges. Determine strategic allocations to asset classes and tolerance for underweighting and overweighting asset classes relative to targets.

Tactical asset class tilts. Establish the process for identifying opportunities for tactical tilts in asset classes.

Manager guidelines. Create expectations for managers in terms of regulation, leverage, strategy, minimum organizational requirements, and related restrictions.

Monitor the program. Describe the procedure for monitoring and rebalancing asset classes and managers.

Maintain Diversification Maintenance of diversification is a first step in portfolio construction, but it is even more important in alternative investments. The concept of diversification in traditional investing usually applies to balancing between two factors: equity and fixed income. Diversification in traditional investment terms extends with great articulation into style analysis. This approach includes diversification among equity styles, such as growth, value, international, and capitalization size. Similarly, fixed-income diversification includes a careful eye toward a range of duration, credit, and geographic exposures. However, many of these exposures carry high correlations to one another in normal times, and some exhibit even higher correlations during times of market stress.

When adding alternative investments to a portfolio of traditional asset classes, or when creating a freestanding portfolio of alternative investments, diversification is an equally important goal. Alternative investments, when considered through their factor drivers of return and risk, may be more easily diversifiable than traditional asset classes, which may have a majority of their explainable returns and risks hinged simply on two or three factors (e.g., equity, interest rates, and credit spreads). Indeed, a well-diversified alternative investment program may have a greater number of factor exposures, and therefore be better positioned for attaining true diversification. In addition to traditional betas such as equity and interest rates, alternative investments may be diversified through exposures to other esoteric betas, such as volatility and commodity exposures. An important element for maintaining diversification in portfolios that include alternative investments is the appropriate measurement and monitoring of the true factor beta exposures that are embedded in the investments. Moreover, identification of the true drivers of return for alternative investments may change over time and acquire new characteristics. Determination of these exposures is not as straightforward as it is with traditional asset classes. Therefore, a fair amount of effort and skill is required to appropriately identify these elements and maintain diversification among them.

Diversification also includes the proper evaluation of spurious correlation during normal times on one hand and the potential for high correlations during crisis events on the other hand. Either of these situations requires analysis. The avoidance of an alternative investment because of its spurious correlation with another alternative investment represents a lost opportunity. One strategy may correlate to another coincidentally, perhaps because both exhibit consistently positive results. Over the long term, avoiding spuriously correlated strategies may represent a diversification opportunity cost. Alternatively, an investment may not be properly evaluated because of an overlap of its underlying factors that may correlate with other assets during periods of market stress. There may also be qualitative considerations that cause certain alternative investments to correlate during periods of stress, such as episodic illiquidity.

In addition to the identification of quantitative factor determinants of return and risk for alternative investments, identification of qualitative sources of correlation also help to ensure true diversification. This aspect may be an area where traditional investment portfolios pay little heed. For instance, consider an institution with concentrated counterparty risk in the form of having one custodian for all of its investment portfolio assets and corporate assets. Another example is a corporate pension plan with a large investment it its own publicly traded securities. In this latter case, if the corporation has an inability to fund its pension plan through new contributions, then its corporate securities are likely also to have declined in value. In contrast, an approach to alternative investments takes more of a 360-degree view of risk and the desire to diversify away as much quantitative and qualitative risk as possible. Therefore, maintaining diversification in alternative investments also applies to qualitative exposures such as counterparty risk, deal flow concentration, and the identification of large amounts of notional leverage that may not be determinable through quantitative evaluation.

Maintain a Growth Orientation   Maintaining a growth orientation is important for a range of different types of investors. For institutional investors, growth defends against inflation and maintains the purchasing power of assets. Inflation for pension plans may be more tied to the cost of providing health care benefits rather than other broader measures of inflation. Too great an allocation to lower growth assets can lead to a higher-than-expected future unfunded liability for some pension plans. For high-net-worth investors, maintaining purchasing power also is a key concern. However, this risk is often overlooked in favor of current income generation from low-growth assets. High-net-worth investors run the risk of underestimating the need for growth in their assets in order to maintain purchasing power of assets for future family generations. Growth also has implications for a restraint on portfolio reliance. Investors must understand the long-term growth that is required of their asset pools and adjust current spending and income generation accordingly. In some instances, expense control can have a greater impact on accomplishing future asset requirements than investment returns from growth-oriented assets.

The concept of maintaining a growth orientation in asset allocation is both a quantitative and qualitative endeavor. Quantitatively, asset optimizations have forward-looking estimates for return that should be built on assumptions for growth. In many asset-class assumptions, for instance, an allocation to venture capital might have the highest assumed return. However, to extrapolate that expectation to equate venture capital as having the highest growth rate might be incorrect. A more conceptual approach to the notion of growth includes asset classes that benefit from certain secular influences. For instance, growth can be observed in areas such as emerging market investing, where fixed-income investments may exhibit return and volatility figures that one might expect from equity. Maintaining a growth stance may not include exclusive allocations to low-volatility, relative-value-type hedge fund investments that generate stable returns. In fact, the presumption of having a long-term growth orientation includes the willingness and ability to accept volatility. Indeed, from a factor perspective, the ability to maintain a growth exposure may include a factor-specific orientation to equity and volatility. These exposures might be found in venture capital private equity and global macro hedge funds, respectively. Exposure to growth does not necessarily equate to a large allocation to long-only investment in equities as much as it may relate to an exposure to the equity factor. The difference lies in the creation of more of an asymmetrical return pattern that benefits from the higher growth and higher expected returning equity factor when it is performing well, but does not receive the losses associated with its cyclical declines. In this fashion, the assumption for returns from the equity factor are maintained, but the assumed volatility component of the returns may be truncated with the proper casting of the equity factor in an alternative investment vehicle. Breaking down barriers between classical asset-class silos enables an investor to maintain a portfolio with a growth orientation.

Fidelity to Rebalancing Rebalancing allocations in order to maintain portfolio optimization is as important to do with alternative investments as it is with traditional asset classes. However, the use of ranges around strategic allocations may be even more useful with alternative investments, because of their illiquidity. Alternative investments can be used in the context of range-bound strategic allocations, which grant an investor the latitude to make tactical decisions regarding asset allocations and practical decisions owing to the illiquid nature of alternative investments. Tactical decisions relate to under- and overweighting allocations based on information. Practical decisions include handling the timing of cash flows from alternative investments as well as the decision-making timeline for many investors, which can be slower than expected and difficult to predict.

There are at least three approaches to rebalancing: strategic, tactical, and sensitivity oriented. Not all of these are desirable, and moreover, not all of these are well suited to an investor's capabilities and culture. Strategic rebalancing is the approach taken by most investors. It is simply the creation of asset allocations in an investment policy statement and the rebalancing to these mean points at regular, but somewhat infrequent, intervals. The importance of rebalancing among alternative investments is little different than it is for traditional investments. However, it can be more difficult to accomplish. The liquidity features of alternative investments and their private partnership structures render them less hospitable to precise timing for rebalancing. Nevertheless, for the maintenance of long-term-oriented strategic rebalancing goals, the ability to succeed in this task typically requires planning and a sound process for understanding liquidity windows, redemptions rights, and reinvestment opportunities. There are two primary aspects to strategic rebalance of alternative investments: (1) implementation as it pertains to partnership liquidity provisions and (2) alternative ways to rebalance among factors. It should be remembered that there are many proxies to facilitate synthetic exposures to certain traditional as well as esoteric betas.[3]

Many consider tactical rebalancing to be the equivalent of market timing. An investor may find this task to be counterproductive. Although there are successful investment managers focused on pursuing global tactical asset allocation, it is an extremely difficult endeavor to accomplish from an investor's perspective, unless it is a task explicitly outsourced to an investment manager. Compared with global tactical asset allocators, an investor may be unlikely to be successful in tactical rebalancing, whether among traditional or alternative factor exposures. The sophistication, skill, and rapidity of professional asset managers in this category tend to be superior to what investors might hope to replicate on their own. Furthermore, similar to the difficulties in strategic rebalancing of exposures to alternative investments, the structure of these investments can make it very difficult to execute short-term tactical rebalancing moves.

Sensitivity-oriented rebalancing really is a combination of strategic and tactical rebalancing. Sensitivity rebalancing is reactionary in regard to severe market changes. Rebalancing alternative investment exposures shortly after a market shock could be considered reattaining strategic asset allocation targets as well as market timing associated with tactical rebalancing. In any event, it is a highly unusual circumstance, but one that is important to be prepared for. Indeed, inaction during such times can represent a significant opportunity cost by not taking advantage of inexpensive factors when they become available. Again, the complexity for acting on this in a short time frame is similar to the complexity of enacting tactical rebalancing, which includes the illiquid nature of alternative investments. One way to accomplish this is through liquid proxies that can be purchased or sold in an effort to rebalance factor exposures on a short-term basis. When factor risk premiums change in a rapid fashion, that is exactly the time to rebalance in order to take advantage of momentary market lapses.

A high frequency of rebalancing is not within the capabilities of most investors. Frequent rebalancing requires investor sophistication, accurate monitoring, and execution capability and presumes market liquidity in all environments. Furthermore, it presumes mean reversion of alternative investment categories and the traditional asset classes on which they often are derived. This approach is vulnerable to not identifying secular change. It also has some style bias in the form of preferring value over growth. An investor following high-frequency rebalancing constantly is buying poor-performing asset classes and selling strong-performing classes. As such, there are implications of rigorous rebalancing that are inconsistent with maintaining a growth posture. An example of a flawed mean reversion approach to rebalancing is the decline that Japan's equity and real estate markets experienced in the 1990s. Another example might be the permanent credit improvement that can occur for some sovereign debt based on rising current account balances and an accumulation of foreign reserves. Not identifying secular change can result in fidelity to asset class rebalancing that is not appropriate and can lead to poor choices. Put in another light, the length of cycles for mean reversion may be misjudged. The length of time required for mean reversion to occur may be difficult to predict. Therefore, while a strict adherence to rebalancing to strategic policy guidelines for alternative investments is important, it is not an absolute process; ranges around policy targets are useful; and tactical judgment based on qualitative and quantitative factors is important for each investor to consider.

Most Favored Nation   Most favored nation (MFN) clauses in investment management agreements ensure the equal and fair treatment of investors. Registration of hedge funds with the Securities and Exchange Commission (SEC) in the United States is a step toward the principle behind MFNs. The SEC seeks for registered investment advisers (RIAs) to treat all investors fairly and that each investment manager has one set of fees and terms for its investors. However, for investment managers who are not RIAs, the need for MFNs remains. These agreements essentially state that an investor will be treated no worse than the best-treated investor that enters the fund thereafter. The context of these agreements is such that the investor seeks to ensure that hard-won negotiated terms and fees with the investment manager are not undercut by even better terms negotiated by another investor at a later date.

Careful Tactical Moves when Changing Strategic Targets   At times, investors find they are in a position of receiving a large amount of new assets, perhaps through a gift to an endowment, a new pension funding, or a bequest to a trust or foundation. Investors also may experience a time when an important change in strategic asset allocation occurs. In these cases, it is important to make incremental changes in accomplishing new asset policy targets. When migrating strategic policy for asset allocation or conducting its implementation through manager changes, it behooves an investor to take a phased or dollar-cost-averaging approach, because of the difficulty of market timing and gauging current and future vintage-year strength. Putting too much capital to work too quickly can overexpose an investor at a certain cyclical point in time. A ramification of this is the risk of potentially derailing certain asset-class exposures. For instance, placing assets into a private equity program too rapidly may run the risk of poor vintage-year diversification, which can cause a lack of interest on the part of the investor for maintaining private equity commitments over the course of cycles. This notion of achieving vintage-year diversification can be applied to the broad array of factor drivers of return that affect other alternative investments. Furthermore, access to investment managers does not always match an investor's time frame. A small-capitalization growth equity firm or hedge fund may have infrequent openings to accept new capital. These are moments when relationships that have been built with managers can be capitalized upon and capacity can be seized. However, this assumes that the investor has capacity in its strategic asset allocation risk budget to add capital to the asset class and has liquidity among its other investment managers to redeem capital and reallocate to the desired area.

In keeping powder dry for hedge fund openings, many investors do not bear at the forefront of their minds that access to the best investment managers in alternative investing is a critical element for success. Applying this notion in practice requires being able to respond to openings in investment firms when they become available. These openings can have certain lead times, such as the formation of a new private equity or real estate fund. They also can have quite short fuses, such as the sudden opening of a hedge fund at the end of the calendar year. Some hedge funds in this instance respond to redemption requests made by their existing investors, or perhaps the indecision of a current investor to adequately absorb previously negotiated capacity. In such a case, the investor who may be new to such a fund will need to be prepared to make a quick decision to invest. This sort of decision making is foreign to the typical culture and decision-making process of many investors. For example, most institutional investors require very long lead times, constituent involvement, approval procedures, and documentation to make investments. Therefore, in an effort to have a vibrant alternative investment program, it is important for investors to have the organizational framework and financial wherewithal to make these types of short-lead-time investments. This requires that manager selection and due diligence work have been conducted on target investments well in advance, and that this material be kept fresh. Furthermore, it requires that provisional approval by the investor's governing body or oversight board has been granted well in advance of the potential investment opportunity. In this case, a conference call or reaffirmation of prior approval may be the only requirements to actually implement such an investment. Such investment responsiveness requires available liquidity. In order to respond to a highly desired hedge fund opening when given scant opportunity to prepare for such an opening, an investor must be able to produce funds at short notice to be able to fulfill an investment. This concept is not very different from an investor's having liquidity on hand to fund capital calls from private equity or real estate fund investments.

Implementation

The cornerstones for implementing an investment program are asset allocation and investment manager selection, due diligence, and monitoring. An investor's asset allocation should reflect a predetermined strategic policy profile. The most efficient asset allocation position from a quantitative perspective may not be optimal for each investor. Therefore, an implemented asset allocation must be constructed within the confines of strategic asset allocation policy targets, ranges, and restrictions. The implementation of an asset allocation position is accomplished through investment manager selection. The evaluation of investment managers includes a qualitative assessment, due diligence, and monitoring once the manager has been funded.

Asset Allocation   Asset-class allocation is a fundamental element of portfolio management. Optimal asset-class allocations can be derived through a number of techniques, including mean variance optimization, maintaining certain structural allocation as determined by an investor, and through factor-driven models. The traditional quantitative approach to asset allocation using mean variance analysis has certain limitations when applied to alternative investments (see Chapter 10). Nevertheless, this technique still can be a relevant tool for use during an initial asset allocation process. Effective asset allocation requires forward-looking views for asset classes or the factors that drive them. These views pertain to expected returns, volatility of returns, and correlations between each asset class. In order to accomplish this task, benchmarks that represent each asset class must be selected. Furthermore, econometric models can be created to determine forward-looking views for asset classes and investment factors. Monte Carlo simulation is a tool that can be used to determine probabilistic outcomes for certain asset allocations in light of an investor's reliance on its portfolio and the portfolio's cash flow projections. These simulations can be useful to determine the potential efficacy of a current asset allocation profile in terms of meeting an investor's strategic goals for its pool of assets. An investor's liability position or predetermined reliance on its asset pool may effectively determine a great deal of an asset allocation framework.

Manager Selection and Weighting Investment manager selection and weighting is a separate task from investment manager assessment and due diligence. The selection of a group of managers is more of a holistic endeavor. Some managers may be able to replace others owing to their characteristics and attributes. Based on a sound and documented process for manager identification, evaluation, and due diligence, investment managers can be assembled in a portfolio of funds. An advantage of doing this is the ability to risk budget investment managers based on their attributes and the investor's level of conviction for each manager. It may be that a higher probability of success and lower estimated risk is assigned to one investment manager versus another. Although two managers may have similar styles and approaches, one may simply be viewed as more likely to achieve higher returns or lower risk than the other, perhaps because of a perception of possessing higher-caliber staff or some investment advantage. Risk budgeting of managers also can occur through an assessment of a manager's relative portfolio liquidity, risk concentrations, and quality of securities or deal exposure. Manager weightings in a portfolio also can be driven by capacity and cash flow considerations. Some investment managers may be sized in smaller allocations, because of a restriction in their available capacity. Others may be sized larger than average, because of an ability to capture capacity with them at an opportune moment.

As a de facto principle, an alternative investment program must have access to top investment managers in order to be successful. Many of the best investment managers in this realm charge high fees, require long periods of investment prior to allowing redemption of investor funds, and claim to be closed to new investors. Furthermore, in some areas of alternative investing, such as venture capital, there is performance persistence associated with access to attractive deals or the possession of specialized technical or industry knowledge. In this area, consider the repeated strong performance of certain Silicon Valley venture capital firms with access to knowledgeable personnel as well as proximity to newly emerging technologies and the people who create them. Another example is value-added real estate. Consider local operators in certain areas of the United States that have unique access to and knowledge of neighboring real estate parcels and opportunities for repositioning properties based on pending events such as municipal redevelopment or corporate investment. A further case in point is a hedge fund manager who utilizes complex trend-following strategies using a large amount of leverage applied to global currencies and commodities. Such an investment profile may see a majority of its transactions generate small losses and a minority generate sizable gains. In this instance, although it may seem to be a simple skill, the existence of and adherence to risk controls focused on minimizing losses for this manager may set him well apart from his peers on a performance basis, because of the substantial leverage involved in the strategy. Whether it is in their access to deal flow, possession of unique knowledge, or strict adherence to risk controls, the best alternative investment managers are typically separated from others in their sectors. Therefore, it behooves investors using alternative investments to spend a considerable amount of their energies in garnering access to the best managers in each of the alternative investment areas.

Manager Assessment and Due Diligence   Another key element to sustaining a successful alternative investment program is conducting sound evaluation and due diligence regarding the investment managers used to populate a program. There are a number of approaches to the assessment of investment managers. However, all approaches tend to have a focus on assessing the capabilities of an investment organization, the qualities and rigor of its investment strategy, and the qualifications and experience of its personnel. Organizational risk assessment is a science not dissimilar to the due diligence that is required for financing or purchasing a company. An assessment of an investment management company includes a review of its legal, accounting, and regulatory standing as well as the systems and processes that are in place from a business, operational, and management perspective. A qualitative assessment of personnel and investment strategy may center on investment or security selection methodology and any competitive advantage that may exist in this endeavor. Furthermore, portfolio construction and risk management go hand in hand. Transparency into techniques for portfolio construction and ongoing measurement of risks, leverage, and factor exposures in a portfolio are mandatory in any manager assessment.

Similarly, is it crucially important to evaluate staff qualifications and experience for conducting security selection, portfolio construction, and risk management pertaining to a portfolio of assets. Additionally, due diligence into the individuals' backgrounds must be conducted.

Not only does due diligence apply to making an initial investment but it also applies to monitoring the investment over time. Due diligence on alternative investments often is best conducted by a fund of funds or consultant, unless the investor has staff and resources to accomplish this endeavor in a consistent and experienced fashion. It is more likely that the breadth and depth of such experiences across a range of alternative investments may be found through a third-party adviser. Due diligence requires prior experience for information to take on context and relevance. For instance, if due diligence is conducted on a hedge fund engaged in distressed debt investing, it is helpful for the analyst conducting the due diligence to have had prior experience in this field. This familiarity facilitates an understanding of the strategy, its techniques, and the hedging that may be employed. Furthermore, prior experience may yield association with traders and investors in a specific field, who can provide references in order to gather a better understanding from a peer perspective as to the skill, style, and market reputation of a manager being considered. This situation also can apply to private equity or real estate investment managers, where competition for deals is keen and coinvestment among funds may occur from time to time. In such instances, references from peer firms can be illuminating and provide very informative insights. From a monitoring perspective, such market contacts can prove useful in evaluating the ongoing performance, risk management, and personnel continuity at an investment manager. Chances are that if an investment manager is operating out of his skill set or beyond prior norms, then market participants will learn of it as quickly as or more quickly than an investor.

Manager Monitoring   Effective monitoring leads to periodic manager turnover. Monitoring detects a decline in skill, risk controls, and internal operations for investment managers over time. Because access to top-performing managers is such a critical issue for investing in alternative investments, it is all too easy to ignore warning signs that are determined through monitoring of managers. Top-performing managers tend not to be the ones who are relinquished most easily by investors, especially when there is the real possibility of not being allowed to reinvest with the manager at a later date. However, there is urgency associated with the identification of manager lapses through monitoring, because of the potential volatility associated with alternative investment managers and illiquidity that can occur from the structure of the investment or through coincident redemptions by other investors. Decisions to fire managers must be made decisively. But in order to do so with comfort and no second-guessing, it is important for an investor to have a strong pipeline of new investment managers. These replacements must be cultivated over time, and this effort takes advance planning and discipline to maintain. Furthermore, creating such a pipeline requires skill in manager identification and capability in evaluation.

SUPPORT FROM INVESTMENT MANAGEMENT FIRMS AND CONSULTANTS

Some investors choose to rely on outsourced solutions, because of the difficulty in attaining all of the necessary ingredients for a successful alternative investment program. There is a level of complexity in creating and maintaining the basic ingredients for success, including requirements for an effective organization, experienced portfolio management, and skilled implementation through asset allocation and investment manager evaluation and monitoring. All of the steps that relate to the necessary ingredients for a successful program can be outsourced to or augmented by an investment management organization or in some cases specialty consulting firms. Benefits from doing so include fiduciary support, expertise and experience, consolidated reporting and risk management, and potential efficiencies through economies of scale.

Fiduciary Support

The foundation for a relationship between an investor and an investment management firm acting in a fiduciary capacity is good governance. A documented investment policy statement delineates roles and responsibilities, strategic goals for a portfolio including asset allocation ranges, performance benchmarks, rebalancing procedures, and expectations for managers through guidelines. Adhering to the elements of an investment policy statement can be facilitated in conjunction with utilization of a third-party fiduciary. In this role, the third-party fiduciary makes investment decisions in accordance with the preset policy and implements asset allocation and manager selection decisions.

There are certain organizational benefits associated with this approach for an investor. Often, boards that represent investors are populated with trustees, beneficiaries, and various ad hoc representatives. While good intentioned, many boards find that they are vulnerable to being less effective than they wish. Problems can develop with sophisticated board members or investors who may not be expert or experienced in certain investment fields, thereby causing hesitation or reluctance to approve certain investment decisions or diversification measures. For example, a claim of prudence can wrongly lead to a lack of diversification. Furthermore, the shape of boards may be too large or swayed by one strong but misguided voice. There are many board issues that can be resolved through the insertion of an external service provider who acts in a cofiduciary capacity, thereby allowing an investor to serve in its best capacity, which is one of oversight rather than one of implementation with too few internal resources. In effect, this partially outsources the investment office for an investor while enabling it to retain its fiduciary oversight.

Additionally, external fiduciary relationships provide constant surveillance of an investor's portfolio and adherence to investment policy guidelines. An external investment manager acting in this role is more likely to be objective in executing investment decisions. In contrast, an investor's trustees are susceptible to turnover, and human nature of new committee members can cause hesitation in the face of contrary investment actions, such as rebalancing and acting on secular changes in asset classes that require policy adjustment.

Expertise and Experience

Another benefit that should be expected from an external resource, such as an investment management firm or consultant, is expertise in the areas of investment that are required as well as past experience in implementing that expertise. Skill and prior experience provide for capability in tactical investment decisions. Often, it is difficult for an investor to take advantage of tactical opportunities for tilting asset allocations toward the high or low ends of approved ranges, because of infrequent committee meetings that are required to achieve consensus and approve changes. An outsourced provider of investment services also can use proprietary advantages to accomplish certain tactical moves. For example, although full disclosure is required, an adviser's internally managed or assembled investments can capture certain proprietary products that possess access to unique opportunities or deal flow. This might be found in garnering capacity with hedge funds or private equity partnerships, entry into merchant banking or coinvestment opportunities, or the ability to tactically hedge against prospective asset-class moves or rebalance an asset class that has experienced a sudden unexpected move. While maintaining fiduciary sensibilities, outsourced cofiduciaries sometimes can utilize investment and market insights for tactical asset-class tilts and investment manager openings more efficiently than investors who have slow decision-making processes.

In addition to expertise in asset classes and tactical opportunities, prior experience is necessary for implementing these changes. Cofiduciaries must have prior dealings in decision making that may be contrarian in nature and have experience in rebalancing and rigor in portfolio construction. Other critical elements to seek in a cofiduciary are experience in asset allocation and access to market intelligence that informs forward-looking expectations. Furthermore, implementing these decisions through manager selection requires access to high-caliber investment managers. Manager access must be complemented by competent manager evaluation skill, due diligence prowess, and prior trading and other investment strategy experience. Manager monitoring systems and processes should be rigorous and entail thorough qualitative and quantitative ongoing assessment.

Consolidated Reporting and Risk Management

A benefit of having a unified asset management program for a portion of an investor's assets is the ability to aggregate reporting statements and risk assessment profiles. As it pertains to alternative investments, a reporting and risk assessment function also pertains to investment cash flows. The treasury function for cash flow management and accounting of capital calls and return of capital and profits also require the calculation of internal rates of return for private equity partnerships. For an investor with a small accounting staff, tracking these transactions can be cumbersome, as can the management of documents for entering and exiting alternative investments. For taxable investors, international tax withholdings and federal and state tax filing can be awkward to track and reconcile. Minimizing taxes and investing tax efficiently also can be managed by an external resource. Compliance with certain foundation, pension, and fiduciary regulations may require documentation. Individual investment decisions, due diligence, and adherence to investment policy statements and guidelines often must be documented. All of these areas can be outsourced through the hiring of a third-party investment manager acting in a cofiduciary role.

Economies of Scale

An additional advantage for an investor using a third-party cofiduciary for multi-asset-class implementation is benefiting from certain economies of scale. Efficiencies include the notions that small investors stand to receive better diversification in commingled multi-asset-class products, and large investors in either commingled or separate accounts should benefit from lower frictional costs, operating expenses, and fees. At the same time, these investors stand to achieve better liquidity through the use of a large provider of asset management services who benefits from a constant flow of investment assets. These providers can spread their operating costs over a much larger asset base, and therefore provide a cost benefit to investors. Economies of scale can be achieved regarding costs for accounting, legal, reporting, technology, and regulatory supervision. Many of these services can be achieved by hiring top providers acting on an aggregated basis. Additionally, a large multiproduct financial services company that serves in a cofiduciary role should have experience in negotiating management agreements with third-party investment managers, accomplishing effective transparency, and utilizing comprehensive risk management systems.

INVESTORS DECIDING TO MINIMIZE THE USE OF ALTERNATIVE INVESTMENTS

Some investors who have made portfolio allocations to alternative investments have trouble moving beyond initial allocations of perhaps 5 percent each to real estate, private equity, and absolute-return strategies represented by hedge funds. This inability, which may not relate to a specific view on asset allocation, tends to be governed by a number of process issues, including: absence of a quantitative portfolio construction methodology that appropriately deals with alternative investments, organizational discomfort and lack of understanding alternative investments, inadequate staff depth for handling the mechanics of private placements, and a possible perception of lack of suitability of certain alternative investments with an investor's profile. Investors deciding to minimize the use of alternative investments in their portfolios usually do so for one or all of the following three reasons:

1. A perception that the organization may not have the skill set or appropriate access to quality investment managers in order to effectively execute a diversified program of alternative investments.
2. A perception that the increased use of alternative investments represents a ratcheting up of risk in a portfolio, which may not be suitable for the institution or to which the fiduciaries of the portfolio may not have an appetite.
3. A structural mismatch of the terms and conditions of alternative investments when used in larger allocations versus the liabilities and required liquidity of an investor's portfolio.

Investor Skill Set and Manager Access

Some investors do not view alternative investments as being suitable because of a perceived lack of investor skill or access to high-quality investment managers. There may be little arguing this issue with an investor, because it may speak to the overall sophistication of the organization and also to an innate comfort level that may simply be out of the cultural norm for the investor. However, in this instance there may be ways to accomplish exposure of an investment portfolio to alternative investments through funds of funds. Although funds of funds may have illiquidity characteristics that also are undesirable for the investor, manager diversification available through funds of funds provides for a reduction of risk. Funds of funds using any of the alternative investment categories still provide the general return and correlation attributes that are the primary characteristics sought by an investor in alternative investments.

Staff Depth for Handling Mechanics There are some basic learning curve aspects associated with the procedures for implementing alternative investments. This notion also applies to more advanced investors who either accept higher allocations and lower constraints to alternative investments in optimized portfolios or those who employ factor analysis to be able to better inform their alternative investment allocations.

One aspect is measuring, anticipating, and balancing the timing of cash flows into and out of these investments. Capital calls and the return of capital can be anticipated given the historic norms for these investments. However, investors also benefit from forecasting tools in order to clarify the frequency of these capital flows (see Chapter 8). Another consideration is familiarity with private placement documentation. The navigation of subscription agreements, partnership agreements, and private placement memoranda often requires prior experience or specialized legal assistance. Furthermore, infrequent pricing, side pockets, coinvestment capability, gating provisions, and performance fee calculations of alternative investments require fluency, which depends on previously attained knowledge and the perspective of experienced judgment.

A sometimes heard exasperated complaint by staff representatives of midsized institutional investors is spending 90 percent of the time on the 10 percent of the portfolio's assets that is allocated to alternative investments. Although this lamentation often is exaggerated, it does highlight the increasing need for investors to develop dedicated staff with prior experience with implementing alternative investments. Maintaining experienced staff does not only pertain to familiarity with alternative investment mechanics, it also relates to the need to generate and maintain access to top investment managers in this field. Indeed, in spite of high fees as a deterrent for demand, top alternative investment managers often have restricted capacity and only seldom offer capacity to new investors. Access to highly sought after alternative investment managers and the cultivation of these relationships requires a certain amount of focus and commitment. This endeavor should occur with enough frequency and in-person contact to maintain these relationships in order to garner new or additional capacity.

Other full-time-job aspects of maintaining an alternative investment program include the need to conduct due diligence on investment managers and their portfolios. This task is time intensive and requires repetitive procedures. Ongoing due diligence conducted on alternative investment managers' portfolios also may require negotiated transparency in order to conduct valid risk measurement and monitoring. Although due diligence and monitoring can be facilitated with the use of an experienced fund of funds or consultant, they nonetheless must be supervised and evaluated by the investor. These duties can be reduced by using third parties, but they cannot be eliminated.

Lack of Quantitative Methodology A lack of quantitative methodology is a significant impediment for the inclusion of more than simple nominal allocations to alternative investments. To the credit of many large investors, initial allocations to alternative investments have been adopted for the sake of diversification. However, beyond the acceptable token investments, there is little concrete cartography that is available for investors to use for making larger strategic allocations to alternative investments. The adoption of factor analysis and risk measurement systems has been limited to the largest institutional investors. The vast middle tier of institutional and high-net-worth investors still are saddled with more antiquated tools, such as style analysis, limited asset class definitions, and long-only asset-class exposures.

Perception of Risk and Related Investor Suitability

The perception of risk may also pertain to cultural fit. An organization should ascertain whether it is considering real versus perceived risks of alternative investments. For example, the use of leverage in alternative investment strategies often is associated with risk by investors. However, leverage is not always risky, and unleveraged strategies may actually have more risk than they appear. For instance, a market-neutral equity hedge fund strategy that is leveraged two-to-one may not be as risky as one might think, because of the nature of its matched long and short securities. Alternatively, a hedge fund using no cash leverage but a large quantity of futures, options, or credit derivatives has embedded notional leverage that could become quite risky under certain circumstances (see Chapter 9).

The perception of risk is relevant, even if risks do not pose a material financial threat. For example, a well-diversified portfolio of hedge fund investments may have one problem hedge fund. Although the impact of this may be inconsequential from a financial perspective, the perception of risk in the portfolio may overwhelm reason. Although an investor in such a circumstance may be well suited from a portfolio perspective to use alternative investments, the investments may not be suitable owing to the way in which the investor processes the perception of risk. One reason for taking additional theoretical risk—perhaps better described as organizational, cultural, or employment risk—is a funding gap between an investor's assets and associated projected liabilities. Such a situation, an example being an underfunded pension plan, may lead to a desire for higher returns even if associated with more perceived risk (e.g., headline risk). Investors who invest in alternative investments with this as their motivation may be those most in need of education to differentiate between perceived and real risks. However, some of these investors will not be able to make this transition, and therefore are not well suited to adopt alternative investments.

Organizational Discomfort The adoption of alternative investments almost always causes consternation among trustees, board members, and beneficiaries of investable assets. This discomfort typically is borne of a lack of familiarity with the instruments, which is exacerbated by hearsay and media stories that fuel the flames of doubt. Even after education sessions that occur for constituents, the natural term-limit feature of most fiduciary boards often causes the need for ongoing education and a documented investment policy statement that delineates the reasons for an allocation to alternative investments. These steps support a perpetual program of annual commitments to alternative investments, which sometimes is required in good and bad times in order to rebalance and maintain allocations to individual alternative investment strategies at predetermined strategic levels.

Structural Mismatch

The third point of dissuasion, a structural mismatch, is focused on the broad parameters that qualify an investor's suitability for alternative investments in general, which include the following: the size of a portfolio, portfolio reliance to pay liabilities, and associated liquidity requirements.

Investor Suitability—Size The overall size of an investment portfolio is a significant consideration for any investor considering a robust and well-diversified allocation to alternative investments. Furthermore, the fact that an investor has an ability from a size perspective to invest in alternative investments does not always mean that it should be done. Determining the suitability for alternative investments lies in the aforementioned issues of skill, culture, and perception of risk. Although the growth in offerings of diversified investment vehicles by funds of funds has enabled ever-smaller investors to gain access to alternative investments, direct programs of properly diversified alternative investments require substantial sums of money.

In part, this is due to the fact that most alternative investment managers have minimum investment amounts of $1 to $5 million and in some cases much larger amounts to gain access to their funds. Therefore, in order for an investor to have a diversified portfolio of perhaps 15 direct investments in hedge funds or private equity funds, a total alternative investment allocation of $15 to $75 million often is required.

Investor Suitability—Portfolio Reliance   Portfolio reliance is another structural consideration for an investor seeking to determine compatibility with the use of alternative investments. Many foundations have a required spending rate of 5 percent per year of total assets. Some pension plans find themselves with varying degrees of assets meeting the present value of projected future benefit liabilities. Pension plans may be vastly underfunded vis-à-vis these liabilities, regardless of the amount actually spent on an annual basis to pay benefits to beneficiaries. Investors have many different situations that determine the annual cash flows into and out of their asset pools. The impact on portfolio construction from these cash flow considerations is varied as well. Some investors use high-growth alternative investments regardless of the fact that their funds may not specifically require higher rates of return, and cash inflow into their portfolio may far outweigh required cash outflows. In these cases, the use of alternative investments is still applicable based on a rationale of sound portfolio diversification and construction. Alternative investments may be used in heavier doses in the event that an investor is vastly underfunded relative to its projected liabilities.

Investor Suitability—Liquidity, Lockups, and Duration   Alternative investments tend to have an important feature in common: illiquidity. The investment vehicles and the investments themselves can be much less liquid than traditional investments. Liquidity considerations for alternative investments and their associated irregular cash flows must be considered in view of the periodic demands on an investor's portfolio of assets. The concept of liquidity requirement dovetails into an investor's portfolio reliance. A greater reliance on a portfolio's assets to meet annual liabilities is typically associated with a greater amount of liquidity that must be kept in a portfolio. This generalization depends on the amount of new cash flows entering the portfolio annually. Nevertheless, since alternative investments generally are far less liquid than traditional investments, they may not be viewed as a good match for a portfolio that must maintain high levels of annual liquidity. For example, an investment in timber may be a multiyear, if not multidecade, proposition prior to experiencing liquidity in the investment. Furthermore, there are pitfalls in the assumption of liquidity from certain alternative investments. Hedge funds often state the liquidity that they offer to their investors on a quarterly or annual basis. However, in certain circumstances, hedge funds have the right to lengthen the liquidity windows afforded to investors through a gating mechanism that restricts total fund redemptions to perhaps no more than 20 percent of the fund in any one quarter. Gating restrictions on a fund's assets supersede any individual investor's redemptions rights.

Another instance of faulty liquidity assumption is in the case of private equity funds, whether they contain leveraged buyouts, venture capital, or real estate. These funds may draw capital from investors more quickly or pay it back more slowly than an investor originally anticipated. Furthermore, a nuance of private equity investing, regardless of the type of investments in the partnership, is that often the investor must overcommit to these funds in order to achieve a desired level of invested exposure for a portfolio (see Chapter 8). Private equity partnerships draw down committed funds from investors over time, even while the partnerships are returning invested capital and profits to investors. Therefore, these funds usually do not actually have more than perhaps two-thirds of investors' committed capital drawn down into the fund at any point in time. This need to overcommit to these funds, in order to achieve a targeted portfolio allocation, places investors in an uncertain future liquidity position. It may be that multiple funds accelerate their capital calls simultaneously, perhaps because of macroeconomic or market events. In this case, the investor would become overcommitted and perhaps be placed in a vulnerable position of illiquidity. This risk, even if remote, speaks to an oft-observed discomfort of some investment committees with making overallocations to certain private funds operating in private equity, real estate, and timber, in order to actually achieve an allocation to the asset class that is consistent with the organization's asset allocation model or investment policy statement.

An ironic aspect of some investors not being comfortable with the lockups for private placements (often 7 to 10 years or longer for private equity and real estate and 3 years for some hedge funds) is the fact that most large investors have liabilities that have long durations, too. In this sense, the duration of many alternative investments is a better match than the duration of many traditional investments. For example, public equity, which in many investors' portfolios has the largest allocation of any asset class, effectively is a very liquid investment that essentially is a mismatch for the long-dated liabilities of pension plans, endowments, and foundations. Even fixed-income investments for many investors are overseen by professional investment managers who disregard the liabilities of their investors and, for instance, reduce the duration of a portfolio of bonds in a rising interest rate environment in order to avoid interim-period mark-to-market losses. Most investors appreciate that tactic. However, there is a loss of yield in doing so and a loss in total return to maturity relative to owning longer-dated bonds and accepting interim periods of volatility.

SUMMARY

An important element for laying the foundation of a potentially successful alternative investment program includes the construction of an effective oversight and management structure that includes an investment policy statement that delineates a portfolio management approach and implementation methodologies for asset allocation and investment manager selection. Goals for this sort of structure include maintaining diversification, retaining a growth orientation that provides an investor's portfolio with long-term preservation of purchasing power, and a rebalancing functionality that is facilitated through program and manager monitoring. Alternative investments can be applicable for all types of investors. However, investors must understand the potential mismatch they have with the idiosyncrasies of these investments. Suitability of alternative investments for specific investors should be based on an investor's skill set, cultural fit, and structural compatibility. An investor's requisite skills in evaluating and securing access to better investment opportunities are critical characteristics that are necessary to facilitate a successful implementation of alternative investments. Additionally, an investor must have a cultural ability to evaluate the nature of risk in alternative investments and embrace risk as a source of return, rather than becoming paralyzed by perception and negative connotations of risk. This cultural ability may transcend investment staff members and be projected toward other constituents, including: investment committee members, trustees, fiduciaries, beneficiaries, union leaders, faculty, political appointees, or corporate executive officers. The structural compatibility of an investor's portfolio and its related liabilities should be viewed in light of some of the nontraditional characteristics of alternative investments and how these fit with the investor's portfolio size, reliance, and liquidity requirements. Nevertheless, certain skills and investment tasks can be augmented by an investor's use of external advisers. It behooves an investor to correctly gauge its suitability to an alternative investment program prior to pursuing it independently or with advisory assistance, in spite of the pressure the investor may have for improving returns, reducing volatility, or emulating its peers.

CHAPTER 3

Hedge Funds

The four main groupings of hedge strategies include long/short equity, relative value, event-driven approaches, and tactical trading. As components of these strategies, there are many hedge substrategies, and new ones are created on a frequent basis. The primary substrategies are described in this chapter along with a discussion of their factor drivers of return and the appeal and risk of the substrategies for investors. While the quantitative factor drivers of return for these substrategies are delved into with more depth in Chapter 11, this chapter seeks to provide an overview of the substrategy factor drivers as well as highlight the qualitative drivers of return and risk. This is not representative of a conclusive list of either quantitative or qualitative factors that inform returns and risk. While quantitative factors can be modeled through regression analysis, qualitative factors cannot easily be modeled. Nevertheless, qualitative factors may be as important, or in certain circumstances more important, for the total return of a substrategy or hedge fund than the associated quantitative factors.

PERFORMANCE AND DIVERSIFICATION ATTRIBUTES

As is the case with most other alternative investments, two key attributes that support the inclusion of hedge funds to a portfolio of assets are the prospect for performance enhancement and diversification. A difficulty in generalizing about absolute-return strategies is that they are heterogeneous and numerous. Moreover, new strategies are developed on a consistent basis, often with the help of derivatives based on other asset classes. For instance, the migration of hedge funds into private equity, real estate, and secured lending provides for returns and risk factors that necessitate a more exacting approach to the analysis of returns and correlations (see Chapter 7). Nevertheless, a review of historical performance and correlations is an appropriate starting place to describe the basic appeal of these investments for most investors.

Table 3.1 illustrates the historical performance that has been generated by hedge funds. This data, which is based on index strings, has been fairly positive across most strategies over the past decade. Furthermore, the volatility associated with this performance has been relatively low, with some notable exceptions (Table 3.2). Although the length of this data is fairly short from which to draw conclusions, it simply illustrates the type of performance and volatility statistics that many investors have in mind when considering hedge funds. The experience of hedge funds relative to traditional asset classes on average over this time frame, which included a period of high volatility for the U.S. equity market, is a point of attraction for many investors. Similarly, there is data to support the expectation of low correlation benefits from hedge funds when added to a portfolio of traditional assets to improve diversification. Table 3.3 portrays the historical correlations among the various hedge strategies and some of the major traditional asset classes. From a correlation perspective, the hedge strategies indicate some noncorrelated attributes vis-à-vis

TABLE 3.1   Hedge Strategy Investment Performance as of December 31, 2006

	1 Year	3 Years	5 Years	10 Years
HFRI Convertible Arbitrage Index	12.16	3.66	5.96	9.19
HFRI Distressed Securities Index	15.95	14.27	15.28	11.85
HFRI Equity Hedge Index	11.72	9.99	8.86	13.20
HFRI Equity Market Neutral Index	7.27	5.88	4.19	7.06
HFRI Event-Driven Index	15.41	12.51	11.31	12.11
HFRI Fixed Income (Total)	8.99	7.62	8.16	7.47
HFRI Macro Index	8.19	6.54	9.55	9.82
HFRI Merger Arbitrage Index	14.26	8.11	6.13	8.83
HFRI Regulation D Index	6.84	8.41	7.74	13.38
HFRI Relative Value Arbitrage Index	12.34	7.94	7.79	9.41
HFRI Short Selling Index	−2.82	0.08	0.26	1.50
HFRI Statistical Arbitrage Index	13.62	7.55	4.49	6.10
HFRI Fund of Funds Index	10.41	8.25	7.42	7.87
90 Day Treasury Bills	4.80	3.00	2.34	3.70
LB Aggregate Index	4.33	3.70	5.06	6.24
LB U.S. Treasury: U.S. TIPS	0.41	3.85	7.19	N/A
Citigroup High Yield Mkt Index	11.49	8.63	9.82	6.75
Russell 2000 Index	18.37	13.56	11.39	9.44
Russell 3000 Index	15.71	11.19	7.17	8.72
MSCI World	20.65	15.22	10.49	8.08

Source: RogersCasey; HFR, Inc.

TABLE 3.2 Hedge Strategy Standard Deviation of Returns as of December 31, 2006

	1 Year	3 Years	5 Years	10 Years
HFRI Convertible Arbitrage Index	1.97	3.39	3.36	3.47
HFRI Distressed Securities Index	2.93	3.47	4.26	5.60
HFRI Equity Hedge Index	5.81	5.73	6.06	9.33
HFRI Equity Market Neutral Index	1.62	1.82	1.82	3.09
HFRI Event-Driven Index	4.28	4.66	5.66	6.63
HFRI Fixed Income (Total)	0.92	1.23	1.90	3.17
HFRI Macro Index	4.77	4.38	5.14	6.45
HFRI Merger Arbitrage Index	3.13	3.33	3.12	3.88
HFRI Regulation D Index	7.45	6.21	6.71	7.22
HFRI Relative Value Arbitrage Index	2.06	2.27	1.99	3.19
HFRI Short Selling Index	5.19	7.13	10.77	21.11
HFRI Statistical Arbitrage Index	2.41	3.07	3.38	3.84
HFRI Fund of Funds Index	4.68	4.11	3.59	6.01
90 Day Treasury Bills	0.13	0.44	0.41	0.52
LB Aggregate Index	2.70	3.25	3.82	3.56
LB U.S. Treasury: U.S. TIPS	4.39	5.22	6.30	N/A
Citigroup High Yield Mkt Index	2.38	4.17	7.98	7.93
Russell 2000 Index	13.61	13.95	17.16	20.09
Russell 3000 Index	6.38	7.62	12.52	15.48
MSCI World	7.25	7.73	12.51	14.47

Source: RogersCasey; HFR, Inc.

traditional asset classes, which make them attractive for use in portfolio construction.

The problems that occur when using index returns to describe the performance, volatility, and correlation of hedge fund strategies are common among most alternative investments. Hedge fund indexes are subject to biases, including survivor bias, backfill bias, and reporting bias. These biases can overestimate or underestimate performance of the indexes. This can impact the historical volatility of the indexes as well. Furthermore, the correlations among the hedge strategy indexes and other assets can be underestimated. In spite of all these problems, hedge fund indexes are in some cases investable, which renders them useful for realistic portfolio construction and benchmarking purposes. Having investable benchmarks provides an investor with a passive alternative to measure the performance of active investment through the selection of individual hedge funds.

TABLE 3.3 Hedge Strategy Correlation Matrix (1996–2006 Q2)

	Cash	Core FI	ILBs	High Yield	U.S. EQ	EMN	EQH	SS	ED	MA	DS	RV	CA	MI
Cash	1.00													
Core fixed income	0.20	1.00												
Inflation-linked bonds (TIPS)	−0.06	0.73	1.00											
High-yield	−0.25	−0.16	−0.20	1.00										
U.S. equity	−0.04	−0.41	−0.49	0.60	1.00									
Equity market neutral	0.59	0.16	−0.04	−0.04	0.16	1.00								
Equity hedge	0.11	−0.39	−0.34	0.36	0.83	0.26	1.00							
Short selling	0.20	0.44	0.34	−0.46	−0.86	0.03	−0.85	1.00						
Event-driven	0.00	−0.44	−0.34	0.63	0.81	0.30	0.79	−0.71	1.00					
Merger arbitrage	0.39	−0.26	−0.34	0.34	0.62	0.62	0.64	−0.42	0.75	1.00				
Distressed securities	−0.25	−0.43	−0.19	0.54	0.59	0.10	0.59	−0.59	0.87	0.51	1.00			
Relative value	0.25	−0.17	−0.12	0.39	0.45	0.48	0.57	−0.37	0.74	0.75	0.72	1.00		
Convertible arbitrage	0.35	−0.08	0.00	0.35	0.30	0.35	0.43	−0.25	0.56	0.59	0.53	0.82	1.00	
Macro investing	−0.06	−0.06	−0.01	0.32	0.52	0.23	0.67	−0.48	0.61	0.36	0.53	0.43	0.29	1.00

Note: Cash is represented by 90-day T-bills; core fixed income is the LB Aggregate; high-yield is the Citigroup High Yield Index; U.S. equity is the Russell 3000; and the hedge strategy indexes are the HFR, Inc. categorizations.
Source: RogersCasey.

Qualitative Factor Determinants for Hedge Funds

Quantitative factors that can be attributed as determinants of hedge fund return and volatility are identified in Chapter 11. In addition to quantitative factors, there are unique qualitative factors that contribute to the performance, volatility, and correlation of hedge funds. Although these qualitative factors are numerous and not easily quantified, they may at times contribute heavily to the total return of individual funds operating in this realm. The qualitative influences on hedge funds are described through examples for each individual hedge strategy described in this chapter.

MARKET SEGMENTATION

Hedge fund strategies have proliferated as the hedge fund industry has matured. Both the number of different strategies that exist and their asset size have increased over time. As Figure 3.1 illustrates, during the time period from 1990 through 2006, the shape of the hedge fund industry changed materially. From its initial critical mass of assets amounting to US$38.9 billion at the end of 1990, hedge fund assets grew to US$1.427 trillion at the end of 2006. Also during this time frame, the allocation of assets invested in hedge fund strategies has changed. The composition is more diverse, and there is no longer a majority of assets focused in the global macro strategy. Although a majority of assets have migrated to long/short equity, allocations are spread more equally over all hedge strategies. However, some of these strategies have finite capacity. For example, while long/short equity and global macro have deep capacity in the worldwide markets in which they invest, convertible bond arbitrage is constrained by the size of the convertible bond market.

HEDGE FUND STRATEGIES

Hedge funds and their strategies are heterogeneous. However, they can be divided into a number of categories. Four chief categories are long/short equity, relative value, event-driven approaches, and tactical trading. Long/short equity includes the substyles of long-biased and short-biased. The relative value category incorporates the subcategorizations of market-neutral equity, convertible bond arbitrage, and fixed-income arbitrage. Event-driven components consist of merger arbitrage, event arbitrage, and distressed debt. The tactical trading area encompasses global macro, commodity trading advisers, and statistical arbitrage. This is not meant to be a comprehensive discussion of all hedge fund styles, but rather a general overview of some of

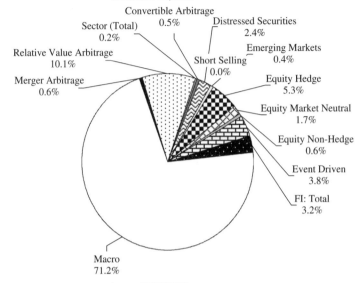

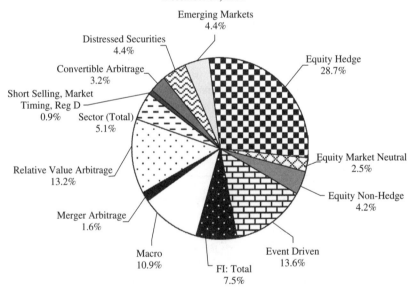

FIGURE 3.1 Hedge Strategy Capital Allocation, 1990 versus 2006
Source: HFR, Inc.

the main areas. Furthermore, certain substrategies can be described as fitting into more than one of the four main categories that have been identified. There also are miscellaneous strategies, including those focused on geographic sectors such as emerging markets, insurance types of investments, and crossover investments into other types of alternative investments such as private equity and real estate.

Long/Short Equity

The long/short equity strategy represents the classic investor concept of a hedge fund. Even though the hedge fund industry was historically driven more by global macro funds, long/short equity funds have become the lion's share of the total capital deployed by investors into hedge funds. The basic premise of investing in equities on a hedged basis is best described by the long/short equity strategy. Long/short equity funds are by their nature directional, which indicates that they tend to have some correlation to the markets in which they trade. The degree of their directionality is a function of net exposure, or gross long positions netted against gross short investments. A higher net exposure, which is the case for long-biased funds, indicates more directionality and higher correlation to public equity markets. A near-zero net exposure, which is the case for market-neutral equity funds, indicates net zero directionality and a theoretical noncorrelation to equity markets. As such, for the purposes of this book, market-neutral equity is considered in the context of relative value strategies. Negative net exposure, or the situation of a portfolio that has a greater dollar amount of short positions than long positions, is the condition for short biased funds.

Long-Biased

The long-biased construct is the primary approach to long/short hedged equity. This strategy is the logical extension of traditional long-only investment management. The evolution to long/short equity from long-only equity investing has certain important nuances. However, the basic execution of this strategy is founded on the same principles that most long-only equity portfolio management is organized. Many securities analysts and portfolio managers have migrated to hedge funds from the long-only investment world and are utilizing similar techniques. However, the higher fee structure for hedge funds versus long-only equity funds is such that hedge funds can afford to spend significant amounts to acquire leading-edge research. Furthermore, the high turnover of hedge funds causes the securities brokerage industry to be solicitous and provide hedge funds with research and investment banking products. With these benefits and in light of their ability to leverage capital and generate returns from both long and short investments, long/short hedge funds are more flexible than long-only equity funds. This is one of the basic appeals for most investors considering long-biased equity hedge funds.

The drivers of return for long/short equity are similar to those for the overall equity market. General economic strength has a beneficial effect on corporate profits, operating margins, and debt reduction, all of which tend to benefit equity owners. Technological advancement also has implications for corporate productivity. Also in terms of long-biased equity funds, low volatility in the equity market can be a boon. Alternatively, when these factors are weak, the short portion of long/short equity portfolios can benefit. However, there are other considerations that affect this investment strategy that are beyond these sensitivities. Since security selection based on strong research should be a hallmark for long/short equity hedge funds, these funds benefit from a rational performance of the equity market that rewards quality companies through stock price appreciation and penalizes poor-quality companies through stock price depreciation. Therefore, equity markets that have low correlation among individual equity prices are beneficial to the security selection approach of long/short equity hedge funds. Alternatively, in the case of a falling equity market with high correlation among individual securities, fundamentally attractive securities that are crowded with hedge fund investors may see larger relative price declines as hedge funds seek to reduce risk and sell securities regardless of merit. Therefore, issues such as institutional ownership and short interest ratios also may be drivers of return for long/short equity hedge funds.

Another basic attraction for investors in long-biased equity hedge funds is the prospect of over the long term achieving a return equal to or better than the overall equity market but with less volatility. The ability to generate a return commensurate with the overall equity market but with less volatility gives an investor a higher probability of experiencing asset growth that meets the need to fund liabilities. This might be the case for a pension plan seeking to grow its assets at such a rate that the asset pool would be able to meet pension liabilities over a long time frame. A benefit of doing this with greater assuredness is the reduction in likelihood that the pension sponsor would have a shortfall in assets and therefore be required to fund additional assets to support pension liabilities or reduce associated pension benefits.

A primary risk for an investor investing in long/short equity is substantially focused on manager selection risk. Because of the nature of long/short equity managers using leverage and short sales, there is the potential for portfolio risk management to break down. In such an event, leverage used in such a fund may be excessive and may combine with portfolio directionality or concentrated securities positions. These combinations can cause catastrophic outcomes. Therefore, the selection and monitoring of managers with sound portfolio risk controls and agreed-upon guidelines for leverage, gross and net exposure, and security diversification is vital for an investor's success. In the event that leverage and shorting are used in instances of security selection that is incorrect in its directional exposure, the potential for loss is multiplied relative to a long-only equity portfolio. Therefore, the dispersion of returns among long-biased equity hedge funds in any given year can be wider than the dispersion among long-only funds. Accordingly, the importance of manager selection that exists in other types of alternative investments is also present in the selection of long/short equity hedge funds.

Short-Biased Short-biased equity hedge funds are similar to long-biased funds, except for the reverse directionality and the implication this has for risk management. The problems that exist for long-biased hedge funds in terms of managing short exposures are more pronounced, because the short positions represent a larger portion of a short-biased portfolio. When short positions move against a hedge fund, the positions become larger and have a greater impact. A critical element to successfully managing either a long-biased or a short-biased fund is the difficulty in security selection and portfolio management as it pertains to the short portion of the fund. A significant problem in achieving profitability through short sales is the fact that over the long term the equity market has a positive bias. The success in selling a security short is achieved in the face of the position typically having a positive beta to the equity market. Therefore, security selection in short sales often is focused on fundamental events or characteristics such as flawed business models, fraudulent accounting practices, earnings shortfalls, or product delays. As important as the discovery of these characteristics is to the success of a short sale, the timing of the market's appreciation of these events and the initiation of a hedge fund's short position are equally important. At times, short investments made by hedge funds can be correct in fundamental analysis but misjudged in timing. The synchronicity of timing an event and the perception of the event by the marketplace are paramount. A sensitivity to timing in part relates to the risk of short squeeze, which is a rapid appreciation in price of a security that otherwise has poor fundamental characteristics. A short squeeze can occur when a security has a high percentage of its shares sold short by the investment community, and a sudden rise in the share price becomes self-sustaining as those who have sold the security short desire to cover their short positions through purchases. Furthermore, brokers and investors can cause a change in the availability of shares to borrow, which may force further purchases of the security to cover short sales and thereby exacerbate a rise in price.

Important qualitative factor drivers of return and risk for short-biased equity hedge funds relate to similar security selection considerations that apply to long-biased equity hedge funds. Furthermore, the portfolio management and risk controls that affect long-biased hedge funds are also relevant for short-biased funds. Risk management may have greater importance for short-biased funds, because of the open-ended nature of short sales. Significant return and risk factors for short-biased equity hedge funds include avoiding short squeeze, having accuracy in research and timing of short sales, and sizing positions in such a way as to control risk.

Because of the natural tendency for equity security prices to appreciate rather than depreciate and the technical difficulties of being successful in shorting equities, there has not been an enormous number of short-biased equity hedge funds that have been successful over the long term. Nevertheless, the attraction for investors in choosing these managers is the potential ability to hedge directionality from other long-biased investments. Short-biased hedge funds may potentially dampen volatility in a portfolio of multiple hedge fund investments. However, the risk of including short-biased hedge funds in such a portfolio is that they may not provide a profit over the long term because of the equity market's positive directional bias.

Relative Value

Relative value hedge strategies include market-neutral equity, convertible bond arbitrage, and fixed-income arbitrage. Relative value is one of the least homogeneous groupings of hedge strategies. It generally relates to nondirectional strategies that attempt to capture a pending convergence in valuation between securities. As such, the securities positions typically are paired and therefore tend to have a natural hedge in place. For instance, a relative value position might include a long position in one security paired with a short position in another security with the securities being similar in asset class but disparate in valuation. A relative value arbitrage might be conducted among different voting classes of securities issued by a common public entity. Furthermore, relative value strategies may use securities with different seniority from the same or different issuers and attempt to capture arbitrage spreads among them, sometimes with the assistance of derivatives on the securities. This endeavor also is called capital structure arbitrage. Typically, relative value strategies are sensitive to the absolute level of short-term interest rates, to the extent that the risk-free rate is the starting point from which the expected return from a relative value trade is constructed. A hedge fund will not seek to capture a discrepancy in valuation between two securities unless that discrepancy incorporates a spread above the risk-free rate of return. Another feature of relative value strategies that particularly differentiates them from event-driven strategies is their often ill-defined terminal points. The spread between two securities that is being captured from a relative value perspective does not have to close during any predetermined time frame. Granted, a hedge fund manager would like the spread to have as short a duration as possible, but typically there is nothing inherent in these trades that defines duration. Furthermore, some relative value strategies are perpetual in nature, where it is not so much the spread in valuation between securities that is being captured on a completed basis as it is the volatility of the spread that is being captured through dynamic changes to the amount of exposure to the short or long portion of the securities involved in the trade.

Market-Neutral Equity Market-neutral equity is a natural extension of long-only equity investment, and could very well be included as a substrategy of long/short equity. This substrategy represents the matching of an equal amount of long exposure to short exposure with no material positive or negative directionality to the equity market. While simple in concept, there are pitfalls in the execution of this approach that can render it not to be market neutral in certain environments. Beyond having an equal dollar amount of long and short equity exposure, portfolios in this area must ensure market neutrality as it also pertains to sectors, styles, and betas of the long versus the short portions of the portfolio. A near-zero net exposure implies little if any directionality or correlation to equity markets. However, this is not always the case if, for example, the market-neutral fund is constructed without regard to the individual betas of its underlying securities. Although a fund may be constructed equally long and short from a dollar perspective, the betas to the equity market of the longs may on average be smaller than the betas of the equities that have been sold short. Beta neutrality is an important element of ensuring market neutrality, particularly during moments of sharp market volatility when the movements in higher-beta stocks are greater than the movements in lower-beta stocks. In some cases, it may be that beta, neutrality requires being slightly non–dollar neutral. In addition to ensuring beta neutrality, market-neutral funds must ensure industry, geography, and style neutrality. Industry neutrality indicates that on a beta-adjusted basis the portfolio is long an equal amount of corporate issuers in one industry as it is short the securities of issuers in the same industry. Geographic neutrality is the discipline of being zero net exposed to any one country or market, thereby indicating the state of being long on a beta-adjusted basis an equal amount as short in those areas. Style neutrality measures the state of having neutral exposure on a beta-adjusted basis to growth; value; and small-, mid-, and large-capitalization stocks, the descriptions of which sometimes change over time as the size or characterization of securities is altered.

If one assumes that market-neutral investing has no beta to the equity market, then in a one-factor regression model the strategy should have no source of return other than a unique return, or alpha. Of course, this disregards the potential for any other fundamental factor betas to exist, such as elements of the fixed-income market (see Chapter 11). Additionally, volatility of the markets in which market-neutral equity funds trade also can have an impact on returns. Although perfectly market-neutral portfolios should not be affected either by declining or rising equity markets, short-term movements in individual securities prices enable these funds to capture discrepancies in valuation that they have identified.

The basic qualitative factors that drive returns for market-neutral equity funds relate to security selection, portfolio risk management, trade execution, and expense management. Security selection is perhaps the most important aspect of this investment style. A variation of market-neutral equity is the trading of discrete pairs of securities in more concentrated portfolios, rather than building a portfolio of a larger number of securities that may span an index. The success in security selection is even more relevant and apparent in pairs trading. Approaches to security selection in market-neutral equity include fundamental, quantitative, and technical. The ability to be successful using any of these approaches is critical for generating returns in a portfolio that is beta neutral. This is important since the market-neutral environment does not benefit from the underlying directional movement in the equity market.

Portfolio risk management can be an area where market-neutral investing is vulnerabe to failure. Maintaining a neutral balance through portfolio risk management is a focal point for success. Appropriate diagnostics must be established and monitored to ensure neutrality of a market-neutral portfolio's exposures to beta, sector, and style, for example. These diagnostic systems should be overseen by someone with judgment and perspective, such that new risks that are security specific or systemic in nature can be identified and neutralized. Examples of security-specific risks are market capitalization or industry creep that can occur as issuers gain or decline in value or change their industry sensitivity through mergers or divestitures. An example of systemic risk is the notion that some market-neutral funds have a quality bias, if they purchase securities with strong fundamental considerations and sell short those with relatively weaker fundamentals. These market-neutral funds may be vulnerable to certain rallies in the equity market that favor lower-quality, higher-beta equities at the expense of higher-quality, lower-beta equities. Some of this risk can be managed through the control of beta neutrality on a dynamic basis.

Trade execution and expenses represent a frictional cost to market-neutral equity investing that must be minimized. Assuming that the approaches to security selection and portfolio risk management to ensure market neutrality are equal among market-neutral equity funds, which they are not, a differentiator that affects relative performance at the margin is trading execution and related cost management. Trade execution seeks to minimize market price impact and commission expense. Market-neutral equity funds that are based on fundamental security selection typically have higher trading expenses than those based on quantitative security selection. A fundamental approach often has a reliance on investment research that carries with it higher commission expenses, while quantitative and technical approaches are either not associated with premium commissions charged by brokers or are executed through electronic systems that bypass full-service brokerage firms. The fundamental security selection approach may actually benefit through net investment performance in spite of higher commissions, if quality research enables the fund to conduct its security selection in a more effective manner. However, in the quantitative realm, brokerage is less well differentiated, except for speed and perhaps volume, and therefore is driven more by price considerations.

Investors find attraction in market-neutral equity investing owing to the strategy's consistent performance, low correlation to the equity market, and low volatility. The allure of market-neutral equity is its promise to generate bondlike returns with more stable standard deviation and less symmetry of these returns than is the case for bonds, with their sensitivity to interest rates. A basic risk for investors regarding market-neutral equity is in the event that the premise of neutrality for the strategy fails, and it becomes directional to the underlying equity market. Such a potential failure could manifest itself as positive or negative correlation to the equity markets. Unintended correlation may have a positive outcome (positive correlation to a rising equity market or negative correlation to a falling market) or more likely a negative outcome (positive correlation to a falling market or negative correlation to a rising market). Indeed, negative correlation to a rising equity market was the case for many market-neutral equity funds during the last part of the twentieth century, when market neutrality became unhinged by a value-style dependency. In the environment of the late 1990s, a rising equity market driven by low-quality, highly speculative growth stocks, which occurred over a sustained period, was a mismatch for many market-neutral equity funds that tended to be short these securities. In the evolution of market-neutral investing, this experience gave way to the inclusion of style and beta neutrality in portfolio construction rather than the prior somewhat sole focus on dollar neutrality.

Convertible Bond Arbitrage   There are at least three types of convertible bond strategies in which hedge funds engage: volatility trading, credit-oriented investments, and special situations that can include private investment in public entities (PIPEs) that are structured as convertible bonds. Each of these approaches to owning and hedging convertible bonds has different determinants of return and risk. Furthermore, each possesses different features of desirability and risk for investors. Some of these traits overlap other types of hedge strategies as well as other types of alternative investments. These commonalities are at the root of the need for more accurate measurement of the components of return and risk that can be determined through factor analysis. However, some of the factor sensitivities for convertible bond arbitrage are more qualitative than quantitative. These environmental considerations can hold equal importance as quantitative regressable factors. Although qualitative factors are difficult to specifically transform into metrics that can be used in algorithms, they are important to measure by investors when evaluating the desirability of these strategies at any point in time.

Volatility Trading   The classic approach to convertible bond arbitrage relates to volatility trading. In this strategy, a hedge fund is long a convertible bond and short a position in the issuer's common equity. The amount of short relative to the bond position relates to the degree to which the hedge fund wishes to hedge the convertible bond and the common stock into which it is convertible. In this strategy the investor receives several sources of income and capital appreciation, including: a current coupon payment from the convertible bond, the potential for appreciation in the price of the bond, and the potential for depreciation in the short equity position. There are also certain expenses, such as the cost of financing leverage associated with the strategy as well as the cost for paying dividends on short common stock positions. An appreciation in the price of the bond might be stimulated by a rise in the common stock price, since the bond is convertible into common stock, or by a decline in interest rates, which should benefit the bond as its yield becomes relatively attractive and its price adjusts upward. The hedge in this configuration of securities is a short position in the common stock. It also is where much of the return from the strategy is generated as well as where the volatility moniker is derived. A potential decline in the common stock may occur on an incidental basis. When it does occur, a portfolio manager using this strategy should benefit from the short position in common stock, while the convertible bond should not decline as much, because its par value and yield provide a floor to its price. In contrast, if the stock price rises, then the short position should generate a loss. However, this loss should be reduced by the long position in the convertible bond, which may rise based on the value of the underlying common stock into which it is convertible. During these gyrations, the portfolio manager may adjust the amount of short common stock to reflect changes in the underlying securities prices, thereby adjusting the hedge ratio. The more volatile a stock price on a short-term basis, the more there may be an opportunity in this strategy to capture return. Thus, short-term volatility is a key driver of returns for this approach. As such, since volatility usually is associated with a decline in stock prices, a convertible bond arbitrage strategy built on volatility trading holds attraction to investors because of its natural diversification benefit when added to assets that have more directionality with the equity market. The strategy also has had a historical tendency to generate consistent returns in most environments. A risk for investors in this strategy is that it generally requires leverage, which can exacerbate losses when they do occur. An additional risk is that hedge funds operating in this area tend to be correlated and tend to dominate the ownership of all convertible bonds. If a problem develops for one sizable hedge fund, it can impact the liquidity of and market price for all convertible bonds and therefore all hedge funds in the strategy.

There are myriad other influences that impact the return-enhancing environment for the convertible bond volatility trading segment. For instance, the availability of convertible bonds in the marketplace is a key consideration, because this strategy has finite capacity as defined by the market size of all convertible bonds. The level of convertible bond new issuance is an important factor that determines the supply of available bonds. An increasingly chronic problem for this strategy is the ability to generate consistently high returns, because of limited capacity and more capital entering the strategy than it is capable of handling. Another aspect of this problem is that the crowding of capital into the strategy can produce undesirable volatility. Therefore, the amount of capital and leverage devoted to the convertible arbitrage strategy relative to the market for convertible bonds is another factor to evaluate.

Credit Trading   The credit trading aspect of convertible bond arbitrage is similar to the distressed debt strategy in the event-driven category, since it largely depends on credit research. As such, the factor drivers of return and risk have some identical parallels with the distressed credit area, and many investors may choose to consider credit trading of convertible bonds as a dimension of that strategy. The essence of trading convertible bonds with a credit approach is the purchase of bonds hedged through the short sale of equity or the purchase of credit default swap protection. However, the money-making aspect of this strategy is not as focused on the volatility of the underlying stock price as is the case for volatility trading of convertible bonds. Rather, it is focused on the correct credit analysis of the bonds. The bonds under consideration may be trading at a discount based on the market's perception of the issuer's low credit rating or prospects. Astute credit research may identify a discrepancy between the true credit merit of an issue versus the market's pricing of the bond. In this way, a potential profit is captured through the purchase of a convertible bond with the hope that the bond price will rise as the primary source of return for the trade. A short equity position in this instance represents either a hedge in the event that the credit analysis is incorrect or an outright profit generator in the instance that an improvement in the credit outlook for the bond for some reason benefits the bondholders at the expense of the common shareholders.

The return drivers for credit trading of convertible bonds are focused on the movement in overall credit spreads across all credit instruments in the marketplace, as well as issuer-specific changes in fortune. Accurate security selection, credit research, and appraisal of convertible bond issuers are paramount for success in this strategy. Credit-driven convertible bond investing is oriented toward securities that may be near or in default, the security selection mechanics of which essentially are similar to the distressed strategy in the event-driven category. Access to bonds that may be difficult to acquire also may be a consideration. Furthermore, there can be an event aspect to the return from credit in convertible bonds. Financial restructuring, operational reorganization, potential spin-offs, and mergers and acquisitions also may have a bearing on the return from these investments. In some cases, these events improve the credit quality of convertible bonds, and in others they diminish credit quality. The prospect for these events and the environment that fosters a high or low incidence of their occurring are important contributors to return and risk in this strategy. Meanwhile, the basic appeal of the credit-oriented convertible bond strategy for investors lies in the same kind of appeal for other types of credit strategies, which is focused on absolute return through security selection–specific skill. The risk for investors is the potential for this skill to be errant, thereby leading to negative returns from security selection regardless of the movement in overall credit spreads that may positively or negatively affect the market for credit-influenced securities.

PIPEs Private investment in public equities, or PIPE transactions, often are structured as privately sold convertible bonds issued by public companies. At the time of the initial investment by purchasers of these bonds, this strategy has a long-only quality. The common stock into which the convertible bonds are convertible is initially unregistered. Hedging can occur through the short sale of peer groups that may have similar operating characteristics as the issuer of the PIPE. However, the short sale of common stock in advance of PIPE securities becoming registered is against securities regulations in the United States. The drivers of return in this strategy relate to deal flow and the discount between the PIPE securities and the price of the common equity into which they are convertible. Both of these return drivers depend on the skill of the investment manager who is securing, evaluating, and negotiating these transactions. Manager skill defines the attraction of this strategy for investors. An additional appeal of this strategy for investors is the ability to purchase public equities at a discount from their market price. However, a risk is that this discount cannot be monetized prior to a decline in the market price of the securities. Furthermore, the PIPE area has historically been fraught with regulatory issues. PIPE transactions can provide a unique source of return that is not dependent on the overall movement of the equity or bond markets. This unique source of absolute return also relates to another risk to investors in this strategy, which is the event that deal sourcing, researching, and negotiating by investment managers is not adequate and ultimately leads to returns that do not justify an investment. (For more on PIPE investments, see Chapter 7.)

Fixed-Income Arbitrage   Leveraged fixed-income arbitrage is a strategy that seeks to capture perceived relative value spreads among fixed-income securities. The leverage involved in this strategy can be accomplished notionally though futures or through cash borrowings generated from brokers or through term loans and revolving credit agreements. Often, leverage is accomplished through repurchase agreements with brokerage firms, which generate cash that is used for the purchase of other higher-yielding securities. Typically, operators of this strategy identify valuation discrepancies among fixed-income securities that may be of different durations or different issuers. To capture yield differences among these securities, leverage can be 10 times or more of the equity capital invested in these funds.

   The essential return drivers for this strategy are the absolute level of interest rates, the slope of the yield curve, and periodic shifts in the yield curve. Furthermore, the availability of capital and the ability to leverage invested equity is a critical aspect to ensuring the viability of these portfolios. This strategy often is associated with the basic carry trade, which is the sale of short-duration bonds and purchase of leverage and capturing the yield differential b are many variations on this concept, including hedging techniques that incorporate swap cont and currencies. However, the key return driver to fixed-income relative value investing is th A greater slope indicates a larger interest rate short-duration bonds, and therefore a greater ret yield curve warrants a lower return, owing to the smaller interest rate spread between long- and short-duration bonds. The key determinants of the slope of the yield curve can include U.S. Federal Reserve Bank monetary policy, the market demand for long-dated bonds, and the strength or weakness of the economy including the rate of inflation. The bond futures market allows for speculation regarding each of these drivers and can add speculative premiums or discounts to the market, which can marginally affect returns as well. Furthermore, the ability to borrow capital is significant for funds involved in this strategy. It is the leverage of bonds that enables the returns from this strategy to be attractive. For instance, if the interest rate spread between long- and short-dated bonds is 100 basis points, this represents a fairly unattractive return per annum. Thus, leverage is required to multiply the equity invested in these funds by investors. The narrower the interest rate spread, the greater the amount of leverage that is required to generate an attractive absolute return for investors. Tight credit conditions can stimulate a lack of lending capacity by brokers to funds that invest in this style, which can have a diminutive effect on returns from the strategy.

The appeal of this strategy for an investor is its fairly consistent performance, especially during periods of steep or flattening yield curves. When long-term interest rates are declining, the strategy benefits from yield capture and capital gains from leveraged long positions in long-duration bonds. A risk in this strategy for investors relates to a cyclical rise in interest rates, unpredicted changes in interest rates, and the early prepayment of debt securities by their issuers, which can have the effect of shortening duration and changing prices of the securities. All of these risks are exacerbated by the substantial leverage used in this strategy. Each of these risks, when manifest, can cause far greater losses than expected for this strategy. Losses in this strategy, when they occur, can be many standard deviations away from historical mean returns.

Event-Driven Approaches

Event driven is a category that generally includes hedge funds that utilize merger arbitrage, event arbitrage, and distressed debt. The success of each of these strategies tends to be contingent on business events unfolding that cause securities prices to change. Approaches to securities can be either long, short, or a combination of these in a hedged fashion. Representative events include the closure of a merger or acquisition offer in the case of merger arbitrage, the completion of a spin-off or recapitalization in the case of event arbitrage, and the successful emergence from bankruptcy reorganization in the area of distressed debt investing. There are many variations on these themes and ways in which hedge fund managers wager that events come to fruition, fail to materialize, or experience a change in expected timing. Furthermore, these positions can be simple in time frame or occur over long time frames with multiple periods, thereby offering combinations of trades and entry and exit points.

Merger Arbitrage   Merger arbitrage is one of the pillar strategies for hedge fund investing. This event-driven approach is a classic area for spread capture. The event aspect of merger arbitrage is the fact that an acquisition of one company by another has been disclosed to the public marketplace and completion is anticipated. Spreads, inclusive of a risk-free rate of return, are created through the difference in valuation between the securities of an acquiring company and those of the company being acquired. In the basic case, an acquiring company's common equity is priced at a slight premium to the company it is purchasing, assuming that the transaction is based on the purchasing company's exchange of its newly issued shares at some ratio to the shareholders of the target company. There are many variations for any specific merger or acquisition, including: transactions that represent exchanges for cash rather than equity, the stipulation that some transactions are only valid subject to securing financing, and the possibility for a change in the entire transaction in the event that a third party seeks to pay a premium to purchase the target company.

Numerous factors drive the merger arbitrage strategy. Chief among them is the volume of deals, as measured by the number of available transaction and the market capitalization of companies involved in the transactions. Furthermore, the amount of capital invested in the merger arbitrage strategy relative to the volume of available transactions is an important determinant for returns. To the extent that the volume of available transactions is much larger than the available investment capital in the merger arbitrage strategy, this is a stimulus for wider spreads and therefore higher returns on capital. The reverse can be said as well. Another key determinant of absolute returns in the merger arbitrage space is the level of short-term interest rates. Short-term rates are the core starting point for a merger arbitrage spread. These spreads, which usually are referred to on an annualized basis since the duration of a merger arbitrage transaction typically is a year or less, incorporate a risk-free return. The amount of spread above the risk-free rate is a function of the aspects of each specific deal, such as: the expected duration of the deal, the credit quality of the involved entities, the risk of the deal not closing, financing risks, and cash versus stock transactions. These bottom-up deal-specific characteristics also represent key drivers of returns for the merger arbitrage strategy.

The merger arbitrage strategy serves a multifaceted purpose for market participants. If transactions are priced too inexpensively, sometimes negative spreads will occur, thereby signaling a valuation discrepancy. Merger arbitrage spreads also price risk associated with transactions. This risk can be sold by investors in the securities of the companies involved in transactions. The buyers of this risk, the merger arbitrage hedge funds, serve the purpose of providing liquidity and the removal of risk for an investor who does not wish to hold the securities to fruition of a merger transaction, possibly out of concern that the transaction will not close and the related securities prices will decline in value. For investors in the merger arbitrage strategy, returns tend to be very stable and highly predictable. The low volatility of merger arbitrage returns is an attractive component to use in portfolio construction. Astute and experienced merger arbitrage portfolio managers maintain diversification among deals in which they are invested. They conduct rigorous research into the aspects of each transaction, which enables them to fairly price the risk associated with each deal. The inherent risk in this strategy is potential correlation among deals when there is a shock to the equity markets that can cause an unanticipated widening of spreads. Although not a deal-specific risk, such systemic shocks to the market can in a worst-case scenario cause some merger arbitrage transactions to fail altogether. In the event that a number of merger or acquisition transactions are canceled, the potential losses associated with an investment in the strategy can be significant relative to the expected return from the spreads associated with the strategy.

As with an insurance contract, often it is the provider of the insurance who collects a premium, while the purchaser of the insurance pays a premium. It is this serially returning aspect of the merger arbitrage strategy that is at the heart of the attraction for investors. An investor who sells stock in an acquisition target prior to consummation of a deal is giving up or paying the last few percentage points of return to an arbitrageur who is assuming the risk that the transaction may not close. As hedge funds migrate into property and casualty reinsurance, these efforts may not be as out of place as one might think, given the familiarity of many hedge funds with the risk insurance concept.[1]

Event Arbitrage Event arbitrage can in some cases be very similar to merger arbitrage. However, it tends to have fewer constraints in terms of the types of transactions that characterize it. Event arbitrage may include the purchase of securities based on speculation or the announcement of an acquisition, restructuring, corporate share repurchase, spin-off, or recapitalization. Rather than a pure spread strategy, event arbitrage often is directional in nature. Many events are difficult to exactly hedge. Therefore, hedges may not exist or may be in unrelated securities. For example, an event arbitrageur who wishes to invest in a company based on a subsidiary that is expected to be spun off might use as a hedge a short position in a peer company that competes with the issuer or the subsidiary. In this fashion, the arbitrageur can neutralize an industry-specific risk associated with either the issuer or the subsidiary. The important drivers of return for event arbitrage tend to be idiosyncratic and include research that is required to discover pending events, creativity to be able to visualize value that may be stored in certain securities or corporations, and possibly activist skill to unlock value in target investments. The appeal of the event arbitrage strategy for investors is the prospect for strong performance, as well as performance being unique and uncorrelated to the capital markets. A primary risk in this strategy is that the research and creative hypothesis building, on which the strategy depends, may be faulty or face unwilling management teams or boards of directors associated with corporate issuers. In this case, the events on which this strategy is based may not transpire. Event risk may represent an opportunity cost for investors in this strategy, or it may result in capital losses. The risk for investors in the event arbitrage strategy is twofold: unique negative performance that is uncorrelated to the capital markets and market-related risk, since often the event strategy has an inherent directional exposure.

Distressed Debt The distressed debt strategy utilizes an array of securities that are in various stages of distress. Securities can range across the debt capital structure, including secured loans, unsecured bonds, and private trade claims. Various levels of distress can include stressed credit with ratings below investment grade, debt originally issued by solvent companies that has fallen into default, and direct loans to nonstandard borrowers in novel transactions. Hedge funds engaged in this strategy make loans or purchase debt that has been well researched and appears creditworthy relative to the duration and expected yield at which it has been priced. Distressed debt often is a long-biased credit investment. However, short credit investments can be made through borrowing and shorting bonds or loans. A difficulty in conducting a short distressed debt strategy is the prospect for paying interest to the owner of the borrowed debt, unless it no longer is paying interest. An alternative for expressing short credit exposure is through the purchase of credit derivatives, the market for which has become robust.

Important factor drivers of return for distressed debt include the expansion or contraction of credit spreads on a marketwide basis, as well as unique research and access to distressed securities that can provide profit. Proprietary research and access to loans and bonds can distinguish one distressed debt fund from another. Unique sources of return may relate to relationships in the marketplace or specialized skill at certain distressed debt hedge funds. For example, a fund may have personnel with certain legal expertise in bankruptcy proceedings. Aside from discrete manager-oriented skill, market return drivers for distressed debt largely are oriented toward the movement in credit spreads. Narrowing credit spreads benefit owners of below-investment-grade debt. A narrowing of credit spreads indicates a decline in the yield premium for non-investment-grade credit over investment-grade corporate credit or risk-free government debt. A change in credit spreads can be influenced by overall economic health and the amount of capital in the market seeking non-investment-grade debt for purchase or sale. Corporate cash flow, interest rate cycles, and movements in capital markets also can impact credit spreads. Furthermore, a robust debt issuance market can enable issuers with nearly delinquent debt to sell less senior securities in order to repay secured credit. In addition to creating refinancing avenues, buoyant capital markets can facilitate the sale of subsidiaries or operations to generate proceeds for the repayment of liens and other obligations.

The attraction of the distressed debt strategy for an investor is the potential generation of high absolute returns. The risk associated with the distressed debt strategy for investors is focused on the directional aspect of the approach. To the extent that credit spreads widen across the market for all below-investment-grade securities, even attractive investments in the distressed debt sector will witness a similar negative shift in valuation. An additional risk pertains to the hedging instruments in credit portfolios. If single-issuer credit default swap derivatives are used to hedge long positions in distressed securities, then there is an element of counterparty risk. A risk is the failure of a counterparty, in which case the hedge fund would not be able to capture the hedge on its long position in a credit.

Tactical Trading

The major components of tactical trading are global macro, commodity trading advisers, and high-volatility trading methods such as statistical arbitrage. These strategies incorporate the use of currencies, equities, and fixed-income securities, often expressed through futures, forwards, options, and swaps. Through their frequent low-correlation attributes, these strategies can make complementary additions to diversified portfolios of alternative investments. During high-volatility periods that can affect traditional asset classes, particularly the equity markets, some of the tactical trading strategies can offer positive performance because of their association with commodities and sovereign bonds. During a flight to quality, commodities as well as sovereign bonds denominated in creditworthy currencies often are sought as a haven from uncertain markets. In spite of periods of higher volatility that can occur in some of these strategies, their diversification benefits during negative market cycles are such that investors consider their use. Tactical trading strategies can act as a form of insurance for a diversified portfolio of hedge strategies. They may provide an opportunity cost during normal periods through their volatility, but offer the prospect for strong countercyclical benefits and performance during high-volatility periods in the markets.

Global Macro   The global macro strategy is a significant area of capital in the hedge fund industry. It also historically represented the largest segment of capital allocated to hedge funds. Over time, its prowess has diminished on a relative basis, because of the advent of new hedge strategies. Capital flowing into hedge funds has sought strategies that are less volatile than global macro and have fewer of the risks inherent in the leverage and types of securities that it employs. The typical global macro strategy uses considerable amounts of real and notional leverage to execute positions in fixed-income securities. Many discretionary approaches to global macro are broadly dependent on either mean reversion or trend-following concepts. Although similar to leveraged fixed-income trading, global macro is conducted on a global scale, thereby exposing this strategy to currency returns and risks. It also is directional by nature, unlike relative value fixed-income arbitrage, which is more hedged and tends toward the market-neutral end of the directional spectrum. The drivers of return for the global macro style relate to international interest rates and credit and their impact on bond prices and currencies. Trades are represented through futures, options, and swaps as well as straight bond positions. Since there are myriad potential directional as well as hedged combinations of positions in this strategy, performance and risk are more determined by the skill and risk management techniques possessed by investment managers. Furthermore, as is the case with the relative value fixed-income strategy, access to leverage either through debt or notionally through derivatives is an important component of return.

The allure of the global macro strategy for capital allocaters relates to its global blend of securities, ability to handle large amounts of capital, and the prospect of generating significant returns. Furthermore, the strategy offers diversification benefits, particularly during periods of high market volatility. However, many of the aspects of the strategy's potential for return generation are symmetrical in their potentiality for loss. The fact that this strategy utilizes significant amounts of leverage implies risk in the event that the investments deployed are incorrect in their directionality. Furthermore, risks lie in the potential for sovereign regulation that may affect the markets and securities in which these funds trade.

Commodity Trading Advisers   Commodity trading advisers (CTAs) benefit from various styles of trading futures contracts on commodities, including systematic and discretionary. The systematic approach is based on computer systems that generate signals on which a hedge fund acts. These signals can be fundamental (based on supply-and-demand metrics) or technical (based on price movements). Each of these approaches may also employ trend-following, mean reversion, or other price-predictive techniques. Most CTAs have branched out to include futures on other assets, including currencies, equities, and fixed-income securities. The CTA, or managed futures, moniker now pertains more to a general style of trading, rather than a pure focus on the commodity asset group. Chapter 6 contains a specific approach to analyzing the return drivers for commodities and currencies in the context of portfolio construction using alternative investments. From a trading perspective, the drivers of return and risk in this strategy typically relate to the cycle or frequency of price movement. The length of periods of volatility and directionality of price movements create gains for this strategy. A critical aspect for investors to consider regarding commodities and currencies is the fact that they do not have an inherent return. Currencies are simply a transfer of wealth mechanism. Commodities also have no dividends or interest payments that enable investors to calculate their value. They are affected more by cyclical supply-and-demand influences. Therefore, the fundamentals of supply and demand are important price determinants, as is speculation, which also can determine price movements over surprisingly sustained periods of time.

The basic attraction for investors in CTA-type investments is their tendency to have low correlation to traditional asset classes and alternative investments, especially during periods of volatility in the equity–, credit–, and interest rate–sensitive markets. During periods of market shock, investors typically seek shelter in commodities such as gold and energy as well as certain currencies. Volatility in these assets can provide either sharp gains or losses, depending on whether the CTAs invested in these assets have long or short positions. Moreover, the style of trading these instruments can determine profit or loss from price movement in these assets. Sudden price changes may provide opportunity for gain or loss, and trending price movements may do the same. The risk for investors in these types of investments is that they do not always represent long positions in commodities. It may be that an investment in a CTA can produce losses during periods of rising commodities prices, depending on the trading style and directional approach taken by the investment manager. CTAs can generate high standard deviation of returns. This volatility can make an investment in this area less predictable than strategies that are more market neutral by nature. Furthermore, an investment in a CTA is a high-fee alternative to the passive approach of investing in a commodities index, which represents another way to achieve a commodities investment for diversification benefits in a portfolio of mixed assets.

Statistical Arbitrage   Although statistical arbitrage could also be considered a relative value strategy, its high-frequency turnover is such that for the purposes of this book it is included in the tactical trading sector. This strategy often is based on the trading of equities through computer models, which entails the rapid execution of small-sized trades, both long and short, as determined by algorithmic formulae. Computer systems measure the sensitivity of securities to certain signals. These signals include fundamental ratios relative to a security's price (e.g., price to book value) and technical ratios relative to a security's price (e.g., relative price strength). Signals that are above or below certain absolute or relative thresholds may trigger trades that are executed through electronic, fully automated trading systems.

As is the case with CTAs, the approach of statistical arbitrage is that of a trading style rather than a generalization about fundamental or quantitative factor return drivers. The complexity in these styles includes the fact that funds may be positioned to benefit from short- or long-term positive or negative movements in fundamental or technical factors. As such, there is an inability to generalize about the directionality of these funds as a group. Accordingly, the basic return drivers for statistical arbitrage funds, and what sets one firm apart from another, typically is the quality and technical superiority of their computer models and the applied quantitative research that enables them to discover and model signals that have variable frequencies. The basic lack of transparency and secrecy of these funds in terms of the identification and frequency of their trading signals as well as the nature of the computer-generated algorithms that enable them to identify these signals is far more restrictive than is the case for most other types of alternative investment styles. The methodology represented by these signals is considered to be proprietary by these firms. The veracity of each signal typically has a finite life, until the market and its participants discover the opportunity as well and dissipate any return potential from the inefficiency. Thus, the return drivers for the statistical arbitrage strategy are temporal by nature. The firms that trade using this approach are required to re-create return drivers on a constant basis through the sophistication of their staff and systems.

The appeal of statistical arbitrage for investors is its prospect for low volatility and consistent returns. It is the more sophisticated firms with top resources in personnel and computer systems that can generate consistent returns with little variance. A basic problem for investors accomplishing this exposure is one of capacity and risk monitoring. The better firms in statistical arbitrage typically limit their acceptance of outside investor capital over time. As each accomplished firm in this strategy gains profits and reinvests in their funds, over a period of time the general partner and its employees tend to represent the largest investors in their own fund. A result is that capital often is returned to limited partners, since the inefficiencies that the funds exploit have finite capacity. Therefore, accomplishing and maintaining an investment in the best-performing funds in statistical arbitrage can be problematic for investors. Alternatively, investors willing to accept mean-performing funds in this strategy, as are represented by the performance and volatility of indexes that track this area, may be unlikely to achieve exemplary results. Mid-tier funds in this area may actually provide profit to top-tier funds, to the extent that the mid-tier firms create statistical inefficiencies in the market that the more sophisticated firms can identify and capture. Another area of risk for investors in statistical arbitrage is the potential inability to conduct due diligence and monitor the portfolios in which they are invested. Although organizational due diligence can be accomplished on statistical arbitrage firms, the secrecy of the signals that drive investment decisions in these funds does not always afford investors transparency into the investment processes. This should be significantly disconcerting to most responsible investors. An inability to gauge portfolio composition and investment style can place an investor in the position of forsaking their fiduciary duty. Therefore, statistical arbitrage may not be well suited to all investors.

Other Strategies

There are a number of other strategies in the broad domain of hedge funds. These include sector funds that focus on certain industries or geographic locations such as emerging markets and construct portfolios using a range of instruments including debt and equity. Some of these strategies migrate into variations of other hedge strategies, such as fixed-income arbitrage and long/short equity. Other strategies also include more inventive areas such as property reinsurance, life insurance settlements, and other alternative investment strategies such as leveraged buyouts, venture capital, real estate, and commodities. Each of these other areas is idiosyncratic in its qualitative and quantitative factor determinants of return, appeal to investors, and the specific risks it introduces to an investor's portfolio. These strategies may only be incidental in an overall portfolio of hedge fund investments or act as diversifiers in multistrategy hedge funds. Some of these strategies disappear prior to gaining much critical mass, based on regulation, capacity constraints, or difficulty in execution. Since many of these strategies are difficult to generalize, lack depth in order to invest significant amounts of capital, lack broad investor appeal, or do not have well-defined parameters, they are not discussed in depth.

Multistrategy Hedge Funds   Multistrategy hedge funds package hedge fund strategies in a blend of allocations. These funds are focused on bottom-up security selection, which generally informs their asset allocation in portfolio construction. Multistrategy hedge funds generally make investment decisions based on specific return objectives and do not construct trades unless they meet certain return expectations. This bottom-up focus on return from investments tends to be the primary driver of portfolio construction and asset allocation for multistrategy hedge funds. It is not to say that multistrategy hedge funds pay no heed to macroeconomic factors that affect hedge strategy asset allocation decisions when constructing their portfolios, but these considerations are apt to have less influence on their security selection endeavors.

THE CONSTRUCTION OF A SEGREGATED PORTFOLIO OF HEDGE FUNDS

Hedge strategies can be used in a portfolio of diversified assets or in a portfolio that is dedicated only to hedge funds. In a blended portfolio of all types of assets, the inclusion of hedge strategies can provide performance enhancement as well as risk reduction through diversification. There are numerous factors that determine the returns and volatility in hedge strategies and that also are present in traditional asset classes, which is discussed in more detail in Chapter 11. When considering the use of only hedge strategies in an optimized portfolio, some of the same principles are present as is the case in other asset optimizations. For instance, the use of constraints for the maximum allowable allocations to any one hedge strategy generates an efficient frontier that is optimized in its risk and return output. As illustrated in Figure 3.2, a lack of constraints in an optimizer using these strategies provides an efficient frontier that has an extended risk spectrum relative to the amount of commensurate return that is expected. In comparison, Figure 3.3, which utilizes a constraint of a 25 percent maximum allocation to any one strategy, provides a truncated efficient frontier. Although the use of constraints in this instance decreases the opportunity for the highest possible levels of return, the benefit from doing so is avoidance of incremental levels of risk. These higher levels of risk appear to be associated with relatively small incremental amounts of compensation. The riskier portfolios tend to seek greater allocations of long/short equity and distressed debt, while the lower-risk portfolios have high allocations to relative value, equity market neutral, and merger arbitrage. All portfolios in these examples have fairly constant allocations to event-driven as a strategy. There is little allocation that is demanded by the optimizer for convertible bond arbitrage, short selling, and global macro, which relates to the relatively lower risk-adjusted

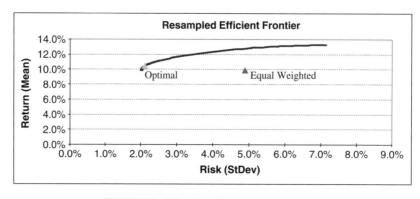

	Optimal Portfolio	Equal Portfolio	Optimal Portfolios -- by Rank					
			1	11	21	31	41	51
Equity Market Neutral	7.5%	11.1%	22.7%	2.7%	0.2%	0.1%	0.0%	0.0%
Equity Hedge	0.6%	11.1%	0.0%	1.7%	6.4%	13.4%	28.8%	56.0%
Short Selling	4.3%	11.1%	5.8%	3.4%	1.8%	1.2%	1.6%	4.4%
Event Driven	36.6%	11.1%	32.8%	37.3%	38.2%	40.7%	40.1%	29.9%
Merger Arbitrage	21.9%	11.1%	12.4%	20.3%	6.7%	1.6%	0.2%	0.0%
Distressed Securities	1.0%	11.1%	0.0%	4.0%	16.4%	27.2%	24.3%	9.1%
Relative Value	27.9%	11.1%	26.2%	30.0%	28.5%	13.3%	3.3%	0.4%
Convertible Arbitrage	0.0%	11.1%	0.0%	0.0%	0.0%	0.0%	0.0%	0.0%
Macro	0.3%	11.2%	0.0%	0.6%	1.6%	2.4%	1.8%	0.2%
Total	100.0%	100.0%	100.0%	100.0%	100.0%	100.0%	100.0%	100.0%
Average Annual Return	10.4%	9.9%	9.9%	10.7%	11.5%	12.3%	12.9%	13.3%
Standard Deviation	2.1%	4.9%	2.0%	2.2%	2.9%	3.9%	5.2%	7.1%

FIGURE 3.2   Portfolio Optimization of Hedge Strategies (Unconstrained)
Note: Model is unconstrained. Data is 1996 through June 2006.
Source: RogersCasey; Resampled Efficient Frontier™ provided by New Frontier Advisors LLC.

returns for these strategies. Nevertheless, the low pairwise correlation attributes of many strategies still render them viable for some inclusion in any diversified portfolio of hedged strategies. The optimal portfolio indicated in the efficient frontiers in these figures represents the portfolio with the highest Sharpe ratio, which may or may not reflect any one investor's risk and return goals. Furthermore, the use of the Sharpe ratio and the entire mean variance optimization approach are flawed in this context, because of the non-normal return distributions that can emanate from hedge strategies. Nevertheless, they remain helpful illustrative tools.

Optimization Issues

There are some significant drawbacks to the use of mean variance optimization for the creation of portfolios of hedge fund strategies. These include

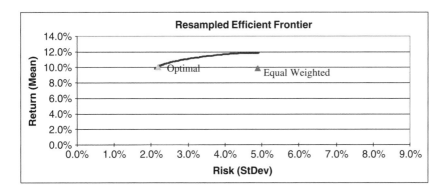

FIGURE 3.3 Portfolio Optimization of Hedge Strategies Constrained at 25 Percent
Note: Model allows for a maximum of 25 percent allocation to any one hedge strategy. Data is 1996 through June 2006.
Source: RogersCasey; Resampled Efficient Frontier™ provided by New Frontier Advisors LLC.

the fact that returns for hedge strategies tend not to be normal in their distribution and are prone to events that fall multiple standard deviations from mean observations. Furthermore, there are numerous biases involved in the index strings that are used for this sort of analysis. These and other shortcomings are discussed in more detail in Chapter 11. A more exacting approach to building portfolios that utilize allocations to alternative investments based on factor analysis is contained in the second section of this book.

Hedge Funds of Funds

Hedge funds of funds are a primary implementation vehicle for the construction of portfolios of hedge funds and hedge strategies. Funds of funds manage more than one-third of all assets invested in hedge funds.[2] Funds of funds may indefinitely represent the platform of choice for certain investors seeking exposure to hedge funds, owing to their capabilities in the following areas: manager access and due diligence, access to transparency from hedge funds, liquidity arbitrage, and portfolio construction using different types of hedge funds and hedge strategies. Some funds of funds construct portfolios of hedge funds through the use of factor analysis and security level transparency pertaining to hedge funds in order to identify factor sensitivities. Increasingly, investors may see the applicability of factor analysis to their hedge fund portfolios and to the rest of their traditional and alternative investments as well.

Investor Suitability   There are characteristics of some investors that cause them to be compatible with hedge funds of funds and the capabilities they offer. Characteristics that may suit investors well to funds of funds include limited expertise, desire, or inability to add resources required to manage a direct hedge fund investment program. These investors may lack enough size to achieve proper diversification in a portfolio of hedge funds, or they may not have a network of relationships to be able to identify promising hedge fund managers and garner access. However, this group also may include even the largest investors. Investors turn to funds of funds for an additional layer of security that they provide in portfolio construction, hedge fund manager selection, and due diligence. The appeal of hedge funds of funds also lies in their specialized products, which can offer exposure to certain market segments that an investor might not otherwise be able to efficiently achieve. Specialized or niche-type products include hedge funds of funds that have a focus on emerging hedge funds, emerging markets, Asia-only, Europe-only, and difficult-to-analyze strategies.

Capabilities in manager selection and access to some of the best hedge funds is a clear benefit to investors who may not have access to apparently "closed" hedge funds. As investors adopt hedge funds, they ultimately seek the same level of transparency and oversight that is commonly attained in traditional investments. A degree of this comfort may be achieved from a fund of funds. Some funds of funds gather security-level transparency either from their hedge funds or from third-party risk aggregators and can use that information in their risk management and portfolio construction tasks. Transparency of risks in portfolios of hedge funds enables an analysis of factor exposures and facilitates portfolio construction by funds of funds. This attribute is attractive to investors.

Liquidity Arbitrage   Another attractive characteristic of funds of funds is liquidity. Liquidity is a significant issue pertaining to investment in hedge funds. Hedge funds are becoming less liquid, which is a function of hedge funds investing in less liquid investments and extending their lockup and redemption periods. Matching redemption periods to the duration of investments is appropriate. However, hedge funds that have less liquid investments and longer redemption periods present a problem for investors. Most asset allocation models used by investors have different return and risk assumptions for hedge funds versus private equity investments. As hedge funds begin to migrate toward less liquid private equity investments, they force investors to rethink the illiquidity risk premium that they should be paid for investing in hedge funds. Perhaps illiquid hedge funds should not be modeled under hedge fund assumptions but rather private equity assumptions. Although some investors are better suited to long lockup hedge funds than other investors, from an asset allocation perspective investors may find that they are not appropriately compensated by hedge funds for the longer lockup. In contrast, hedge funds of funds provide an arbitrage for investors who do not want the illiquidity exposure presented by some hedge funds. Most funds of funds provide liquidity terms that are more generous than the illiquid hedge funds in which they may have an investment. In turn, a portion of the fee that a fund of funds commands might be considered as payment for this liquidity arbitrage that is offered to investors.

Portfolio Construction Skill   Skill in portfolio construction also should be an important part of the value proposition provided by hedge funds of funds. In addition to constructing portfolios of hedge funds with various risk and return attributes, hedge funds of funds usually generate forward-looking views on the hedge strategies that they use. This process enables tactical allocation and rebalancing among hedge strategies, which can be an important contributor to overall performance. The funds of funds that are particularly good at this are able to make the argument that they add value in a way that an investor simply picking multistrategy hedge funds is unable to do. Skill in portfolio construction is an example of a significant differentiator for funds of funds. An important component of portfolio construction is factor analysis. Factor analysis provides funds of funds with the ability to quantitatively analyze their portfolios and conduct scenario analysis based on changes in interest rates, credit spreads, volatility, equity prices, and other factors that contribute to hedge fund returns. The fact that some funds of funds are able to create forward-looking estimates of these factors can be a differentiator as well. Funds of funds make positive and negative allocations to factors such as volatility, credit spreads, and liquidity. Most investors invest in hedge funds only with the modest goals of performance enhancement and diversification. The skills that some funds of funds have in portfolio construction can provide considerable value to investors seeking more accurate and robust factor-based performance, measurement, and diversification.

The Use of Factor Analysis   The use of factor analysis increasingly can be a catalyst for the adoption of hedge funds and funds of funds by investors. Factor analysis is the basis for strategy allocations for better hedge funds of funds. The more that hidden equity beta is identified in hedge funds, the more investors should become aware enough to appreciate the unique other factor betas offered by hedge funds and their ability to invest long or short in these factors. As investors grasp the concept of multifactor analysis for evaluating their own portfolios, the stark lopsidedness of many long-only factor exposures to the equity and bond markets should become more evident. This type of realization, such as having a 60 percent portfolio exposure to one factor (equity) and long-only at that, has led many endowments to drastically diversify their factor exposures through the greater use of alternative investments. Hedge funds and hedge funds of funds are entering the mainstream of portfolio construction, and the foundation of that pathway is a better definition of the unique return drivers captured in the open architecture of hedge funds. Expert hedge funds of funds may have created a prototypical portfolio platform, to which the most sophisticated investors ultimately will migrate, and some already have.

The question of whether hedge funds of funds are the platform of choice for investors has a deeper meaning than their structural fit with certain investors. Hedge funds of funds are not merely an easy way to implement a hedge fund investment. They represent a new way to think about investing through factor exposures. Hedge funds of funds seem to have created the platform of choice. Not only can it be populated with unique hedge fund factors, but also with traditional betas. This way of looking at portfolio construction transcends investor types and the more limited notion of style exposures. Ultimately, it can be the way in which all investors evaluate their portfolios of all types of asset classes.

SUMMARY

In spite of not being homogeneous, hedge funds and their strategies can be divided into sectors that have common return drivers. Long/short equity, relative value, event-driven approaches, and tactical trading are groupings that enable consideration of most individual hedge strategies. Each of these has primary qualitative determinants of return and risk. For example, long/short equity can be dependent on the quality of research used in making investment decisions. Relative value strategies tend to find their success or failure linked to security selection, risk management, trade execution, and strategy capacity. Returns from event-driven approaches are sensitive to the availability of securities, the quality of credit research, and event prediction and precipitation. Tactical trading has as its foundation tactics that focus on risk management, the availability of leverage, and the quality of computer models. The use of these strategies can provide performance enhancement, risk reduction, and diversification to a portfolio of mixed assets. Furthermore, portfolios that are dedicated exclusively to hedge strategies can be constructed. These portfolios consist of allocations to hedge strategies that can benefit from unique factors. Factor exposure also may relate to the inclusion of traditional asset classes. The numerous ways in which hedge strategies can be used to establish exposures to various return and risk factors render them suitable for portfolio construction. Hedge funds of funds can be used as implementation vehicles for this purpose and may have created the platform of choice for doing so.

CHAPTER 4

Private Equity

T he two main areas of private equity are venture capital and leveraged buyouts (LBOs). In addition to these core regions, other private equity strategies include mezzanine debt, distressed, secondary investments, special situations, and funds of funds. The primary private equity strategies are described along with their return and diversification attributes. This chapter seeks to provide an overview of these strategies as well as highlight the qualitative drivers of their return and risk. The independent variables that influence these strategies from a quantitative perspective are discussed in Chapter 11.

In appraising the various private equity strategies, the analysis of quartile segmentation is germane. There is a wide dispersion of returns among the investment managers that operate in these strategies. As a result, an investor's ability to replicate the performance of quartiles may be more relevant than modeling the mean performance and volatility characteristics for any single strategy. Furthermore, private equity strategies can be combined in optimized portfolios. A balance between venture capital and LBO investments can be used in portfolio allocations to achieve a broad range of targeted return and risk.

PERFORMANCE AND DIVERSIFICATION ATTRIBUTES

The primary attraction of private equity for investors is performance. Most investors associate private equity with outsized gains from venture capital and LBO deals. However, the domain of private equity is complicated by issues such as access to high-quality investment managers, vintage year performance, and competing sources of capital for transactions. Although historically the investment performance of private equity, broadly speaking, has enabled early investors to reap outsized gains, the field has become more efficient than it once was.[1] This efficiency has occurred because of the degree to which institutional investors have flocked to the area. The ability for an investor to be successful in private equity relates to the maturity of relationships that can identify and provide access to the top investment managers in the field.

Furthermore, embarking on a private equity program requires a multi-year approach of investing over broad private equity cycles. Commitment of capital to this area is required to be consistent through good times and bad, in order to smooth performance over different market environments. A tricky aspect of private equity investing is that the point in time when commitments to funds are made does not necessarily reflect the conditions under which those commitments will be either invested or harvested. There is significant lead time for committed capital to be called and subsequently liquidated during the life of a private equity fund. Private equity funds typically are structured as closed-end limited partnerships with 10-year terms and possible extensions thereafter. Human nature is such that there is natural reticence to make new commitments to private equity during poor market environments, in spite of the fact that the new commitment often will not actually be invested and monetized until future market cycles. A program of exposure to multiple vintage years provides diversification and defends against this element of human nature. Nevertheless, new commitments should be sized based on the outlook for cash flow from and carrying values of existing private equity investments (see Chapter 8).

Beyond cyclical considerations, there are secular changes that have occurred in the private equity realm that should cause an investor to view attractive historical performance data from these funds with a cautious eye. Other providers of capital, such as hedge funds, have entered into this market (see Chapter 7). The impact from this change potentially permanently changes the long-term expected return in the various private equity strategies. It also potentially alters the number of available transactions, to the extent that other sources of capital can change the configuration of transactions. For example, a hedge fund might provide a loan for the recapitalization of a company through which a dividend is paid to its owners, rather than that company seeking a financial partner for an LBO. Nevertheless, with the assumption that these hurdles can be surmounted, private equity remains an attractive component for the overall construction of an investment portfolio.

Table 4.1 shows the performance of private equity strategies over multiyear periods. Robust historical performance is a significant source of allure that private equity provides to investors in general. Although Table 4.1 also alludes to the volatility that can occur in performance over various time intervals, this risk is acceptable within the context of risk budgeting in the construction of an investor's portfolio. That is to say, when proportionally allocated, the volatility of returns from private equity is acceptable as long as

TABLE 4.1 Private Equity Investment Returns as of September 30, 2006

	1 Year	3 Years	5 Years	10 Years	20 Years
All venture	7.0%	9.1%	−1.2%	20.5%	16.5%
All buyouts	21.6%	15.6%	9.1%	8.8%	13.2%
Mezzanine	−0.4%	4.8%	2.9%	5.9%	8.4%
All private equity	16.5%	13.1%	5.8%	11.2%	14.0%

Source: Thomson Financial: 1,814 U.S. venture capital and buyout funds formed since 1969.

TABLE 4.2 Private Equity Correlation Matrix 1996–2006 Q1

	Cash	Core FI	ILBs	High Yield	U.S. EQ	PE	Venture	LBO
Cash	1.00							
Core fixed income	0.20	1.00						
Inflation-linked bonds (TIPS)	−0.06	0.73	1.00					
High-yield	−0.25	−0.16	−0.20	1.00				
U.S. equity	−0.04	−0.41	−0.49	0.60	1.00			
Private equity	0.13	−0.40	−0.31	0.25	0.71	1.00		
Venture capital	0.26	−0.33	−0.25	0.09	0.53	0.93	1.00	
Leveraged buyouts	−0.08	−0.42	−0.32	0.42	0.79	0.83	0.57	1.00

Note: Cash is represented by 90-day T-bills; core fixed income is the LB Aggregate; TIPS are the LB U.S. Treasury Index; high-yield is the Citigroup High Yield Index; U.S. equity is the Russell 3000; and the private equity indexes are the Venture Capital Economics categorizations.
Source: RogersCasey.

it is in relation to positive performance that meets risk premium expectations. The other underpinning for the appeal of private equity for use in portfolio construction is its diversification attributes. This nonstandard correlation, which is more fully explored through factor analysis in Chapter 11, is illustrated in simplified terms in Table 4.2. A primary observation regarding the correlation of private equity to traditional asset classes includes the fact that it offers some benefit as a diversifier. Nevertheless, some correlation is exhibited between the various categories of private equity and a broad measure of public U.S. equity, in this instance as measured by the Russell 3000 index. Nevertheless, because the correlation of private equity to U.S. equity is not 1.0, it therefore offers some diversification benefits. More importantly, the performance enhancement potential of private equity is such that some correlation with public equity is tolerated by investors as they include private equity into a diversified portfolio.

Qualitative Factor Determinants for Private Equity

Quantitative factors that can be attributed as determinants of private equity return and volatility are identified in Chapter 11. In addition to quantitative factors, there are unique qualitative factors that are involved in the determination of the performance and diversification merits of private equity. Although these qualitative factors cannot easily be modeled, they may at times be more important to the total return of a fund in this area than quantitative factors. Private equity strategies have some distinctive qualitative factors in common with each other. These include deal flow, manager skill, team stability, longevity, and entrepreneurial incentives.

The ebb and flow of available deals that represent private equity transactions can vary for specific investment managers and for the private equity industry as a whole. Furthermore, manager skill is a factor that may in some cases be persistent for certain private equity managers, but nonetheless is a qualitative feature that is difficult to quantify. The entrepreneurial incentive system that is present at each private equity fund and underlying portfolio companies represents another factor for which it is difficult to assign a metric, but which has an important bearing on the attraction and retention of high-quality professionals.

Venture Capital–Specific Qualitative Factors There are qualitative issues that have a specific relationship to venture capital transactions. Some of these considerations affect supply of venture capital opportunities, such as high unemployment in certain industries, low capital gains taxes, and research and development tax incentives. Ironically, high unemployment may stimulate entrepreneurial activity that can lead to the creation of new ventures. Low capital gains taxes also may provide an environment in which entrepreneurs believe that there is additional incentive to attempt to commercialize new technologies. Research and development tax incentives also may stimulate entrepreneurial activity. Other considerations may affect demand related to the venture capital industry, such as the number of venture capital fund offerings in the marketplace and the strength of the initial public offering (IPO) market for exits. For instance, many venture capital funds in the market can reduce overall returns for that vintage year.[2] An overheated IPO market can enable venture capital companies that are not generating profits to come to market, which may not be a sound investment for the buyer, but for the venture capital seller it can enable a higher velocity of money. A quicker turnaround of investors' money and a faster return of capital mean a higher internal rate of return (IRR) for the venture fund investors. Other specific factors that can have an overall affect on venture capital include new scientific breakthroughs, which can cause high demand for nascent venture-backed companies. In this environment, small companies that may show promise for new developmental products can experience high private equity prices. High prices paid for unproven companies give corporate buyers competitive or technological advantages over their peers and provide venture investors with handsome returns.

Although the source of risk and return for venture capital may be closely aligned with the public equity market (a notion that is more fully explored in Chapter 11), deal-specific sources of return that are qualitative in nature focus on the skill of operating management teams. Venture-backed companies derive financial success from business concept identification, product and service development and expansion, market identification, manufacturing and sourcing, staffing, and the development and management of financial controls. Since these items include essentially all aspects of business creation, growth, and management, they are critical to the success of individual companies that are backed by venture capital funds. In light of all of the myriad aspects that are required to make a venture business successful, it is not surprising that many fail along the way. Therefore, those that are successful are required to produce handsome enough returns in order to make the overall venture capital pursuit worthwhile.

Leveraged Buyout–Specific Qualitative Factors LBOs often have a number of qualitative issues that create either attractive or poor environments for success. Examples of this pertain to the receptivity of financial markets in certain environments. An important consideration for the success of LBO transactions is access to financial markets in order to consummate deals. This access can be limited at certain times either by illiquid markets or stringent lending standards by banks. Furthermore, capital may not be available at certain times for the recapitalization of buyouts or the payment of special dividends to LBO funds. Depressed public equity prices may either make the availability of inexpensive target LBO companies abundant, or make access to the public markets for the purpose of monetizing LBO equity investments unavailable. Furthermore, as with venture capital transactions, supply and demand considerations are important to evaluate. Healthy economic environments may provide strong corporate cash flows that increase the ability to borrow capital or generate higher LBO exit prices. Strong economic environments, while a positive for existing buyouts, may provide less hospitable environments for new LBO transactions.

Such an environment may supply too much capital chasing too few deals, thereby raising purchase prices multiples of cash flow and depressing future returns.

Other qualitative considerations include: loose labor and pension regulations that facilitate restructuring of related agreements and improvement in cash flow to service debt; changes in product pricing that cause industry consolidations; and high equity prices or cash accumulation by companies that lead to acquisitions. Each of these can create opportunities that benefit buyout funds.

Additional qualitative factors for LBO performance are deal specific.[3] Deal-specific sources of return can be grouped into financial, valuation, and operating elements. Financing elements include the ability for debt to be repaid and the deal-specific cost of borrowing. The benefit from repayment of debt in an LBO investment accrues directly to the equity investors in the transaction. Therefore, in the event that a general partner finds ways to generate cash through asset sales or refinancing of the entity's balance sheet, the reduction in leverage ratios shift enterprise value toward equity and away from the remaining debt in the entity. Similarly, if high-cost debt can be replaced with lower-cost debt, because of a decline in the business's borrowing rates or an improvement in its operating condition, then the equity holders benefit. Even in the event that the public markets do not represent a viable current exit avenue for the equity investor in an LBO, the recapitalization of an LBO through the sale of additional debt used to pay a substantial dividend to the equity owners is another source of financial value that a general partner can bring to an LBO transaction.

Valuation and operating improvements are other deal-specific sources of return. Often, valuation and operating enhancements to a business are intertwined. Valuation tends to improve as the operating condition of a business is improved, either through a reduction in expenses or growth in revenue. Cost reduction and an increase in revenue also can be stimulated through subsequent acquisitions that are added to the initial business. Ensuing acquisitions can change the nature of the original business that was purchased. In turn, these types of improvements can have a bearing on valuation. Valuation can improve because of growth in revenue, earnings, and cash flow net of additional financing costs. Additionally, an improvement in valuation can transpire due to an expansion of the multiples paid by the public marketplace for a business.

Expanding multiples may be a phenomenon of the changing appetite for an industry in the marketplace. This may be because of a change in interest rates or general economic conditions that affect an industry. However, multiple expansion also may be due to specific value added that is created by a general partner who is managing a transaction. For instance, the addition of acquisitions to an existing LBO may cause a revaluation of the business. Acquired lines of business may reduce the cyclical nature of an existing business; the introduction of new product lines may improve the growth potential of a company; new operations may provide synergies through economies of scale that reduce costs associated with manufacturing, overhead, or distribution; and the addition of divisions may provide an expanded customer base to which products and services may be cross sold. These types of alterations to the nature of a company can cause the market to change its risk assessment, which can lead to an increase in valuation through higher multiples of earnings and cash flow. Permanent multiple expansion is a significant source of value creation that can be provided by the general partner of an LBO fund. Being able to decipher and achieve multiple expansion provides an incremental rate of return on initial equity invested in a leveraged buyout.

Mezzanine Debt–Specific Qualitative Factors   Mezzanine debt funds have deal specific sources of return that are fairly mundane in comparison with venture capital and LBOs. Mezzanine debt is not as invasive an investment as venture capital or LBOs. The mezzanine lender rarely is involved in business building, as is required in the other main private equity categories. If all goes well, the mezzanine investor collects interest payments, receives a repayment of principal, and enjoys a small equity return. It is only in the instance of an investment that has trouble in meeting its mezzanine debt covenants and cash flow requirements that the general partner of the fund becomes a hands-on investor in the entity. In this event, some mezzanine funds are ill equipped to conduct the type of management-intensive nursing that is common practice among LBO and especially venture capital funds. Nevertheless, the best mezzanine funds have developed this capability or can attain it through management consulting firms. This area of potential skill represents a qualitative source of return for mezzanine debt funds.

DISPERSION OF RETURNS

An important consideration to bear in mind when evaluating the performance statistics associated with any alternative investment strategy is that they usually are based on indexes that represent average or median fund results. Some of these indexes are equal weighed and some are dolla weighted to reflect the size of assets under management for the repor funds. In either event, however, the notion of mean fund reportin provide for some distortions.

Mediocrity Pulls Down Averages

Average returns become more muted as more mediocre managers enter an investment field. Presuming that skill is limited and capital is less so, constrained capacity in highly qualified funds can lead to capital inflows to private equity, causing a decline in average performance results for all funds. The fact that allocated capital is successfully deployed in private equity despite restricted capacity in better funds can only mean that the funds with available capacity are funded.

One ameliorating feature in this event is the marginal funds' entering into new areas of operation. For instance, it may be more palatable if open capacity funds compete through different industry types or sizes of deals. This might be the case in the LBO realm, where new capacity is more easily developed than is the case in venture capital. Compared with LBOs, venture capital funds are more sensitive to higher expected IRRs, which require a limited use of capital. The greater amount of capital that is showered on a venture capital transaction may actually reduce returns to an investor.

Who Wants to Be Average?

There is some performance persistence in private equity, compared with other types of investments. This is more often associated with top-quartile performers and may relate to deal access or a particular skill in evaluating opportunities. One could envision that this particularly could be the case with venture capital firms that may have a certain expertise in science, technology, or medical fields. The dispersion of returns in private equity is such that depending on which quartile a fund resides, the result for an investor could be far better or worse than the assumptions used in an asset optimization. Misalignment in this regard can render the assumptions used for investment returns in a portfolio structure fairly inaccurate and therefore can cause allocations to asset classes to be quite misguided. In fact, one could go as far as to say that if an investor is certain of having access to only mediocre private equity funds, then that investor might be more accurate in modeling third- or fourth-quartile performance for the private equity ean index performance.

1 could be made for investors with access to
1gh seemingly unrealistic and overly aggressive,
ccess to top funds might use vastly higher return
tions to private equity. Alternatively, by using
ity, and correlation figures that are reflected by
facto assuming that its access to private equity
This may be accurate or inaccurate based on the
uly has to the range of quality firms in venture

capital and LBOs. Furthermore, an investor's access to LBO versus venture capital funds may not be the same. Better-performing funds in these two areas are not represented by the same firms, and relationships and histories that an investor may have with one group versus the other may differ for various reasons.

The Importance of Manager Access

The concept of having average index returns either understate or overstate an investor's actual experience highlights the importance of both attempting to achieve access to superior managers and accurately measuring the true quality of the managers to which an investor has access at any point in time. The private equity asset class has tremendous exposure to manager-specific risk by virtue of the wide dispersion of returns among managers. This concept is illustrated in Table 4.3, which depicts the wide range of performance among quartiles in the venture capital and LBO categories. The table shows the extent of variability in returns by fund managers of the same vintage year. A fund manager's expertise is crucial in identifying investment opportunities, growing companies, and taking advantage of exit opportunities in order to earn substantial returns for investors. Variability in these skills often divides managers among these quartiles of performance. This can be said for investment managers of both venture capital and LBO funds.

Table 4.3 illustrates the greater volatility of year-to-year returns for venture capital compared with buyouts, and it shows that the range of annual quartile results for venture capital is generally wider than the range for buyouts. Wide dispersion of quartile returns in private equity in general compared with traditional assets also relates to the nature of deal busts and home runs in this arena. In contrast, investment in traditional asset classes using public securities seldom offers the same severe results. Furthermore, this boom/bust phenomenon is more pronounced among venture capital funds than buyout funds, owing to the nature of venture funds investing in less mature companies than is the case for buyout funds. However, a differentiating feature for top-quartile funds in both venture capital and buyouts often boils down to only one or two significantly successful deals that can enable the funds to vastly outperform their peer groups.

PRIVATE EQUITY STRATEGIES

As depicted in Figure 4.1, the vast majority of private equity capital is represented by LBOs and venture capital, with capital commitments to LBOs representing the larger portion between the two. The depicted growth

TABLE 4.3 Dispersion of Private Equity Returns (IRRs) by Quartile

Vintage Year	Venture Capital					Buyout Funds				
	Max	Upper	Med	Lower	Min	Max	Upper	Med	Lower	Min
2005	41.10	-0.40	-8.90	-19.80	-46.20	61.40	-2.10	-11.40	-17.80	-95.70
2004	13.20	-6.70	-15.00	-20.20	-54.70	79.50	11.90	4.90	-6.30	-21.40
2003	31.50	0.60	-6.10	-8.50	-27.50	54.10	21.30	6.70	3.20	-6.00
2002	10.60	3.40	-3.70	-5.70	-20.90	100.00	24.70	4.90	—	-28.80
2001	33.80	6.80	-3.20	-7.10	-27.80	109.50	17.40	7.50	-3.50	-20.00
2000	39.10	0.40	-6.10	-10.10	-33.70	112.10	17.00	6.70	-2.00	-22.10
1999	140.20	0.10	-9.10	-19.50	-100.00	62.00	8.70	0.90	-4.80	-16.30
1998	721.00	11.40	2.40	-4.10	-44.80	37.30	13.10	5.30	-3.50	-26.00
1997	296.00	61.20	21.00	-0.60	-39.90	65.30	10.90	2.90	-1.50	-20.80
1996	454.90	114.30	34.30	1.60	-20.00	81.50	10.20	5.00	-0.90	-12.40
1995	247.80	64.90	20.80	3.50	-31.80	48.00	13.10	7.90	0.20	-12.80
1994	112.90	41.30	20.10	4.00	-47.90	91.30	21.60	12.50	0.60	-7.80
1993	116.40	39.50	12.90	0.20	-25.00	57.00	26.00	15.70	8.70	0.20
1992	102.30	38.10	14.20	11.30	-47.20	60.10	29.80	18.50	11.40	-23.50
1991	61.40	25.60	17.90	4.40	-0.80	14.60	13.80	8.90	2.40	-0.20
1990	74.90	29.30	14.00	0.40	-10.00	20.70	12.40	6.50	-0.80	-28.80

Source: Cambridge Associates LLC.

in private equity commitments highlights the fact that the capital flows into this alternative investment category have been robust and beyond prior cyclical norms. This type of growth creates various uncertainties for investors attempting to predict portfolio outcomes using alternative investments. The question arises whether the capital that has been committed to this realm will experience similar returns as in prior years when there was less capital available to invest in deals. The risk is that an environment occurs where excess capital is invested in transactions with less-than-hoped-for expected returns, simply in an effort to deploy capital. While more seasoned private equity general partners may restrict capacity in their funds, new untested general partnerships nevertheless receive capital commitments, under the condition of capital allocaters seeking capacity in the area.

Figure 4.1 also highlights the fact that the depth of the investable opportunity set for private equity is quite limited in terms of the different types of strategies that can provide diversification to a portfolio solely comprised of private equity. One might make the argument that it is the demand for rather than the supply of noncore private equity strategies that is limited. Nevertheless, there is a limited number of funds in more esoteric private equity strategies, and these funds have limited capacity. Investors who construct dedicated private equity portfolios often will include portfolio diversifiers that move beyond classical private equity (e.g., venture capital and LBO) types of return and risk characteristics, such as oil and gas properties, timber, and special situations. However, for the purposes of portfolio construction in this book, these other types of alternative

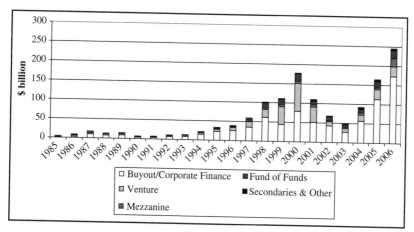

FIGURE 4.1 Annual Capital Commitments to Private Equity Funds
Source: The Private Equity Analyst.

investments are considered separately from private equity and are discussed in more detail in Chapter 6.

Venture Capital

Venture capital investing represents an area of private equity that is focused generally on equity investing in young private companies. The equity investment aspect of this is more in name than in essence. Many venture investment rounds are structured as series of preferred stock offerings. Often, these preferred issues have liquidation preferences, antidilution rights, and other protections that render them almost debtlike in their seniority. Because many young companies do not have much in the way of debt, aside from equipment leases or other physically secured loans, preferred stock issuances typically have the most senior positions in the capital structure of these companies. As such, they may represent a small amount of the total equity shares of the firms, but a significant amount of the diluted ownership over time. Venture capital investment may be further segmented into seed, early, late, and pre-IPO stages.

Seed Stage   Seed-stage venture investments typically represent very small dollar amounts for initially large equity stakes in start-up companies. This is the highest-risk form of venture capital, and it is fraught with failure. Professional venture capital funds usually spread these small investments over many start-up companies in hope that the many anticipated failures will be offset by several significant winners. Nevertheless, because of the nature of these funds making small-sized investments, their capacity can be very constrained. The aggregate size of these funds typically is among the smallest of any area in the alternative investment universe.

The appeal for investors in seed-stage funds is the home runs that can occur in this area. However, the lack of capacity in these funds render them of limited use in large-sized investment portfolios, where even home runs on small initial investments may not have a very meaningful impact on the total value of a diversified portfolio. Moreover, the ability to gain access to the best fund managers in this end of the venture capital market may be limited for most investors. It is these outperforming managers that positively skew the mean performance of seed-stage venture funds, thereby making this alternative investment area a potential mirage for some investors.

Early Stage   Early-stage venture capital represents investments that are post seed stage. These investments have similar risk and return dynamics as seed-stage opportunities, but are somewhat less extreme. Companies in this stage often require capital to complete product development and initiate distribution. Typically, each venture capital company has multiple rounds of investment, as the company becomes more seasoned and requires new capital for different stages of its development. Therefore, early-stage investments can benefit from aspects of the home run appeal that is associated with seed investing, but the available investment opportunities can be more varied. Early-stage venture companies often are more viable, and therefore less risky, than seed-stage companies. Early-stage investments tend not to have as many failures as seed-stage venture investments. Moreover, competent early-stage venture capital firms are adept at controlling their portfolio companies at an early stage of capital formation. Therefore, each subsequent round of financing often is at terms that are acceptable to the early-stage venture capital firms. This thereby enables them to protect their initial investments from dilution, while still allowing them to add new capital to the subsequent financing rounds. Meanwhile, portfolio companies that are not destined for success are summarily culled during the life of early-stage venture funds.

Late and Pre-IPO Stages Late-stage private equity is the least-risky form of venture capital, but it also provides an investor with the smallest return. Typically, this stage of investment is well beyond the proof period that determines the viability of an entity. By the time of a late or pre-IPO round of financing, most of an enterprise's venture risk has been dissipated. Moreover, the time period of investment for late-stage venture capital is far more truncated than earlier rounds of finance, and the exit point is much more visible. The viability of the entity and the proximity to a point of exit are both determinants of the expected return and level of risk for this stage of venture investment. Often, the preexisting providers of venture capital to entities being financed will participate in late-stage rounds, but this usually occurs only by necessity in order to maintain a percentage equity ownership or to encourage new investors in the entity.

Funds that exclusively focus on investment in late-stage venture capital may find themselves somewhat marginalized by competition for this level of finance. Furthermore, diversified venture capital funds may be less desirous of participating in these rounds, since the expected returns for late-stage venture capital are among the smallest within the venture category. Most venture funds are broadly benchmarked, such that lower-returning invest-ments reduce IRRs against which these funds are measured. Therefore, some venture funds do not invest in late-stage rounds, which can reduce aggregate IRRs for the funds. Meanwhile, other sources of capital, such as hedge funds and high-net-worth investors, participate in the late-stage realm, owing to the short time frame for liquidity and relatively low risk. Investment banks also compete in this area by providing bridge loans to pre-IPO candidates.

Leveraged Buyouts

LBOs represent the largest pool of capital in the private equity area. Moreover, once this equity capital is committed to private partnerships, it then is leveraged. Often, this leverage can be three to five times the amount of LBO equity provided to a transaction. Accordingly, the amount of LBO equity capital that is available in the marketplace at any point in time actually represents a far larger figure as it pertains to leveraged buying power. When considered in this light, one can view the comparison of private equity strategies in Figure 4.1 and realize the magnitude of the buying impact for the LBO strategy compared with all other private equity strategies combined. Part of the allure of LBOs is the impact that leverage can have on the return on equity in these types of transactions. While the total return on the value of an LBO transaction (i.e., equity plus debt) can be modest, the use of leverage has a multiplier effect that increases the return on equity capital. Once deals have been negotiated, the entities being acquired raise debt capital through the public or private offering of secured and unsecured debt. This debt capital also can be provided by the LBO investor, sometimes achieved through side funds to their primary equity investment vehicles.

The LBO marketplace not only represents the largest slice of the private equity pie, it also acts as a counterbalance to the public equity market. Inclusive of the leverage that LBO funds command for their transactions, this source of capital presents a significant parallel market that facilitates public equity market equilibrium. Private equity LBO capital is one element that helps to resolve the undervaluation or overvaluation that occurs in public markets. LBO capital gravitates toward undervalued public companies when they become too inexpensive, and LBO portfolio companies seek liquidity when the public markets are fairly or overvalued. This ebb and flow of private equity capital provides for a cyclical facet to this investment style. This has an impact on vintage-year returns and on the cash flow considerations for investors in these funds (see Chapter 8).

LBOs can be considered along a size spectrum. There is a stratum of expected returns and risk associated with large, middle-market, and small company buyouts at any point in time. Although middle-market LBOs can represent unique opportunities with strong expected returns and medium risk, the ability to deploy large amounts of capital in these types of funds may be limited at any point in time. Conversely, large-sized LBO funds are able to accept significant sums of capital. The ability to spread LBO investments across funds that specialize in different-sized transactions offers an additional element of diversification for an investor. Each of these areas may be more or less attractive than the others at any point in time.

Mezzanine Debt

Mezzanine debt investments are loans to private or public companies or in support of real estate properties. Typically these loans are second in security to some other sort of senior loan that the borrower has received. As a second lienholder on the assets of the entity, mezzanine lenders often command a premium expected return through a combination of interest payments and an equity payment in the form of options, warrants, or a stake in the appreciation of a property. Although these loans are debt in nature with a focus on cash flow and leverage ratios, they can become equity in nature if the borrower defaults. As such, the risk and return profile of mezzanine debt falls in between that of secured debt and equity.

The environment for mezzanine debt funds in the private equity realm has changed relative to their historical norms for expected return and risk. Mezzanine debt is a prime example of a private equity strategy that has seen encroachment from other sources of capital. Historically, mezzanine funds often enjoyed the position of being a lender of last resort. If a borrower could not find a lender because of an inability to provide collateral to secure a loan, there may have been few institutional lenders willing to provide credit based solely on the strength of cash flow. This is a void filled by mezzanine debt funds, which accept cash flow loans with second-lien collateral. In part, because of the long lockups for mezzanine funds (often 7 to 10 years), they can extend medium-duration loans to borrowers and have some flexibility in accepting interim-period cash flow shortfalls. However, the growth in hedge funds has provided significant additional capital available for mezzanine transactions. This dynamic has made competition for these transactions more intense, and may have permanently slightly reduced the expected return on short duration mezzanine debt transactions.

Furthermore, the duration of these loans may have been altered. Whereas private equity mezzanine funds operate with 7- to 10-year locked-up capital, hedge funds offer more liberal redemption terms. Accordingly, the duration of the loans that hedge funds are willing to make tend to be shorter. This shorter-duration influence also potentially reduces the expected return for some mezzanine transactions.

Secondary Private Equity

Secondary investments in private equity represent the purchase of limited partnership interests from original investors. To the extent that these interests are associated with active funds still making new investments, the purchase of the limited partnership interest includes the invested assets in the partnership as well as the outstanding amount of committed but as yet uncalled capital. Therefore, there are asset and liability features to these investments. Secondary transactions generally serve two purposes: access to relatively mature private equity investments for the buyer and access to immediate liquidity for the seller. Nevertheless, the general partner of a partnership being transferred usually must approve any prospective transaction prior to its occurrence.

The broad purpose of a secondary investment for the buyer is to reduce the J-curve effect on investment returns. The J curve relates to the tendency for private equity investments to be net users rather than producers of capital for investors in their early years. The result is that the carrying value of initial private equity investments typically declines in value during the first several years of investment prior to rising in value as investments mature and appreciate. Although a private equity partnership may carry its initial investments at cost, it also is charging partnership fees, which can cause the overall net asset value (NAV) of a partnership to decline in its early years. The attraction for investors placing capital with funds that focus on the purchase of secondary investments is accomplishing a reduction in the J-curve effect. However, this approach primarily relates to investors making initial private equity allocations. Once vintage-year diversification is reached for a seasoned private equity program, the investor likely should experience little overall portfolio impact from the J curves that occur for each of its new private equity commitments, since these would be smoothed by the returns from older vintage-year allocations. For perennial private equity programs, vintage-year diversification renders secondary investments somewhat less relevant. Nevertheless, investment managers that have proprietary secondary deal flow may provide unique value for private equity investors at any stage in their programs.

Funds that purchase secondary interest are a form of funds of funds. One of the additional attractions for an investor in a fund of funds that purchases secondary limited partnership interests is improved visibility pertaining to the underlying partnerships. The initial seasoning of these partnerships beyond their inception affords an investor a more accurate gauge of the profitability of existing portfolio companies in each underlying fund. This also enables the investor to more precisely calculate expected future capital calls that may occur for these funds. Therefore, not only is the estimation of assets improved, but so is the assessment of future liabilities.

An investor also must be mindful of the fact that investments in secondary funds are correlated with the other venture capital and LBO investments. Although secondary investments provide vintage-year diversification, they represent substantially similar attributes as other private equity investments to which an investor may have exposure. Therefore, a potential negative issue associated with an investment in secondary funds is possible redundancy they may have with other venture capital and LBO investments in an investor's portfolio, since this is what underlies the secondary partnerships.

An additional approach to secondary investments is the direct purchase of portfolios of companies by private equity funds of funds. In this instance, a fund of funds acquires a group of investments from a sponsor, rather than investing in limited partnership interests of separate private equity funds. In the completion of these transactions, the fund of funds often is required to form a general partnership around this portfolio purchase in order to have the organizational capability to manage these investments as any other venture capital or LBO fund would be managed. Typically, these opportunities arise from corporate sellers of portfolios of developmental business lines. Often, these prospects are shed by corporations that are undergoing reorganizations, perhaps precipitated by a management change, merger, or financial restructuring.

Whether for financial or strategic reasons, the sales of developmental businesses often are not associated with a diminished view of the quality of the ventures. Furthermore, in order to facilitate the sales of these portfolios, the sponsors may be willing to grant preferential treatment in the form of scientific, sales, distribution, or other assistance to foster the development or launch of the ventures. It is not uncommon for these portfolio opportunities to arise on an exclusive basis. Often, the buyers of these sponsor-originated secondary portfolios have some sort of preexisting relationship with the sponsor, such as investment banking or investment manager. As a result, these opportunities may lack a competitive bidding process and enable the buyer to achieve a more customized transaction. This may afford the buyer some latitude in picking over the portfolio to select the investments that it most desires, in creating an operating agreement that specifies the continued strategic assistance by the corporate sponsor, or in reducing the risk of the transaction to the buyer through certain financial provisions with the seller. Each one of these conveniences are attractive to potential investors in these types of secondary products. Investors may find these types of secondary private equity purchases more attractive than secondary investments that are represented by the purchase of preexisting limited partnership interests.

A difficult aspect for all types of secondary private equity investments is a lack of consistency in benchmarking. There is difficulty in measuring secondary funds as a group, because there is not a deep pool of these types of funds relative to other areas of investment, and secondary funds are not homogeneous. Individual secondary funds include different allocations to different private equity strategies; secondary funds have different durations for the maturity of the portfolios that they purchase; and secondary funds differ on the quality of their portfolios, with some having a better chance of becoming profitable and others being laden with investments that may not be successful. Furthermore, the price paid for these portfolios can vary widely. Variation in price-to-NAV discounts paid can be a function of a specific investment manager's deal access, or it can be related to cyclical influences at the time of the purchase.

Indeed, secondary private equity funds are subject to vintage-year sensitivities in the same way as are other forms of private equity. Purchase prices paid by secondary funds also can be influenced by the supply of capital for these funds, trends in the targeted rate of return for these funds, and economic conditions that influence the level of distress for sellers of secondary portfolios. The cash flow nuances of secondary private equity investments are discussed further in Chapter 8.

Special Situations

Special situations in private equity investing tend to represent opportunistic areas in venture capital, LBOs, mezzanine debt, and secondary funds. Special situations can include a certain geographic focus, such as Israel, Russia, or Asia. They also can have an industry focus that from a secular perspective is nascent and opportunistically prone to growth, such as portfolio companies focused on the development of alternative energy. The purpose of these types of funds is to add diversification to a private equity program. Investors who consider special situation investments likely already have mature private equity programs where an investment that is out of the ordinary may have some appeal.

An important benefit of these funds for investors, besides diversification, is the prospect for incremental performance on an opportunistic basis. Investment in these funds can be tactical in nature, based on investments that avail themselves during the course of a private equity program. The risk in these funds is that generally they are very untested and have few peers against which to compare. Managers of these funds also often do not have prior track records to substantiate their success in these areas, since the areas themselves frequently are new to investor capital. Furthermore, as new opportunities, the underlying investments in these funds may not be successful. Lack of success can be more pronounced in these types of funds, since their portfolio companies often are engaged in similar types of industries, geographic regions, or market opportunities, and therefore are correlated.

Other Categories

Other investment strategies that often are used in dedicated private equity portfolios include: funds that offer to their limited partners the opportunity to coinvest directly in their portfolio companies; equipment lease finance provided to venture companies; private investments in public companies (PIPEs); distressed debt; oil and natural gas investments; timber; infrastructure; and real estate. A benefit from these investments is their ability to provide diversification and performance enhancement to a private equity portfolio. However, most of these investments can be categorized elsewhere in the alternative investment universe. The risk of lumping them together in an overall allocation to private equity is that their returns and risks may overlap other investments, including traditional asset classes, venture capital, LBOs, hedge funds, real estate, and other dedicated hard-asset investments.

THE CONSTRUCTION OF A SEGREGATED PORTFOLIO OF PRIVATE EQUITY

Most private equity investors, or investment managers that operate funds of funds, build portfolios of private equity investments in a robust and diversified fashion,[4] but they do so in isolation from traditional asset classes and other types of alternative investments. As such, these isolated constructs run the risk of overlapping other types of investments, especially when considering the common factor drivers of returns and risk that occur across these investments. The creation of a dedicated private equity portfolio enables an investor to achieve some diversification in this alternative investment area.

The main private equity strategies used in this endeavor are LBOs and venture capital. These are the two largest areas of capital in the private equity world, because they are the areas that have the greatest number of funds offered by investment managers. LBOs and venture capital strategies are well developed, and there are many underlying investment opportunities for each of them. Meanwhile, more ancillary private equity strategies also can be used in portfolio construction. Such areas include mezzanine debt, secondary investments, and special situations. These other strategies offer diversification. However, the ability to place capital in these strategies is relatively constrained when compared with LBOs and venture capital.

Many of these ancillary investments have common characteristics with other distinctly separate alternative investment strategies. As such, for the purposes of the construction of a dedicated private equity portfolio in this example, these supplementary investments are excluded. An analysis that blends multiple alternative investments into one portfolio is examined further in Chapter 11.

Private equity funds of funds provide value to their investors in the form of underlying private equity fund access, evaluation, and due diligence.

In terms of portfolio construction, funds of funds offer a range of products including those that are diversified across the various private equity types of strategies and those dedicated to one strategy or another. The benefit from diversified products is the reduction in volatility that they provide versus single-strategy funds of funds as well as additional vintage-year diversification. A simplistic approach to diversified private equity portfolio construction includes only a two-asset model split between venture capital and LBOs. This approach limits potential factor redundancy, and it removes strategies that have restricted depth of investment opportunity.

Figure 4.2 depicts an optimized portfolio using only two assets: buyouts and venture capital. This simple example illustrates that the low-volatility characteristics of leveraged buyouts have a very strong pull during allocations to private equity for many investors. In the figure, the optimal risk-adjusted point (as defined by the highest Sharpe ratio) on the efficient frontier has an allocation of 91.4 percent to buyouts and 8.6 percent to venture capital. The data for the illustration is based on the time period 1996 through March 2006. Although the utilization of the mean-variance

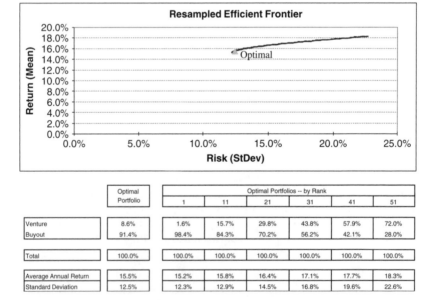

	Optimal Portfolio	Optimal Portfolios -- by Rank					
		1	11	21	31	41	51
Venture	8.6%	1.6%	15.7%	29.8%	43.8%	57.9%	72.0%
Buyout	91.4%	98.4%	84.3%	70.2%	56.2%	42.1%	28.0%
Total	100.0%	100.0%	100.0%	100.0%	100.0%	100.0%	100.0%
Average Annual Return	15.5%	15.2%	15.8%	16.4%	17.1%	17.7%	18.3%
Standard Deviation	12.5%	12.3%	12.9%	14.5%	16.8%	19.6%	22.6%

FIGURE 4.2   Portfolio Optimization of Venture Capital and Buyouts
Note: Model is unconstrained. Data is 1996 through March 2006.
Source: RogersCasey; Thomson Financial; Resampled Efficient Frontier™ provided by New Frontier Advisors LLC.

optimization (MVO) technique for alternative investments has certain short-comings, it is a tool that can act as a starting point for an allocation to private equity (see Chapter 11).

One issue with using MVO in determining the amount of venture capital versus LBO exposure to have in an allocation to private equity is that the optimal point in the MVO analysis presumes that the investor is seeking the highest risk-adjusted return rather than the highest absolute return. This is a key differentiator in how an investor might construct a portfolio of private equity and how an investment manager might construct a fund of funds. On one hand, an investor may be willing to accept a generous dose of volatility in returns for a private equity portfolio as long as the risk is accompanied by relatively high returns. In this sense, the investor is expending a portion of its risk budget, and most likely would accomplish this through a higher allocation to venture capital relative to LBOs. On the other hand, an institutional money manager perhaps running a private equity fund of funds may be less willing to create a portfolio with high amounts of expected volatility, because of a desire to generate consistent returns in order to keep most investors satisfied most of the time. An issue with volatility in venture capital is that it can be symmetrical, thus leading to the potential for both large positive and large negative returns.

The optimal portfolio point illustrated in Figure 4.2 is optimal only from an inherently risk-averse perspective. The optimal frontier is a better depiction of the range of allocation opportunities available to investors. When considering this frontier, an investor who is comfortable with assuming significant volatility in order to maximize potential returns would be placed well to the right on this curve. The implication from this positioning is a much higher allocation to venture capital than is the case for the optimal point that has the highest Sharpe ratio. By contrast, a more risk-averse investor, perhaps a private equity fund of funds manager who was seeking more balance in a portfolio, would be on the left half of this spectrum.

SUMMARY

Private equity strategies span core and ancillary approaches. Core strategies, such as LBOs and venture capital, account for the vast majority of assets that have been committed to private equity funds. Meanwhile, many non-core private equity strategies also can be used in the construction of diversified private equity portfolios. However, these satellite investments often are better evaluated when defined by their underlying assets, such as energy, real estate, and timber. All private equity funds possess certain qualitative factors that hold great importance in determining their likely success. These elements include deal access and manager skill in business building and incentive creation, which can have an impact on growth, profitability, and valuation of underlying investments.

When compiling forward-looking estimates for returns, volatility, and correlation for portfolio optimization of private equity strategies, investors must be candid in assessing their relevant access to investment managers. If access to better-performing managers is not available, then expectations should be modeled on the quartile of performance to which access is available. In any case, mean returns and their volatility and correlation figures should be used with great caution. They may have little bearing on the characteristics of actual investments, because of the relatively wide dispersion of performance among investment managers operating in the venture capital and LBO strategies. During the construction of portfolios of private equity investments, there is a natural tendency to overweight LBOs, because of their lower historical and expected future volatility of performance compared with venture capital. Nevertheless, this presumes that an investor is seeking a balanced return rather than a maximum potential return, in which case an increased allocation to venture capital would be required.

Real Estate

R eal estate equity can be segmented into five primary investments: real estate investment trusts (REITs), core, core-plus, value-added, and opportunistic. These approaches to real estate provide investors with a range of returns and risk. They also have different proportions of total return that are generated from current income compared with potential capital gains. A prime benefit from investing in real estate is its prospective stability as a physical asset. Real estate provides to a portfolio of assets an additional element of diversification, and it does so through the trait of generally low correlation of returns to other asset classes. There are qualitative sources of returns for real estate operators, some of which are pronounced and can account for a large portion of results. This chapter highlights some of these qualitative drivers of return and risk and gives an overview of real estate investment strategies. (The quantitative factor drivers for these strategies are evaluated in Chapter 11.) The attributes pertaining to real estate can be garnered when added into a diversified portfolio of traditional asset classes and alternative investments. Real estate investment strategies possess a wide range of tendencies. These differing characteristics also enable an investor to construct a dedicated portfolio of real estate that has style diversification. Such an isolated portfolio that contains only real estate assets can be constructed in a fund of funds setting.

WHAT IS THE ATTRACTION?

Real estate is a foundation asset for many investment portfolios. Its simplicity as a hard asset pertains to its value retention and cash flow generation. These traits tend to provide investors with consistent and stable results. Although there are exceptions to this characterization based on the type of strategy employed and geographic exposure, real estate generally is an asset class that can be fairly predictable in its value retention and cash flow generation over complete business cycles. However, the general overarching purpose for real estate in a diversified portfolio is similar to the rationalization for including most other alternative investments, which are the benefits to be derived from performance enhancement, volatility reduction, and diversification.

Performance Enhancement

The inclusion of real estate into an investor's portfolio offers the potential for performance enhancement. Real estate as an investable asset is more intuitive to most investors compared with other sorts of alternative investments, such as currencies, timber, hedge funds, and private equity. This familiarity lends itself to the inclusion of real estate as an acceptable alternative investment for many investors. The low-volatility characteristics of returns from the more conservative types of real estate strategies, such as core and core-plus, also contribute to the likelihood of these returns being realized. As an asset class, real estate has generated fairly consistent returns over a relatively long period of time, compared with the time measurement periods that are available for most other alternative investments. As indicated in Table 5.1, the returns from core real estate (measured by the National Council of Real Estate Investment Fiduciaries [NCREIF] National Property Index) as well as REITs (measured by the National Association of Real Estate Investment Trusts [NAREIT] Index) have been competitive with the major traditional asset classes. In comparison with core real estate, historically REITs have provided higher returns with higher volatility. As

TABLE 5.1 Traditional versus Real Estate Historical Returns and Risk (1996–2006 Q2)

Asset Type	Average Annual Return	Standard Deviation	Compound Return
Cash	3.77%	0.93%	3.77%
Core fixed income	6.00%	3.61%	5.94%
Inflation-linked bonds (TIPS)	6.74%	4.30%	6.65%
High-yield	6.99%	7.77%	6.70%
U.S. equity	10.74%	17.79%	9.30%
Real estate	11.67%	2.11%	11.65%
REITs	15.24%	14.85%	14.28%

Note: Cash is represented by 90-day T-bills; core fixed income is the LB Aggregate; TIPS are the LB U.S. Treasury Index; and REITs are the NAREIT Index.
Source: RogersCasey.

publicly quoted securities, REITs exhibit greater equity-like price fluctuation than is the case with privately quoted core real estate. Noncore real estate strategies can prospectively offer even higher rates of returns than core real estate or REITs. Value-added and opportunistic strategies focus on less well-established properties, which can generate higher levels of both risk and investment performance. Unfortunately, indexes for value-added and opportunistic real estate have not been finalized by NCREIF. Therefore, the ability to approximately measure the performance, volatility, and correlations from value-added and opportunistic real estate is difficult.

Volatility Reduction

Beyond the natural volatility-reducing tendency that occurs through diversification from the process of adding uncorrelated assets to a portfolio, real estate as a freestanding investment also offers its own isolated low-volatility attributes. While the amount of volatility in returns that occurs for a real estate investment depends on the type of real estate strategy employed, the generalization of real estate returns having lower volatility than some other asset classes over the long term has merit. As illustrated in Table 5.1, both core real estate (measured by the NCREIF National Property Index) and REITs (measured by the NAREIT Index) experienced lower volatility of returns than U.S. equity from 1996 through the second quarter of 2006. During the same time period, core real estate also registered lower volatility of returns than inflation-linked bonds (Treasury inflation-protected securities [TIPS]), the high-yield bond market, and the U.S. bond market.

Diversification

A key element that supports the volatility-reducing capabilities of real estate as a diversifier when added to a portfolio of other assets stems from its lack of high correlation with many of these other assets. As indicated in Table 5.2, core real estate and REITs have historically low correlations to some of the more significant traditional asset classes. Core real estate has exhibited low or even negative historical correlation to some asset classes. Although the correlation figures for REITS are higher than they are for core real estate, they still are relatively low on an absolute basis. The low correlation figures for both core real estate and REITs offer support for their use in investment portfolios as diversifying assets. However, these correlation figures can be sensitive to shorter time frames and episodic events. Nevertheless, over longer time periods, the low correlation statistics for real estate are fairly constant. An encouraging feature for investors who include real estate in their portfolios is the long historical data measurement offered by real

TABLE 5.2 Real Estate Correlation Matrix (1996–2006 Q1)

	Cash	Core FI	ILBs	High Yield	U.S. Equity	Real Estate	REITs
Cash	1.00						
Core fixed income	0.20	1.00					
Inflation-linked bonds (TIPS)	−0.06	0.73	1.00				
High-yield	−0.25	−0.16	−0.20	1.00			
U.S. equity	−0.04	−0.41	−0.49	0.60	1.00		
Real estate	0.19	−0.02	−0.20	−0.05	0.14	1.00	
REITs	−0.16	0.09	0.16	0.38	0.37	−0.01	1.00

Note: Cash is represented by 90 day T-bills; core fixed income is the LB Aggregate; TIPS are the LB U.S. Treasury Index; and REITs is the NAREIT Index.
Source: RogersCasey.

estate. The lack of correlation for real estate and an explanation for what correlation exists can be analyzed using the different return and risk factors that are inherent in real estate. This notion is further examined in Chapter 11.

Cash Flow Considerations

In addition to the attributes of performance enhancement, volatility reduction, and diversification, real estate also often provides improved cash flow for an investor. (Real estate cash flow is more fully explored in Chapter 8.) Cash flow from real estate can be robust, but it may not be relevant to all investors. Unlike most other alternative investments, certain types of real estate investments—REITs and core real estate, for example—generate a majority of their expected returns in the form of current yield. However, this feature may not be desirable for all investors. While certain investors find real estate cash flow to be advantageous, particularly as an alternative to fixed-income cash flow, other investors may consider significant cash flow to be a problematic. Some investors may find the current-yield aspect of some real estate investments to be undesirable, because it provides them with a reinvestment risk. These investors may have difficulty in reinvesting this income back into real estate assets at advantageous terms. Nevertheless, other types of real estate strategies, such as opportunistic, generate a majority of their expected returns through capital appreciation rather than current income. In this case, cash flow from the investment is more incidental.

Idiosyncratic Return

Another benefit of real estate is that it provides an additional source of idiosyncratic return from active management. Idiosyncratic return is the return from a fund invested in a strategy that is not related to the average return from that strategy in general. To the extent that real estate indexes represent the average return for real estate, performance that is different from this is unique. It is very difficult to apply the concept of active versus passive investment management to real estate. Each real estate parcel is unique. Although there are indexes for real estate strategies, many are not investable. Therefore, they are passive alternatives only to the degree that a derivatives contract can be issued that relates to them. Nevertheless, from a statistical perspective, real estate managers can be measured against their benchmarks, and relative performance can be measured. This relative under- or overperformance represents real estate alpha. The greater the number of independent active management alphas that can be added to an investor's diversified portfolio should be associated with greater diversification. Discrete returns that are separate from the beta associated with a benchmark represent idiosyncratic alpha.

Qualitative Factors for Real Estate Investment

As is the case with other types of alternative investments, there are a series of qualitative factors that determine success in real estate investment. Real estate, more so than many other types of alternative investments, can be very dependent on local market considerations. For instance, the characteristics that are required to be successful in an urban area in Europe are very different from those that are required in a suburban Washington, D.C., market. Qualitative considerations include access to significant buyers and sellers of properties, experience in local zoning regulations, and knowledge of how to position properties to appeal to local market needs. Often, these issues are so important in determining the success in local real estate markets that national or international real estate investors seek exclusive local market partners in order to facilitate their market penetration. Adept local market partners can make the difference between success and failure in executing an expansion into certain geographic regions. These qualities cannot easily be modeled, as is the case for quantitative macroeconomic factors. Nevertheless, many qualitative features can be of greater significance than quantitative factors in the performance of local real estate investments. For example, manager skill can be a significant qualitative factor in certain strategies of real estate. Particularly as it pertains to opportunistic real estate, manager skill can be the single most important determinant of success. In these types of properties, new development and repositioning properties can have high risk and uncertain return expectations. Manager skill in creating unique solutions for these types of properties and securing tenants often is distinctive and may be repeatable. Therefore, securing investment capacity with these operators is coveted.

Additionally, local markets often have their own economic factors that are more important in determining the occupancy and rental rates for properties than are national economic trends. Industry sectors may have a greater impact in certain local markets than is the case nationally. For example, the state employment for the U.S. automobile industry may be of greater importance to the real estate market in Detroit than is the national level of employment. Another financial consideration for local markets is tax abatements or deferrals. In some instance, municipalities seek real estate developers to build in areas that can benefit from job creation and new business. These localities may provide financial incentives for developers to built new structures or refurbish existing structures in order to accomplish the goal of an improvement in the local economy. Many of these factors may not be revealed by a standard quantitative factor analysis of real estate.

REAL ESTATE STRATEGIES

Differentiation among real estate strategies tends not to be demarcated by property types as much as it is defined by the expected rates of return and potential volatility of returns from specific strategies employed. Prospective returns and risk from the various real estate strategies tend to be determined by considerations such as occupancy, leverage, and physical alteration of properties. Investment real estate equity tends to be bucketed in five major strategy areas: REITs, core, core-plus, value-added, and opportunistic. REITs are more of an investment packaging than an investment strategy. Nonetheless, REITs represent a high-current-income strategy that generally is invested in properties and securities. REITs can be very diverse in composition. In comparison, core real estate tends to embody a classic real estate exposure with a majority of returns coming from current income, as represented by the NCREIF National Property Index benchmark to which investment managers in this strategy track. The core-plus strategy represents a step up in risk and expected returns from core real estate and accomplishes this generally through the use of higher levels of leverage and slightly lower initial levels of occupancy. Value-added investing in real estate assumes still higher levels of risk, return, and leverage through the purchase of properties that may require repositioning or restructuring and new tenants. The riskiest and highest-potential-return type of real estate is opportunistic, which is reliant on new development or redevelopment of highly leveraged properties that may be distressed or previously controlled by distressed owners.

Tables 5.3 and 5.4 display a variety of generalized terms for real estate using the REIT, core, core-plus, value-added, and opportunistic approaches. This information is based on observations from investment managers and funds operating in these areas, rather than hard-and-fast rules about the strategies. Table 5.3 illustrates the trend in return and risk traits that characterize each type of real estate investment strategy. Alongside the migration up the return-and-risk spectrum, there generally is a coincident increase in leverage, a decrease in occupancy, and a rise in the requirement for additional capital to be invested in properties once they are acquired. One should note that the expected returns and risk for REITs and core real estate that are indicated in Table 5.3 are different from the historical returns and standard deviation of returns that these two strategies generated in Table 5.2. This disparity stems from the many influences that support any estimation of future returns for an asset. In this case, the estimates for future returns and volatility (contained in Table 5.3) represent point-in-time generally accepted estimates. However, the basis for this sort of estimation is largely subjective. This highlights the need for factor analysis to determine the historical sources of returns and volatility that may be repeated in the future. With this type of quantitative factor identification, forward-looking factor estimates can be established that should have greater veracity in determining the outcome for a dependent asset class than is the case for subjective opinion (see Chapter 11). From an investment fund perspective, Table 5.3 reveals that as strategies rise in expected returns and risk, they also generally experience a decline in liquidity, a decline in the proportion of total return that is expected to occur from current income versus capital appreciation, and a rise in investment management fees.

TABLE 5.3 Sample Real Estate Strategy Characteristics

Strategy	Expected Return	Expected Risk	Property Leverage	Property Leased/ Occupancy	Additional Capital Requirement
REITs	6%–7%	Low–Med.	40%–50%	High	Low
Core	8%	Low	0%–30%	85% +	Low
Core-plus	8%–12%	Low–Med.	30%–50%	70% +	Low
Value-added	10%–15%	Medium	50%–70%	Medium	Medium
Opportunistic	15% +	High	70% +	Low	High

Note: Data represent sample observations, not hard-and-fast rules.
Source: RogersCasey.

TABLE 5.4 Sample Real Estate Fund Terms

Strategy	Fund Terms	Fund Initial Investment Period	% of Return from Appreciation	% of Return from Income	Management Fee	Performance Fee	Fund Hurdle Rate
REITs	Open-end	Immediate	35%	65%	55–85 bps	0%	None
Core	Open-end	Immediate	15%	85%	75–125 bps	0%	None
Core-plus	Open/closed-end	0–3 years	30%	70%	75–125 bps*	0%–20%*	None*
Value-added	Open/closed-end	0–3 years	50%	50%	100–125 bps	20%	8%–9%
Opportunistic	7–10 years	3 years	75%	25%	125–150 bps	20%	9%–10%

Note: Data represent sample observations, not hard-and-fast rules.
*Core-plus funds that are open end typically have fees that are similar to core funds, while closed-end core-plus funds have fees that are similar to value-added funds.
Source: RogersCasey.

Real Estate Investment Trusts (REITs)

REITs are very diverse, from both a property type and an instrument perspective. The properties in which REITs invest range across all industries and types, including: office buildings, shopping centers, residential properties, industrial facilities, health care, lodging, warehousing, and new development. Furthermore, the instruments through which REITs gain exposure to these property types vary and include: equity interests, commercial mortgages, and residential mortgages. It can be difficult to generalize about the investment considerations for REITs, since they invest in a broad range of properties and real estate securities. However, the main generalization that can be made is that the substantial portion of total return from these entities is provided by current income. REITs are mandated to pass through to unit holders a majority of their operating income. As a pass-through entity, a REIT is allowed to convey its pretax income to its unit holders before the application of income taxes. The unit holder then is taxed on the dividends from the REIT at the unit holder's rate of taxation.

REITs generally are unified by the common theme of cash generation, which is passed through to unit holders. The Real Estate Investment Trust tax provisions of 1960 created REITs in the United States. For an entity to qualify as a REIT from a U.S. Internal Revenue Code perspective, it must pay a minimum of 90 percent of its annual taxable income to its unit holders in the form of regular dividends. Access to REITs typically is accomplished by investing in active investment management funds that are dedicated to investing in publicly traded REITs. Investment managers who build portfolios of these REIT exposures are able to achieve diversification through publicly traded REITs that are invested in a range of properties, securities, and geographies.

Although the benefits of REITs for an investor's portfolio include their unique return, volatility, and correlation characteristics versus other types of assets and other types of real estate strategies, one of the main utilities of REITs for investors is their securitization structure. A central problem for investors seeking exposure to real estate is the illiquid nature of individual properties and the substantial effort involved when purchasing, maintaining, and leasing properties. The mechanics involved with this market do not fit well with the capabilities of most institutional investors. Although real estate funds exist for core, core-plus, value-added, and opportunistic strategies, they can be difficult to enter (i.e., queues) or difficult to exit (i.e., lockups). The packaging of real estate in REIT structures enables access to the public market for equity interests in these properties. The liquidity provided in the public market for these securities facilitates the creation of open-end funds that are akin to traditional equity and fixed-income funds. In comparison, an investment in and redemption from an open-end core real estate fund is

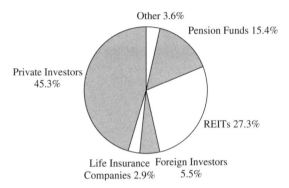

FIGURE 5.1 Total Equity Capital Invested in U.S. Institutional-Quality Real Estate
Source: Urban Land Institute and Pricewaterhouse Coopers LLC, *Emerging Trends in Real Estate 2006.*

reliant on liquidity being granted by the fund. This access is provided by matching redemptions and subscriptions to the fund, using liquid capital on hand to fund redemptions, or using lines of credit that are in place to fund redemptions.

Liquidity in open-end funds that are not REITs is very sensitive to the fundamentals for the real estate market. Weak real estate markets can cause the invoking of gating procedures that limit the ability of investors to redeem their capital. Strong real estate markets and investor demand create queues of investors seeking access to funds. However, queues also represent liquidity to meet periodic redemptions by investors seeking to exit these open-end non-REIT funds. Alternatively, investors in REITS, whether directly or through REIT funds that are managed by investment managers, have more immediate market liquidity through the status of most REITs as publicly traded entities. A final inevitable aspect of REITs is the simple fact that more than one quarter of all equity investment in institutional-quality U.S. real estate is invested through REIT structures, which is illustrated in Figure 5.1. Therefore, exposure to REITs is almost unavoidable, particularly as investors increase the breadth of property types in which they invest.

Core Real Estate

Core properties tend to be described as the most conservative type of real estate investment, since they typically have low or zero levels of debt associated with their capital structure, are fully occupied with strong-credit-rated tenants located in major markets, and have leases with long lives. Core real estate properties also typically are characterized as larger-sized properties that are located in major metropolitan areas.[1] Furthermore, these parcels often are contained in open-end investment funds that offer investors good liquidity and relatively low risk. Nevertheless, some investors consider core properties to have a built-in future risk that is associated with a potential loss of the desirable features that make these properties considered as core (e.g., close to full occupancy). However, the strong present financial condition and predictable cash flow from worthy tenants make core properties the most desirable form of real estate in terms of current risk.

Core buildings are the most efficiently priced, and they are priced with the smallest implied rate of return on capital. Although the expected return from capital appreciation is a small portion of expected total return for core real estate, current income in the form of rental income after expenses represents a significant majority of the expected total return. The NCREIF calculates the primary real estate index (the National Property Index [NPI]) used by many investors. This quarterly index for private equity real estate is based on performance and appraisals of individual properties put forward by approximately 70 investment managers. The NPI benchmark is used by investors to calculate relative performance, and some real estate investment partnerships state their targeted returns as a basis-point premium to this index. Nevertheless, the NPI is a core real estate index, and it represents only about 5 percent of the investable institutional real estate universe from a U.S. dollar perspective.

Core real estate properties are considered to have the lowest cap rates among the various sorts of real estate types. Real estate cap rates are the ratio of net funds from operations for a property divided by the appraised value or purchase price of the property. Cap rates for core real estate typically are several hundred basis points above risk-free rates. In some regards, core real estate cap rates are similar pricing mechanisms to current yields for bonds and have somewhat similar correlations to interest rates. However, other elements such as occupancy rates, lease terms, and local market economic strength play as much, if not at times more, of a role than the direction of overall interest rates in determining the cap rates of individual properties.

Core-Plus Real Estate

The core-plus real estate strategy is simply a step below core in the investment gamut. The differences between the core and core-plus approaches are slighter in comparison than the differences between the core strategy and other more aggressive strategies such as value-added and opportunistic. A chief reason for the development of core-plus as a distinct strategy is the desire to marginally exceed the expected returns from core real estate funds. The development of investment funds in the core-plus area has been in reaction to performance measurement of core funds against the NPI benchmark. The potential ability of core-plus funds to surpass the NPI by more than the amount that a core real estate fund might hope to achieve is a distinct competitive advantage in garnering investors' assets. Core-plus real estate funds might be expected to exceed the NPI in performance by perhaps 200 to 300 basis points, by utilizing somewhat less stringent standards than are found in the more pristine core real estate strategy.

In terms of accomplishing this higher rate of expected return, core-plus operators usually expect that a slightly larger proportion of total returns will be derived from capital appreciation on properties than from ordinary income. One way in which this additional appreciation is accomplished is through purchasing properties at slightly lower prices relative to core real estate parcels; the second way to accomplish the higher prospective equity return is through the use of a greater proportion of leverage in each real estate transaction. In spite of the competitive nature of real estate, lower prices for properties typically are associated with lower occupancy rates. Core-plus real estate funds target the purchase of properties that are not fully leased and may be 20 percent or more unoccupied. The additional leverage used in property acquisitions for the core-plus strategy may be as high as 50 percent of the total transaction value. Returns from capital appreciation generate a higher rate of return on equity capital invested in core-plus transactions, since there is less equity invested in each transaction than is the case for core real estate. However, core-plus real estate funds might be expected to have a significant majority of their individual properties classified as core properties.[2] Thus, the enhancement to returns that these funds seek to achieve is focused on a series of specific properties where the aforementioned techniques are employed.

Value-Added Real Estate

Value-added real estate results in an expected risk-and-return profile that is more aggressive than either the core or core-plus strategies. Properties in this category of real estate usually are not fully leased and may require renovation or complete redevelopment. Investment in properties of funds with this classification offers unique benefits for investors, compared with other forms of real estate. These investments receive a large portion of their total return from idiosyncratic elements that are separate from the basic drivers of the real estate market in general. The return and risk associated with this form of real estate become very deal specific. Returns associated with these properties are discrete and are oriented toward capital gains over the long term. As such, these investments are dependent on the expertise of the managers of funds that control them, their local market knowledge, and their general business acumen.

Typical tactics employed by value-added real estate managers include: retenanting, recapitalization, repositioning or rehabilitation, redevelopment, and new development.[3] The concept of retenanting a property has a focus on increasing occupancy and upgrading tenants, either in terms of the credit quality of the tenant pool or the pricing and length of the leases with tenants. Higher occupancy rates increase funds from operations and raise a property's overall appraised value. Higher-credit tenants, higher lease rates, and longer leases improve property cash flows and reduce risk, thereby raising the price that other operators are willing to pay for the facilities. Recapitalization of properties relates to reducing the interest rate on debt associated with a building, thereby increasing net funds from operations, or reducing the total amount of leverage on a property, thereby improving the equity value and credit rating of the property. Repositioning or rehabilitating properties include taking a real estate parcel and changing its physical appearance. For instance, refurbishment of an office building's lobby and elevators should lead to higher rents from new tenants and higher renewal rates from existing tenants. Redevelopment of existing properties is an area that can border on or invade opportunistic real estate investing. An example of redevelopment is an investor who purchases a warehouse and reorganizes the property into condominiums for sale as residential housing. A characteristic of redevelopment is that it can require significant interim-period capital expenditures following the initial capital outlay to acquire the original property. New development is similar in many respects to redevelopment, since it can enter the opportunistic style of real estate investment. New development also requires significant interim-period capital during the course of construction. The embedded risks in new development include the estimation and realization of construction costs and associated raw materials, the changing market price and cap rates for real estate during the period from the start of construction to the final lease up or resale phase, and the competitive market for capacity and its impact on occupancy and leases rates in the type and location of the facility being developed.

Most value-added real estate funds limit their exposure to opportunistic types of investments (especially new development) to 20 percent of invested assets. However, small allocations to opportunistic real estate enable a value-added fund to enhance returns with some additional risk, while not changing the overall complexion of the fund. The dynamic approach of value-added real estate investing is in sharp contrast to the core and core-plus strategies, which essentially operate within the bounds of a property's original tenanting and physical positioning. Nevertheless, value-added real estate is not as risky as opportunistic properties, which tend to be focused on allocations to new development, redevelopment, and distressed properties.

Opportunistic Real Estate

Opportunistic real estate is yet another degree more aggressive than the value-added, core-plus, or core strategies. It would not be uncommon for an opportunistic manager to sell a property to a value-added operator with local market access. Similarly, the value-added manager might sell the same property to a core-plus or core investor once it is released or redeveloped. The opportunistic region is the most aggressive of real estate investment and therefore is perhaps one of the most difficult to characterize through generalizations. The types of properties involved in these transactions are varied. Some unifying themes are that they tend to be existing real estate that is either distressed or highly leveraged, or they are new developments of speculative buildings. As such, the return and risk for these properties can vary widely from the overall real estate market. Investment managers operating in this area of the real estate market often exhibit a propensity to "flip" properties. The average holding periods for these properties can be shorter than is the case with other types of real estate investment.[4] As is the case for value-added real estate, operators or managers of opportunistic investments are required to have unique knowledge and access to buyers and sellers in local markets. An additional requirement for opportunistic real estate managers is expertise in the areas of unique deal flow and access to financing. For example, whereas an investment manager in the value-added space may have a keen eye for renovation or redevelopment of a local property, the opportunistic investor may have found a property through a relationship with a national bank seeking to monetize a nonperforming mortgage. In this instance, both the opportunistic and value-added managers are operating from different points of access in finding and securing transactions in the same local market. Additionally, the opportunistic manager may have to conduct an immediate refinancing of a property, which may require unique relationships with financial institutions.

Opportunistic real estate investments include those with the following attributes: the use of greater than 70 percent leverage, purchases of distressed properties, and purchases from distressed sellers. Distressed sellers of real estate may be distressed because of a combination of the distressed nature of a specific property and the limited capital resources of the owner, or simply the property's specific problems. Examples of specific problems that might render properties distressed include real estate with environmental contamination; properties located in blighted areas; properties that require substantial redevelopment and repositioning; new types of specialty properties serving emerging industries; greenfield developments in areas that require substantial construction of original infrastructure and associated regulatory or zoning approvals; and real estate in developing market areas that have substantial geopolitical risk. In many of these cases, the distressed nature of the properties can be resolved, but only with considerable effort and expense. Indeed, it is the technical inexperience of the original owners, their limited financial flexibility, or their lack of interest in going through the trouble that renders them sellers of these properties.

Examples of distressed sellers include the following: a highly leveraged operating company that possesses a facility that has become distressed or is of marginal utility to the company in its ongoing business; a real estate operating company that is in default to its lenders and is forced to sell properties into a weak market; two companies that have merged and are forced to liquidate some properties in order to raise cash, eliminate redundancies in overlapping markets, or resolve antitrust concerns; and a large company that has a strong credit rating and good financial flexibility but that owns a small property with significant distress, in which case the corporation may wish to liquidate the parcel perhaps at any cost in order to limit the risk of contingent liabilities spreading from the property to the corporation and jeopardizing its pristine financial condition.

Infrastructure Properties

From an investment perspective, real estate is more often defined by its strategy approach than its property type. Nevertheless, it is clear that operators must have very different skills and experience to be successful in one type of property versus another. For example, an investment manager who owns office buildings has very different business considerations than one who owns industrial sites, shopping malls, or residential rental units. These property types can be utilized across the various investment strategies. For instance, office buildings can be contained in REITs, core, core-plus, value-added, and opportunistic funds. In each case, a discussion of the property type is better defined by the investment strategy than it is by the characteristics of managing the property. Although this chapter focuses on how real estate is situated in the investment strategy landscape, rather than how property types are managed, an exception is infrastructure properties.

Infrastructure real estate, such as toll roads and airports, is unique in the sense that the properties are captive assets with a forced utilization. This characterization makes infrastructure quite different from other prop- erties types that are based on at-will utilization by occupants. Stabilized, or later-stage, infrastructure assets are similar to core real estate, which has high current income as a proportion of expected total returns and gen- erally high-quality occupancy rates. However, infrastructure investments are different in the potential higher levels of debt that are used to finance their purchase and the small amount of flexibility they have in setting future prices. Nevertheless, because of their long-term revenue contracts and captive occupant demand, infrastructure investments are well suited to match long-dated liabilities. A long-term liability can be debt used to finance the purchase of the project, or it can be a pension sponsor seeking to match pension liabilities to the cash flow from the project that is unencumbered by debt. This liability-matching suitability has stimulated investor demand for infrastructure assets. This is especially true for investors utilizing liability-driven investing strategies by matching future liabilities with similar-duration assets. Infrastructure investments also should be considered in light of their potential stability and predictability of returns. However, the historical data from these types of properties as investable assets is limited. There are long-term eminent domain risks that may affect the stability of these investments in the future.

THE CONSTRUCTION OF A SEGREGATED PORTFOLIO OF REAL ESTATE

A portfolio of traditional asset classes can benefit from the addition of real estate. Real estate has generated fairly low historical correlation to traditional asset classes. Furthermore, when added to a diversified portfolio, real estate can contribute benefits of performance enhancement and volatility reduction. Examples of this are contained in Chapter 11. However, there are enough distinct styles of real estate investment that can be used to construct a diversified portfolio that contains only real estate. REITs, core, core-plus, value-added, and opportunistic real estate all can be utilized in a dedicated real estate equity portfolio. This type of combination can be accomplished through a fund of funds that has allocations to active investment managers. An investor who makes an allocation to real estate through a blend of strategies is likely to experience enhanced diversification from this approach. As a result, the volatility of returns from any one of these real estate strategies should be muted through the addition of multiple strategies and multiple investment partnerships.

The perspective taken in constructing a portfolio of real estate investments is one that uses funds (except as it pertains to the use of the NCREIF NPI, which is based on actual properties) rather than direct properties. Direct investment through the outright purchase of buildings requires a large amount of capital and can represent a process that is difficult to evaluate and manage. Fund investments offer the ability for most investors to access this market with reasonable skill and property diversification, whereas direct property investments require substantial skill, depth of staff, or external resources, which may apply only to a small portion of the largest investors. In terms of diversification, a similar rationale applies: only the largest investors can hope to deploy the sums of capital required to accomplish diversification across individual properties. The perspective in portfolio construction using real estate also is one of investing in equity rather than fixed-income real estate investments. Equity investments are considered at the exclusion of debt investments in the belief that debt investments are a subcomponent of traditional fixed-income investing. Although backed by real estate investments, as a generalization, debt investments in real estate provide similar risk-adjusted returns to other sorts of fixed-income investments that have equal credit ratings.

The Use of REITs in Real Estate Portfolio Construction

The analysis of the diversification benefits from REITs within a portfolio of real estate investments can be time-period specific. Some studies suggest that REITs may be redundant when used in a portfolio of direct real estate investments.[5] However, significant periods of time do not support this. For example, as illustrated in Table 5.2, from 1996 through the first quarter of 2006, REITs and core real estate exhibited nearly zero correlation. Nevertheless, this observation should be considered more deeply though an analysis of the independent factors, which REITs and core real estate may or may not share. The factor analysis approach is conducted in Chapter 11.

REITs versus Core Real Estate   REITs generally depict a structure rather than an investment strategy. Nevertheless, because of their growing importance in the real estate investable universe, it is difficult to ignore using REITs in real estate portfolio construction. As depicted in Table 5.3, both REITs and core real estate seem to offer similar traits in high occupancy and low requirements for additional capital. Furthermore, REIT funds fall near core real estate in terms of their expected return, level of expected risk, and nature as open-end funds, also shown in Table 5.3. More specifically, at times REITs can offer a slightly less attractive expected return but a higher level of expected leverage than what is assumed for core real estate. Based on this information in isolation, an investor might question why an investment in REITs should be made rather than one in core real estate. REITs seem to be close in nature to core real estate but at times can offer a less attractive expected return profile and higher potential risk through the use of greater leverage.

In addressing this question, one must clarify the premise that REITs are expected to generate returns that are less than core real estate. A qualification must be made that there is a wide range of REITs in the public and private market in the United States as well as in many other countries around the world. These entities are invested in a broad range of property and security types. It is very difficult to generalize about REITs. Furthermore, REITs have had periods of performance that vastly exceed the estimated target of 6 percent to 7 percent used in Table 5.3. However, these periods have been associated with a general compression in cap rates during a low-interest-rate environment that coincided with strong operating fundamentals for real estate, including falling vacancy rates. A return assumption in the 6 percent to 7 percent range depicts a long-term average assumption during economic cycles.

Reasons for the appeal of REITs, in spite of potentially lower returns and more leverage risk than core real estate, involve the following: diversification, fees, income, investment size considerations, liquidity in entering and exiting the investment, and the J-curve phenomenon. The generalized differences between REITs and core real estate that are depicted in Table 5.4 include management fees and the proportion of total return that is expected to be achieved from current income rather than capital appreciation.

REITs Provide Diversification   In terms of diversification in comparing core real estate funds and REITs, REIT funds have vastly greater property diversification than core real estate funds. While a core real estate fund may have as few as 8 to 12 properties, REIT funds are populated with minority investments typically in publicly traded REITs that have numerous properties and investments contained in their funds. Thus, an investor's actual exposure in a REIT fund may number hundreds of properties. This broad diversification from a property perspective that is offered by REIT funds has implications for risk. Lower risk accomplished through diversification of properties may enable REITs to utilize a greater amount of leverage than core real estate funds without a commensurate increase in overall expected volatility of returns. Moreover, this perception of diversification and its relationship to risk reduction may cause investors to demand less compensation in the form of expected returns from REITs.

Fees for REITs versus Core Real Estate   Although neither REIT funds nor core real estate funds tend to charge performance fees (therefore neither has a hurdle rate), they do both charge management fees. The expected management fee for a REIT fund is expected to be half to two-thirds what the management fee is for a typical core real estate fund. The lower fee structure for REITs is an attractive feature that may cause greater demand for this type of product than is the case for core real estate funds. If so, this would result in downward pressure on expected returns for REITs versus core real estate funds.

Current Income for REITs versus Core Real Estate Approximately one third of total returns from REITs might be expected to be derived from capital appreciation, whereas the proportion of capital appreciation expected for core real estate funds is perhaps closer to 15 percent. There is greater risk associated with capital appreciation over a long time period than there is with current income associated with short time periods. Current income from net operating funds is more predictable than the realization of forecasted capital appreciation or the sale of properties at profitable levels. Accordingly, the risk associated with expected total returns for REITs should be higher than core real estate funds. Higher risk associated with a greater proportion of an investment's total return being derived from capital appreciation versus current income should translate into a higher level of total expected return. However, this does not appear to be the case for REITs versus core real estate funds. This implies that perhaps other factors involved in the pricing of expected returns for these two types of real estate structures may have heavier weights than the unpredictable nature of capital appreciation versus current income.

Size of Investment Investment size is an additional consideration that may provide a source of excess demand for REITs and therefore create downward pressure on expected returns relative to core real estate. Size relates to the minimum acceptable investment by a REIT investment manager versus a core real estate fund. While core real estate funds may require up to a $5 million or larger minimum investment, REIT funds tend to have minimum investment amounts of $1 million and potentially much less than this. Part of this dynamic relates to the fact that REIT funds are well suited to being registered investment companies with the Securities and Exchange Commission (SEC) in the United States, while few open-end core real estate funds are registered. REIT funds are invested in publicly traded REIT securities, whereas core real estate funds are invested in actual properties. As registered investment companies, REIT funds are capable of accepting investors who do not meet high-net-worth standards. From an institutional investor's vantage point, these investor restrictions are less of a concern. However, the ready access to REIT funds by small investors may create a dynamic in the pricing of these instruments such that the required average return demanded by investors is reduced. This ease of access subjects REIT funds to a far greater number of investors than can gain access to core real estate funds. On one hand, smaller-sized investors may be somewhat less discerning in measuring expected returns versus expected risk. On the other hand, smaller-sized investors simply may not have access to as broad a selection of investment choices in real estate as larger-sized investors. In order to gain access to certain asset classes, these investors may simply have no choice but to accept the selections that are available to them. This may be in spite of there being more attractive risk-adjusted returns available in similar assets offered elsewhere, but to which they do not have access.

Open Access for REITs versus Core Real Estate In addition to these considerations, another important difference between REITs and open-end core real estate funds is the concept of a queue, which tends to exist for investors seeking access to core real estate funds but not for REIT funds. A queue for some open-end core real estate funds results when demand exceeds available capacity. Existence of a waiting list for investment in core funds is in stark contrast to the ease of access that investors have to REIT funds, which are very liquid and able to accept new investor funds fairly readily. This difference represents a liquidity gap that may have implications for expected returns when comparing these two investment options. Core real estate funds may pay a price for the less liquid access that they provide. In other words, investors may be compensated for a higher illiquidity risk premium related to the entry into core real estate funds in the form of an extra expected return. (For more discussion on the pricing of illiquidity as a risk factor, see Chapter 10.)

Other Aspects of Liquidity for REITs versus Core Real Estate The REIT investment model not only offers better liquidity for access to and redemption from funds versus core real estate; REITs also offer a consistency of liquidity. In other words, the presumption of liquidity is not expected to change. The access to and redemption from REIT funds is expected to remain constant in a variety of market circumstances. However, the same cannot necessarily be said for core real estate funds. Indeed, core real estate investor queues can disappear in certain environments, such as when cyclical fundamentals are poor for this type of asset or when substantial capacity is created for these types of funds. Lack of an investor queue could hamper investors seeking to redeem from core funds by using liquidity provided by a queue. Although most core real estate funds have cash on hand and even lines of credit in place to facilitate investor redemptions in the event that a queue was not available, there are scenarios that can be constructed where investors' demands for redemption might overwhelm these funds' ability to provide for them. In this case, delayed redemptions, forced sales of properties, and potential pressure on the market for prices of core buildings could occur. While admittedly this would have an impact on REIT pricing as well, the concept illustrates that core real estate liquidity and the presumption of its existence is far less certain than the liquidity associated with REITs through their public market nature. This uncertainty regarding the presumption of consistent liquidity for core real estate may plausibly have some bearing on setting the expected returns for core real estate slightly higher than for REITs.

J-Curve Differences for REITs versus Core Real Estate   A benefit of investing in REITs is the shorter or nonexistent J curves that they have compared with the possible presence of J curves in core real estate funds. Although the J-curve phenomenon typically is associated with private equity funds (e.g., venture capital), it nonetheless can be present in real estate funds. The J curve, or the period of flat or down performance in the very early stages of any private fund, may be more pronounced for a core real estate fund than for a REIT fund. Granted, the nature of an open-end core real estate fund is such that an investor may be entering the fund after its initial years of operation when it is well seasoned and therefore past any J-curve effect. However, a REIT fund that is comprised of numerous publicly trade REITs offers broad diversification across enough mature investments that a J curve is not expected to be present, whereas for a core real estate fund in its early stages, a J curve could be present. The absence of J curves for REITs may cause higher demand for this type of real estate product and therefore lower returns. Meanwhile, the potential presence of J curves in core real estate may represent another risk that requires compensation in the form of higher expected returns.

The Use of Core and Core-Plus in Real Estate Portfolio Construction

Core and core-plus funds tend to be representative of the overall risk and return characteristics of the real estate asset class in general. As a result, it may be counterintuitive to use many of these funds in the construction of a portfolio of real estate assets. The reasoning is that the potential benefit from using multiple selections of these funds is limited, because of the low variability of outcomes for one core fund versus another. The potential correlations among these funds are likely to be high, in which case it is difficult to accomplish much diversification benefit by adding many of them to a portfolio. The benefit from diversification among these sorts of funds is likely to be reached quite soon from the incremental addition of funds in this area. Core funds are not required to have a large number of properties in their funds, because of the limited benefit derived from diversification among these similarly situated lower-risk properties. However, some core funds have many core properties, because of a desire to accept a large quantity of investor assets. Meanwhile, core-plus funds often simply are core funds with the minor addition of some value-added or opportunistic property exposure.

There is some basis to consider the veracity of small samples in real estate portfolio construction. Because of the generally stable nature of property as a physical asset, one could argue that real estate has inherently lower-volatility characteristics than some other types of assets that might be more volatile due to market pricing influences. The infrequent pricing through appraisals of real estate properties does not allow for much short-term over- or underpricing of property based on market psychology or volatility, such as can be the case in certain equity markets. There is evidence to support the notion that as few as 10 properties can be effective for accomplishing a reasonable mirroring of expected average outcomes of portfolios holding 100 properties.[6] Although volatility of performance is higher for smaller portfolios, some diversification is accomplished with smaller number of properties included in a portfolio. Furthermore, this research is based on specific properties, whereas the methodology considered in this chapter is based on a combination of commingled funds, each of which has numerous underlying properties.

The expected volatility of returns from investments in core real estate is quite low, because of the stable attributes of the properties. As a result of expected low volatility and low returns, core real estate can be a stable yet not high-performing asset to use in the context of constructing portfolios of real estate. While core real estate is a fundamentally sound investment in its own right, alternatively, the concept of using properties or funds with somewhat higher-volatility characteristics strikes at the heart of capturing the benefit of diversification. These benefits are garnered through the dilution to risk when multiple risky assets are combined into one portfolio. Because of the already low-risk features of core real estate, these properties do not contribute as much benefit from diversification as other types of investments.

This light being shed on core real estate is not meant to disparage its utility as a source of diversification when combined with traditional asset classes. Rather, when considering a portfolio that consists of only real estate assets, the more speculative real estate strategies are the ones that can benefit more greatly from diversification. There is less opportunity for core real estate to generate high returns that are associated with unique value creation, such as found with the opportunistic and value-added real estate strategies. Core real estate has low capitalization rates, since it is a low-risk asset that has a preponderance of total return comprised of current income. By contrast, returns associated with opportunistic and value-added real estate, while receiving some impact from current income, are more strongly driven by the potentially volatile nature of capital gains. The active management and resulting alpha that is generated by a manager of a property is less apparent in core real estate.

Furthermore, if an investor chose to invest in a portfolio of real estate funds as constructed by a fund of funds, then the benefit from the use of core real estate in such a product would be proportionately more greatly diminished by the fund of funds' fees than would be the case for value-added or opportunistic funds. In other words, in a fund of funds setting, the required return target for an individual subfund investment has to be high enough that, net of the fund of funds' fees, the underlying investment still contributes both to risk reduction and performance enhancement of the total fund of funds' portfolio.

The Use of Value-Added and Opportunistic Properties and Funds in Real Estate Portfolio Construction

Value-added and opportunistic real estate properties and funds represent relatively high return and risk segments of the real estate investment area. These sectors of the real estate universe are appealing for portfolio construction, where risk can be reduced through diversification. The potential for a wide range of outcomes in actual returns from these properties results from their high expected volatility. Therefore, the utilization of a portfolio approach to these investments and their inclusion in diversified portfolio of real estate can be beneficial. Diversification has the benefit of lowering the risk of these value-added and opportunistic assets while retaining their relatively high real estate returns. A typically wide dispersion of returns from the top- to the bottom-performing properties and funds that can be classified as value-added or opportunistic highlights the benefit of diversification in this area of investment. Because of the likely range of potential outcomes, careful due diligence in property and manager selection in these sectors are endeavors that also can yield strong relative returns.

Benefits from Atypical Real Estate Factors   Elements of the value-added and opportunistic styles create new attributes for real estate as an investable asset. Some of these characteristics are shared with other types of alternative investments. For instance, value-added real estate derives a greater portion of its return than core real estate from investing in properties where there is a less liquid market. The expected return and volatility of returns associated with these parcels becomes somewhat dependent on an illiquidity risk premium. These properties also are dependent on credit. Credit as a source of return is present in other alternative and traditional assets, such as distressed debt and high-yield debt. When applied to real estate, the credit factor can be as important, if not more important, in determining total returns than are other basic real estate sources of return. This overlap and commonality of factor drivers of returns illustrates the need for a deeper understanding of the sources of returns and risks that exist across investment types.

Limitations of Data Measurement and Benchmarking One significant problem in conducting an analysis of real estate for portfolio construction is benchmark selection. Although the NCREIF NPI is a fairly well accepted proxy for core real estate and there are several indexes that measure publicly quoted REITs, there are not many widely accepted indexes that represent value-added or opportunistic real estate. However, NCREIF is planning to make these available in the future. It is precisely the value-added and opportunistic real estate strategies that hold special intrigue for real estate portfolio construction, because of the potential inefficiencies that abound in these regions. The unique industry and market niches in which the value-added and opportunistic strategies operate hold substantial potential for operators in these areas to generate discrete returns above the beta returns represented by core real estate. This is observable on a fund-by-fund or property-by-property basis. However, it is difficult to make generalizations about value-added and opportunistic real estate without the aid of widely accepted indexes. In the absence of obvious opportunistic and value-added real estate indexes, an approach is to create surrogate indexes. One such effort is to take properties that report results to NCREIF but that do not meet NCREIF's qualification standards for the NPI. Because they do not meet the quality traits of core real estate, these non-NPI properties de facto qualify for some form of core-plus, value-added, or opportunistic classification.[7] However, there are difficulties in rendering these properties useful for index creation because of uneven appraisal periodicity and leverage profiles. It is uncertain whether this group is a better fit with core-plus, value-added, or opportunistic real estate.

Sample Optimization Using Only Real Estate

Figure 5.2 contains an optimization of a two-asset portfolio that utilizes only the NCREIF NPI and REITs. Value-added and opportunistic real estate have been excluded in the absence of well-vetted indexes that measure these strategies. The model in Figure 5.2 is unconstrained and allows for significant or minute inclusion of either of the two assets. The optimal point on the frontier is defined by the highest Sharpe ratio portfolio. However, this point may not be optimal for each investor with differing return and risk objectives. Furthermore, the optimal point does not fully reflect the benefit from diversification that can be derived through the use of REIT investments and core real estate investments in a portfolio that includes additional assets. The data used in the exhibit is historical and includes only a span of approximately 10 years. Therefore, it is illustrative in nature, since data using different periods of time may show altered results.

One observation from the results for this optimization is the fairly long efficient frontier, which illustrates the wide risk spectrum. Meanwhile, the

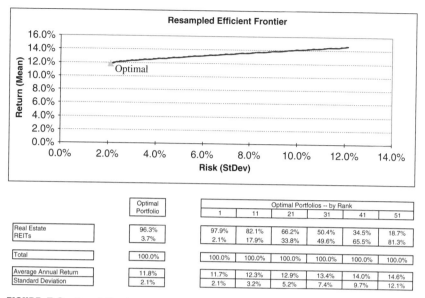

FIGURE 5.2 Portfolio Optimization of Real Estate and REITs
Note: Model is unconstrained. Data is 1996 through June 2006.
Source: RogersCasey; NCREIF; NAREIT; Resampled Efficient Frontier™ provided
by New Frontier Advisors, LLC.

opportunity for incremental gain in returns for each unit of additional risk
appears to be small. The reasoning for this is the relatively close returns
for the NCREIF NPI and the utilized REIT index over the time period
but a relatively wide difference in volatility. The REIT index during this
time frame exhibited sizable volatility of returns relative to the NPI. This
is not surprising considering the infrequent and estimated valuations of the
properties contained in the NPI, compared with the public market pricing
of REITs. Points farther to the right side of the efficient frontier include
higher allocations to REITs.

SUMMARY

The inclusion of real estate in a diversified portfolio can provide return
enhancement and volatility reduction. There are numerous real estate strategies and structures through which this can be accomplished, including:
REITs, core, core-plus, value-added, and opportunistic. Real estate also can
provide an investor with a source of current income, which is a unique
attribute compared with most other types of alternative investments. Other

benefits from real estate include its stability as a physical asset that typically does not exhibit as much pricing volatility as many traditional asset classes. Real estate also provides an investor with access to different types of returns. Real estate has its own beta return, which typically is depicted by core real estate. Furthermore, there are different types of real estate strategies, such as value-added and opportunistic, which offer unique manager-specific returns. Therefore, an investor can hope to capture additional diversification through real estate because of its uncorrelated beta and alpha generation compared with other types of investments.

As a result, real estate can be included in an investor's overall portfolio, and different types of real estate strategies can be combined to provide a portfolio that consists of only real estate. Benefits in each case are expected to be realized from diversification and a resulting reduction in volatility, while robust and unique returns remain. Once the various real estate strategies and their sources of return and risk are understood, an investor can utilize these investments in portfolio construction. This process is explored from a quantitative perspective in additional detail in Chapter 11.

CHAPTER 6

Currency, Commodities, Timber, and Oil and Gas

A final area of alternative investments includes those assets that do not fit neatly into hedge funds, private equity, or real estate. The various investments that are sequestered into this noncategory are not easily generalized in terms of traditional asset classes or alternative investment characterization. The investments included in this chapter are currency trading strategies, liquid commodities exposure, and private partnerships devoted to timber or oil and gas properties. These assets have distinctive qualitative attributes that contribute to their total return. These qualitative characteristics are in addition to the quantitative traits that are evaluated in Chapter 11. Currency and commodity trading as well as timber and oil and gas investment have benefits in the form of performance that is derived from unique sources. Furthermore, they generally exhibit low correlation to traditional asset classes and to other types of alternative investments. Therefore, currency, commodities, timber, and oil and gas can provide diversification to a portfolio of assets. When added to a portfolio of assets, they also tend to provide a reduction in overall volatility of returns.

THE QUALITATIVE DETERMINANTS OF RETURNS

In addition to the quantitative factors that affect investment managers operating in currencies, commodities, timber, and oil and gas (see Chapter 11), there are qualitative factors that may be difficult to measure but are important to evaluate. Qualitative factors that influence returns from the various alternative assets discussed in this chapter share some characteristics with those for private equity, real estate, and hedge funds. They include two distinct areas, one that relates to private investments and one that relates to more liquid securities such as the currency markets.

Private Investments

In the private investment realm, access to promising transactions is an important determinant of future returns. Many of these alternative assets are even less efficient than certain areas of the real estate and private equity markets. For instance, the timber market is very idiosyncratic. The tracts of timber that become available sometimes are not auctioned, but sold to a very small and select group of potential bidders. Many of these properties are sold by forest products companies seeking to divest themselves of these assets, while retaining the logging rights to the properties. Therefore, there is a continuing business relationship that may exist after the sale of these parcels, and the selection of buyers often is in view of this extenuating circumstance.

Similarly, oil and gas properties are very sensitive to insider knowledge of the oil leases that are available as well as specific skill required in geology. The ability to properly gauge the expected success of extracting reserves from a producing property is highly complex and requires prior experience. Even in downstream oil and gas endeavors, such as distribution and refining, sound knowledge of regulation, engineering, as well as market dynamics is essential for success. Much of this knowledge also relies on strong industry contacts and relationships that are required to facilitate transactions. Furthermore, as is the case with leveraged buyouts, investment in both timber and oil and gas can be sensitive to financing. Not only can availability of lenders provide entrance into some of these transactions, but posttransaction financing may be required for recapitalizations and dividend payments. Public market access to liquidity at the time of exit for these investments also may play a factor in total return, as do relationships with possible strategic purchasers of these investments for resale.

Liquid Securities

Commodities and currency trading are areas that are less deal sensitive and more dependent on discretionary and systematic qualitative factors. Discretionary traders in these areas are those who have strong risk controls, but essentially are using their experience and judgment in placing the investments that they make in these markets. Skill and success therefore relate to prior experience, informational advantage through local market contacts, and sound research. In terms of systematic traders, skill often relates to robust computer models that inform trading decisions. The cost of maintaining these systems and sophisticated personnel who develop the algorithms that run them often are the main drivers of relative performance. This is an area where there is a close linkage between market winners and losers. Unlike the production of commodities or timber, trading commodities and currencies can be more of a zero-sum game where each winner produces a loser. In this sense, being better skilled or having an edge in computational power and speed of execution can generate profits at the expense of other market participants who lag in these areas.

In these liquid strategies, risk controls also are necessary and pose an important qualitative factor for total return. The importance of risk systems lies in the fact that often a majority of individual trades in currency and commodities trading are unprofitable, and losses from them must be stemmed. Meanwhile, profitable trades are allowed to remain in place to their fruition. Cornerstones for risk management are the existence of securities management systems, the identification of triggers to cut losses or instigate hedges, and the existence of management oversight that ensures that they are utilized. Integrity of management holds promise that risk measurement systems are used and that limits that trigger risk reduction actions are followed with strict discipline.

THE ATTRACTION OF CURRENCY

The worldwide currency market is the most liquid single market in the world, with daily turnover of some $1.9 trillion.[1] As Figure 6.1 illustrates, the worldwide currency market is far larger than the turnover for the New York Stock Exchange, the London Stock Exchange, or the market for U.S. Treasury securities. In addition to the sizable asset area it represents for investors in alternative investments, there are certain structural inefficiencies in the currencies markets, and there are lags in currencies attaining equilibrium with each other. These issues create opportunity to generate profit for currency traders. Such idiosyncrasies manifest themselves from a

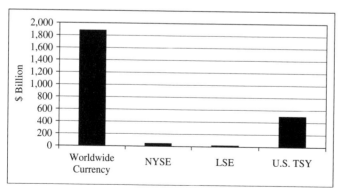

FIGURE 6.1 Worldwide Daily Currency Turnover (U.S. $1.9 Trillion in 2004) Copyright 2006 by Goldman, Sachs & Co.; data as of 2004.

quantitative perspective by currency trading managers having few, if any, repeatable factor sensitivities during regression analyses of their returns (see Chapter 11).

Structural Inefficiencies Created by Market Participants

Underpinnings for potentially considering currency as an investment are its unique structural return considerations. The currency exchange market has many participants, as Figure 6.2 illustrates. Some of these participants are involved for practical exchange purposes, rather than specifically being motivated by trading profits. For example, the fact that major multinational corporations are constantly in the marketplace buying and selling currency on a regular basis to facilitate the normal course of their business often creates a price-inelastic participant. Multinational corporations must make their purchases and sales of currency in order to run their businesses, and their core business is neither the making of markets in currencies nor the most efficient buying or selling of currencies. Furthermore, government central banks that are in the market buying or selling currencies may be even less price sensitive. Central banks often are in the position of making purchases or sales that may be counterintuitive to the market direction of their currencies. Central bank intervention may provide market pressures that are opposite to the fundamental direction of the currencies that they are supporting or depressing. Meanwhile, an investment manager that is in the business of capturing spreads between buyers and sellers in the currency market may find an ability to profit from these types of structural inefficiencies. Furthermore, this approach combined with leverage can provide a rate of return on investment that is attractive.

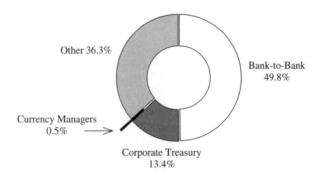

FIGURE 6.2 Worldwide Currency Market Participants
Source: First Quadrant, LP.

Another aspect of the inefficiency embedded in the currency markets is the participation of long-only international equity investors who hedge their currency exposures. These investors may be less focused on the dissipation of their currency risk than they are on the analysis and execution of their bottom-up fundamental research investments. A notable irony in this is the fact that the very spark of interest in these equity investments for a fundamental investor may be fostered by local country macroeconomic environments. These environments, which may support the fundamental company-specific analyses conducted by these investors, might be at odds with the implied impact they have on the local currencies. In other words, accommodative monetary policy such as declining interest rates and rising money supply often are precisely the macroeconomic stimulants that generate corporate activity. This activity is likely to send a wave of higher expectations for corporate profits and cash flow. Nevertheless, these same stimulants often are the undoing of fundamental strength for domestic currencies. Indeed, declining interest rates, expanding money supply, and generally accommodative monetary policy are stimulating influences that can negatively affect the valuation of domestic currencies. Therefore, such an environment may be good for an equity investor but poor for a currency investor. This potentially creates a trading opportunity for currency investors taking advantage of equity investors.[2]

Part of the inability of traditional long-only international equity managers to take advantage of the opportunities to retain currency exposure is a limitation on their mandates by their investors. Although there are funds that retain local currency exposure, the ones that do not may find themselves "paying" profits generated by currency investment to currency trading counterparties who capture the market inefficiencies that are provided. These types of inefficiencies create returns for currency trading managers that have low correlation with other asset classes and distinctly different return drivers and sources of volatility.

Macroeconomic Influences

In addition to structural inefficiencies that can be captured by investors, there are fundamental factors that dictate the strength or weakness of various currencies. Although currency is a transfer of wealth mechanism rather than an asset per se, the volatility in valuations among different currencies creates opportunities for trading profits. In this sense, currency volatility is a potential source of return. There is no implied rate of return for currency as there is in equities, which can be valued through the dividend discount model. Nevertheless, there are macroeconomic influences that cause currency exchange values to fluctuate. Macroeconomic factors that affect currency exchange rates tend to be focused on two areas: country-specific inflation and real growth in gross domestic product (GDP). Although a critic might say that an investor benefits from an appreciation in the value of bonds that are denominated in a country's currency rather than the value of the currency itself, there are both currency and fixed-income components of this total return. Furthermore, a currency-only investment can be made through futures or forward swaps with dealers or counterparties.

There are global pressures that affect all countries, currencies, and their purchasing power. More specifically, there are domestic macroeconomic factors that lead to realized inflation in individual countries. The ability to identify and forecast these factors as leading indicators of future inflation may be a source of return for currency traders. Fundamental analysis and forecasting are areas of active management that potentially can add value. This area of potential unique return is in addition to the opportunity for return that is created by market-wide inefficiencies, such as the existence of participants in the currency market who do not specifically seek to profit from their transactions.

Purchasing Power Parity and Its Lag

Another element of discrete return in currency trading relates to the lag that purchasing power parity (PPP) can have during its affect on currency equilibrium. The PPP concept dictates that all currencies over time will find equilibrium, such that a country with high inflation will see its currency depreciate versus a country with low inflation. Therefore, over time and after conversion of currencies, goods in one country always will be valued the same as in other countries. In its essence, PPP implies that currencies will always be in equilibrium. Therefore, the premise for investing in or trading currencies should not exist. However, the key determinant of PPP is time. PPP requires a sufficient period of time for equilibrium to be realized. In spite of technology and communications, time realization in the context of the completion of PPP seems to rely on the recognition of current inflation in one country versus another. PPP assumes equilibrium among currencies. However, this is perhaps a longer-term phenomenon. Over short-term periods of uncertain information, inefficiencies may exist where the logic of PPP has not yet taken hold. PPP may not resolve the existence of short-term friction in the marketplace that offers the opportunity to capture inefficiencies.

THE ATTRACTION OF COMMODITIES

Commodities, like currencies, have limited inherent return-generating capability. Commodities may exhibit positive or negative price movement based on the inflationary pressure that exists for each commodity, which is determined by forces of market supply and demand. However, the commodities futures markets also offer certain structural sources of returns. Investment in commodities is largely accomplished through the purchase and sale of futures contracts. Futures entail notional leverage. Buyers are required to deposit only a small amount of an initial purchase price to accomplish fairly sizable exposure. This concept of notional leverage is common in the derivatives marketplace, whether involving futures, options, or swaps. Regardless of whether the reference entity in the transaction is a commodity, a currency, an equity, an interest rate, or a credit, in each case the use of notional leverage is similar. Furthermore, these instruments have finite time periods. Unlike other forms of assets, futures contracts have predetermined dates at which they expire. Rolling an exposure to commodities from futures with one expiration date to another can offer unique "roll returns."

The Benefit of Long Roll Return in Backwardation

An investment in commodities futures contracts typically involves a purchase or sale of the right to receive delivery of a commodity at a specified time in the future. Often, producers of commodities use the futures market to hedge against price fluctuation. A party entering into a futures contract may be offering a commodity for sale at a future price, ostensibly because they expect to have a long position in the commodity in the future. The price of the referenced commodity in the current spot or cash market relative to the price of the futures contract may vary. If the price of the futures contract is lower than the price of the commodity in the spot market, this is a configuration known as backwardation. In the case of backwardation, a perpetual buyer of futures contracts is constantly enjoying the appreciation of futures contracts, as the futures price discount to the current spot price closes over time. This creates the opportunity for roll return, which means that every time the buyer of the futures contract is rolling their futures positions into the next dated contract, they are enjoying a return on initial investment. Of course, this assumes a fairly constant spot price from the present to the future when the futures price is realized. Backwardation frequently is the normal situation that occurs in futures markets for heating oil, for instance.

The Benefit of Short Roll Return in Contango

If the price of the futures contract is higher than the price of the commodity in the spot market, this configuration is known as contango. Contango represents an environment where a futures buyer is experiencing a dissipation of premium from the point of purchase to the point of the futures expiration date, assuming a constant spot price. However, a short seller of contangoed futures is in a position of collecting premium similar to the case of long buyers of backwardated futures. Therefore, there is opportunity for "roll return" in perpetuity by shorting contangoed futures contracts. Contango frequently is the situation that occurs in futures markets for gold, for instance.

Roll Return versus Spot Price Return

Roll return and spot price return are two dynamic components of futures return. Each can be positive or negative. However, the roll return for both backwardated and contangoed futures normally tends to be a larger portion of return than the spot price movement. Indeed, the roll return in one observation was estimated to have contributed 91 percent of cross-sectional variation of commodities futures returns from December 1982 through May 2004.[3] If roll returns can be found to be a significant portion of returns for commodities futures contracts, then this may be the source of much alpha for this investment strategy. However, roll return is significantly dependent on time period and price movement, which may be tied more closely to supply and demand dynamics for each individual commodity and an overall rate of inflation. Any one commodity price is affected by a myriad of local and global price pressures. Commodity prices often have low correlation to each other. However, taken as a group, diversified commodities indexes tend to show some relationship to inflation factor proxies such as inflation-adjusted bonds.

CURRENCY AND COMMODITY STRATEGIES

Investment strategies that are used to implement an exposure to currencies or commodities can be simple long-only index investments, or they can be more complex views that are expressed through both long and short positions. An expansion into positive and negative directional investments in this realm also can unlock further sources of unique returns. The four major approaches to trading currencies and commodities include systematic, discretionary, technical, and fundamental. Elements of these approaches include trend following, mean reversion, and volatility capture. Furthermore, these approaches can be executed over short, medium, or long time frames. These strategies also may be employed with other types of investment instruments, including futures, options, and swaps on equities and fixed-income investments.

Systematic

Systematic traders rely on computer-based models to determine their entry and exit points in securities. Often, these models can be very complex and opaque to the average investor. Systematic approaches seek to discover small discrepancies in markets that are repeatable. After back testing the historical veracity of these anomalies, computer programs are written in an attempt to capture them when they recur in the future. Systematic programs may have elements of fundamental and technical analysis. They also may adopt trend-following, mean-reversion, and volatility trading tactics. Managers using this style view their edge as being the proprietary signals that they use to determine trading points and the way in which they create computer algorithms that conduct these calculations. Many of these managers have developed their own trading systems that execute numerous trades electronically in rapid-fire fashion. A benefit from this adjunct is the immediate expression of a systematic view in an attempt to be competitive with other systematic traders using similar techniques. These systems generally execute trades at rock-bottom commission rates. However, they possess the specter of risk associated with the use of an automated system to move large sums of capital with limited human intervention.

Discretionary

Discretionary managers use their own subjective judgment when purchasing and selling securities. These investors rely on their past experiences to inform their current decisions. This approach can be applied through fundamental or technical analysis. The discretionary approach also may utilize trend-following, mean-reversion, and volatility trading methods. Although discretionary traders may be criticized for being unable or slow to recognize and act upon trading patterns and fundamental signals that systematic traders are able to distinguish through their computer-generated decision making and execution, the human element of discretionary traders purports to make them more risk aware of new market developments that might cause past quantitative relationships to become unhinged. Moreover, from a trading perspective, while they are less efficient than systematic traders, discretionary traders can be more subjective in altering their rate of trade execution. During their trading, they can bring the process to a halt if need be, owing to intraday changes in fundamental or technical outlooks.

Fundamental

Fundamental investors are traditional in their approach. Their decisions tend to be triggered by macroeconomic or microeconomic factors, which they believe will determine the value of investments. Whether used in a discretionary or systematic context, fundamental investing relies on the association of economic factors to securities prices. Discretionary traders using a fundamental approach make decisions based on their perception of linkages between economic data and securities prices, while systematic traders identify similar connections through the use of computer models. Both the discretionary and systematic use of fundamental analysis can be executed using short, medium, or long periods of time, during which the relationship between the fundamental factors and their effect on securities are expected to take hold. A contra approach to fundamental analysis for informing investment decisions is technical analysis.

Technical

Traders who follow technical analysis are commonly referred to as chartists. Those who follow technical analysis base their investment decisions on observations about securities using their price movement and associated graphical charts over different time periods. The basic belief that supports technical analysis is that it is difficult to determine the fundamental influences that truly are controlling the price movement of various securities. Therefore, it makes more sense to seek and predict repetition of certain patterns of price movements. Identifying and capturing these price movements more often than not can potentially reap profits. Many traders who employ technical analysis also must limit losses on unprofitable investments, in order to protect against the predicted price patterns changing from their historical guides. Both discretionary and systematic approaches may utilize technical analysis. From a discretionary perspective, technical trading decisions are made based on judgment pertaining to historical security pricing movement. Systematic computer programs also can use price information to create triggers for investment action. Some of the types of tactics that may underlie technical analysis include trend following and mean reversion.

Trend Following   The trend-following tactic, whether used by systematic or discretionary traders, is focused on the identification of and investment in securities that have exhibited persistence in price movement. Investing based on the detection of a security's price direction also is considered momentum investing. The trend-following method is technical in nature. It is based on securities price movements, rather than fundamental signals. Often, trend followers will make many investments based on nascent trends, only to eliminate those that do not blossom into sustainable movements. The trends that exhibit longevity and continuity provide opportunity for these traders to increase their investment in these securities. Trend followers tend to change course only after trends have ended. Therefore, they tend to experience some negative performance at the point of a trend's reversal. Once the trend ends, the securities are eliminated. The rationale for sustaining end-of-trend losses is the presumption that gains prior to trend reversals will more often than not offset end-of-trend losses.

Mean Reversion The concept of mean reversion represents another technical analysis tactic. Investors using mean-reverting techniques base their decisions on the assumption that price action for securities has a tendency to return to the mean of a normal distribution following deviations from the mean. Deviations may amount to as much as one standard deviation or more from the mean, which often triggers initiation of an investment. All of this assumes that future price distributions will parallel historical distributions. Some investors also may marry technical analysis with fundamental analysis when using mean-reverting trades, in order to consider whether the fundamental underpinnings for the investment have changed and therefore warrant a new price distribution. Inherently, mean-reversion investors tend to initiate securities positions that oppose those of trend-following investors. Rather than seeking trends in securities to continue, the mean-reversion approach believes that the trends will reverse themselves and attempts to predict this. Mean-reversion investors believe that the reversal point in an extended trend will occur sooner or later. It is that trend reversal from which they hope to profit.

Volatility Capture

A volatility capture approach to investing is common across many hedge fund strategies. In currencies and commodities, volatility-based traders use a technique similar to certain types of hedge funds as they invest in underlying securities and related derivatives contracts. A typical trade might be a position in a security and a directionally opposite position in an option on that security, which is adjusted as the underlying security exhibits volatility. The desired result of the transaction is to capture periods of volatility in the price movement of either the underlying security or its derivative, while being hedged through the existence of a contradirectional security. This type of approach can be informed either through discretionary or systematic decision making. It also can be derived from fundamental or technical information.

Time Frames

Systematic and discretionary traders, whether using fundamental or technical styles, express their positions over various time frames. A short-term time frame, which might entail a backward-looking view of less than one day to as many as 10 days, is used to inform and instigate a current investment to last about the same time period into the future. A medium-term time frame is likely to be 10 to 30 days in duration, and likewise it relies on signals that have backward-looking durations of a similar length. Long-term time frames tend to be from one month to as long as multiyear or market cycle–length durations, and they are based on historically similar periods that inform expectations for securities' prices in the future.

THE ATTRACTION OF TIMBER

What is the inherent rate of return for a commodity? The answer to this question for most commodities is that prices are determined by forces of market supply and demand, rather than any intrinsic rate of return. However, some commodities have certain embryonic returns at their point of creation. Biological growth is at the heart of a return on the production of perishable commodities, after planting and harvesting expenses. The size of this profit is also a function of spot prices for a commodity net of all expenses incurred for production. The difference between the cost to produce a commodity and its spot price should equal a certain rate of return. For instance, the production of wheat, cotton, and orange juice should exhibit certain sensitivity to market equilibriums. Ideally, supply approximates demand, and profits approximate compensation for risks associated with managing a perishable commodity's biological growth. Of course, a caveat is that some commodities are supported by government price incentives that encourage domestic production and discourage importation.

One example of a commodity that tends to generate some unique inherent return is timber. Timber has a very long growth cycle, which gives it certain appreciation characteristics that are distinctive. Timberland that is in a growth and harvest mode is an area of direct commodity exposure that has found a certain degree of investor acceptance. The majority of the return from timber has been observed as occurring through the growth of the trees themselves. It has been estimated that the returns from timber investment can approach 60.5 percent from biological growth, 33.3 percent from product price changes, and 6.2 percent from land price changes.[4] Timber yields per acre tend to rise with time and the age of the planted crop. The veracity of a majority of timber's return occurring through organic growth is dependent on long investment periods. Over shorter periods, the volatile nature of inflation and market pricing of timber can have a larger relative influence. Thus, over short periods of time, timber returns may well correlate to economically sensitive asset classes, even though they tend not to do so over long periods of time. Furthermore, timber's organic growth rate can vary from region to region and depending on the species of tree. For example, it has been cited that pine growth in the southeastern United States can approximate 6 percent to 12 percent per ton per year, whereas the annual growth rate in the Northeast can be as low as 1 percent.[5]

Timber is one of the few commodities that has a lasting organic growth contributor to return. Timber can grow for a long period of time, during which it continues to appreciate in value. (There always will be some minor timber losses associated with fire, insect infestation, storm damage, and environmental regulation.) However, this sense of durability is not a shared trait with most other crops. For instance, cotton, corn, wheat, oranges, coffee, and oil seeds are more perishable than timber and have limited growth cycles. The short duration of growth cycles for these crops causes a significant portion of their return to be dependent on short-term movements in commodity spot prices. Shorter-duration commodities are vulnerable to having a lower proportion of total returns associated with biological growth. Therefore, it is less viable to consider their organic growth as an independent factor in a factor optimization framework. However, a basket of these commodities might be considered in this regard, since diversification of their individual crop prices may make their unique growth characteristics more relevant in determining their overall implied rate of return.

One significant difference that timber has versus other crops is its longer growth cycle term. Timber can be left standing for decades prior to harvesting, while other crops are subject to shorter-term crop growth cycles. Timber is not immediately perishable. Unlike other types of commodity crops, timber's long growth cycle affords its owner flexibility in points of harvest. While perishable crops are subjected to market-pricing conditions at their time of harvest, timber harvests can be delayed if market conditions are unfavorable. The owner of a tract of timber can choose not to harvest during a period of poor demand and market prices, while the owner of land devoted to grains, cotton, or orchards must harvest during an annual cycle or essentially lose its annual yield. The yield on timber may be deferred almost indefinitely. In fact, timber continues to appreciate through biological growth if a decision to delay harvesting is made.

Biological growth is a factor that is a unique driver of returns. It is independent of most other factors that might exist in a factor model. Although it is fair to say that at any point in time investors may overpay for timber and thereby eliminate any benefit from the natural appreciation of this asset through organic growth, this does not negate its independent and innate return characteristics. Other return drivers for timber that are more common include economic growth, local housing starts, employment, and inflation. Furthermore, there are other exogenous influences on timber that are of a geopolitical nature, such as currency exchange rates, trade tariffs, and trade quotas.

Where Does Timber Fit in the World of Alternative Investments?

Often, this alternative asset is considered within the realm of real estate, which in fact it includes. However, the majority of returns from timber tend not to be associated with real estate strategies or economics. Timber has some very different return attributes than many other categories of real estate. Most forms of real estate investment are evidenced by structures. Whether the strategy in real estate is core, value-added, or opportunistic, in each case the real estate is generally in the form of buildings that generate rental income and the potential for capital appreciation. It may be that the cash flow is attractive or even insufficient, but the common thread in real estate as an investment tends to be the existence of buildings that generate rental income from tenants. In contrast, timber is not a man-made asset but a natural resource tended and harvested by man. Although timber has exhibited a recent correlation of 0.64 to core real estate, it also has shown correlation of 0.52 to LBOs and 0.45 to all private equity. (A full correlation table for assets appears in Table 11.2.) While the returns from timber exhibit similarities to some other types of alternative asset classes, the return dynamics for timber appears unique, such that it should be considered in an independent fashion.

The factor drivers of return for timber are potentially different from traditional forms of real estate (see Chapter 11). Some of the main macro-economic determinants of returns for real estate investments include interest rates; inflation; occupancy rates that tend to be tied to local and national employment levels; GDP and regional levels of economic activity; and the active management of a real estate property in terms of renegotiating leases, upgrading buildings, or redeveloping properties. Meanwhile, only a few of the same economic drivers are at work in determining returns on timberland. Some of those include inflation, interest rates, and general economic activity. Other factors at work for timber include building permits, local and national housing starts, the value of the domestic currency to the extent that it affects exports and imports of lumber, and regulations and tariffs that also may have an impact on exports and imports. A similarity between timberland and real estate is the residual value of the land that is used to grow timber. This land may ultimately have an alternative use in the form of development for residential, commercial, or industrial use. The potential for redevelopment represents an area of close comparison between timberland and certain real estate strategies, such as value-added and opportunistic.

Timber also may be depicted as having similarities to oil and gas in terms of the characteristics of depletion and imputed costs to realize a commodity. In spite of some parallels to oil and gas, timber has exhibited a negative correlation of −0.21 to this asset, likely because of their different supply-and-demand forces. Furthermore, oil and gas do not have the same biological growth traits as timber. Nevertheless, timber and oil and gas can make complementary components in a portfolio of private assets because of this negative correlation. In the case of oil and natural gas reserves, a well must be drilled, fractured, and pumped in order to extract the value of the natural resource. Similarly, timber must be produced. It must be sprayed for insects, tended against fire, culled, logged, replanted, and reduced in a sawmill in order to extract cash flow from it as a natural resource. Timber also could be compared with cropland, orchards, and mining interests for minerals or precious metals. However, timber tends not to correlate to other commodities and has shown negative correlation to commodities of −0.09.

One of the most significant factors that determines investment returns for timber is the growth of the trees during the period of investment. This factor may be responsible for a majority of the return on an investment in timber. It is a unique factor determinant of return and perhaps one of the prime reasons that timber offers a portfolio of investments important diversification characteristics. With such a differentiating determinant of return that accounts for a majority of its return, biological growth can be clearly seen as a unique characteristic for timber that the rest of real estate does not possess.

TIMBER STRATEGIES

The general approach to investing in timber is through private partnerships. Private partnerships can be constructed as commingled funds or as separate accounts for only one large investor. These vehicles typically invest in tracts of timberland and benefit from the current production and appreciation of the timber over time. Investments also usually include operating companies that manage timberland properties. Timber operating companies are engaged in tending the timber crop, managing the timberland, and negotiating with production companies seeking to harvest the timber. These endeavors can be conducted in domestic and international forestlands. Local experience and regulatory expertise typically are required in these areas.

Other exposures to timber can be accomplished through master limited partnerships (MLPs), real estate investment trusts (REITs), royalty trusts, and direct purchase of timber parcels. Benefits of MLP or REIT structures for the ownership of timber include the pass-through of income and tax benefits to investors. Furthermore, MLPs and REITs offer liquidity since they usually are publicly listed closed-end funds. Appraising these funds is similar to evaluating REITs. However, a potential negative aspect of placing timberland in one of these pass-through structures is an implicit requirement to maintain certain yield levels for investors. This need may cause the manager of the timber properties to harvest timber in both positive and negative lumber price environments. This forced regular harvesting may be incompatible with timber because of its slow growth cycle.

Timber Investment Management Organizations

Access to timber often is accomplished through timber investment management organizations (TIMOs). TIMOs are engaged in the purchase, sale, and management of timber and timberlands. TIMOs create funds that accept capital from investors to use in these endeavors. Qualitative attributes of TIMOs include their ability to purchase and sell timber and timberland at attractive prices, harvest responsibly, exhibit responsible seedling replenishment practices, manage crops, improve yields, and add value in the process of harvesting trees and by-products.

Because timberland is a relatively new investment category, there are not many TIMOs in which to invest. Furthermore, most TIMOs are periodic in the capital formation cycles of their funds. As is the case with private equity, there may be lulls in the market for timber funds seeking to raise capital. Therefore, there may not always be private timber funds that are available to accept new investor capital at all points in time. The formation of timber funds also can be opportunistic and in response to tracts of timberland that are available to purchase. Many of these sales are by forest products manufacturing companies, governments, and estates seeking divestment of acreage. The market for these properties is very illiquid. The ability to purchase these properties often is driven by relationships, conservation concessions, and supply agreements.

TIMOs serve as the general partners of funds that accept limited partner investments. Often, some of the qualitative aspects that differentiate one timber investment from another include the types of wood stands involved. The selection of timberlands can include different maturities and species trees, which have different growth cycles, price points, and somewhat different end users. These differences also relate to variations in prices paid per acre for these properties.

THE ATTRACTION OF OIL AND GAS

The energy marketplace is a significant portion of the investable universe for commodities. For example, a majority of the Goldman Sachs Commodity

Index (GSCI) is represented by energy. The GSCI is representative of the worldwide market for commodities. Therefore, one attraction for considering oil and gas as an investable area simply is its significant size. Simple entry to this market can be achieved through the commodities markets. While almost all commodities are available to investors through the spot and futures markets, access through private equity structures that invest in producing properties and operating companies provides for an additional type of return. This value-added return is separate from spot price speculation or roll returns associated with futures contracts. A fairly well established private equity area has developed for oil and natural gas investments because of its size and appeal to investors. While investment in other types of commodities through private equity can be scarce, energy private placements have been available for some time. Furthermore, tax-advantaged oil and gas pass-through funds, such as MLPs, also are available for investors.

Speculation has long been an attraction of oil and gas for investors. For instance, wildcat exploration is associated with the possibility for enormous returns on invested capital. Nevertheless, exploration for new energy reserves also is associated with volatility of returns since dry holes tend to be more common than successful wells during exploration. However, through technology, this ratio has improved over time. Beyond speculation, an important appeal for investment in energy is the reliable demand that exists for this commodity. The end use primarily for heat and transportation provides stability of demand. Furthermore, there is a perception of an eventual scarcity of energy products, because of their finite nature. Oil and natural gas have no real inherent return, such as the biological growth that is innate for timber. However, unlike perishable commodities that must be regrown, oil and gas are storable.

In spite of the attraction of market size, speculative exploration, demand for energy, and limited supply, an investor still can overpay for energy assets such that the return becomes unattractive or negative. An important determinant of returns for investments in the energy marketplace is the commodity price for oil and natural gas. Often, the commodity market price is the most volatile and difficult to determine of all of the drivers of return for energy. The volatile nature of this market and the impact of speculation on these commodities can at times be a pronounced factor in setting the market price. Nevertheless, if an investor purchases reserves for production, a stable rate of return can be determined with the help of fixing a market price through the selling of futures, which entitles the producer to deliver its commodity in the future at a set price. Even longer-term contracts can be arranged through the sale of forward swap agreements with counterparties and dealers.

Beyond energy prices and their influence on the return from an investment in oil and natural gas, essential drivers of returns relating to the acquisition of producing properties are an increase or decrease in production yields and the ultimate sale of the properties. A benefit from producing properties is the current cash flow that they can provide to investors. Nevertheless, a portion of this cash flow must be considered as a return of capital, to the extent that reserves are being depleted. The ultimate value that is realized for the properties upon sale relates to an increase in or depletion of proven reserves.

Approaches to oil and gas investment tend to be focused on either producing properties or operating companies. Production can range in strategy from high-risk speculative exploration to lower-risk purchase of proven reserves. Meanwhile, investment in operating companies can range in risk from start-ups to LBOs of existing companies. In this sense, there are similarities between this approach and private equity with an industry focus.

OIL AND GAS STRATEGIES

As is the case with an investment in timber, exposure to oil and gas can be accomplished through private partnerships, MLPs, royalty trusts, the direct purchase of oil and gas property leases, or the purchase of operating entities. Private partnerships that hold oil and gas investments can be configured as commingled funds or as separate accounts for sizable investors. The main strategies for investment in oil and gas are focused on exploration and production; the acquisition of reserves; and investment in operating companies that may be engaged in drilling, oil field services, processing and refining, transmission, and distribution. These approaches offer various degrees of risk and return as well as different cash flow dynamics. Although these strategies can offer diversification when used in conjunction with each other, they all tend to have some basic dependency on oil and natural gas prices.

Reserves Acquisition

On the low-risk and relatively low-return end of the spectrum for energy investing is the acquisition of proven and producing reserves of oil and natural gas. The return on these properties is fairly low, because the reserves and their rate of production have been fairly well delineated. Reserves acquisition is a strategy that can be more passive in nature, although it does require strong technical and geological expertise. This is a very competitive market space with rivalry from many of the largest multinational exploration and production companies. Success often relies on a niche market focus or specialty strategies. An example is the acquisition of small regional properties that require negotiation with multiple beneficial owners, which is a labor-intensive task that many larger competitors might not pursue. Another example is the acquisition of mature reserves that have declining production rates, but through the application of new technologies in conjunction with locking in product prices, the properties can provide strong relative returns on capital. Typically, reserve acquisition strategies are focused on cash returns on capital through production, rather than an expectation for capital appreciation through the resale of the properties. Because of their relatively predictable nature, the expected returns for reserves acquisition are lower than that for the exploration and production strategy or the creation of operating companies.

Exploration and Production

The exploration and production (E&P) approach has a focus on the creation or acquisition of companies engaged in exploring for and producing energy reserves. Often, substantial amounts of initial capital are required to identify, drill, and prove reserves. However, once reserves are identified and delineated, the resulting value of the reserves or cash flow produced through the extraction of the reserves can be rewarding. Substantial technical and geological expertise is required for the operation of these entities. The E&P strategy is among the riskiest in the oil and gas private equity segment. A significant portion of the returns from this strategy may be derived from capital appreciation.

Investing in energy exploration and production has an array of risk and return opportunities. A medium return and risk opportunity in energy is represented by development drilling of proven and probable reserves. The additional delineation of proven reserves in these properties and an increase in their rate of production is an area of value-added that carries a higher degree of return and risk than straightforward reserves acquisition. At the upper end of the return-and-risk spectrum resides exploratory drilling of unproven reserves. Although diversification of properties in wildcat drilling can help to lower risk, the area still is speculative and prone to volatile returns on invested capital.

Operating Companies

Another section of the energy investment opportunity is operating companies that can be built from the ground up, through multiple acquisitions, or through the lift-out of a services component of an E&P company. Examples of operating strategies include those engaged in production services such as refracturing wells, exploration services such as drilling, pipeline operation, other types of transportation services, and refineries. These services companies can be well suited to private partnership structures. Liquidity for the private investors in these funds typically is achieved through the initial public offering or sale of the operating companies. Success in this realm demands operating expertise in the form of strong management teams and experienced investment managers that have a deep prior history in the relevant energy areas. Typically, a majority of the expected return from these investments is through capital appreciation. Therefore, these investments are very sensitive to conditions for exit, such as public market investor demand and market multiples of cash flow. The expected return on investment is higher for these opportunities than for reserve acquisitions because of their venture capital and LBO characteristics.

THE CONSTRUCTION OF A SEGREGATED PORTFOLIO OF CURRENCIES, COMMODITIES, TIMBER, AND OIL AND GAS

Currencies, commodities, timber, and oil and gas have provided a range of historical returns and volatility characteristics that are depicted in Table 6.1. In general, their risk-adjusted returns have been competitive with some of the more prominent traditional asset classes. Although the currency fund index that is illustrated has exhibited somewhat less competitive returns, currencies still have generated less than half of the volatility of U.S. equities with an acceptable return. Currencies, commodities, timber, and oil and gas also have produced relatively low correlation figures to traditional asset classes and to each other, as is depicted in Table 6.2. This low correlation attribute supports the notion that a diversified portfolio can benefit from their use.

A benefit from the use of currencies, commodities, timber, and oil and gas in a segregated portfolio is the generally separate return drivers that each has. Each of these alternative investments provides new sorts of asset betas and opportunity for unique alpha provided by active managers. Some of these quantitative factor determinants are discussed in further detail in Chapter 11. A greater number of independent betas and alphas added to a portfolio should benefit overall risk reduction through enhanced diversification. Furthermore, there are distinct strategies within currency, commodities, timber, and oil and gas that offer additional sources of discrete return associated with value-added approaches to each type of investment. Additionally, most of these alternative investments appear capable of adding to overall portfolio performance through their absolute returns.

TABLE 6.1 Traditional versus Commodity, Currency, Oil and Gas, and Timber Historical Returns and Risk (1996–2006 Q2)

Asset Type	Average Annual Return	Standard Deviation	Compound Return
Cash	3.77%	0.93%	3.77%
Core fixed income	6.00%	3.61%	5.94%
Inflation-linked bonds (TIPs)	6.74%	4.30%	6.65%
High-yield	6.99%	7.77%	6.70%
U.S. equity	10.74%	17.79%	9.30%
Commodities	9.20%	14.02%	8.30%
Currency	5.75%	7.16%	5.50%
Oil and Gas	16.93%	13.05%	16.20%
Timber	8.27%	5.76%	8.12%

Note: Cash is represented by 90-day T-bills; core fixed income is the LB Aggregate; TIPS are the LB U.S. Treasury Index; high-yield is the Citigroup High Yield Index; U.S. equity is the Russell 3000; commodities are the Dow Jones AIG Commodity Index; currency is the Parker FX Index; oil and gas is the Alerian MLP Index; and timber is the NCREIF Timberland Index.
Source: RogersCasey.

The mean variance optimization model in Figure 6.3 is unconstrained, and it allows for large or small inclusion of any of the four assets considered. The data used in the exhibit is historical and only includes a span of approximately 10 years. It should be considered illustrative in nature. The use of data with longer or shorter time periods may show different results. Furthermore, optimizations using additional assets would show changed allocations. The efficient frontier that is depicted is fairly long and steep. This indicates a wide range in terms of both returns and risk for portfolios of currencies, commodities, timber, and oil and gas that can be constructed using mean variance optimization. The optimal portfolio, as defined by the portfolio with the highest Sharpe ratio, generates a historical return of 10.6 percent and volatility of 5.7 percent. This outcome is fairly attractive given the individual risk-and-return characteristics of currencies, commodities, timber, and oil and gas listed in Table 6.1. The more conservative portfolios on the efficient frontier are mostly comprised of currency trading and timber. The low volatility of returns from these strategies is a primary determinant of this allocation. As risk and return for portfolios rise along the efficient frontier, greater proportions of oil and gas and commodities are utilized. Nevertheless, commodities do not experience a very significant allocation at any point in the optimization. This avoidance relates to the relatively

TABLE 6.2 Commodity, Currency, Timber, and Oil and Gas Correlation Matrix (1996–2006 Q1)

	Cash	Core FI	LBs	High Yield	U.S. Equity	Commodities	Currency	Oil and Gas	Timber
Cash	1.00								
Core fixed income	0.20	1.00							
Inflation-linked bonds (TIPS)	−0.06	0.73	1.00						
High-yield	−0.25	−0.16	−0.20	1.00					
U.S. equity	−0.04	−0.41	−0.49	0.60	1.00				
Commodities	−0.19	−0.18	0.17	−0.09	−0.16	1.00			
Currency	0.13	0.26	0.26	0.04	0.03	−0.19	1.00		
Oil and Gas	0.06	0.31	0.31	0.41	0.02	0.11	0.02	1.00	
Timber	0.09	0.01	−0.09	0.06	0.18	−0.09	0.11	−0.21	1.00

Note: Cash is represented by 90-day T-bills; core fixed income is the LB Aggregate; TIPS are the LB U.S. Treasury Index; high-yield is the Citigroup High Yield Index; U.S. equity is the Russell 3000; commodities are the Dow Jones AIG Commodity Index; currency is the Parker FX Index; oil and gas is the Alerian MLP Index; and timber is the NCREIF Timberland Index.
Source: RogersCasey.

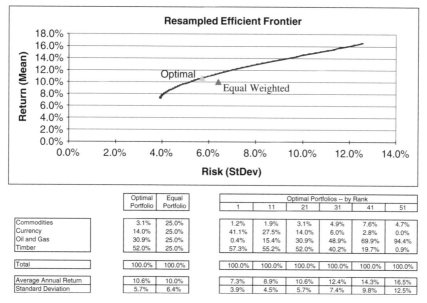

FIGURE 6.3 Portfolio Optimization of Commodities, Currency, Oil and Gas, and Timber

Note: Model is unconstrained. Data is 1996 through June 2006.

Source: RogersCasey; Dow Jones AIG Commodity Index; Parker FX Index; Alerian MLP Index; NCREIF Timberland Index; Resampled Efficient Frontier™ provided by New Frontier Advisors, LLC.

high historical volatility from commodities relative to the level of returns generated. Nevertheless, the unique negative correlations that commodities exhibit both to U.S. equity and to core fixed income as well as positive correlation to inflation-linked bonds implies its diversification benefits and inflation hedging attributes.

SUMMARY

The utilization of currency, commodities, timber, and oil and gas in a diversified portfolio has strategic merit. Rather than making a generalization that these tangible assets represent a hedge against inflation, the perspective of this chapter is that they offer unique sources of return for a diversified portfolio. These investments have discrete factors that can improve a portfolio's diversification. This diversification benefit is also apparent in a comparison of the low correlations of these investments with traditional asset classes such as long-only equity and fixed income. Furthermore, these alternative investments generally exhibit low correlation to each other. Therefore, currency, commodities, timber, and oil and gas can provide increased diversification for a portfolio of assets and a reduction in overall volatility of returns.

In addition to the benefit of utilizing these assets for diversification, currency, commodities, timber, and oil and gas provide opportunity for performance enhancement. These assets display unique attributes, and some have structural inefficiencies in their markets. Currency trading can generate return from the participation in currency markets by counterparties that exchange currency for business or banking reasons, rather than for profit generation. These participants therefore can create opportunities for profit by currency traders. Commodities futures markets offer structural return characteristics related to rolling forward existing futures positions. Timber offers distinctive return in the form of a biological growth characteristic that is unique among other types of sources of return. Investments in oil and gas benefit from a number of atypical sources of return, including the nature of this commodity as a finite resource and the demand for energy products relating to the necessity of heating and transportation. Furthermore, currency, commodities, timber, and oil and gas are available for investment through many different sorts of structures and investment manager participants. Whether the investment advisers are pursuing systematic, discretionary, fundamental, or technical styles, they all offer access to strategies that are able to provide an investor with additional diversification and sources of risk and return that augment investment portfolios.

Two

Alternative Investments in Traditional Portfolios

The legacy of alternative investing is one of ad hoc methodology. As it pertains to asset allocation, most investors have added alternative investments to their portfolios in a haphazard fashion. For these investors, traditional investments often have been constructed in portfolios using the well-worn path of risk budgeting through mean-variance optimization. By contrast, most alternative investments are acquired on an incidental basis. This is partly because of an inability to fit alternative investments into a traditional asset allocation approach. Of course, hedge funds, real estate, and private equity, for example, can be modeled using expected returns, volatility, and correlation.

However, non-normal return distributions, wide dispersion of returns, and incomplete peer groups are obstacles. For many investors, the use of these investments is artificially capped in their overall portfolios. This setting of constraints usually is done for a combination of reasons that may be qualitative in nature. For instance, a desire for liquidity in a portfolio might limit the use of illiquid private investments. When considered versus the duration of their liabilities, most investors such as high-net-worth individuals and families, endowments, foundations, and pension plans tend to have more liquidity in their strategic asset allocations than is warranted. The utilization of factor analysis can foster a more integrated approach to the use of alternative investments in conjunction with traditional asset classes.

The chapters included in Part Two address topics such as the migration of hedge funds into the realm of private equity, alternative investment cash flow and its implications for portfolio rebalancing, the use of leverage, and portable alpha techniques. Alternative investments are considered in terms of their relationship to each other, their interaction, and the redundancies that may exist among them. Factor drivers of return and risk, which are identified through regression analysis, are central in this evaluation. A by-product of this analysis is a narrower definition of alpha as well as its active and passive components. This approach is extended to risk budgeting using factors. The methodology opens the door to creating synthetic portfolios of alternative investments.

CHAPTER 7

The Migration of Hedge Funds into the Private Equity Realm

The mathematics of uncontrolled growth are frightening. A single cell of the bacterium E. coli *would, under ideal circumstances, divide every twenty minutes. That is not particularly disturbing until you think about it, but the fact is that bacteria multiply geometrically: one becomes two, two become four, four become eight, and so on. In this way it can be shown that in a single day, one cell of* E. coli *could produce a super-colony equal in size and weight to the entire planet Earth.*
—Michael Crichton, *The Andromeda Strain* (Dell, 1969)

This quote from *The Andromeda Strain* encapsulates by analogy the viral growth occurring in hedge funds as they migrate into other areas of alternative investment. Not only are hedge funds growing by moving into these marketplaces, but the environment appears fertile for them to continue to do so. In spite of there being certain inefficiencies and misfit considerations for hedge funds to be successful in doing this, a lack of structural impediments for hedge funds enables them to embark on this migration. Hedge funds have evolved into increased users of less liquid investments. Examples of the types of private investments that hedge funds are making in this area include the following: real estate, private equity, mezzanine debt, secured loans, and revolving credit lines. One outcome of some of these investments is that hedge funds increasingly are becoming corporate activists through illiquid investments that create control or significant influence positions in private or public companies.

This migration necessitates a more careful analysis of the sources of return and risk in hedge funds. In addition to measuring hedge fund return factors and their overlap with other alternative investments, there are structural issues to evaluate when contemplating the merit of a hedge fund investing, for example, in private equity or real estate transactions, such as matching the duration of investments to hedge fund liquidity terms offered to investors. Moreover, a basic consideration for investors to gauge when appraising a hedge fund that has an allocation to private equity is the ability of the hedge fund to manage the investment. Managing these investments is a distinctly different endeavor than making an initial private equity investment, and it may take different skills and personnel. Furthermore, investors must ask themselves whether the management of private equity assets in a hedge fund is relatively cost effective from a fee perspective versus the alternative, which is to invest with a pure private equity manager to achieve the investor's private equity asset allocation.

ARE HEDGE FUNDS GAINING MARKET SHARE FROM PRIVATE EQUITY?

The infiltration of hedge funds into private equity investing is a phenomenon that has been in existence on an infrequent basis for some time. However, this trend has become more systemic throughout the hedge fund industry in recent years. In part, this is because of the sheer growth in the number of hedge funds in existence and the growing amount of assets that they control. It is also because of the increased utilization of hedge strategies that are comprised of quasi-private securities, such as the following: secondary purchases of distressed debt, which includes bank debt, revolving credit agreements, and receivables; primary lending on a secured basis, which includes all forms of extending credit secured by collateral; and activist investing in public companies, which requires the accumulation of public securities either in such size or with such intent that the positions are rendered illiquid from a regulatory perspective.

The structural pathway for certain private equity or real estate transactions may have changed, either temporarily or permanently, because of the participation of hedge funds. An example of such a structural change might be a financially stressed public company that may not have access to public markets or banks for new financing, but does have access to hedge funds looking to make a restricted and temporarily unregistered investment. Were it not for these investors of last resort, such a company alternatively may have gone to a private equity fund and considered engaging in a management-led leveraged buyout (LBO). Another example of a structural change is a group of merger arbitrage hedge funds that successfully block an acquisition of a public company by a private equity firm, in order to realize a higher price that might be paid by a strategic buyer of the company, such as another public company that may be in a position to use its own securities as partial currency to compensate public shareholders.

A final example of a change that may be reducing the deal flow for real estate equity or mezzanine investors are hedge funds that make debt and equity investments in real estate, thereby possibly taking advantage of a secured lending position. In each of these cases, while displacing and likely undercutting the pricing that might be offered by providers of private equity capital, hedge funds still are accomplishing attractive deal terms relative to expected returns for hedge funds.

The Quantitative Evidence

Indeed, as indicated in Table 7.1, the recent trend in capital formation for private equity seems to support some notion of structural change. During the six-year period ending in 2006, the venture capital, LBO, and mezzanine debt marketplaces recovered from a bubble in private equity that occurred in the preceding six-year period. During the six years of recovery, the average size of funds in these areas has increased. The increase in average size of funds for venture capital occurred in an environment where the number of firms able to raise new funds was limited. For the LBO and mezzanine category, an increase in the average size of funds occurred in conjunction with a general increase in the number of funds formed.

In both instances, whether limited venture firms raising larger funds or more buyout funds raising larger funds, private equity has migrated to larger pools of assets to manage. Accordingly, many of these funds may be forced to complete larger-sized deals than has been the prior norm. Furthermore, in the case of venture capital with moderate funds being formed relative to the past, this may represent a data point that supports the concept that venture firms are getting crowded out of the private equity markets, or at least becoming more selective about the types of deals they accept. Also, some private equity capital may be getting pressed into larger-sized transactions

TABLE 7.1   Private Equity Capital Commitments

	2001	2002	2003	2004	2005	2006
Venture capital ($ billion)	60	18	17	29	48	45
Venture capital (funds)	746	462	319	388	430	332
Venture capital (average per fund, $ million)	80	38	55	75	111	137
LBO and mezzanine ($ billion)	72	40	55	71	164	152
LBO and mezzanine (funds)	201	152	158	208	270	179
LBO and mezzanine (average per fund, $ million)	361	264	347	343	608	847

Source: Thomson Financial.

because of ample alternative funding sources for deals. Alternative sources of capital include hedge funds, direct investments from high-net-worth investors, and strategic investors. The resulting trend may be that some small private companies skip the classical venture capital funding route altogether in their growth life cycle.

Although data show an increased utilization of hedge funds by segments of the investment community as well as relatively stronger recent asset growth in hedge funds compared with some other alternative investment categories, there are caveats to be mentioned prior to making generalizations about the wholesale market share growth in hedge funds at the expense of other alternative asset choices. There are a host of other issues at play here. A rise in assets invested in hedge funds does not necessarily mean that this asset flow has been at the expense of or reduction in allocations to private equity or real estate, for example. This may more accurately illustrate a reduction in asset allocation to long-only equity and fixed-income asset classes (see Chapter 2). Furthermore, a periodic reduction in the invested amounts in private equity and real estate may simply represent a cyclical point in time. Such a reduction also is only the tip of the iceberg, since these figures typically exclude total commitments to these funds and include only the portion of commitments that may have been called by the general partners to fund portfolio investments.

A key time period for the attraction of assets to hedge funds at the expense of allocations to other asset classes was shortly after the peak in equity markets in 2000. Following this market peak, while investors continued to contribute capital to other alternative asset classes, the cumulative contributions to the hedge fund category began to outweigh other alternative asset groups. For example, as depicted in Figure 7.1, the cumulative growth in assets invested in hedge funds of over $900 billion was nearly twice that for private equity, broadly speaking. Although an inexact science, these figures reflect new capital inflows and appreciation for hedge funds and new commitments of capital in private equity, excluding the return of capital and changes in the market value of preexisting funds.

In addition to some quantitative evidence that hedge funds may be gaining market share on a secular basis from other forms of alternative investments, anecdotal evidence of this may be present in the sometimes habit of private equity funds reducing the size of their funds and releasing their investors from committed amounts. Admittedly, it is difficult to truly differentiate whether this tactic is a function of cyclical environments for these investments or the initiation of a longer-term secular trend that may become more apparent during cyclical declines. Private equity funds may be finding fewer attractively priced deals to do, especially among mid- and

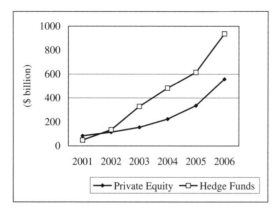

FIGURE 7.1 Cumulative Change in Committed
Assets
Source: Hedge Fund Research (HFR), Thomson
Financial, National Venture Capital Association.

small-sized transactions. Another movement that may have implications is
the increased incidence in the LBO sector for the raising of mega funds.

The inference from this development may be a crowding out of
middle-market buyouts possibly caused by hedge funds. Of course, there
could be other influences, such as a consolidation of private equity
investment dollars among the largest or most appealing buyout firms.
Nevertheless, hedge funds provide more choices to companies seeking capital. A middle-market company considering selling itself in an LBO might
choose an alternative path of refinancing its balance sheet through a hedge
fund lender who may not be seeking control. A migration to larger fund sizes
by buyout investment managers might reflect no choice but to seek larger
game. This also may be corroborated by a tendency of some buyout funds
to syndicate large-sized transactions. A ramification of a potential bunching
of LBO money toward the top of the capitalization spectrum could be that
the age of super-sized LBOs may once again be on the corporate landscape.

A large quantity of capital committed to private equity funds at any
point in time may not be captured by the figures for invested assets. A
possible accumulation of committed but unused capital may imply that
investment opportunities for private equity firms at their required rates of
return are not available. Another way to express this concept is that at
times the volume of investable transactions might be low. Yet a reduction in
deal flow also may be attributable to poor economic activity, closed capital
markets, or high interest rates. However, it may be that there are deals
occurring but not at adequate rates of return for all types of funds. This

last point could have its roots in market share gains by hedge funds seeking private equity or real estate investment opportunities that may have return characteristics that are less than the standard rates of return for private equity or real estate funds but greater than the targeted return for hedge funds. If this is the case, then it might not be that there are fewer quality real estate or LBO opportunities, but that these opportunities have taken on different return characteristics because of investment encroachment by new market participants, such as hedge funds.

The Diminished Availability of Venture Capital as an Asset Class

There may be other aspects of a self-inflicted basis that are assisting in the possible marginalization of venture capital as an asset class. These include the unilateral decision by some venture capital firms to progressively limit their availability. Although there has been a long-term trend for highly sought-after venture funds to limit allocations made available to investors, some venture firms are eliminating new capacity altogether for some long-term investors in their prior funds. This trend toward increased selectivity is in some cases at the expense of independent funds of funds that cannot offer any bilateral value-added relationship. The rationale for a venture capital firm's finding certain investors' capital of higher monetary value than others is rooted in a desire to be closer to the end investor. There also appears to be a desire to limit competition from other venture capital firms for high-quality deals as the venture capital funds of funds base has grown. Funds of funds have been successful in raising capital based on their underlying allocations to highly sought-after venture firms, which draws large amounts of capital to funds of funds from investors who do not have access to the desired venture firms on their own. Since funds of funds' capacity with the desired venture funds tends to be inelastic, additional capital that a fund of funds may raise based on this appeal may be invested in a different venture capital firm. The result is more capital invested in new venture firms chasing a limited number of venture deals and increasing competition for deals with the more established venture firms. Private equity funds of funds with a strategic advantage in garnering capacity with the better venture capital funds tend to be those with a range of synergistic business lines that can benefit the portfolio companies contained in these funds.

Venture capital as an asset class is inherently capacity constrained, which is why attaining capacity directly or through funds of funds should become increasingly vital. There are a finite number of solid investment ideas and venture deals that are created in any one year. This is further evidenced by the venture capital community's having only a very limited ability to accept new investors or create new funds. Not only are top tier funds created infrequently, they are limited in dollar size, and often only preexisting investors in earlier funds are granted access to the very best partnerships when new funds are launched. In fact, one might say that venture capital is slowly losing its legitimacy as an asset class for most investors. Access to venture capital is becoming the privileged domain for certain investors because of its limited investment size and availability of truly skilled general partners.

Additionally, venture capital firms are becoming more reluctant to accept assets from public pension plans. Many United States public pensions are subject to the Freedom of Information Act (FOIA) of 1966 or similar state statutes. These laws can require public pensions to divulge upon request the information underlying their venture capital investments. Such information pertaining to private equity can be a competitive disadvantage for the portfolio companies in these funds or for the funds themselves. A result is that some venture capital funds are cutting back on acceptance of public pension assets in general. One consequence of limiting public pension plan access to venture capital funds is to increase the importance of access through certain funds of funds. Venture capital as an asset class is increasingly becoming an elite strategy rather than a robust investable asset class that is accessible to all types of investors.

HOW WELL SUITED ARE HEDGE FUNDS TO PRIVATE EQUITY INVESTMENTS?

A broad generalization regarding the migration of hedge funds into private equity and real estate investments needs to be more finely parsed. The main area of infiltration by hedge funds relates to lending. Hedge funds by their nature are risk averse. Where they cannot hedge, they tend to gravitate toward secured positions with collateral. This area of secured lending is a more effective one for hedge funds to apply in the private equity realm. The skills and proclivity that hedge funds have are easily applicable to what historically may have been private equity or bank lending opportunities. The core of this skill is basic credit analysis, understanding cash flow and leverage ratios, and vetting collateral. These types of transactions, typically evidenced by a loan agreement and possibly with control of a corporation's cash flow, are more mechanical in nature. They differ greatly from an equity investment. This distinction describes the areas in private equity and real estate where hedge funds may be more successful, such as lending and credit, and those areas where hedge funds may be less successful, such as equity investments. Equity participation in a private transaction that has a long expected time to exit requires a certain focus and management resources that may not be readily available to hedge funds.

The ability exists for hedge funds to structure LBO deals and invest in restricted private equity or debt in public companies. However, hedge funds may be less adept at the more nuanced skills of building and nurturing companies. Such expertise requires unique capabilities that take years of prior experience in management, technical fields, industry relationships, and strategy. These represent barriers to entry that are not easily overcome by hedge funds. These resources arguably are out of the core competencies of most hedge funds. The types of skills housed at hedge funds tend to be characterized as deal-centric rather than company-centric. Most hedge funds that employ private securities are transaction focused, followed by arm's-length forecasting of cash flow, maintenance of lending covenants, and monitoring collateral.

By contrast, equity investments have a significant focus on asset growth beyond an entity's liabilities and expansion in equity valuation. Equity investing tends to be focused on characteristics such as earnings and cash flow growth, increases in market share and revenue, and expansion of margins and exit multiples. Moreover, a critical element to being an effective private equity investor is the ability to become involved in the management of the entity if it requires assistance, which tends to be the case more often than not.

The role of the value-added equity investor is a critical one for sustaining a private equity investment during periods of transition or hardship. Such circumstances can occur in venture capital deals and LBOs. For example, this level of involvement by an equity investor can include being responsible for replacing management teams, implementing systems and business processes, providing insights into distribution channels and competition, and acquiring or divesting business units. These types of activities can go well beyond simple attendance at board of director meetings, and they can imply regular appearances at the portfolio companies and daily communications with their management teams. Therefore, being an equity investor in a private transaction may require skills in management consulting and often prior experience in operations, manufacturing, and distribution. The sustaining and caring of private equity investments post initial investment can require an entirely different team of professionals than those required to simply conduct the analysis associated with making the original investment. Some hedge funds do not fully realize this, or they have the hubris to believe themselves capable of developing these skills during the course of an investment.

Often, these are the type of private equity investments by hedge funds that do not work well. Hedge funds and their transaction-oriented mentality often are better suited to unallied transactions with companies, similar to the way in which a commercial bank would approach an investment with a company. By contrast, investment teams assembled by competent private equity firms are more focused on the ownership of companies and building those companies over a much longer period of time than the typical targeted duration of an investment made by a hedge fund. An investor in a private equity transaction in most cases enters this investment through cooperation with the management of an issuer, whereas investing in public securities generally is conducted unilaterally without cooperation from a corporate issuer.

An exception to hedge funds being less well suited to making private equity investments relates to those hedge funds that invest in control situations in distressed debt as their primary business. Often, the well-skilled firms in this area have established management groups to focus exclusively on their portfolio companies that incur or already have operating problems. In fact, investing in troubled companies is a primary source of return for these investors. However, the expected time frame for the resurrection or immediate resuscitation of these portfolio companies often is shorter than that for a comparable investment made by a private equity investor, who might be looking to grow a portfolio company over a longer time frame. Furthermore, the performance bounce from buying an investment at a distressed level is able to mask less robust performance that is attributable to fixing or healing a troubled company through operating skill.

THE POWER OF COMPOUNDING: A COMPARATIVE ADVANTAGE FOR PRIVATE EQUITY

An area worthy of contemplation relating to the infiltration of hedge funds into private equity is the length of time required for investments to mature. Although hedge funds are capable of making any sort of duration investment that they choose, the propensity is for the prospective maturity of a private equity investment made by a hedge fund to be much shorter than a similar investment made in a private equity partnership. One reason for this is the rough matching of the maturity of underlying investments with the liquidity provisions for funds in which the investments reside. With hedge funds having lockups of perhaps one to three years, in general most private equity investments made in hedge funds tend not to have expected maturities much longer than three years. However, there are always exceptions to this.

For private equity funds with expected terms of 10 years and usually with extensions thereafter, the maturity of investments may be much longer and are more governed by a desire for higher internal rates of return than the concept of matching underlying investment maturity with fund maturity. The importance of this difference in appetite for duration between hedge funds and private equity funds is that an investment may perform better when given a longer time to mature. The cyclical nature of industries, capital markets, and interest rates can affect the fundamental conditions of an investment, its exit liquidity window, and its exit multiple. Therefore, having more time to select an exit for an investment can be a tactical advantage that private equity firms have over hedge funds in private equity investments.

The premature exit of an investment can represent an enormous opportunity cost. The difference of a relatively short period of time can be responsible for the entirety of performance on certain investments. Having greater flexibility regarding the timing of exits for investments can represent the difference between breakeven returns and significant gains on invested capital. The norm is for hedge funds to have much shorter lockups than private equity funds. However, this may change in the future. The increased use of less liquid investments by hedge funds is causing pressure on the funds to make their redemption terms less liquid. It is probably presumptuous to assume that anything relating to hedge funds will remain static. The current norm for lockups of one to three years may be one of those items that may change. If hedge funds lengthened their lockups, they could avoid the handicap of having some inherent pressure to exit private investments earlier than perhaps what is optimal. Furthermore, some hedge funds have "side pockets" for investments in illiquid private equity investments. These side-pocket investments have redemption features that are less liquid than the overall redemption features of the hedge funds. Side pockets could become increasingly used for a growing portion of hedge fund assets under management, perhaps done in tandem with lengthening lockups for hedge fund structures in general. In this fashion, hedge funds that are increasingly engaged in private equity transactions may be better able to equalize the mismatch between the duration of their investments and the liquidity of their funds.

THE FEE DIFFERENTIAL BETWEEN HEDGE FUNDS AND PRIVATE EQUITY

The analysis of fees is a critical component in the relative appraisal of funds that operate in different alternative investment strategies. An investor should want to pay the lowest possible fee per unit of quality for access to alternative investment strategies. As alternative investment strategy–specific managers engage in style drift and invade each other's domains, fees can be a significant differentiator in determining an investor's expected return. With the increasing incidence of alternative investment managers overlapping in strategy allocation, the accepted norms for structures of their funds should be challenged by investors. For instance, if the terms and conditions of one fund operating nominally in a specific strategy (such as a large-capitalization equity hedge fund) are less attractive than another fund operating nominally in a different alternative investment strategy (such as large-capitalization LBOs), but both funds are investing in similar transactions and benefiting from identical factor drivers of return and risk, then the investor should pit these managers against each other from a fee and terms perspective. This seems to be done rarely, because of the accepted norms for terms and conditions of one alternative investment structure versus another. Furthermore, the segregation of alternative investment strategies by specialization sometimes results in separate investor personnel evaluating one type of fund (e.g., real estate) versus another (e.g., hedge funds). This silo effect can cause a lack of cross-disciplinary analysis, in which case investors do not consider different types of alternative investments to accomplish similar return and risk exposures.

As investors increasingly identify a commonality of factor determinants across the range of alternative investment strategies, they will be well armed to speak in these terms and select the investment structures having fees and liquidity terms that are most advantageous. In the future, there may be a bifurcation in the categorization of alternative investments. First could be a separation by strategy exposure across all nominal types of alternative investments, such that, for example, a hedge fund is partially defined as a real estate fund if a portion of its investments is driven by real estate factors. Second could be the cross-disciplinary ranking of these funds by the most to least attractive structure, as defined by fees and terms for investors.

Have the Economics of Hedge Funds Laid the Seeds for Domination over Private Equity?

Another consideration when evaluating hedge funds entering private equity investments is a comparison of hedge fund business economics with those of private equity firms. On one hand, hedge funds may be driving down returns for private equity partnerships, because of their willingness to accept lower targeted returns on transactions. On the other hand, there may be a mixed result in performance for these hedge funds, based on the level of operational expertise for the kinds of private equity investments they are making. But perhaps a more important determinant of long-term market share potential for hedge funds in private equity transactions is simply their fee economics compared with private equity firms. Fees may ultimately influence the competitive positioning of hedge funds in this area. This is not because fees are lower for hedge funds, but because hedge funds are empowered by their generally higher fee income paid with greater frequency versus that for private equity funds.

A great irony is that investors, who generally prefer lower fees, become fee insensitive in this instance. This is because most investors do not consider hedge fund and private equity investments side by side when making an investment decision. Rather, they compare fees of one hedge fund to another and one private equity fund to another. They do not consider that the drivers of return and risk in these different investments may be similar or even identical in the case of hedge funds investing in private equity transactions. This is another reason why the utilization of factor analysis should be a critical element in leveling the playing field and enabling a more accurate comparison of investment opportunities.

The fee economics for hedge funds often are more lucrative and timely than those for private equity firms. Therefore, in the future, it may be likely that hedge funds will command greater economics to develop better resources, such as staff with varied expertise. Over time, this could lead to hedge funds becoming more competitive in execution, able to generate better returns on private equity investments once made, and a permanent catalyst for lower expected returns on private equity investments made by traditional private equity firms. The ability of hedge funds to offer enormous platforms with deep resources and more lucrative compensation than private equity partnerships may enable these types of hedge funds to simply hire the best new investment professionals who might otherwise have sought employment with private equity firms. The ubiquitous and viral nature of hedge funds and their ability to be unbounded by style or form make them the great equalizer in driving down investment returns and volatility during normal times and potentially contributing to a consolidation in the private equity investment business.

Often Fee Structures Are Better Aligned with Investors in Private Equity versus Hedge Funds

The general components of fees for hedge funds are a management fee, a performance fee, and usually a charge against the fund that is associated with the fund's operating expenses. Private equity funds also charge management fees and performance fees. However, the management fee, while it is charged on committed but unused capital, typically will decline in later years of the fund. Furthermore, performance fees in private equity are subject to profits that are in excess of a preferred rate of return. In contrast, hedge funds usually do not have hurdle rates that they must achieve prior to receiving their performance fees. Additionally, hedge fund performance fees are collected annually, while private equity performance fees are not paid until later years in a fund's life when successful investments are exited. Furthermore, private equity performance fees often are subject to clawback provisions, which enable limited partners to receive prior-period performance fees paid to the general partner, in the event that the predetermined preferred return is not realized by the limited partners. One observation from this is that on a relative basis the private equity fee structure may be better aligned with the interests of investors than is the case for hedge funds.

Examples of these terms are displayed in Table 7.2. This table illustrates two of the important differentiators of fees for hedge funds and private equity funds. The preferred rate of return in private equity is an important threshold above which the fund must perform. In contrast, while hedge funds usually do have high-water marks, they do not have preferred rates of return that must be achieved prior to being able to charge their performance fees. Furthermore, the clawback provision for private equity funds is an important element of potential fee savings in the event that these funds are not profitable over the long term for their investors. The length of time it takes for private equity funds to receive their performance fees, the preferred returns offered to investors, and the clawback provisions each represents an alignment of interests between the general partner of a private equity fund and its limited partners. However, they also represent economics that disadvantage the private equity firms versus hedge fund operators in terms of building their businesses, attracting and keeping staff, and marshaling resources.

Although investors may find it less expensive from a fee perspective to invest in a private equity partnership versus a hedge fund, this ignores the fact that hedge funds usually are far more liquid than private equity partnerships. An additional caveat is that hedge funds often place their private equity investments into side pockets that charge fees more akin to private equity fees. Although capital in hedge fund side pockets may be charged normal management fees, performance fees usually are deferred until a point in time when the investments are exited. Nevertheless, organizationally, hedge funds still benefit from ongoing performance fees on their hedge fund assets, which can be used to pay the private equity personnel at hedge funds a higher rate than what they might experience at private equity funds. In this sense, hedge funds can use their hedge fund business to subsidize their private equity efforts and any other type of investment businesses they choose, as they also migrate into real estate and long-only investment funds.

TABLE 7.2   Fee Comparison of Hedge Funds versus Private Equity Funds

Sample Fee Schedule—Hedge Fund	Sample Amount	Features
Management fee	1.50%	Management fees range from 1% to 2% and potentially higher.
Hurdle rate	N/A	Hedge funds typically do not have hurdle rates.
Performance fee	20%	Performance fees for some hedge funds are even higher than this.
High-water mark	TBD	No performance fee is paid while a hedge fund's net asset value is below its annual high point.

Sample Fee Schedule—Private Equity	Sample Amount	Features
Management fee	1.75%	Management fee paid on committed capital, but declines over time. Venture capital funds average 2% and larger buyout funds 1.5%.
Hurdle rate	8%	Returns above this preferred rate are charged a performance fee.
Performance fee	20%	Performance fees can range higher or lower than this in private equity.
Clawback	TBD	Performance fees paid early in a fund's life are retroactively returned, if net performance later in the life of the fund dips below the hurdle rate.

Note: Figures exclude other operating expenses that may be passed through to the funds.
N/A, not applicable; TBD, to be determined.

ALTERNATIVE INVESTMENT FEE AND TERM COMPONENTS

In order to better understand the differences in fees for the various alternative investment categories, an investor must have a grasp of the features and components that are contained in the fund agreements. There are significant differences in the generally accepted methods for charging fees in hedge funds versus private equity funds that are invested in LBOs, venture capital, real estate, or hard assets. An appropriate way to discuss these differences is through the definition of these component features.

General Partner versus Limited Partners

The existence of a partnership structure in one form or another is common-place for alternative investment private funds. Although there are certain registered investment funds, separate accounts, onshore limited liability companies (LLCs) domiciled in the United States, and offshore investment companies domiciled in various tax havens across the globe, the basic structure for most alternative investments is a private partnership. Limited partners invest in entities that are managed by general partners, who control the partnerships and are responsible for their operation. For simplicity's sake, investors are referred to as limited partners and the investment managers are referred to as general partners, even though they may often be represented as LLC members and managing members, respectively.

This separation creates several nuances when considering the alignment of interests between limited partners and investment professionals who represent general partners and usually have two forms of economic incentive: (1) fees that are paid to the general partner or investment operating company and (2) the investment that the general partner has in the fund itself. Hedge funds can roll a portion of their fees into the funds they manage, which also may have certain tax advantages for the general partner. The incentive that a general partner and its principals have as an investor in their fund may be a two-edged sword. On one hand, passive outside investors often prefer to see a general partner and its principals as investors in their fund. For example, in private equity and real estate funds, it is virtually a requirement for the general partner to invest its own capital in its fund in an amount that represents at least 1 percent of the fund's total size.

On the other hand, some limited partners in hedge funds must elbow their way into maintaining positions in funds as general partners' assets become so enormous that outside investors' assets are returned annually, such that an increasing portion of the fund is represented by the general partners' assets. The conundrum is that an investor must question whether the assets that a general partner has invested in a fund act as an incentive for its investment personnel to perform well or as a disincentive to take risk. It is the latter issue that can become a problem for investors over time. A general partner may become more risk averse as its assets become a larger portion of a fund's assets and a larger portion of the general partner's principals' personal net worth. This phenomenon may be more of a concern regarding hedge funds than private equity or real estate, which tend to have serial funds. An excess preservation-of-capital mentality by a general partner may discourage risk taking below the risk budgeted for a fund by limited partners. This phenomenon may contribute to a reduction in risk taking by hedge funds over time, as the largest and most successful hedge funds seek to protect the capital they have accumulated in the past.

Term

The term for private equity funds tends to be finite, whereas the term for hedge funds is less finite. In spite of the trend for hedge funds to have increasingly elongated lockup periods, they tend to be considered open-end funds. Private equity and real estate funds generally are closed-end funds from which investors cannot withdraw their capital. However, there are open-end versions of these funds. The general partners of closed-end private equity and real estate funds remit investors' assets as a return of capital and profits during the specific life of the funds. This return of funds occurs as income is generated and capital appreciation is realized through asset sales. The typical life span for a closed-end private partnership is 10 years, but may be as short as seven years for certain debt-oriented funds, usually accompanied by one or two one-year extensions at the discretion of the general partner.

Management Fee

For private equity or real estate funds, depending on the type of strategy and amount of capital employed, management fees may range from 1 percent to 2 percent per annum on committed capital and decline over time. The type of private equity or real estate fund and its size tend to dictate the reasonableness of these fees and the way in which they decline over time. For instance, large-sized buyout funds tend to have lower fees than smaller-sized venture capital funds, which relates to the basic economics of the ongoing overhead for the general partner in making and managing these investments. The larger buyout funds might have fees in the 1.0 percent to 1.5 percent range, while the venture capital funds often demand fees closer to 2.0 percent, particularly for those in heavy demand by investors. In any case, these fees are applied to committed capital and decline over time. Typically, management fees applied to committed capital begin to decline in the fifth through seventh year of the life of a partnership. Rates of decline may be straight line as a percentage of the original management fee, or applied as a percentage of each preceding year's management fee once the decline begins.

It should be noted that management fees are different in a number of respects for hedge funds, which also fall in the 1 percent to 2 percent range but can be higher. Management fees for private equity and real estate funds are applied to committed capital, not invested capital, as they are for hedge funds. In some regards, this might lead one to consider private equity management fees to be more expensive from a scrupulous perspective than hedge fund management fees. However, the fact that the norm is for private equity management fees to decline over time tends to ameliorate this. This decline in management fees as private equity funds mature is clearly not the same case for hedge funds, which charge their management fees annually based on assets under management with no decline over time.

Performance Fee

The performance fee concept is one that is fairly unique to alternative investments. In fact, in the United States, there are securities law restrictions contained in the Investment Advisers Act (1940) against the application of performance fees, except for an exemption contained in Rule 205-3 of the Act that applies to investors who meet certain asset and income levels. Generally speaking, the performance fee or carried interest concept is common in its existence across each type of alternative investment strategy. However, there are features that adjust this fee using certain mechanisms, such as high-water mark, hurdle rate, preferred return, catch-up, and clawback.

For hedge funds, performance fees are calculated as a percentage of gross profits generated by a fund, which the general partner keeps as a profit incentive. For private equity funds, the carried interest term is used to denote the performance fee paid to the general partner. Unlike the case for hedge funds, however, the carried interest is paid to private equity general partners only at the conclusion of profitable transactions (American style) or at the conclusion of the life of the fund (European style). Many private equity and real estate funds calculate their performance fees via a waterfall methodology (as described later in this chapter). In contrast, performance fees are paid to the general partners of hedge funds on an annual basis and based on the profit (net of management fees and fund expenses) generated by the fund each calendar year. While a 20 percent performance fee or carried interest is fairly standard for many alternative investment strategies, it can range far higher for certain hedge funds or venture capital funds that view themselves as having limited capacity in the face of strong investor demand that appears to be fee inelastic.

Capital Call

A capital call applies to many types of private equity funds, whether invested in venture capital, LBOs, real estate, timber, oil and gas, or any other sorts of hard assets. While an investor makes a capital commitment to a fund at its inception, this committed capital then is intermittently called by the general partner and drawn down from limited partners over the life of the partnership in order to fund investments. Capital calls are conducted at points in time when the general partner has found investments that it seeks to make or augment on behalf of the partnership.

High-Water Mark

A high-water mark describes the high net asset value (NAV) that a fund has attained in any annual period. High-water marks typically relate to open-end funds, such as hedge funds, currency funds, or commodities funds. The high-water mark is the NAV that must be exceeded before a fund may accrue and pay a performance fee on annual gains. For instance, if a fund saw its NAV decline to 95 at the end of a year from 100 at the end of the previous year, then that fund would not be able to pay a performance fee to its general partner for that year. In this example, the fund would be required to experience a rise in its NAV to above 100 in a subsequent year before it once again could apply a performance fee calculation.

Hurdle Rate

A hurdle rate, which sometimes is used in conjunction with hedge funds, is similar to a preferred return, which is used with private equity funds. More often, a hurdle rate is applicable to hedge funds of funds. A hurdle rate is the gross return above which a fund must earn before its general partner may charge its performance fee. In the event that a fund earns less than its hurdle rate, then no performance fee is granted to the general partner. In comparison with a preferred return for a private equity fund, hurdle rates typically are lower than preferred returns. Often, hurdle rates equal a risk-free rate, whereas preferred returns in private equity usually are a fixed rate (e.g., 8 percent).

Preferred Return

Typically, private equity and real estate funds have preferred rates of return. Profits from these funds must exceed the preferred rates in order for the general partner to capture any performance fee. The rationale for a preferred return is to provide an enticement for investors to lock up their capital for an extended period of time in what amounts to a blind pool closed-end fund. Preferred returns also are an attempt to align the incentives of a general partner with the interests of limited partners. General partners are required to generate enough return to meet the limited partners' preferred return, so that the general partners may then begin to enjoy performance fees applied to gains on the fund. In many cases, the preferred return is compounded annually.

Catch-up

In most private equity funds, the general partner benefits from a catch-up of its carried interest once the limited partners have been paid their preferred returns. (See Figures 7.2 and 7.3 later in this chapter.) In American-style private equity funds, as profitable investments are exited, the limited partners are paid their capital plus a promised preferred return on each transaction, which often has been accruing on a compounded basis since the associated capital was called. Once the preferred return is paid, the general partner then can apply its carried interest to the preferred return. In other words, the cash that is distributed to the limited partners and associated with the preferred return is multiplied by the general partner's carried interest percentage (e.g., 20 percent). That figure then is deducted from the proceeds of the exited investment and paid to the general partner. In this sense, the general partner has caught up its carried interest, but only after the limited partners have received their preferred returns.

Clawback

The term *clawback* indicates an instance when performance fees previously paid to a general partner are returned to limited partners. This occurs when, over the course of a fund's life, it does not generate an agreed-upon preferred return or an overall profit for its limited partners. The existence of a clawback feature is common among private equity funds, but more so among U.S. funds and funds that may not offer a preferred return to limited partners, such as some venture capital funds. Hedge funds rarely, if ever, have clawback provisions. The concept of a clawback is to protect investors in the event that performance fees have been paid to the general partner through the life of a fund, but due to losses on deals toward the end of the fund, the limited partners end up either losing capital or not being paid an agreed-upon preferred return on an aggregate fund basis.

In spite of the unique aspects of this feature and its benefits for investors, clawbacks are not always a desirable outcome. Clawbacks clearly are not a desirable outcome for general partners and their principals. Additionally, limited partners may not want to resort to enacting a clawback of prior carried interest payments made to general partners for several reasons. First, clawbacks usually are net of income taxes paid by the general partner's principals. In other words, at the time when a general partner's principals receive (through the general partner) their carried interest on exited investments, the principals pay income taxes. In light of this money going unilaterally to the tax authorities, the convention is to only claw back previously paid carried interest payments net of this income tax payment. Second, invoking a clawback assumes that the principals of a general partner still have assets to repay. It may be that a clawback is difficult to collect from some principals. Although in Europe escrow accounts often are created to hold carried interest payments made to general partners (in order

TABLE 7.3 Cash Flow Example of Private Equity Clawback of General Partner Performance Fee (American-Style Fund)

Deal 1	Cash Flow Limited Partner	General Partner
Capital called	−20.0	
Return of capital	20.0	
Gross profit = $20		
Preferred return paid to limited partner	9.4	
Catch-up paid to general partner		1.9
Carried interest paid to general partner		2.1
Profit allocation paid to limited partner	6.6	
Net cash flow	16.0	4.0

Deal 3	Cash Flow Limited Partner	General Partner
Capital called	−10.0	
Return of capital	10.0	
Gross profit = $10		
Preferred return paid to limited partner	4.7	
Catch-up paid to general partner		0.9
Carried interest paid to general partner		1.1
Profit allocation paid to limited partner	3.3	
Net cash flow	8.0	2.0

Total Fund	Cash Flow Limited Partner	General Partner
Capital called	−20.0	
Return of capital	20.0	
Gross profit = $20		
Preferred return paid to limited partner	9.4	
Catch-up paid to general partner		1.9
Carried interest paid to general partner		2.1
Profit allocation paid to limited partner	6.6	
Net cash flow	16.0	4.0

Deal 4	Cash Flow Limited Partner	General Partner
Capital called	−10.0	
Return of capital	10.0	
Gross profit = $10		
Preferred return paid to limited partner	4.7	
Catch-up paid to general partner		0.9
Carried interest paid to general partner		1.1
Profit allocation paid to limited partner	3.3	
Net cash flow	8.0	2.0

Deal 5	Cash Flow Limited Partner	General Partner	Total Fund	Cash Flow Limited Partner	General Partner
Capital called	-40.0		Capital called	-100.0	
Return of capital	0.0		Return of capital	60.0	
Gross profit = $0			Gross profit = $60		
Preferred return paid to limited partner	0.0		Preferred return paid to limited partner	28.2	
Catch-up paid to general partner		0.0	Catch-up paid to general partner		5.6
Carried interest paid to general partner		0.0	Carried interest paid to general partner		6.4
Profit allocation paid to limited partner	0.0		Profit allocation paid to limited partner	19.8	
Net cash flow	-40.0	0.0	Gross cash flow	108.0	12.0
			Net cash flow	8.0	12.0
			Implied limited partner compound return pre-clawback	0.8%	
			Clawback test = 0.8% is less than 8.0%		
			Nominal Clawback	**12.0**	**-12.0**
			Real clawback (post general partner income taxes)	7.4	-7.4
			Revised gross cash flow	115.4	
			Revised net cash flow	15.4	
			Revised limited partner compound return post-clawback	1.5%	

Note: Figures exclude management fees and fund expenses. Figures are in $ millions and rounded.

to fund clawback provisions should they be triggered), for U.S. funds this typically is not the case and only personal guarantees are made by principals of general partners. Third, the enactment of a clawback likely would render a general partner tarnished and in a compromised position in its ability to raise next-generation partnerships. If limited partners believe that a general partner still has merit—for instance, because of a belief that only one or two bad deals caused a prior fund to be in a clawback position—then the reputational and financial damage possibly inflicted to a general partner by the enactment of a clawback may be undesirable.

An example of a clawback calculation is contained in Table 7.3. In this example, five deal transactions are used to illustrate an instance where a private equity fund with profitable transactions early in its life can succumb to poor performance from a transaction late in its life. In the table, profits garnered in the first four transactions are outweighed by a loss in the last transaction, in terms of the overall contribution to a preferred return calculation. The loss in the last transaction has the impact of triggering a clawback feature for the fund, because the cumulative profits for the fund do not surpass the required preferred return for the total fund. This is in spite of the preferred return's being exceeded in the earlier deals for the fund on a deal-by-deal basis. Therefore, previous-period carried interest payments made to the general partner are clawed back, but they are done so net of income taxes paid by the general partner's principals.

Table 7.3 **Assumptions:**   Total limited partner capital called over life
    of fund = $100
Assumed limited partner compound preferred return = 8 percent
Assumed life of fund = 10 years
Assumed general partner carried interest = 20 percent
Average maturity for a deal = 5 years
Assumed general partner income tax rate = 38 percent

Private Equity Clawbacks May Also Contribute to Market Share Growth by Hedge Funds   The threat of clawbacks reducing or eliminating performance fees that were paid in prior periods has an impact on the behavior of private equity general partners compared with hedge fund general partners. The clawback risk for private equity may cause general partners to be relatively conservative in their financial behavior. The risk of having to return performance fees may cause the hiring and compensation patterns of private equity firms to be more conservative than a comparable hedge fund that has no clawback provision. The risk of a clawback also may cause fewer talented individuals to be attracted to the private equity firms versus the hedge funds because of the long-tailed personal liability that it poses.

Indeed, once a clawback provision is enacted, individual general partners who may have been paid a performance fee have to return the fee to the limited partners. Therefore, the existence of clawback provisions may be another intricacy of fees for alternative investment funds that contribute to long-term gains in intellectual capital by hedge funds at the expense of private equity funds. This may support long-term gains in market share of assets under management by hedge funds.

The Clawback as a Free Option Offered to Private Equity Investors The clawback provision is unique to private equity partnerships and offers an investor great value. Clawbacks are not part of the terms and conditions of most hedge funds. In private equity funds, clawbacks offer investors the ability to see a return of prior-period performance fees that had been paid to a general partner, in the event that the cumulative net returns for the limited partners become negative or fall below a predetermined preferred return late in the life of a partnership. The clawback provision has like characteristics. Investors rarely consider the potential value that this option holds. This effective hedge regarding the payment of performance fees can have a material consequence for an investor in the event that a fund's cumulative profits dissipate in future years. However, as an option, the clawback also may have no value in the future, if the fund is profitable and no return of prior-period performance fees paid to the general partner is warranted.

It is perhaps easier to think about a clawback's value when it is applied to a secondary investor who purchases a limited partner's stake in a private equity partnership. If a secondary purchase is made and assuming no contingent payments are owed to the seller of the position, then the new investor effectively receives through the clawback provision a free call option on performance fees that were paid to the general partner in prior periods of the partnership. Obviously, the seller of a secondary interest in the partnership has this benefit embedded in its ownership of the partnership as well. Although the clawback when enacted is simply a reduction in net losses to the investor (or shortfall in preferred return), prior to the end of the partnership the clawback can be seen as having a present value of this potential payment. This potential future payment can have a positive impact on an investor's performance from a private equity fund relative to a hedge fund. Furthermore, the present value of the clawback has market value that can affect the secondary market purchase price of a private equity limited partnership interest. However, rarely do sellers of secondary interests in these partnerships apply quantitative options pricing theory to value this feature.

There are several ways to assess the value of a clawback for investors. One might interpret the payment of the performance fees to the general partner prior to invoking a clawback simply to be an opportunity cost for the limited partner, or something akin to an interest-free loan that the limited partner has made to the general partner. Another approach is to consider the cash flow that the return of performance fees represents. The cash flow for a limited partner does not occur until the clawback is triggered in the last year of a fund. The value of the clawback for an investor can be calculated as the present value of this expected future cash flow.

An additional way to evaluate a clawback is to consider that it has variable value at different points in time. This variability depends on several factors, including the time left for completion of the fund, the cumulative performance fee that has been taken by the general partner at that point in time, and whether the fund appears likely to meet its obligation to return invested capital to its limited partners plus a preferred return. The clawback is a natural hedge for the long position that a limited partner holds in a private equity fund. If a fund performs poorly late in its life, then the clawback becomes more valuable. Conversely, if the fund becomes increasingly successful later in its life, then the clawback becomes less valuable to the limited partner.

Waterfall Calculation

A waterfall calculation in private equity relates to the prioritization of cash flows from an investment. The waterfall sets the order of recipients of cash flows from individual deals or from a fund in total. Waterfalls include the return of invested capital, preferred returns, catch-ups, carried interests, and profit allocations. The essence of a waterfall is that the general partner must pay to limited partners a preferred return, possibly compounded annually, prior to the general partner being able to pay itself a carried interest. A waterfall also illustrates the ability of a general partner to catch up its carried interest on the amount of preferred returns paid to limited partners. The final piece of a waterfall is the normal profit split between the general partner receiving its carried interest and the limited partners receiving their profit participation. In total, waterfalls represent potentially cumbersome calculations both for a general partner and its limited partners.

Figures 7.2 and 7.3 illustrate different cash flow constructs pertaining to waterfalls for American versus European styles of private equity funds. The basic difference lies in the fact that American-style private equity funds tend to calculate their preferred return, catch-up, and carried interest on the basis of capital calls for and performance of individual deals or transactions, whereas European-style funds calculate these figures based on the total capital called over the life of a fund and the performance of the total. Accordingly, the notion of a clawback often does not apply to European-style private equity funds, since the need for a clawback usually

Net Cash Waterfall

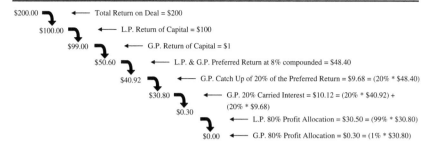

FIGURE 7.2 Private Equity Cash Flow Waterfall Example—American Style Per Deal

    Assumptions. Gross return on invested capital = $200
Limited partner invested capital = $100
General partner invested capital = $1
Total capital invested in deal = $101
Assumed life of deal = 5 years
Assumed limited partner compound preferred return = 8 percent
General partner carried interest = 20 percent

Net Cash Waterfall

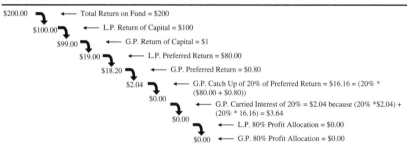

FIGURE 7.3 Private Equity Cash Flow Waterfall Example—European Style Per Fund

    Assumptions. Gross return on invested capital = $200
Limited partner invested capital = $100
General partner invested capital = $1
Total capital invested in fund = $101
Assumed life of fund = 10 years
Assumed limited partner simple preferred return = 8 percent
General partner carried interest = 20 percent

is superseded by the fact that the carried interest for these funds is not paid until the conclusion of the fund and not on an interim basis during the life of the fund.

SUMMARY

The migration of hedge funds into private equity investments may very well be changing the return dynamics for classic private equity as an asset class. A continued flow of assets into hedge funds that have private-equity–like investments might contribute to a degradation of returns for traditional private equity funds. Private equity funds may increasingly find it difficult to secure transactions with the type of return characteristics required to meet the performance objectives that have been delineated to their investors. In turn, this would exacerbate a restriction in the capacity of private equity firms to accept assets from investors. There appears to be some statistical support to the notion that hedge funds are gaining market share from private equity funds. Although there are questions surrounding the ability of hedge funds to manage private equity investments, the fee structures for hedge funds generally provide them with an economic advantage over private equity funds. For instance, the clawback provision contained in private equity funds is a clear benefit for investors, but may be an indirect contributor to market share growth by hedge funds at the expense of private equity funds. Nevertheless, longer-duration terms provide private equity funds some advantage in being able to offer better performance in their investments. Furthermore, fee structures for private equity funds appear to be better aligned with investor interests than is the case for hedge funds.

A hedge fund that invests in private equity transactions may offer lower returns, less private equity management skill, and structural inefficiencies in terms of shorter investment time frames and higher fees than a comparable private equity fund. Yet investors are attracted, because of better liquidity terms pertaining to their investment in hedge funds and perhaps more likely because of a lack of comparative analysis. Therefore, the use of factor analysis to understand the commonality of one form of alternative investment with another must increasingly be part of an investor's overall due diligence process. Without this approach, it is all too likely that investors will bucket alternative investments in their classical definitions and therefore not consider alternative investments on an equal fee and terms basis. This potential misstep is exemplified by investment in relatively high-fee partnerships, funds with relatively inferior skills, or partnerships with liquidity terms that are not well suited to the duration of their underlying investments.

CHAPTER 8

Cash Flow Forecasting and Its Implications for Rebalancing

Investors using alternative investments are required to implement a framework to manage cash flows from these assets. Unlike most traditional asset classes, the cash flow characteristics of alternative investments are difficult to administer. These investments have three distinct periods of cash flow: entering the investment, managing cash flows into and out of the entities during their life, and redeeming the investment at its conclusion. Furthermore, the complexity of managing alternative investment cash flows has at least two collateral ramifications. The first relates to the investor's ability to achieve its strategic asset allocation targets. The second is the ability to rebalance. There are two tools that may be used for managing cash flows and for rebalancing. They are cash flow models and the utilization of proxies to emulate certain alternative investments. Therefore, this chapter focuses on the following three topics: (1) the forecasting of cash flows to manage alternative investment liquidity, (2) the ability of an investor to meet strategic asset allocations for alternative investments and effectively rebalance these allocations, and (3) quantitative tools to help with these tasks, including cash flow models and the use of alternative investment proxies during periods of mismatched cash flows.

ALTERNATIVE INVESTMENT CASH FLOW

Cash flow associated with alternative investments is not easily generalized, because the situation is quite different for hedge funds; private equity; various real estate investments, including real estate investment trusts (REITs); commodities; and currency investments. The key demarcation when considering the cash flow characteristics of different sorts of alternative investments is a comparison of open-end funds, closed-end funds, separate accounts, and direct investments. Cash flow in alternative investing has a closer relationship to liquidity than is the case in traditional investing. That is to say, for alternative investments, cash inflows and outflows partly define liquidity, since they can be large and contain a component of return of capital. In traditional investments, cash flow often is simply a dividend, an interest payment, or the return of all invested capital on demand from an open-end fund or separate account. In traditional investments, dividend payments and interest income represent cash flow that may or may not be a significant component of the total return on an investment. However, alternative investment cash flow payments and timing have larger importance from three perspectives: (1) the cash flows into and out of the investment can be sizable and have uncertain timing; (2) the cash flows back to the investor can represent an important component of total return on the investment; and (3) the cash flows from alternative investments often include the return of capital to the investor, which makes accounting more complex than is the case in traditional investment cash flows. (The concepts of cash flow and liquidity are separated for this discussion. Alternative investment cash flow is discussed in this chapter, while liquidity is approached as a distinct factor in Chapter 10.)

Hedge Fund Cash Flow

Hedge funds can have various types of fund structures, including open-end funds, closed-end funds, and separate accounts. Hedge funds have no direct investment opportunities per se, as is found with private equity, real estate, and hard assets where there is an ability to directly invest in portfolio companies and properties. In terms of open-end fund structures for hedge funds, there are several subgroupings, including commingled private partnerships,[1] registered investment companies (RICs), and separate accounts. There are closed-end hedge fund of funds products that are publicly listed primarily in Europe and exchange-traded hedge fund indexes in the United States. However, closed-end hedge funds do not yet represent a significant portion of capital invested in hedge funds.

Hedge fund private partnerships and separate accounts can be domiciled onshore in the United States or in an offshore tax haven such as the Cayman Islands or the British Virgin Islands. Nontaxable investors in the United States take advantage of offshore funds and separate accounts. For instance, endowments, foundations, and ERISA (Employee Retirement Income Security Act of 1974) corporate pension plans that are subject to unrelated business taxable income (UBTI) liabilities utilize offshore funds. Offshore tax havens also are suitable for non-U.S. investors seeking safe harbor from their domestic tax laws. Whether onshore or offshore, the difference between commingled funds and separate accounts lies in the fact that separate accounts typically are reserved for the largest investors that commit more than $25 million to a hedge fund.

For commingled hedge funds, although initial cash flow subscriptions can be completely accomplished over a short time frame, redemptions may be less predictable. Redemptions depend on initial lockups, quarterly redemption periods, the ability for the manager to gate redemptions if large numbers of investors seek to redeem, and holdbacks of a small portion of capital upon final redemption until the completion of the fund's annual audit. In comparison, a separate account is dedicated to the beneficial interest of only one investor. Furthermore, the investment manager serves in a discretionary role as the effective agent in the management of investments in the separate account, but the investor also has direct authority over the account as the beneficiary. The benefit of the separate account structure is that the investor often is allowed to make immediate cash contributions or withdrawals from the account, in accordance with an investment management agreement with the hedge fund manager. Thus, separate accounts in hedge funds have among the most flexible and predictable cash flow considerations for the range of alternative investments.

Open-end hedge funds that are RICs are also quite liquid and subscriptions to and redemptions from them tend to be quite facile. Nevertheless, the managers of these funds often make it a practice to erect redemption windows that may require initial lockups and advance notice periods prior to redemption. The structure of RICs, which in many respects mirror traditional mutual funds, is such that they can offer liquid terms to investors. However, the underlying strategies of the hedge funds and the securities that they hold can cause the managers to create constraints to redemption. Therefore, in the area of RICs for hedge funds, cash flows into and out of the funds are fairly predictable but often may require some planning.

Hedge funds with long lockup periods reside in the middle of the spectrum for open-end versus closed-end funds, in terms of liquidity and degree of aggravation associated with cash flow planning. For example, hedge funds with lockup periods of three years, although they are technically open-end funds, might be considered hybrid funds that lie somewhere between true closed-end and open-end funds. Consider a hedge fund with a three-year rolling lockup and redemption periods only up to 20 percent of the investor's assets in any one quarterly period thereafter. This construct is the equivalent of a closed-end fund, particularly if the illustrated fund does not have a cleanup provision. Without a cleanup provision, the 20 percent quarterly redemption limitation is perpetual, such that the investor ad infinitum would be able to redeem only 20 percent of its total investment each quarter, not based on the total value of the investment when the initial redemption process began. Even with a cleanup provision, such as a straight-line 20 percent quarterly redemption based on the total amount of investment when redemption was initiated, this example of an open-end fund would only return the investor's total capital in four and one-quarter years. Many investors who may be enticed into investing in long-lockup hedge funds because of fee discounts may not be fully cognizant of the illiquid nature of these investments. The timing of cash flows out of these investments has the propensity to underachieve the cash flow expectations of investors. A rigorous read of the placement documents for these types of funds and the creation of a detailed cash flow and liquidity matrix by the investor in order to track cash redemption privileges from these investments are required. Without such an approach, an investor with a generous allocation to these types of funds is vulnerable to finding a significant cash flow shortfall that affects the ability to rebalance in future years. An inability to effect rebalancing of a portfolio at a minimum will be an embarrassment to the investor, if not a significant missed opportunity to capture or avoid movements in asset classes.

As far as closed-end funds are concerned, examples are few in the realm of hedge funds, but the area is growing as managers of open-end hedge funds seek sources of permanent capital. An early example of a hybrid closed-end hedge fund is structured products. These devices offer investors tax advantages, the ability to leverage hedge fund returns, and a form of insurance on invested principal. In return, the investor enters into often a five-year investment term, with the caveat that the invested capital is returned early to the investor in the event that the underlying hedge fund generates losses of a certain magnitude. Therefore, although the cash inflows into this type of investment are predictable, the cash outflows from the investment have a chance of surprising the investor. Unplanned cash outflows are likely to occur at disadvantageous times, such as in the face of a loss. This would be unfortunate if the investor believes that ultimately the value of the investment will recover.

Two other examples of closed-end hedge funds are public listings of hedge fund organizations and the classic closed-end fund public offerings. In the former case, an investor in these shares benefits from an investment in the management company that operates the hedge fund, rather than as an investor in the related fund. However, there is a linkage between these two opportunities through the performance fee that is paid to the manager of the hedge fund. Strong returns in the hedge fund cause a performance fee that will be paid to the hedge fund manager. Therefore, the buyer of shares in the management company experiences an alignment of benefits with the investors in the underlying hedge fund. Additionally, the investor in the management company benefits from the stability of the management fee paid to the management company and perhaps some sort of related dividend pass-through to common shareholders. This example yields very predictable timing of cash outflows to the investor, but much more proportionally because of the ability to liquidate an investment in the public markets than an ability to capture dividends. Another variation on this investment is private equity seed funds that invest in hedge funds. Although the lockups for these funds are long, the cash flow from the ownership share in the management and performance fees of the underlying hedge funds typically is paid in regular dividends back to the limited partners in these funds, thereby providing predictable interim-period cash flow.

In the case of the traditional closed-end fund public listing of hedge funds of funds, there are instances of this structure primarily in Europe as well as hedge fund indexes listed in the United States. This form of classic closed-end fund enables good secondary market liquidity for the purchasers of these funds. Therefore, cash flows out of the investment are predictable. Interim-period cash flows likely would be nonexistent, but predictable in that sense. The benefit for a hedge fund manager from this structure is access to permanent capital. However, this benefit comes with the vulnerability of being replaced as manager upon a vote by shareholders. The benefit for an investor in this type of fund is complete liquidity, predicable cash flow for portfolio rebalancing, and ostensibly strong corporate governance pertaining to the public listing status of the closed-end fund.

Private Equity Cash Flow

Private equity funds also are structured as open-end private partnerships. However, these funds have limited open-end terms. Typically, they have 10-year lives with the capability for one- to two-year extensions. In this sense, they are different from traditional open-end funds that have far more liquid terms. Although public closed-end private equity funds are a recent addition to the menu of choices for investors, there is not a wide selection of these vehicles. As is the case with public closed-end hedge funds, either as an investment in the management company or an investment in the underlying fund, these structures when applied to private equity offer the same benefits to the fund manager and investor, including access to permanent capital for the fund manager and good liquidity, predictability of cash flow, and strong corporate governance for the investor.

As open-end private partnerships, private equity funds have some very distinct differences from hedge funds that pertain to their cash flow features. For example, there is a twofold effect on investors from a 10-year term that many of these open-end private equity funds have. First, the investor must be willing to see its funds locked up in the investment for over a decade. Second, the investor will be asked to make capital calls to the investment manager at uncertain times during the life of the fund. The timing and amount of capital calls are difficult to estimate. Capital calls must be funded by the investor as negative cash flow, and they provide a challenge to the investor in terms of maintaining a fully invested commitment to private equity in a portfolio asset allocation model. Furthermore, at the same time that the investor is continuing to allocate more cash to meet capital calls from private equity funds, it also is seeing the return of invested capital and profits on that capital during the life of private equity funds.

Open-end private equity funds also are able to offer onshore and offshore domiciles, similar to hedge funds. To the extent that the private equity partnership does not use leverage, there is no need to have an offshore version of the fund. The lack of leverage means, in most cases, that there is no UBTI liability imposed in the United States for nontaxable investors. Accordingly, a fund invested entirely in equity investments in venture capital deals would be unlikely to generate profits from leverage. However, funds using leveraged buyout (LBO) investments are more likely to generate profits from leverage, as are funds investing in mezzanine debt or real estate.

Another difference for private equity funds is cash inflows to the investor during the life cycle of these funds. Most U.S. closed-end private equity funds return capital and profits net of fees to investors on a per-deal basis during the life of the fund. Each investment is a discrete transaction with a series of cash calls and a return of capital and profits through dividends during the life of the investment and through a return of total remaining invested capital at the conclusion of the investment. In contrast, some non-U.S. open-end private equity funds conform more in spirit to a traditional closed-end fund. Although these funds have finite periods of life, proceeds from the refinancing or the sale of investments are retained by the fund. These proceeds may be reinvested in new investments in the fund or retained until the end of the life of the fund. Therefore, the cash flow features of these funds are far more predictable for an investor. Once the investment has been made by the investor, there is no worry about the timing of cash inflows to the investor or about the reinvestment risk associated with this return of capital. As such, the investor is in a better position to maintain a stable allocation to private equity as an asset class in an overall portfolio optimization. On the other hand, the investor is somewhat at a disadvantage in terms of rebalancing the allocation to private equity. Without frequent returns of capital from the private equity funds, which is the case with U.S.-styled private equity funds, the investor has fewer opportunities to reduce an allocation to private equity should there be a need to do so.

Other examples of open-end funds in private equity are separate accounts and direct investments in portfolio companies. In principle, separate accounts and direct investments are identical. In both cases, the investor is making a direct investment in portfolio companies and is considered the beneficiary of the investment, rather than investing through a fund as a limited partner. In a separate account, the investment manager makes capital calls to the investor to support investments in a portfolio of companies. The investor is the sole beneficiary in the separate account, unlike commingled funds where there are multiple investors and beneficiaries. In a separate account, the investor may have the ability to fire the investment manager and liquidate its investments at will. In practice, liquidating these investments can be very difficult.

Where separate accounts and direct investment in portfolio companies differ is more in the realm of operations, procedure, and oversight, not in the predictability and characteristics of cash flow. Examples of direct investments in portfolio companies include a sophisticated investor with robust technical and operational staff that makes direct investments on its own without the aid of a fund manager, or an investor in a commingled private equity fund who is given the right to make coinvestments on a pari passu basis with the fund in which it is invested. Coinvestments provide an investor with operational and oversight benefits of being able to selectively invest in companies with the aid of the investment manager. However, in either case of sole direct investment or co-investment via access granted by a fund manager, the investor is unilaterally deciding to invest, as opposed to capital calls being made by a fund manager. The benefit from this juxtaposition is that the investor therefore has command of its cash flow destiny as it pertains to cash outflows to the investment. This feature is helpful to an investor in maintaining portfolio allocations to private equity and in rebalancing.

Post initial investment in these direct transactions, however, the investor is vulnerable to interim and ending cash flows. During the middle of the life of these transactions, the investor may choose not to reinvest in the transaction, as further financial support is required. Such a shortfall in support could have a materially adverse outcome on the total economic return on the investment to the investor, in the event that the investor's original investment is diluted by subsequent financings that are supported by other investors in the transaction. Therefore, in exchange for the cash flow flexibility that the investor might gain at the beginning term of these investments, it might lose flexibility from an economic perspective during the middle term of these transactions. Another aspect of altered cash flow characteristics for these transactions is the end period cash flow. A direct investment as a coinvestor participating pari passu with a fund manager in an American-style private equity fund leaves the investor with similar cash flow characteristics as the commingled fund. However, in non-U.S.-style deals where proceeds remain in the fund until the life of the fund has concluded rather than the life of the deal, the investor in coinvestments will witness returns of capital and profits earlier than is the case with the commingled fund. From this perspective, early returns of capital from coinvestments might have ramifications for an investor's private equity reinvestment risk and maintenance of portfolio allocations.

Real Estate Cash Flow

Funds invested in real estate have among the widest variety of investment structures of all alternative investments. Each of the closed-end, open-end, and direct investment structures for real estate has very different return, risk, and liquidity characteristics. These partnerships or funds also range in predictability of cash flows. However, compared with other alternative investment options, real estate tends to have the most regular cash flow features, as it pertains to current income if not in terms of return of principal and related capital gains and losses.

Real Estate Private Equity   Real estate investments that are open-end private funds are similar to most other open-end private equity funds. In this instance, capital calls (negative cash flow for an investor) and return of capital and profits or losses (positive cash flow for an investor) are similar in nature to other types of private equity funds. However, the timing and magnitude of the capital flows may be different. For instance, real estate transactions tend to be more sizable than capital calls that are associated with venture capital funds. Real estate transactions also do not tend to require the same sort of interim-period capital calls as do venture capital funds, which are required to fund the continued growth of portfolio companies. From a cash flow perspective, private funds invested in real estate may have a closer resemblance to LBO funds that make sizable capital commitments to a smaller number of investments than venture capital funds. The cash flow requirements for these investments tend to be focused toward the initial purchase price of a property rather than the ongoing funding of an enterprise. Nevertheless, the need to fund add-on acquisitions that occur in LBOs usually does not happen in most real estate funds. Furthermore, the recurrent positive cash flows or dividends from real estate transactions clearly are different than the irregular dividends from LBOs.

Cash flow from real estate investments is determined by the level of seniority of the investment in the capital structure of a property. The characteristics of cash flows also are defined by the real estate strategy that is employed. The timing and amount of cash outflows and inflows are substantially determined by whether the real estate investment is core, core-plus, value-added, or opportunistic (see Chapter 5). Indeed, the seniority of investment, when overlaid by the type of strategy being employed, creates a mosaic of return, risk, and cash flow expectations, as is depicted in Figures 8.1 and 8.2. For instance, the senior secured direct mortgage lender in an opportunistic real estate property might have the return, risk, and cash flow predictability of an equity investor in a value-added property.

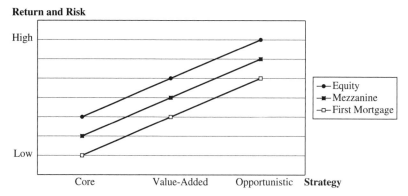

FIGURE 8.1   Real Estate Expected Return and Risk: Seniority versus Strategy
Note: Relationships are generalizations and should not be interpreted necessarily as linear.

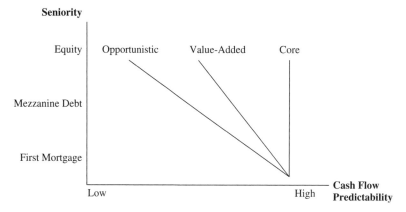

FIGURE 8.2   Real Estate Cash Flow Predictability: Seniority versus Strategy
Note: Relationships are generalizations and should not be interpreted necessarily as linear.

The ability to compare real estate investments across capital structures and strategy types is fundamental for an investor to be able to select the most efficient investment to achieve desired return, risk, and cash flow targets.

Many private equity core real estate funds are open-end funds, which indicates that investors may withdraw their capital on fairly short notice, often quarterly. However, open-end real estate funds that allow for redemption of capital typically have credit lines available to them that help manage client redemptions. Furthermore, these funds usually have quarterly gates that limit the total amount of redemption in any one quarterly period. By contrast, the less liquid strategies in real estate private equity, such as value-added and opportunistic, are approaches that are better suited to longer-lockup open-end funds. Open-end funds have regular redemption periods offered to their investors, whereas longer-lockup open-end funds are more along the lines of private equity funds and have multiyear lives. Furthermore, short-lockup open-end real estate funds tend to be focused more toward properties that are expected to generate most of their returns via current income, or rental income minus operating expenses, rather than through capital appreciation and subsequent sale of the properties.

Real Estate Private Debt   Private funds that invest in debt instruments tied to real estate are some of the more predictable cash flow instruments among alternative investments. These funds have a variety of credit and duration objectives. Initial cash flow considerations in terms of capital calls are similar in nature to real estate private equity funds. Ongoing cash flows in the form of dividends and current income are more predictable than is the case for funds invested in the equity tranches of real estate transactions. As debt instruments are purchased on specific properties, key metrics that characterize ongoing cash flows include the loan term, the general level of interest rates, geographic location, property type, debtholder equity participation rights, and ultimately the credit quality of the property. The credit quality of each building or property is depicted by the amount of financial leverage involved in its capital structure, the occupancy rate of the facility, the credit quality and diversification of its tenants, the local economic conditions, and the facility's state of repair. These characteristics determine the ability of each property to sustain its interest payments and repay or refinance its debt. The ability ultimately to repay the investor is the final cash flow consideration that must be estimated for these types of funds. Nevertheless, the timing and amount of a final exit are far more estimable than other types of alternative investments.

Real Estate Public Debt and Equity   In terms of public real estate, there are a number of avenues for investment offered to a range of investors. In general, these offerings are distinct in comparison with private equity and debt alternatives because of their liquidity traits as publicly traded investments. These opportunities include mortgage securities, REITS, and equity in public companies that have as their main line of business the operation of properties or the development of real estate. The opportunities to invest in public debt in real estate have become numerous and include collateralized mortgage obligations (CMOs), commercial mortgage-backed securities (CMBSs), and corporate bonds secured by real estate.

Public investment in real estate equity, aside from REITs, usually is in the form of common or preferred stock held in real estate operating companies (REOCs) that may be engaged in the development of properties or the management of buildings. Whether as developers or operators, these companies focus on a range of industries, including commercial, health care, education, residential, retail, industrial, leisure, and gaming. The cash flow characteristics from funds that invest in these securities are determined by the investment manager. These securities are quite liquid since they are publicly traded. The dividends and income from properties owned by REOCs can remain in the REOCs and accrue as an increase in the companies' shareholders' value, rather than being distributed to investors. An investor with a portfolio of public equities in real estate operating and development companies can benefit from the availability of total liquidity of such a portfolio. This portfolio approach can experience cash flow from common and preferred stock dividends from its investments and appreciation or depreciation of these securities over time. The current income of such a portfolio of investments should reflect the dividends from companies held and be fairly stable and predictable during most times.

Typically, REITs are structured as closed-end publicly traded funds. However, the funds that invest in REITs may be open-end funds. An investor's beginning period and ending period cash flows related to REITs are the simple purchase and sale of an asset. However, this excludes the situation where an investor is investing in a private fund that is structured as a REIT and is making periodic capital calls from the investor. Whether private or public, REITs typically pay out at least 90 percent of their annual taxable income to unit holders in the form of regular dividends. The forward-looking visibility and predictability of these dividend streams often are fairly good. The total return from a REIT to an investor usually is more weighted toward current income than capital gains. Therefore, an investor in REITs or REIT funds tends to have very good liquidity and predictability of cash flows from these investments once they have been made. An investor in a REIT structure also stands to experience a capital gain in the net asset value of the investment, which tracks the appreciation or depreciation of the underlying property investments over time. Furthermore, changes in the price of publicly traded REITs are influenced by interest rates to the extent that the REIT dividend yield is influenced by interest rates.

A less predictable aspect of cash flows from REITS occurs during bull markets for real estate. During strong real estate markets, gains on property sales can be quite large and REITs may choose to make special dividend payments to unit holders. In this case, principal from and gains on properties in REITs may begin to be returned to unit holders through the sale of properties. REITs can retain or distribute all or part of the capital gain associated with the sale of a property. The proportion of distributions related to gains and return of principal, as opposed to regular dividends associated with funds from operations, is a function of the minimum 90 percent dividend distribution requirement for REITS and the investment manager's current market opportunities for reinvesting capital. If the market environment is frothy for real estate and prices are high, the REIT investment manager may choose to return proceeds from asset sales to the REIT unit holders. This presents the unit holder with unexpectedly large positive cash flows and a resulting reinvestment problem. In a sense, savvy REIT operators in this case force the investor to underweight real estate through a unilateral return of capital and capital gains. This phenomenon is illustrated in Figure 8.3, which represents data from the National Association of Real Estate Investment Trusts (NAREIT) and indicates the historical trend for the breakdown of dividends from REITs between regular dividend versus capital gain and return of capital.

Real Estate Direct Investments The purchase of direct investments in real estate typically is an area that best suits large institutional investors. These

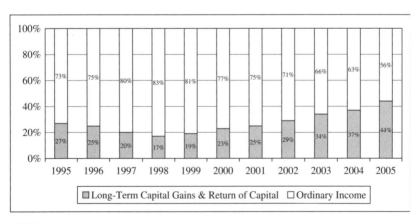

FIGURE 8.3 REIT Dividend Attribution
Source: NAREIT.

types of transactions include controlling real estate properties through the purchase of equity, providing a senior secured or direct mezzanine loan to the equity owner of a property, or the investment in and development of a new property. In any of these cases, but particularly in the case of controlling the equity in a property, the investor must have either substantial internal capabilities in evaluating and managing the properties or must utilize an operator for a fee to provide these services. An alternative approach to solving the need for expertise in property management and development, rather than using an outside service provider for a fee, is for an investor to purchase or create such a service provider as an ancillary investment in and conduit for its real estate investment activities. In the case of providing a direct loan, an investor also requires substantial legal assistance and the ability to analyze the credit quality of any property that is to be mortgaged. However, when providing a loan, after the initial investment, there is less ongoing management responsibility than is the case when the investor is in an equity ownership position.

The cash flow considerations for investors who invest in direct parcels of real estate are widely diverse depending on the seniority of the investment and the investment strategy employed. The degree of seniority of investment is characterized by whether the investor is providing a senior secured first mortgage, a second lien or mezzanine debt investment, a passive direct equity investment, or a control investment in the form of direct equity. Each of these routes has different patterns of cash outflows and inflows for the investor. For instance, the provider of first-lien mortgage debt to a real estate property likely will see a substantial initial cash outflow followed by fairly stable cash inflows in the form of income on its loan until the property is sold or refinanced. At the other end of the spectrum, an investor who is in control of a parcel through an equity investment is likely to see initial and perhaps even periodic cash outflows as the investment is purchased and maintained, which then should be followed by periodic income and a return of principal and capital gain at exit. In this regard, the cash flow characteristics of a direct equity investment in real estate are similar to private funds invested in real estate. However, a benefit from an exit cash flow perspective for investors using a direct investment approach in real estate is that the timing is up to the investor. In comparison, the finite life of a real estate private equity fund limits the flexibility of timing the exit of properties.

Currency, Commodity, and Hard-Asset Cash Flow

Alternative investments in currencies, commodities, and other types of hard assets have a wide range of open-end, separate account, and closed-end opportunities. Investment in currencies, commodities, and hard assets such as timber, oil- and gas-producing assets, and mining interests can be achieved through private equity partnerships, public equity, private debt, direct ownership, public debt, and public and private royalty interests. Similar to private equity, long-lockup open-end private partnerships exist for investment in oil and gas, timber, and mining interests. There is not a great number of short-lockup open-end private partnerships available to gain exposure to these hard assets. Meanwhile, closed-end exchange-traded index funds represent a major source of the hard-asset investable opportunity. Hard-asset investments are also available for direct investment on an individual property basis for larger, more sophisticated investors with capable staff and operating management. Currency investments are most often represented by short-lockup open-end funds and separate accounts, since the currency markets are among the most liquid in the world.

Producing Properties   By and large, investors seeking to allocate capital to commodities and hard assets accomplish this through long-lockup open-end private partnerships, unless the investor seeks greater liquidity or a more passive exposure, in which case the investment frequently is accomplished through a closed-end exchange-traded index fund. Typical examples of long-lockup open-end funds in this area are those invested in oil- and gas-producing properties, operating mines, or timber management. Each of these has similar traits to private equity investments in long-lockup open-end partnerships. The liquidity and cash flow perspectives of an investor in these funds is long-term acceptance of committed capital, but these partnerships tend to have more advantageous cash flow considerations than partnerships invested in private equity. Private equity partnerships invested in venture capital or even LBOs require periodic cash calls to support existing investments as well as new investments, as do partnerships invested in hard-asset-producing properties. However, private partnerships invested in hard-asset properties offer their investors much more in the way of regular interim period cash inflows. Net procedes from the sale of commodities that are produced by these properties are passed back to the limited partners during the life of these funds. This cash flow feature typically is less frequent for long-lockup open-end funds invested in private equity. The result of this characteristic is that investors in hard-asset-producing properties through these private funds are well able to gauge their overall cash flow.

Nevertheless, these investments also are defined by the strategies employed, not unlike the situation with real estate investments. Each type of hard-asset strategy has a distinct expected cash flow pattern. Commodity investments can be focused on different production stages, each one of which offers separate risk, return, and cash flow characteristics.

The various stages for these investments include the purchase and management of royalty interests, participation in net production profits, greenfield exploration, reworking of existing production properties, investment in operating companies versus producing properties, and downstream activities such as refining and distribution. For example, although the purchase of royalty interests has initial negative cash flow considerations for a limited partner in those funds, each of these investments is likely to immediately begin to generate a cash return passed back to the investor. This tends to be a very stable and predictable cash flow generator for the investor. In comparison, an investor in a wildcat oil well exploration operating company is in a cash flow situation akin to venture capital investing. In this instance, the investor expects to experience cash calls for each well being drilled, with an ultimate cash flow payoff on those investment that is very unpredictable.

Investors also may avail themselves of direct investment in producing properties and operating companies. The way in which an investor may accomplish this exposure is similar to the private equity environment. These investments typically are achieved through a direct investment in the equity or debt of these operating properties and companies, based on the knowledge and sophistication resident at the investor, or through a coinvestment alongside a private fund. The coinvestment route has the benefit of oversight by a private fund manager who has granted the investor coinvestment rights as a part of the terms for that investor's investment in the manager's fund. The cash flow considerations for these types of investments are the same as direct investment or coinvestment in private equity transactions. The investor has control over its interim-period cash outflows to these investments, but is subject to potential dilution in the event of abstaining from follow-on investments. Similarly, the asset-weighting and rebalancing-control benefits are the same as with direct investment and coinvestment in private equity transactions.

Closed-End Indexes   As it relates to commodities, indexes represent a simple form of closed-end fund. These index products are unique among alternative investments, in that they truly are representative of the global opportunity set for the asset. Although indexes exist for hedge funds, they do not capture the hedge fund industry in its entirety. Hedge fund indexes are prone to their underlying manager-specific characteristics. In contrast, broad exposure to an asset class is accomplished in commodities indexes. They represent a central way for investors to accomplish exposure to this asset class. Examples include the Dow Jones–AIG Commodity Index and the Goldman Sachs Commodity Index. These indexes are closed-end funds that provide investors with good market liquidity through index linked products. As a result, cash flow estimation for entering, maintaining, and exiting these investments is very straightforward. Therefore, the ability to manage and reweight allocations to commodities through these indexes is fairly simple. The one drawback for investors in these vehicles is the limited ability to customize exposures to individual commodities. Nevertheless, specific commodities index allocations also have been developed in the marketplace, but they offer less liquidity than some of the broader diversified commodities index products.

Royalty Trusts   Another closed-end fund avenue for investment in hard-asset-producing properties is through royalty trusts. These instruments are similar in nature to REITs. They convey the economic benefits and cash flow from underlying investments to limited partners. There are a number of publicly traded royalty trusts that contain oil, gas, mining, and timber properties. However, there are fewer open-end funds that specialize in the management of portfolios of these investments than is the case with the fairly large number of fund managers that specialize in REITs. In any event, investment in these public royalty trust interests represents a steady and predictable cash flow stream for investors in hard-asset-oriented production properties.

Currency Open-End Accounts   The vast majority of investment in currency as a distinct strategy is accomplished through open-end accounts managed by professional fund managers. The goal of a currency allocation can be different from one investor to another. Investors can use currency as a direct source of returns or as an overlay to eliminate currency exposure in certain other assets. The structure of open-end currency accounts can include funds that provide daily liquidity, separate accounts, and hedge funds that offer restricted redemption periods. The instruments used in these vehicles include futures, forwards, and over-the-counter swaps. In all of these cases, the initial cash flow considerations are predictable, as is the end-period certainty of liquidity and cash flow. An area of potential uncertainty is the daily mark-to-market gains and losses in the futures markets that require the posting of collateral. This consideration would not directly apply to an investor who was invested in a commingled fund. In a separate account, the initial allocation of capital to futures contracts and related collateral typically creates ample liquidity for meeting mark-to-market gains and losses on positions. Nevertheless, circumstances can develop where additional collateral is required in separate accounts invested in currencies, which poses a cash outflow for an investor that may be unexpected.

Cash Flow and Maintenance of Collateral for Futures and Swaps   Certain alternative investments allow for the execution of futures contracts and over-the-counter (OTC) swaps. These instruments are used to achieve hedge fund positions and commodities and currencies exposures. Although their use in a commingled fund or closed-end fund should not have an effect on an investor's cash flows, their use in a separate account may have cash flow ramifications. The existence of the OTC swap market for currencies and commodities is enormous and alongside the futures market is the central avenue for investment in credit, currencies, and commodities rather than the cash market. Depending on their guidelines, some managers of separate accounts that are focused on credit, currencies, and commodities actively utilize futures and swaps. The notional leverage inherent in these instruments can lead to uncertain cash outflows for an investor in a separate account. In the event that large losses are posted on these securities, an investor would be required to post additional collateral to the separate account. Although investors are able to directly enter into these derivatives instruments, most are better suited toward investing in these exposures through commingled funds or managed accounts. Exceptions to this rule of thumb are sophisticated investors with depth of staff to execute tactical bets on traditional asset classes, credit, currencies, and commodities. Indeed, a central way for some of the more complex organizations to rebalance asset-class exposures is through futures and swap contracts executed on a daily basis.

Cash Flow at the Initial Commitment to an Alternative Investment

Executing a portfolio investment by an alternative investment fund is done at the timing preference of the investment manager, rather than that of the investor. This idiosyncrasy provides the crux of the problem in maintaining strategic portfolio allocations to these assets. Whether it is an investment made by a hedge fund or a private fund invested in venture capital, real estate, or LBOs, the timing of investments made to these assets is irregular. Although committed capital may take an uncertain period of time to be deployed by the investment manager, the basic asset allocation framework is an aspect that the investor can command. However, investors also are able to make certain tactical decisions pertaining to the cash flow timing of new investments. For instance, certain hedge funds that are desirable to investors are considered soft closed to new capital. Occasionally, these funds will open on short notice to new investors. Investors who have completed their due diligence on these managers are prepared to make an investment and can be nimble in doing so. In the case of private equity investments, the access windows also are infrequent. Disregarding secondary purchases of private equity interests, the availability of most private equity investments is entirely based on the timing of the general partners' formation of new funds. Investors in these funds must wait for the creation of new funds that are sponsored by investment managers they find appealing. Alternatively, some investors make the mistake of forcing an allocation to an alternative asset group using a time schedule that suits them rather than having patience to wait for an opening with investment managers that are deemed attractive.

Cash Flow during the Life of an Alternative Investment

Capital calls and the return of capital and profits during the life of most private partnerships are fairly unpredictable in their timing. Indeed, this phase may require a great deal of attention from a cash flow management perspective. Interim-period cash flow considerations differ from one type of investment to another. For example, there are very different cash flow considerations for hedge funds in general compared with other private investment funds investing in venture capital, LBOs, and real estate. For hedge funds, interim-period cash flow considerations during the life of the investor's investment in a fund are less relevant, because of their generally shorter lockups than private equity and real estate funds. Nevertheless, even hedge funds have initial lockups, quarterly redemption periods, and the ability to impose gates that limit redemptions. Furthermore, hedge funds have nonstandard cash flow considerations such as unilateral return of capital to the investor by the hedge fund in the event that the manager sees limited investment opportunities. Generally, however, hedge funds retain the profits and losses in their funds for reinvestment in the fund, whereas private equity funds effectively distribute invested capital and related profits and losses back to the limited partners.

Cash Flow at the Conclusion of an Alternative Investment

Once most of the cash flows have occurred during the interim periods for alternative investments, final capital calls to and distributions from private partnerships can be fairly anticlimactic. In the private equity and real estate worlds, these late-stage cash flows can range from fairly transparent distributions to administrative nuisances. These events happen quite late in the life of private funds, and they typically represent final augmentation to investments in portfolio companies and the liquidation of remaining interests in investments. Final liquidations range from the sale or distribution to limited partners of public equity interests in successful investments to the distribution of proceeds from the sale of relatively unsuccessful investments that simply require liquidation. In terms of hedge funds, the final liquidation of these investments typically relates either to holdbacks or the sale of illiquid investments contained in side pockets. The payment of holdbacks normally is related to concluding administrative and audit work on the funds, while side-pocket liquidations can be more difficult. However, both events require cash flow planning on the part of the investor. Anticipating these types of end-of-fund cash flow distributions is a worthwhile endeavor, because they can occur with less expedience than most investors expect.

ASSET ALLOCATION: ACHIEVING POLICY TARGETS AND REBALANCING

The proper management and forecasting of alternative investment cash flows enable investors to achieve policy targets and accomplish periodic asset rebalancing. Moreover, improper cash flow management for these investors can lead to under- and overallocations to alternative assets, which can compromise expected return and volatility goals that have been set for these assets. An example of a problem that can develop from this miscue is the cannibalization of liquid hedge fund investments in order to fund private equity capital calls, because of the underestimation of the speed of private equity capital calls relative to committed capital. Another illustration is a real estate or hard-asset program that overestimates a return of capital from the private funds, such that investments in subsequent vintage years are missed in order to not become overcommitted to the asset group.

Cash flows associated with alternative investments can be irregular and can depend on the type of investment under consideration. A critical issue pertaining to the need for cash flow forecasting for private fund investing is the fundamentally unpredictable cash flows associated with these investments. This can be said in varying degrees for private partnerships invested in private equity, real estate, oil and gas, commodities, and timber. The common issue is the ability of the investor to identify the likely cash inflows and outflows associated with the underlying investments in partnerships. Capital calls may be made by the investment manager in a somewhat unpredictable fashion. Likewise, the return of capital and associated profits or losses also may be made with irregular timing.

Overcommitment to Private Funds

The risk for an investor is that predetermined allocations for alternative investments become over- or underallotted, because of the unpredictable nature of the associated cash flows during the life of private partnerships. During certain market environments, these partnerships may find many attractive investment opportunities in a coincidental fashion. In this case, the investor could become overallocated to certain alternative investment categories. The sensitivity to this risk lies in the fact that most investors overallocate in terms of their commitments to private equity–type investments, with the knowledge that the only way to become fully invested to target allocations is to nominally overallocate to them. That is to say, most investors commit capital to private fund investments in an amount that is materially greater than their intended investment, with the knowledge that the cash calls from the partnerships will be slow and will be somewhat offset by the return of capital and profits from the partnerships. A quandary arises in two instances: When cash calls are accelerated due to attractive market situations, the investor will become overinvested in the asset area; and when the return of invested capital and profits occurs more rapidly than expected, the investor will become underinvested in the strategy.

Admittedly, an investor must overcommit to private fund alternative investment, in order to achieve the desired level of invested asset exposure at any point in time. When considering how much to commit to these investments in order to accomplish a constant invested level, there are variables that must be considered that enable an investor to evaluate the expected future cash flows for such a program. Important variables include the type of underlying investments, the vintage year of the private funds, and the quality of the investment managers. At the outset, the type of illiquid assets held in each private fund will set the tone for initial characteristics of expected speed and direction of net cash flows. For example, capital calls by a general partner will have very different characteristics for a real estate fund, which may be making a series of more sizable one-time investments, compared with a venture capital fund, which may be making many small initial and supporting investments in its portfolio companies. An additional plane of consideration is vintage year. Each vintage year will have its own capital market and macroeconomic cycles that will dictate a sizable portion of the velocity of capital calls and return of capital over the life of a partnership. Furthermore, the caliber of the fund management firm will determine many cash flow elements for the investor. Depending on whether the investment manager is in the first, second, third, or fourth quartile of performance among its peers, this will have enormous impact on the NAVs and cash flows associated with the partnership.

Approaches to Managing and Rebalancing Private Fund Allocations

An investor's current allocation to a private fund sector equals the sum of the NAVs of the partnerships at the end of the year. It is this number against which an investor is measured in terms of matching policy targets for an alternative investment sector. NAVs represent the net result of capital calls, capital distributions, and portfolio gains and losses. In this mix of asset valuations and cash flows, an investor can control very little, except for the level of commitments it makes on an annual basis. Meanwhile, the investor must attempt to make estimates of the velocity of capital calls, the return of capital, and the net change in NAVs (the write-up and write-down of investments on an interim basis). The following are various methods used by investors in an effort to estimate the amount of new commitments that they should make to private funds.

Rule of Thumb   One approach to balancing capital allocations to alternative investments (such as private partnerships invested in venture capital, LBOs, real estate, and commodities) is simply a rule-of-thumb approach.[2] This naïve approach suggests that capital committed to a private partnership will experience a capital call rate that is unknown. Therefore, new commitments should be proportionally equal and made on a regular basis. For example, commitments should be a fixed percentage of the total desired allocation and should be made every year or every two years. Although this is not a bad approach in the absence of any substantive information, it is vulnerable to veering off course depending on the actual capital call and distribution rates that are experienced. The rule-of-thumb concept places the investor in the position of being on autopilot when making private partnership commitments. If the rate of capital calls is accelerated or retarded over a sustained period of time, this strategy could create a very unbalanced situation. The investor might find itself in an over- or underallocated position, with no good solution or system for repairing the position. Such a state of affairs could lead to a scrapping of the program because of an inability to properly calibrate the rate of commitments in order to maintain a desired invested position over time.

Ratio of Commitment to Policy Target   Another approach is to focus on capital commitments rather than current invested allocations.[3] In this application, an investor places primary importance on the total amount of its capital commitment, rather than the actual capital invested in various private funds. For example, this approach derives a required capital commitment at any point in time equal to $1.70 for every $1 of desired exposure. For this approach, a monitoring tool is the ratio of committed capital to the policy target. To facilitate this approach, a longer-term time frame is applied to policy targets for the alternative investments. However, this may ignore the possibility of overinvesting in an alternative investment area. Furthermore, if mistakes are made in allocations, they are likely to be larger mistakes than using the rule-of-thumb approach. This approach makes new allocations based on a large ratio at any point in time, rather than focusing on the outlook for actual investments.

Historical Averages   A third approach is one used by Yale University's endowment.[4] In this approach, there is an assumption that the amount of capital in play, or actively called by funds, will average a certain amount over time (e.g., 50 percent of committed capital called in the first two years of commitment). These assumptions are based on actual historical rates of capital utilization versus capital commitments. Furthermore, Yale focuses on the projection of cash flow from each individual fund in which it invests, then rolls these projections into an overall cash flow projection for its illiquid allocations in total. The premise for this strategy is that there is no way to predict all investment environments for each alternative investment (e.g., venture capital, oil and gas properties, and opportunistic real estate).

Short-Term Predictions   Finally, another approach to balancing commitments to private funds with the actual net investment in any one period is through short-term predictions. In most environments, cash flows into and out of private investment funds are fairly predictable when estimated over very short time periods. When they are not predictable, it tends to be during market or economic sea changes. For instance, during market bubbles, it is difficult to maintain invested allocations to certain alternative investments, because capital distributions increase in speed and size. Bubbles also are points in time when investment managers launch many new funds to quench strong demand, sometimes by investors seeking to maintain their allocations. Often, this is precisely the wrong time to add more capital to these partnerships, since they may prove to be poor-performing vintage years.

Another example is during burst bubble periods. In this environment, it is difficult to gauge the length of time required for a recovery in distributions. Furthermore, capital calls also tend to decline. This environment leads to a lack of new funds and in some cases a unilateral reduction in commitments previously accepted by investment managers. An investor's inability to find new fund opportunities in which to invest causes an incapability to keep a constant exposure to committed capital in certain alternative investment categories. In turn, this can lead to negative selection bias. With fewer funds to select, the quality of funds selected may decline as the investor strives to make commitments. Allocations made to funds during these periods may represent sound policy from a strategic portfolio allocation perspective, but may be fairly unwise from a tactical fund selection perspective. An investor's strenuous effort to maintain its allocation to an asset class may lead to selecting active managers who generate negative alpha. Rather than investing in lower-quartile funds simply to fill an allocation to an alternative asset class, it would be a wiser course of action to use a passive approach to the asset class during periods of disequilibrium. This leads to considering passive proxies for alternative investments (see Chapter 11). For example, if factor betas can be used as proxies during disequilibrium, it removes the risk of locking in potential negative alpha from a subpar investment manager. Once the market crisis has passed, the passive proxies could be unwound, and high-quality investment managers with the promise for delivering positive alpha could be selected.

A flaw in portfolio construction using alternative investments is the emphasis on asset allocation rather than manager selection. An investor may be successful in maintaining a strategic asset allocation to an illiquid alternative class, but generate losses equal to or worse than the median experience of managers in the group by doing so. The nuance in alternative investing is that a significant proportion of performance is dictated by manager selection. Therefore, energy focused on maintaining asset allocations may be misplaced. Following this path, an investor might become undercommitted to certain alternative investments relative to its policy allocations. Nevertheless, this should be considered in the context of staying within broad bands for any specific policy allocation. These bands can be proportionately wider for alternative investments than for traditional investments because of their less liquid nature.

CASH FLOW FORECASTING TOOLS

In an effort to describe the basic cash flow framework for alternative investment funds, Table 8.1 illustrates typical cash calls, cash distributions, and net asset values of private funds. Although each of these flows will be quite different in actual timing for a specific private partnership in a particular investment strategy, this illustration is simply to give a stylized view of the metrics. The table shows the likely cash calls for some types of private funds with the pronounced affect of cash calls very early in the life of the funds. This particular example is more indicative of the pattern seen in LBO funds or perhaps real estate funds rather than venture capital funds. Table 8.1 also depicts the return of capital, which might include marketable securities. The return of capital that occurs over time assumes that the funds in fact experience positive outcomes. It is these two streams of negative and positive cash flows that represent one area of required analysis and forecasting for an investor, in order to have the required liquidity to meet cash calls and to have uses for returned capital when these payments occur. Meanwhile, the third component that affects the ongoing invested allocation

TABLE 8.1 Illustration Depicting Private Equity Committed Capital, Cash Flows, and Asset Allocation

Year	0	1	2	3	4	5	6	7	8	9	10	11	12	13	14	15
Capital Commitment Fund 1	100	—	—	—	—	—	—	—	—	—	—	—	—	—	—	—
Capital Commitment Fund 2	—	—	—	100	—	—	—	—	—	—	—	—	—	—	—	—
Capital Commitment Fund 3	—	—	—	—	—	—	100	—	—	—	—	—	—	—	—	—
Capital Commitment Fund 4	—	—	—	—	—	—	—	—	—	100	—	—	—	—	—	—
Capital Commitment Fund 5	—	—	—	—	—	—	—	—	—	—	—	—	100	—	—	—
Capital Commitment Fund 6	—	—	—	—	—	—	—	—	—	—	—	—	—	—	—	100
Outstanding Committed Capital	100	80	50	120	90	57	125	93	59	126	93	59	126	93	59	126
Capital Call Fund 1	—	20	30	30	10	3	2	2	1	1	1	0	0	—	—	—
Capital Call Fund 2	—	—	—	—	20	30	30	10	3	2	2	1	1	1	0	0
Capital Call Fund 3	—	—	—	—	—	—	—	20	30	30	10	3	2	2	1	1
Capital Call Fund 4	—	—	—	—	—	—	—	—	—	—	20	30	30	10	3	2
Capital Call Fund 5	—	—	—	—	—	—	—	—	—	—	—	—	—	20	30	30
Capital Call Fund 6	—	—	—	—	—	—	—	—	—	—	—	—	—	—	—	—
Total Capital Calls	—	20	30	30	30	33	32	32	34	33	33	34	33	33	34	33
Distributions Fund 1	—	—	—	5	5	20	20	25	30	30	35	10	1	—	—	—
Distributions Fund 2	—	—	—	—	—	—	5	5	20	20	25	30	30	35	10	1
Distributions Fund 3	—	—	—	—	—	—	—	—	—	5	5	20	20	25	30	30

Distributions Fund 4	—	—	—	—	—	—	—	—	—	—	—	—	—	5	20	25
Distributions Fund 5	—	—	—	—	—	—	—	—	—	—	—	—	—	—	—	—
Distributions Fund 6	—	—	—	—	—	—	—	—	—	—	—	—	—	—	—	—
Total Distributions	—	—	—	—	5	20	25	30	50	55	65	60	56	65	60	56
NAV Fund 1	0	20	50	78	98	101	98	84	64	41	11	1	0	—	—	—
NAV Fund 2	—	—	—	—	20	50	78	98	101	98	84	64	41	11	1	0
NAV Fund 3	—	—	—	—	—	—	—	20	50	78	98	101	98	84	64	41
NAV Fund 4	—	—	—	—	—	—	—	—	—	—	20	50	78	98	101	98
NAV Fund 5	—	—	—	—	—	—	—	—	—	—	—	—	—	20	50	78
NAV Fund 6	—	—	—	—	—	—	—	—	—	—	—	—	—	—	—	—
Total Allocation (a)	—	20	50	78	118	151	175	202	215	216	214	216	216	214	216	216
Overcommitment (b)	NM	5.0	2.0	2.5	1.8	1.4	1.7	1.5	1.3	1.6	1.4	1.3	1.6	1.4	1.3	1.6
Net Cash Flow	—	(20)	(30)	(25)	(25)	(13)	(7)	(2)	16	22	32	26	23	32	26	23

Note: Illustration is net of fees. Figures are rounded. Figures in $ millions.

(a) Represents the carrying value of the actual asset class exposure at the end of the period, which is net of all cash flows.

(b) Equals (Outstanding Capital Commitment + Total Allocation)/Total Allocation. This represents the implied overcommitment of capital that is required to achieve a desired asset allocation to private equity in this example.

NAV, net asset value; NM, not meaningful.

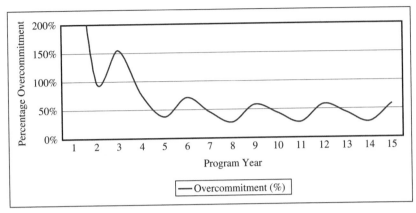

FIGURE 8.4 Sample Private Equity Overcommitment as a Percentage of Invested Capital

to the asset and must be estimated by the investor is the valuation of the net asset values for the private funds. The movement in NAV is positively affected by capital calls, negatively affected by the return of capital to investors, and both positively and negatively affected by the write-up or write-down of investments that remain in the portfolio managed by the investment manager or general partner.

Based on these three inputs along with an assumption for committed capital, Table 8.1 provides a framework for measuring the total allocation to the asset, the amount of overcommitment required, and the net cash flow from the private funds. At any point in time, this table can be used to compare the invested exposure to a private fund asset versus the target allocation from a policy perspective. A key element in using a cash flow tool such as this is to perform new estimates of the inputs on a regular basis. Frequency of estimation should provide for a more realistic outlook for net cash flows and their likely near-term impact on the total allocation to the asset. Figure 8.4 depicts a stylized progression of the overcommitment to private funds that is required in order to maintain target allocations.

PORTFOLIO REBALANCING TOOLS

Rebalancing allocations to alternative investments and forecasting cash flows into and out of these investments are inexorably intertwined. However, most cash flow models for managing alternative investments have flaws over long periods of time, because of the unpredictable nature of investment opportunities and exit windows for the portfolio companies contained in these partnerships. The farther into the future that cash flow models attempt to forecast, the less likely they will be accurate. Alternatively, the shorter the period of time used to predict the likely capital calls and return of capital, the more accurate predictions tend to be. The answer to the problem of inaccuracy of cash flow models over long time frames is to recalibrate cash flow models annually or as often as new relevant information is available. However, there is a mismatch between using a short-term approach to cash flow forecasting for rebalancing and its ability to be executed, because of the nature of the private partnership structures for many of the alternative investments.

A noticeable problem in meeting and maintaining portfolio allocations to alternative investments is the arduously slow process that is required to subscribe to funds, redeem from funds, and contend with the natural life cycle of these investments. In an effort to seek a substitute to this unattractive option for rebalancing, it is in an investor's best interest to consider the question from a slightly different vantage point. What is the true goal for rebalancing? For most investors, rebalancing is undertaken in order to meet a predetermined asset allocation based on forward-looking views for return, risk, and correlation for a series of assets, based on an optimization technique. However, if the asset allocation is based on forward-looking views for a series of passive factor betas that comprise alternative investments, then the rebalancing process is not held captive to the legal structure that happens to house the alternative investments that require rebalancing. Thought of in this vein, the investor is freed to use a number of other investments that perhaps are more liquid but still accomplish a change in exposures.

Consequently, from a practical perspective, the application of methods to affect short-term rebalancing of various alternative investment allocations may be through proxies. Proxies are investable passive assets that replicate a high degree of the return and risk characteristics of the asset class or strategy being emulated. The use of proxies, or synthetic beta replicators through futures and derivatives, are available to tactically rebalance or adjust allocations within strategic policy targets (see Chapter 11).

For example, a desire to rebalance an allocation to venture capital may be accomplished through a surrogate to the Russell 2000. Moreover, these exposures can be positive or negative in direction. For instance, a desire to increase a venture exposure could be accomplished through a purchase of a Russell 2000 index fund, and a desire to reduce the exposure to venture capital could be accomplished through a short sale of an exchange-traded fund (ETF) that replicates the Russell 2000. Not only is this approach more convenient, but it also in some cases could be achieved through the use of futures contracts, and therefore require less in the way of utilized capital.

Another approach to rebalancing alternative investments is through the secondary market. The purchase or sale of private partnership interests that contain alternative investments is one solution to maintaining policy targets. However, a negative aspect for sellers in doing so is the discount that often is paid in this market. Although the discount for the purchase of a secondary interest can benefit an investor who is seeking to increase a portfolio allocation, a discount would be a detriment for an investor seeking to reduce an allocation through the sale of a private partnership interest.

The Risk/Benefit of Forgone Alpha through the Use of Proxies

A disadvantage to using beta proxies is the piece of alpha that is missing from not using active management. In other words, if rebalancing is accomplished through the use of a proxy, the investor would not have invested in a private alternative investment fund. The beta replication is accomplished through a passive proxy that has no active alpha component. However, this is a two-edged sword. Although alpha is being left out of the rebalancing, the alternative choice might have been to select an active fund that was not among the top quartile group, simply because it was open for investment and therefore met the investor's liquidity needs. The outcome from this path might actually have been negative alpha, in which case the net return would decline. In this instance, having selected a surrogate with passive beta would have been the better choice.

For example, if

$$R(\text{Active}) = \alpha + \beta x$$

where

$R(\text{Active}) =$ the return on an actively managed investment
$\alpha =$ alpha
$\beta =$ beta
$x =$ the independent factor in a one factor model

and

$\alpha = -0.5$
$x = +0.05$
$\beta = +0.7$

then

$$R(\text{Active}) = -0.5 + (.7 * .05) = -0.5 + 0.035 = -0.465$$

This would compare with a passive return of

$$R(\text{Passive}) = \beta x$$

where

> $R(\text{Passive})$ = the return on a passively managed investment
> β = beta
> x = the independent factor in a one factor model

and

> $x = +0.05$
> $\beta = +0.7$

so

$$R(\text{Passive}) = .7 * .05 = 0.035$$

SUMMARY

The ability to forecast cash flows pertaining to alternative investments is a key to achieving and rebalancing these allocations. In order to manage the generally illiquid nature of these funds, an investor must be in a position to adequately forecast required cash outflows to these investments and cash inflows as well. The importance of this forecasting is to be able to adjust capital commitments and maintain policy targets within range-bound strategic allocations. Accordingly, various models are available to enable cash flow forecasting. In addition to successful cash flow forecasting, liquidity can be generated through the use of proxies that replicate alternative investments. Although these surrogates are imperfect matches, they represent adequate temporary solutions during periods of low natural liquidity available for the investments. In spite of the ability to make adjustments using proxies, investors using alternative investments should implement a framework for cash flow management of these assets. This type of tool should ensure that appropriate portfolio allocations are met. More importantly, such a framework protects against an unexpected overweighting to these investments. An effective use of cash flow modeling and investment proxies also assists in the avoidance of becoming unbalanced through the cannibalization of one alternative investment, because of its available liquidity, in order to feed the cash flow needs of another alternative investment.

CHAPTER 9

Leverage and Portable Alpha

everage can exacerbate the volatility of returns for alternative investments. Leverage typically is associated with risk, since it can enhance either the return or loss on equity invested in any asset. For some alternative investments, such as real estate or leveraged buyouts (LBOs), the higher ratio of leverage in a transaction equates to higher potential volatility of returns on invested equity. However, as it pertains to other alternative investments, leverage represents a structural component of the strategy. For instance, market-neutral equity hedge funds are leveraged through their short sale of stock. They have borrowed and sold stock in order to achieve a short position that is hedged with an offsetting long position in another security. In this regard, leverage does not directly relate to the classical concept of risk. There are other examples of leverage that affect alternative investments, such as notional leverage through the use of derivatives, portable alpha strategies, and structural leverage in an organizational sense. Each of these instances of leverage holds different opportunities and risks for investors. Leverage also must be considered carefully in regard to its effect on clouding the true sources of returns for alternative investments. The returns that an investor experiences may be more attributable to leverage than to either discrete sources of alpha or factor betas. Furthermore, the ability for alternative investment managers to post highly unexpected and very negative results typically is tied to one form or another of leverage. Another issue regarding leverage pertains to data analysis. It is difficult to separate the degree to which index returns for alternative investments are proportioned between leveraged and unleveraged sources. Therefore, an explicit understanding of the leverage used in an alternative investment and its perceived versus real risks must be determined by an investor.

LEVERAGE

Leverage per se is not a pure determinant of return and volatility. Rather, it is an accelerant or an amplifier of return factors with which it is used. Leverage magnifies volatility and returns, whether they are positive or negative. The key in evaluating leverage when considering an array of alternative investments is to neutralize it. In other words, in conducting a fair comparison of funds or investments, one must attempt where possible to eliminate the use of leverage for a proper "apples to apples" comparison. The use of leverage in generating returns is not necessarily a negative attribute. Leverage is only a part of an investment's return profile that is required to be understood. Once the existence of leverage is identified, a separate determination can be made as to whether the degree of leverage used in any investment is excessive, appropriate, or underutilized. This determination establishes the theoretical tipping point at which too much leverage can destabilize an investment strategy. Leverage that varies from an optimal level can have a negative influence from its overuse or pose an opportunity cost from its underuse.

One question for investors to resolve includes the following: when considering two potential investments with identical factor sensitivities but where one uses leverage and is likely to generate a superior return (although with higher probabilistic volatility and possibly the same expected Sharpe ratio as the investment that has less leverage), which of the two investments, all other things being equal, is superior? For example, a hedge fund manager that possesses a low-volatility strategy may have a parallel product to this that applies twice the leverage. In this instance, one might presume that the superior investment is the leveraged one, because of its higher return expectation in spite of its proportionally higher expected volatility. However, this assumes that the volatility of the higher-leveraged product preserves its proportionality *under all circumstances*. Often, this presumption may be faulty. This is the essence of risk associated with kurtosis. In the example of the identical hedge fund strategy that has a high- and low-leveraged version, the highly leveraged product has a higher likelihood of extreme results than is the case for the lower-leveraged version. Nevertheless, if an investor can tolerate the potential incremental volatility of returns that the higher leverage implies, perhaps this is a suitable choice. For instance, such a leveraged product could be used within the context of a diversified portfolio of alternative investments that through its diversification mutes the volatility of any one single investment. However, there is a risk that the higher-leveraged investment has risk beyond its idiosyncratic risk. Market illiquidity may provide increased overall risk for a leveraged fund under certain crisis scenarios.

Once an alternative investment is considered relative to the predictability of its volatility inclusive of different degrees of leverage, an investor is better able to identify the appropriateness of the investment. There is not a single variable relationship between leverage and the incremental returns and volatility of returns that it produces, because other variables must be considered as well. Key among the other variables that influence the impact that leverage has on returns and volatility are illiquidity and directionality.[1]

Leverage and Directionality

Leverage is difficult to define in risk terms unless the structure of the alternative investment is understood. The degree of directionality of an investment informs this structure. Although the total gross leverage that supports an investment may be sizable relative to the equity invested in the transaction, some alternative investments are hedged. For example, a fixed-income arbitrage hedge fund may utilize 5 or 10 times gross leverage, but it may have largely offsetting long and short positions. The net directional exposure in this regard may be considered quite small. Generally speaking, gross leverage equates to the value of all long plus short positions divided by the equity invested in all the positions, while net leverage equates to the value of all long positions minus the value of all short positions divided by the equity invested in all positions. Under a hedged circumstance such as that expressed by low net leverage, the potential for loss and gain from volatility will be somewhat muted, regardless of the amount of gross leverage employed. Although this concept of low net exposure can break down for security-specific reasons, this portfolio construction tends not to be as risky as the associated high gross leverage might indicate. Unlike the combination of illiquidity and leverage, which can produce severe outcomes during high market volatility, alternative investments that are directionally neutral tend to exhibit less volatility in these environments. These investments benefit on one side of their portfolios (e.g., short) as much as they are hurt on the other side (e.g., long). The offsetting positions tend to neutralize market shocks, and the long-term returns from these neutral strategies depend more on the specific characteristics of underlying securities.

Leverage and Illiquidity

Liquidity, which is discussed in more detail in Chapter 10, can be highly unpredictable. Although an investor may be able to measure the amount of expected return that is attributable to the illiquid feature of an investment, liquidity can materially change for an investment based on the fickle nature of market participants. For instance, a crisis in which all participants back away from a market is a form of severe systemic illiquidity. The assumption that a hedge fund, for example, can repay loans that underlie its investments is based on the investments having a liquid market. When this liquidity presumption changes, investments that are supported by leverage experience pronounced volatility. This situation often is further exacerbated by the fact that falling securities' prices and illiquid markets are situations in which lenders become most unlikely to continue to commit leverage in support of an investment. Although this bleak scenario is associated with negative returns, the same combination of factors can occur with positive return outcomes. An example of this alternative environment is when liquidity is restricted because willing sellers back away from a market, in which case investments that are enhanced by leverage can experience sharp volatility with positive price movement. The essential issue that pertains to leverage and illiquidity is uncertainty. The reliability of liquidity has a material influence on the outcome of leveraged investments. The inability to predict a change in liquidity under all scenarios impairs an investor's ability to accurately gauge leverage as a source of risk. High historical liquidity can lead to the increased use of leverage, under the assumption that liquidity is constant and not variable. Therefore, the careful evaluation of liquidity must accompany any use of leverage in alternative investments.

Cash Leverage

Leverage can assume several forms. It can be represented as cash leverage or notional leverage, or it can relate to the structural way in which an investment is assembled. The most common sort of leverage is the obvious form of cash leverage. Borrowed funds are the primary source of leverage used in many alternative investments. For example, LBOs, convertible bond arbitrage, and leveraged real estate all require cash-producing debt. These examples cannot easily construct their strategies through notional leverage created from derivative securities. As a result, relationships with lenders can be a key consideration for alternative investment managers. In the realm of public securities, cash-producing leverage can be achieved through prime brokerage relationships and sometimes through the attainment of revolving credit agreements and term loans with commercial banks. In the example of LBOs or real estate, cash often is generated through loans from banks and insurance companies or the public sale of bonds in the corporate, mortgage, and private placement markets.

Debt typically is secured by the assets that relate to an investment, such as buildings, securities, and commodities. The amount of leverage that a lender extends to a manager of alternative investments is a function of the creditworthiness of the collateral, its cash flow characteristics, and the implied volatility of the assets that are being used as collateral. For example, a lender might be cautious about providing capital for a loan that is collateralized with more volatile investments such as publicly traded equities that are directional in nature. In comparison, a prime broker might allow much higher leverage to an investment manager engaged in equity pairs trading in large-capitalization equities, because of the hedged and low-volatility profile of this strategy. Nevertheless, an important aspect of leverage when it is secured by liquid securities is the control that a lender can exert. In a situation of price declines and an impairment of equity, lenders with liquid securities as collateral are able to unilaterally sell them over very short time periods.

Notional Leverage

Notional leverage often is created through the use of derivative securities, such as options and swaps. These securities in essence reflect their time value until expiration and the price change but not the principal value of the securities from which they are derived. Notional leverage is an entirely different form of investment enhancement than cash leverage. While cash leverage enables the purchase of a greater amount of an investment, notional leverage represents the embedded price multiplier for an underlying security. As such, notional leverage can be associated with potentially greater volatility than cash leverage. Notional leverage also may not be as readily apparent as cash leverage. The identification of notional leverage during an examination of a portfolio of securities requires knowledge of potentially exotic derivative securities. Furthermore, some derivative securities are custom designed between two counterparties and traded over the counter, rather than on transparent and liquid markets. The illiquid nature of some bespoke securities further highlights their potential volatility. The practice of estimating prices for some illiquid derivatives, in the absence of real market prices, also can be a source of concern.

The importance of considering notional leverage when evaluating an alternative investment is twofold. First, the sole consideration of cash leverage ignores the potentially more potent form of notional leverage. The market value of certain notionally leveraged securities often belies their embedded potential for volatility. Notional leverage is particularly important to measure when comparing investments with similar factor exposures. An example of this is a hedge fund trading volatile oil price futures contracts compared with a private equity fund investing in fairly stable oil and gas production properties. Second, the use of notional leverage can exacerbate the potential volatility of an investment, particularly in an environment with reduced liquidity. An example of this is an unhedged short position in equity puts during a market crisis.

Structural Leverage

Structural leverage may be viewed in two planes. The first is the use of leverage as a fundamental component of a type of investment. The second is the use of leverage in a synergistic sense. In the first case, leverage is used as a structural component in a number of alternative investment strategies that cannot be conducted without leverage. An example of this is LBO investing, which uses leverage as a part of its foundation. An important ability for LBOs to generate returns for their equity investors is the use of cash leverage. Another example of structural leverage is a hedge fund that uses futures contracts on bonds, currencies, or commodities. Futures contracts require collateral, because they have notional leverage. This is a structural aspect of futures that mandates a form of collateralized lending. The collateral in this instance is used to support the frequent mark-to-market pricing for futures contracts. There are few alternatives to owning these securities other than to do so in this way. Although a swap contract can accomplish the same economic exposure as a futures contract, even these instruments require posting collateral during interim periods prior to their expiration date.

The second concept of leverage in a structural meaning is the benefit that may be derived from making an investment in an area where there are synergies to be gained from preexisting investments, relationships, or knowledge. Examples of this type of structural leverage include an investor who has identified a new product trend and made multiple fundamental investments on the basis of this research or a timber investor who has preexisting regulatory relationships in a certain region that might enable the investor to act more quickly in bidding for timberland in the area. The lessons learned in making previous investments can be leveraged for greater impact on future investments. As is the case with cash or notional leverage, if the research or edge that lead to these investments is correct or erroneous, the volatility from this type of leverage can produce outsized gains or losses, respectively.

One might question whether synergistic leverage is really leverage or borrowing in the true sense of the notion. The concept here is that clearly the investor would be borrowing from his prior experiences in launching a new investment. The success of new investments is dependent on the correctness or success of the prior work done by the investor. This prior work could be an industry perspective, a computer model pertaining to volatility trading, or analysis of a regulatory scheme. Not only is the investor borrowing from his prior work, and therefore perhaps making the investment more quickly than the competition, but he is leveraging the foundation of his prior experiences. In this sense, the investments are correlated and have high betas to the particular decision factor on which they were made. This leverage has many of the same connotations as the broader definition of cash or notional leverage. The benefit is that if the investor is correct in the work that has been done, the reward will be multiplied. However, if the analysis or relationships on which the investment niche has been based are faulty, then there could be a cascading negative impact on investment performance. Synergistic leverage might also be seen as an opaque correlation risk that may not be readily identified in a normal evaluation of correlations by industry sectors, strategies, or securities types. Another remote but possible risk for synergistic leverage relates to an investor who has been effective over a long period of time at consolidating a grip on a certain niche, such that the commanding position attracts the attention of regulators. This type of critical mass might have a tipping point that leads to implosion rather than dominance. Tipping points could be represented by outsized profits or the development of a monopolistic position.

PORTABLE ALPHA

Portable alpha is a method of segregating and carrying uncorrelated incremental returns among asset classes. Typically, the implementation of portable alpha investments requires the use of securities that have notional leverage, such as futures contracts. The ideal application of this strategy is in conjunction with efficient asset classes where there is very little alpha and where beta explains the vast majority of returns most of the time. An example of portable alpha is certain types of enhanced indexing, where the passive performance of an index is enhanced slightly by some incremental return. While enhanced indexing generally is considered a game of inches in its ability to add tens of basis points of return, other more aggressive implementations of portable alpha are games of miles that seek hundreds of basis points of incremental return. In either event, there are certain risks associated with portable alpha that often are overlooked, and there are other approaches to replicating beta and generating alpha that may have fewer of the risks that are intrinsic to portable alpha. The use of portable alpha does not necessarily make alpha any more attainable.

WHAT IS PORTABLE ALPHA?

Portable alpha transports the active return, or alpha, of one asset class to another. The asset class to which alpha is ported is passively replicated by a derivative contract. The alpha instrument should be market neutral in relation to the asset class to which the alpha is being ported. The mechanics of portable alpha are that the alpha investment also serves as collateral for the derivative contracts that generate the passive asset-class return. In this sense, the alpha generator is overlaid by a swap or futures contract that generates the passive index return. The alpha component can be as simple as short-duration bonds or as complex as a group of hedge funds.

The Components of Portable Alpha

Alpha refers to the return generated through active management that is in excess of the return that is attributable to a passively managed asset class, which usually is generated by a futures contract on its benchmark index. Beta is the amount of return for an investment that is explained by its benchmark. A passively managed asset class should have a beta of 1.0 to its benchmark. In a simple linear regression model, a single regressor (x) is an independent variable that is used to explain a corresponding response from a dependent variable (y). To the extent that there is a small alpha associated with such a regression, alpha may have little or indistinguishable relevance. In this instance, the majority of the explanatory power for the determination of the dependent variable is from its beta to the independent variable. An example of this is an efficient asset class, where the vast majority of returns can be replicated through a passive exposure to the asset class. Active management of that asset class may produce no credible benefit, and it may in fact produce negative incremental returns, especially when management fees are considered. From a quantitative perspective, the following variables and equation describe this relationship:

y_n = the expected dependent return from an investment
x_n = an independent asset class or benchmark
β_n = beta, which represents the amount of return for y_n explained by its benchmark x_n
α_n = alpha, which represents an exogenous return factor
ε_n = an error term, which represents an element of y_n return that is unexplained

The simple linear regression is represented by:

$$y_1 = \alpha_1 + \beta_1 x_1 + \varepsilon_1$$

and if, for example,

$$y_1 = 0.01 + 0.95x_1 + 0.01$$

then this is an instance of high explanatory power of the independent variable, or asset class, for the outcome of the dependent variable. In this example, if (y_1) represents the average active manager, then ostensibly (x_1) is an efficient asset class. Therefore, it is sensible to passively replicate this asset class, compared with the alternative of selecting among the available active managers. If one did not choose passive management in this instance, then there only could be a hope that the benefit of active return (alpha) would rival the random influences of the error term.

In this example of an efficient asset class and the applicability of passive replication, the notion of portable alpha gives rise to the concept of artificially bringing alpha back into this equation. The presumption in doing so, however, is that whatever new alpha is introduced has little or no beta that is associated with the asset class that is to be passively replicated, such that:

If

$$y_2 = \alpha_2 + \beta_2 x_2 + \varepsilon_2$$

and

$$y_2 = 1.5 + 0.01 x_2 + \varepsilon_2$$

and

$$y_2 = 1.5 + 0.01 x_1 + \varepsilon_1$$

then a portable alpha (y_{pa}) construct can be represented by

$$y_{pa} = \alpha_2 + \beta_1 x_1 + \varepsilon_2$$

In this instance, the newfound alpha has unique characteristics and represents a stable source of return that is not associated with the return of any asset classes under consideration. This enables an investor to port this alpha to another asset class that is passively replicated.

The Theory

The theory behind portable alpha is that some asset classes are efficient and can be improved only through the addition of active returns from a less efficient asset class. Based on this conception, it is not wise to attempt to actively manage these efficient asset classes. Active management of efficient asset classes theoretically can lead to only two outcomes: (1) the payment of active investment management fees, which generally are substantially higher than passive investment management fees; and (2) the incurrence of uncompensated risk. Rather than beating the passive benchmark, active management of efficient asset classes should lead to performance that is below the alternative of simply buying the benchmark through a passive index fund.

Practical Examples

Once an investor identifies an efficient asset class that appears to be suitable for passive replication within the context of portable alpha, a beta mechanism as well as a source of transportable alpha must be identified. The common tools used for the passive replication of asset classes are futures or swap agreements on benchmarks. These instruments generate passive beta returns that may be used in conjunction with returns from alpha generators. In terms of the alpha source, this investment must have a low beta to the passive asset class in the portable alpha program as well as low betas to other asset classes in an investor's overall portfolio. If the alpha product does not have these low-beta considerations, then in reality it is duplicating other elements of an investor's asset allocation. Additionally, the alpha source should hopefully have the characteristic of generating consistent positive returns that do not exhibit high volatility. This quality is desirable and adds to the predictability of returns from the portable alpha program.

Tables 9.1 and 9.2 depict examples of the practical application of portable alpha and its associated notional leverage. In Table 9.1, the

TABLE 9.1   Portable Alpha: Notional Leverage Example 1

	Capital Employed	Notional Capital Employed
Buy S&P 500 futures contracts (or swap)	10%	100%
Invest in market-neutral hedge funds	80%	160%
Cash on hand for futures mark-to-market	10%	10%
Total	100%	270%

TABLE 9.2   Portable Alpha: Notional Leverage Example 2

	Capital Employed	Notional Capital Employed
Buy S&P 500 futures contracts (or swap)	10%	100%
Invest in portfolio of short-duration bonds	80%	80%
Total cash on hand	10%	10%
Total	100%	190%

efficient asset class used in the example is the Standard and Poor's (S&P) 500, which is replicated through a futures contract on that index. Although only a small portion of available capital is employed to purchase this agreement (10 percent in this example and perhaps far less in the event that an over-the-counter swap is executed with a counterparty), the notional exposure to the asset class is 100 percent. This means that the gain or loss for the asset class will be represented in its entirety, in spite of the investor having only a small portion of capital allocated to the area. Although there is a fairly significant notional exposure of 100 percent of capital to the beta portion of the portable alpha program, the majority of the balance of capital is used to invest in a portfolio of market-neutral, long/short equities. However, this 80 percent allocation to market-neutral equities is notionally leveraged two times, since for every dollar invested in long equities, there is a dollar invested in short equities. Therefore, there is a total notional exposure of 160 percent of capital employed in the alpha portion of the portable alpha program. Finally, the remainder of capital is used for collateral and mark-to-market settlement in the account that sustains the investor's purchase of futures on the S&P 500. In total, this example illustrates that for the 100 percent of capital allocated to a portable alpha portfolio, the notional exposure is a total of 270 percent. This is the leveraged expression of the investor's capital across the investment factors to which it is exposed. Perhaps the most important observation about this notional exposure is its embedded susceptibility to enhanced volatility, depending on the volatility of its alpha and beta exposures. This is the linchpin for risk in portable alpha, that is, the degree to which predicted volatility and correlations among typically low-correlated markets and investment factors are inaccurate.

The portable alpha example depicted in Table 9.2 represents a more muted creation of notional leverage than is the case for the example in Table 9.1. The example in Table 9.2 also uses a futures (or swap) exposure to the S&P 500 as the passive beta benchmark that is replicated. However, the alpha portion of the portable alpha construction is supplied by a portfolio of short-duration bonds. The benefit of short-duration bonds is that the performance they contribute should be more normally distributed and less susceptible to kurtosis than hedge fund–oriented assets. Short-duration bonds are simple in nature since they pay par value at maturity and add short-term interest income during the interim periods. They also expose the investor to less interest rate sensitivity than might be the case for longer-duration bonds. Furthermore, short-duration bonds potentially have a higher credit profile than an alpha generator that is comprised of equities. The notional exposure for such a portable alpha construction is far less than when using an alpha generator that is comprised of hedge funds or other portfolios of long/short securities. Nevertheless, notional leverage still exists in this example, and it amounts to 190 percent of capital employed in the portable alpha allocation.

THE BENEFITS AND ISSUES WITH PORTABLE ALPHA

The benefits of employing a portable alpha program lie in the efficient use of capital and the ability to more precisely target asset classes that produce skill and those that do not. The beta component of portable alpha enables an investor to match the benchmark in an efficient asset class, while generating excess return through an alpha element. This entire conception is based on relative performance, which for many investors is a central measurement tool. Portable alpha can enhance the relative performance of an efficient asset class through the contribution of returns from an unrelated asset. Although this endeavor may appear contorted to an investor who is more focused on absolute performance, it nonetheless is an effective approach to meeting relative performance goals, at least most of the time. Furthermore, portable alpha identifies efficient asset classes that can be passively replicated and does so in an inexpensive fashion without the payment of active management fees. Meanwhile, fees may then be spent with greater efficacy on providers of alpha within the context of active management. Thus, portable alpha results in an investor paying active management fees only for alpha and not for beta.

A significant issue of caution that is associated with portable alpha centers on its use of notional leverage. As illustrated in Tables 9.1 and 9.2, the notional leverage often engaged with portable alpha can be fairly sizable relative to the actual capital employed. Indeed, not all fiduciaries associated with portable alpha programs may be aware of the subtle nature of this leverage, since it is less apparent from a financial statement point of view. This issue of concern relative to notional leverage is not so much leverage in itself as much as it is the magnification that leverage may have on performance during certain non-normal circumstances. For instance, what happens when the alpha component of the program has periodic episodes of higher-than-anticipated correlation with the passive beta component? In this event, potential losses from portable alpha programs may exceed expectations.

Furthermore, there are a number of tactical issues for portable alpha programs that could become amplified by the notional leverage involved. One tactical issue of concern related to portable alpha simply is the risk of negative alpha. In the event that alpha is negative, regardless of the contribution to overall performance from the passive beta generator, relative performance from the portable alpha program will be below the relevant benchmark, thereby undermining the rationale for the whole program. Such an instance could occur in spite of the associated time, effort, and costs associated with erecting the portable alpha program. Another area of tactical concern for a portable alpha program is the mechanics of instituting the passive beta exposure. To the extent that this exposure is achieved through the purchase of futures contracts, accomplishing the futures rollover mechanism is not effortless. Rolling over futures contracts can require the investor's involvement, oversight, or outsourcing in order to ensure that a consistent exposure is achieved over multiple time periods that span futures expiration dates. Additionally, futures collateral support must be established and maintained in the form of capital retained for mark-to-market price fluctuations. Furthermore, to the extent that swaps on indexes are used rather than the purchase of listed futures contract to establish the passive beta exposure, these swap agreements have inherent counterparty risk, collateral support requirements, and documentation ramifications. Finally, one last area of tactical concern in portable alpha is the frictional costs associated with such a program. These costs may manifest themselves in fees, tracking error, and internal program expenses. Fees are present by virtue of the commissions or spreads associated with establishing the passive beta exposure through futures or swaps. Fees also are quite evident in certain alpha generators, such as hedge funds or funds of funds. Tracking error may result from the futures or swaps generating returns that are slightly inexact vis-à-vis the returns on the reference benchmark. Furthermore, program expenses may be overt, such as legal fees required to evaluate and to establish such a program, or covert, such as the administrative time required to monitor both the beta replication vehicle and the alpha generator for such a program.

REEVALUATING THE PREMISE FOR PORTABLE ALPHA

The premise for portable alpha is that some asset classes are more efficient than others. Efficient asset classes have little demonstrable ability for active managers to generate meaningful incremental returns above that which can be attained on a passive basis from the asset class. Therefore, these efficient asset classes are suitable for use in portable alpha, since they can be replicated on a passive basis through the purchase of derivatives. However, the premise for portable alpha and the efficiency of some asset classes can be quite time-period sensitive.

For instance, Figure 9.1 depicts the passive versus active management performance comparison for large-capitalization U.S. equities, using the

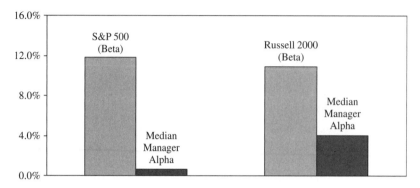

FIGURE 9.1   Beta versus Alpha, 10 Years to June 30, 2004
Notes: The median manager alpha is calculated based on all of the large-capitalization U.S. equity managers (separate accounts and commingled funds) contained in the RogersCasey database and includes large-capitalization core, growth, and value styles.
The median manager alpha is calculated based on all of the small-capitalization U.S. equity managers (separate accounts and commingled funds) contained in the RogersCasey database and includes small-capitalization core, growth, and value styles.
Source: RogersCasey.

S&P 500 as a benchmark, and small-capitalization U.S. equities, using the Russell 2000 as a benchmark. This illustration for a 10-year period ended June 30, 2004, shows what to many investors is intuitive: that large-capitalization equities offer much less opportunity for incremental returns through active management than is the case for small-capitalization equities. However, if the time period for this comparison is altered to a four-and-one-half-year period ended June 30, 2004, the resulting relationship is changed (depicted in Figure 9.2). Although the benefit of active management still is apparent in the performance of small-capitalization equities, it now also is apparent for large-capitalization equities. Even though one might quibble over the relatively short time period for drawing conclusions in Figure 9.2, nonetheless it does illustrate the point that there potentially is active alpha to be forgone through the passive indexation of an asset class in portable alpha. Although the sustainability of this alpha may not be perceived to be as consistent as is the case for an alpha that might be ported from a less efficient area, it is closely related to the asset class or beta to which it originates. This inherent proximity may bring comfort to an investor, who otherwise during portable alpha might be porting alpha from a completely unrelated asset class or alternative investment strategy.

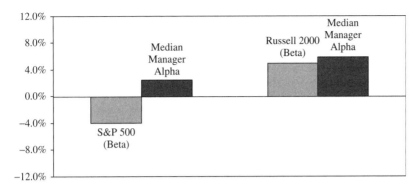

FIGURE 9.2 Beta versus Alpha, January 1, 2000, to June 30, 2004
Notes: The median manager alpha is calculated based on all of the large-capitalization U.S. equity managers (separate accounts and commingled funds) contained in the RogersCasey database and includes large-capitalization core, growth, and value styles.
The median manager alpha is calculated based on all of the small-capitalization U.S. equity managers (separate accounts and commingled funds) contained in the RogersCasey database and includes small-capitalization core, growth, and value styles.
Source: RogersCasey.

The point is that should something go wrong with the combination of alpha and beta, at the very least a local alpha is more understandable in its over- or underachievement than is an alpha that is leveraged and has more distant origins.

THE USE OF HEDGE FUNDS IN PORTABLE ALPHA

Portable alpha programs frequently use individual hedge funds or portfolios of hedge funds to generate the alpha component of the construction. The attraction of this source of alpha is the historical propensity for hedge funds to provide low correlation to many traditional asset classes, their low volatility in performance most of the time, and potential they hold for performance enhancement through the generation of positive alpha. To illustrate these assumptions regarding correlation, volatility, and performance, Figure 9.3 and Table 9.3 depict a selection of historical statistics using the HFR Hedge Fund of Funds Index. Figure 9.3 indicates the bondlike risk and stocklike performance that one would expect from this hedge fund of funds index over one historical five-year time frame, while Table 9.3 indicates the correlation of this performance to U.S. equities

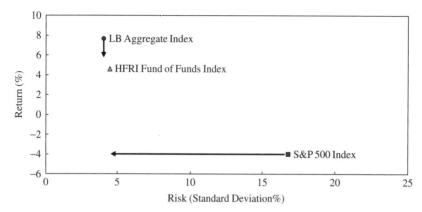

FIGURE 9.3   Risk and Return, January 1, 2000 to June 30, 2004
Source: RogersCasey.

TABLE 9.3   Correlation Matrix, January 1, 2000 to June 30, 2004

	HFRI Fund of Funds Index	S&P 500 Index	LB Aggregate Index
HFRI Fund of Funds Index	1.00		
S&P 500 Index	0.43	1.00	
LB Aggregate Index	0.12	0.17	1.00

Source: RogersCasey.

and bonds. Although this data depicts only a relatively short slice of history, it is representative of the data that supports the use of hedge funds in portable alpha programs.

There was evidence of success during the initial period of time that hedge funds were used more widely in portable alpha constructions. As portrayed in Figure 9.4, a comparison of the performance in the S&P 500 versus the S&P 500 plus the HFR Hedge Fund of Funds Index exemplifies the benefits of portable alpha. The S&P 500 in this illustration is implied to be the passive beta asset class in a portable alpha program, while the HFR Hedge Fund of Funds Index represents the alpha generator. In this example, which also is over a fairly brief time frame, the performance of the S&P 500 added to the alpha generated from the hedge fund index easily surpasses the performance of the S&P 500 by itself. The conclusion drawn from this instance of portable alpha is that it is a worthwhile endeavor. An interesting observation about the example in Figure 9.4 is that the time

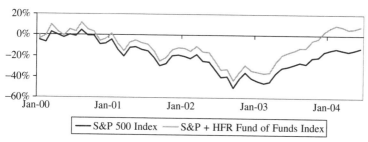

FIGURE 9.4 Cumulative Returns, January 1, 2000 to June 30, 2004
Source: RogersCasey.

frame used represents a period of significant decline for the S&P 500. The fact that the HFR Hedge Fund of Funds Index managed to generate positive cumulative alpha during this period rests on its less than 1.0 correlation to the S&P 500. This thereby further lends credibility to portable alpha using these specific investment examples for beta and alpha.

However, success in portable alpha can be time-period specific as well as alpha-selection specific. Had an investor constructed a portable alpha program with market-neutral equity as the alpha generator during 1999–2000, the outcome for the program may have been much less attractive than the outcome illustrated in Figure 9.4. During the late 1990s, many market-neutral equity funds found themselves in a losing position, because of their tendency to be long value and a short growth. This positioning related to their natural proclivity toward being short expensive stocks and long inexpensive stocks relative to measures of price to earnings, sales, and growth rates. In fact, the historical data for many of these market-neutral funds has been blotted out of existence. Many of the market-neutral funds that performed poorly during this period were discontinued and therefore were dropped from the relevant databases. This phenomenon is also referred to as survivor bias in these databases. Nevertheless, if one were to attempt to reconstruct the landscape of this time period, then a proxy on this environment might be a combination of a long position in the Russell 3000 Value Index and a short position in the Russell 3000 Growth Index, which is illustrated in Figure 9.5. If an investor had chosen an alpha vehicle similar to the depiction in Figure 9.5 during the 1999–2000 period, then a vastly different outcome would have occurred relative to the portable alpha outcome pictured in Figure 9.4.

Beyond the importance of selecting the correct alpha generator and time frame of utilization, the true hidden risk in these programs is maintaining noncorrelation between the alpha and beta instruments used. If one refers back to the example of portable alpha using the HFR Hedge Fund of Funds

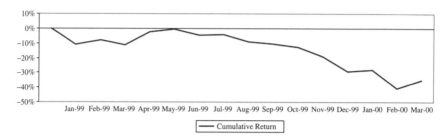

FIGURE 9.5   Long Russell 3000 and Short Russell 3000 Growth, January 1, 1999 to March 31, 2000
Source: RogersCasey.

Index in Figure 9.4, the outcome of this scenario would have been much different had the alpha engine been correlated to the passive beta during this severe period of decline for the S&P 500. For instance, if the narrow time period of the third quarter of 1998 were used, then the correlation between the HFR Hedge Fund of Funds Index and the S&P 500 would have been much higher, as is shown in Tables 9.4 and 9.5. This crisis period was associated with a default by the Russian government on its debt obligations as well as the collapse of the hedge fund Long-Term Capital Management. This occasion was characterized by high correlations among many investment strategies as illiquidity gripped certain segments of the financial marketplace. Although temporary in nature, the mark-to-market declines in many securities and hedge strategies caused a spike in correlation of performance between hedge funds, as exemplified by the HFR Hedge Fund of Funds Index, and the broad equity market, as represented by the S&P 500.

Accordingly, had a portable alpha program utilized the S&P 500 and HFR Hedge Fund of Funds Index during this snapshot of market crisis, results would have been very poor. Figure 9.6 charts the likely course of

TABLE 9.4   Crisis Period (July 1, 1998 to September 30, 1998)

	Return
HFRI Fund of Funds Index	−10.2%
S&P 500 Index	−9.95%
LB Aggregate Index	4.23%

Source: RogersCasey.

TABLE 9.5 Correlation Matrix (Crisis Period Equals High Correlation)

	HFRI Fund of Funds Index	S&P 500 Index	LB Aggregate Index
HFRI Fund of Funds Index	1.00		
S&P 500 Index	0.78	1.00	
LB Aggregate Index	−0.49	0.17	1.00

Source: RogersCasey.

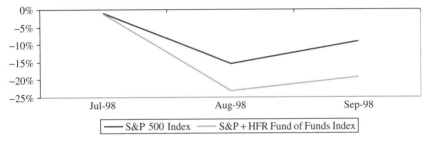

FIGURE 9.6 Cumulative Returns, July 1, 1998 to September 30, 1998
Source: RogersCasey.

such an investment. During this brief period, a portable alpha program using these instruments for beta and alpha exposure would have yielded performance results that were far worse than simply investing in the efficient asset class, which in this case was the S&P 500. Had an investor invested in an actively managed version of the efficient asset class, even this result would not likely have generated as much negative alpha as the illustrated exposure to hedge funds. Moreover, active management of the efficient asset class may have caused the contribution of positive alpha, depending on the specific active exposure selected.

However, as illustrated in Table 9.6, had an investor stayed the course with a portable alpha program through the market crisis in 1998, they would have reaped profits associated with a recovery both in the alpha and in the beta components of this strategy. In fact, the investor in this example would have enjoyed a profit in the peak-to-trough-to-peak cycle that was far greater than having invested only in the passive beta component of the strategy. This analysis indicates that even during a market crisis with high correlation between hedged investments and the market beta, portable alpha in this example might have been the correct strategy to employ over a period that included a recovery to normalcy.

TABLE 9.6 Portable Alpha Requires Staying Power

	Crisis July 1998 to September 1998	Rebound Total Return July 1998 to December 1999
HFR Fund of Funds Index	−10.02%	9.76%
S&P 500 Index	−9.95%	20.45%
100% S&P 500 Plus 100% HFR FOF Index (Portable Alpha)	−19.97%	30.21%

Source: RogersCasey.

Nevertheless, a practical question that surfaces from these observations is whether the investor in this example would have exhibited staying power. In other words, would the all-too-human tendency for intervention have overwhelmed logic and shut down this program right at the bottom of the market? Imagine a decline in a portable alpha program that equaled twice the decline in the broad equity market during some sort of market dislocation, as is depicted in Figure 9.6. The stark realization and naked truth of the inherent leverage employed in portable alpha would be all too obvious, but perhaps occur as a shock to fiduciaries, such as trustees, chief financial officers, union representatives, or political appointees to a pension plan. Furthermore, if human intervention did not occur, would the size of the allocation to the portable alpha strategy cause the investor to receive a margin call from its dealers? Imagine an entire equity program that was reconstituted to have a passive beta and active alpha using the hedge fund example. The magnitude of a correlated decline in a portable alpha program's alpha and beta might trigger dealers to require additional capital to be provided from the investor. The degree to which this might occur largely depends on three ingredients: (1) the percentage of total assets for an investor that is contained in the portable alpha program, (2) the magnitude of the decline in beta, and (3) the degree of correlation between the alpha and beta components of the program.

Using the example in Tables 9.4 and 9.5, which indicates a correlation of 0.78 between hedge funds and the S&P 500, and assuming a stronger decline of 30 percent in the broad market, the associated loss in the portable alpha program could have totaled 55.7 percent (30 percent in beta and 25.7 percent in alpha). This case clearly would have caused a margin call by any dealers that were counterparties involved in the beta overlay portion of the portable alpha program. For a total portfolio that was 70 percent invested in equities through a portable alpha program and 30 percent invested in fixed-income investments, meeting a margin call might not have been possible by posting fixed-income securities. In this example, the loss in the equity program would have amounted to 39 percent of total portfolio assets (55.7 percent of 70 percent = 39 percent), which would have exceeded the 30 percent fixed-income allocation in the portfolio. Meanwhile, liquidating commingled hedge fund investments on short notice to meet a margin call would be highly unlikely, given their typical lockup provisions and liquidity constraints. A more diverse portfolio that included other illiquid assets, such as real estate and private equity, would have had an even more difficult time meeting such a margin call. Nevertheless, most of this doomsday discussion depends on investments declining and correlating with sudden speed and severity. Slower meltdowns would likely give ample opportunity for intervention on the part of the investor, its counterparties, and other market participants to reduce exposures and potential losses.

ALTERNATIVE THINKING ABOUT ALPHA

Rather than thinking about portable alpha in its traditional constructs, there are other ways in which to consider the division of beta and alpha. Identified here are two additional approaches. First is alpha core, which is the consideration of alpha as the primary driver of a portfolio construction, rather than an exposure to asset class betas. The second is the application of "exotic betas" to portable alpha and their fit as it pertains to the premise of portable alpha, which is based on the efficient nature of some asset classes and their ability to be passively replicated.

Alpha Core

As indicated in Figure 9.7, the construction of portable alpha implies two simple tools: a passive beta accomplished through a derivatives contract and an allocation to an alpha generator. However, the construction of portable alpha utilizes notional leverage of at least 200 percent in most instances, which is represented by the 100 percent exposure to gains or losses in beta plus 100 percent exposure to movement in alpha.

If an investor accepts that the premise for portable alpha is still correct, which is to say that some asset classes are efficient and should be indexed, then why add leverage to this? Plenty of cautious investors take the efficient market presumption to a very conservative conclusion, which is to index a majority of their portfolio as it pertains to the presumed efficient asset classes. Another approach is to employ enhanced indexing of the efficient asset class, which is a conservative form of portable alpha. However, a risk is that the efficiency of an asset class is not stable. For periods of time, active

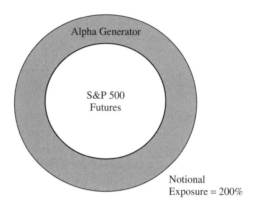

FIGURE 9.7 Portable Alpha

management of efficient asset classes can add identifiable value above the passive benchmark. Therefore, two downsides to portable alpha are the risk associated with its leverage and the asset-class active alpha that is forsaken during periods that the asset class indeed is not efficient.

The concept of alpha core represents an alternative approach to portable alpha. It does not require the use of notional leverage, as is the case with portable alpha, and it allows for periods of efficiency and inefficiency in the asset class that is passively replicated in portable alpha. Alpha core simply is the construction of a portfolio using absolute-return assets at its core and layers onto this actively managed asset classes in concentric rings of rising expected volatility. Such a construct might apply to an investor who believed in the premise of portable alpha (that some asset classes are efficient), but only most of the time and not all of the time, and did not want to use leverage to express this philosophy. In fact, allocations both to active and passive exposures to sometimes efficient asset classes could be utilized. For instance, an allocation to large-capitalization U.S. equity could be represented by a 50 percent apportionment to an enhanced index fund and 50 percent to active management. Constructing a portfolio with concentric rings of asset classes with increasing amounts of volatility creates a portfolio that has a stable alpha core but retains active and passive exposure to asset classes known for higher return potential. Such an alpha core portfolio could be considered a strategic allocation.

An initial step in portable alpha is accepting the notion that alpha exists among various investments and that it can be transported to other asset classes. However, the replication of the core asset class is of primary importance in portable alpha. The simple question that arises from this is: Why would an investor seek as a primary investment objective to preserve a core allocation to a volatile asset class? Doesn't it seem counterintuitive that preservation of volatility is the primary objective, especially when the investor has just accepted the existence of low-correlated alpha that presumably has low volatility? Why not simply reverse this prioritization, make the generation of low-volatility alpha of core importance with lesser emphasis on higher-volatility assets, and place a proportionate portfolio emphasis accordingly?

From this vantage point, an investor using alpha core principles could as its primary goal make a core allocation to low-volatility assets that have low correlation to other asset classes. Around this stable allocation, as depicted in Figure 9.8, an investor then could add allocations to increasingly volatile asset classes that presumably would have higher levels of long-term expected returns. In effect, this approach is similar to the creation of an efficiently optimized portfolio, but with broader inclusion of alternative assets. Furthermore, portfolio construction using the principles of alpha core does not employ notional leverage. Although there certainly would be leverage utilized by providers of alpha (e.g., a hedge fund or hedge fund of funds), there is no notional leverage through the use of swaps or futures at the portfolio level, such as there is for portable alpha. The one stark truth that comes from this exercise is the simple nature of leverage that is the foundation of portable alpha. Indeed, this leverage may be unnecessary for many investors who simply are attempting to achieve an exposure to alternative investment alphas in an optimized portfolio.

Perhaps some efficient asset classes should be indexed. Furthermore, it is accepted that uncorrelated alternative investments with consistent, low-volatility returns exist and deserve an allocation. Portable alpha can be an efficient way to generate both market and excess returns. However,

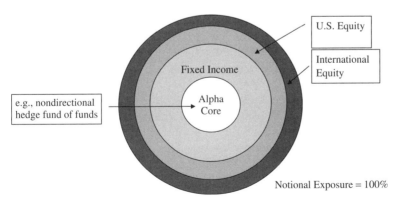

FIGURE 9.8 Alpha Core: Concentric Rings of Increasing Volatility

portable alpha potentially makes a portfolio less reliable, particularly during crisis events, because of notional leverage. Indeed, portable alpha investors must have staying power to weather the risk of losses during interim periods. Although the premise for portable alpha may still be correct, an alternative to leveraging a portfolio two-to-one through portable alpha is to make room in the asset allocation process for high Sharpe ratio alternative assets. Alpha core improves the reliability of a portfolio through diversification with low-correlated and typically low-volatility assets, but without the use of leverage such as through portable alpha.

Portable Alpha Using Exotic Betas

Another approach to the portable alpha concept is its application to alternative investment return factors. In the traditional approach of portable alpha, the beta component is simply the passive replication of a well-known asset class. An extension of this traditional approach is to use the independent return factors associated with alternative investments as the beta components in portable alpha. These independent factors often are referred to as exotic betas. For example, exotic betas can include returns from direct lending, insurance, and capturing risk premiums from other business types of risk rather than classic investment types of risk. Potentially, they are another sort of beta that like traditional betas may be passively replicated. However, a significant assumption is that exotic betas are efficient and should be indexed, which clearly is not the case. Exotic betas usually are considered so inefficient that there is debate over whether they simply are components of alpha. Nevertheless, as investors consider the investment landscape from the perspective of factor exposures, which is discussed in Chapter 11, they also may be able to apply these factors within the context of portable alpha.

How can this be done? How can exotic betas be passively replicated? In principle, exotic betas can be replicated the same way that traditional betas are replicated. Passive proxies on traditional betas are supplied through futures and swap agreements on indexes that represent the traditional betas (e.g., the S&P 500). These futures and swaps are inventions of securities dealers and investment banks. In turn, there is no reason to think that exotic beta cannot ultimately be replicated by these counterparties, assuming that there is sufficient demand for such products. Presently, there are in existence certain exotic beta proxies, such as the ability to invest in derivatives of volatility indexes. Granted, the frictional cost for entering into more prevalent traditional beta proxies arguably is much lower than is the case for attaining exotic beta proxies. Nevertheless, over time, one should expect this differential to narrow or close if greater liquidity, because of demand, is brought to futures and swaps for exotic betas.

When extending the portable alpha concept to exotic betas, two issues arise. First, do exotic betas possess a distinct and associated alpha? Second, is the inefficient nature of an exotic beta (as witnessed by the high frictional cost associated with its derivative replication) mean that it is not well suited to portable alpha construction? Perhaps these two questions are the inverse of the same issue: Does the mere identification and exposure to an exotic beta give an investor the majority of the benefit? One point of view is that exotic betas simply are components of traditional alpha. However, this may not be true if one can passively replicate these exotic betas. Exotic betas appear to exist and in some cases are passively replicable, which therefore indicates that they are separate and distinct from the alpha that is associated with them. Nevertheless, the identification of new betas should come with large associated alphas. This is because of the novelty of the source of returns, the inefficiency of the opportunities, the difficulty in passively replicating the exotic betas, and the lack of investment competition that ultimately will narrow the associated alpha.

Exotic betas are expensive and inefficient to replicate. Therefore, exotic betas seem to fail the initial premise of portable alpha, which is to passively replicate an efficient asset class or investment factor. Furthermore, the alpha associated with exotic betas may be less separable from them, because of few investment players in the exotic beta arenas. Fewer players equate to a greater chance that they represent the fused alpha and beta of the exotic factors. Although exotic betas are less appealing than some traditional asset classes to use in a portable alpha construction, because of their inherent inefficiencies and probable large alphas, it is possible to consider them in this framework for future use as they evolve into more efficient sources of return.

SUMMARY

Leverage comes in many forms and can affect virtually all alternative investment strategies. The ability to enhance potential returns from invested equity can be accomplished through cash leverage, notional leverage, and structural leverage. In all of these cases, the prospective impact from leverage can be difficult to gauge. Leverage can act as a benign performance enhancer. However, when mixed with illiquidity and directionality, leverage can become much more combustible. When correlations among assets sharply deviate from their historical norms, significant amounts of leverage can cause catastrophic losses. Indeed, it is this decoupling of historical correlations married with sizable leverage that has been the source of many historical hedge fund disasters.

The use of leverage through the strategy of portable alpha is effective for the enhancement of returns from efficient asset classes most of the time. However, when alpha generators become correlated to the asset classes to which they are ported, an investor must possess staying power in order to ride out mark-to-market losses. Through this perseverance, investors will be positioned to recoup interim-period losses that might be associated with crisis events that negatively affect portable alpha programs. Portable alpha is revealed to have great intrinsic notional leverage that can exacerbate periods of correlation between alpha and beta. For investors who believe that some asset classes are efficient most but not all of the time, there are approaches other than portable alpha to capture beta and alpha in an efficient manner. One of those approaches is alpha core, which uses uncorrelated, alpha-producing strategies at the core of a portfolio and augments these holdings with allocations to increasingly risky but higher-returning assets. Although the portable alpha strategy may be applied to exotic betas, the inefficient nature of these betas closely binds them to their local alphas and renders them less likely candidates for portable alpha constructions.

CHAPTER 10

Factor Analysis: The Rationale

The dynamic nature of the investment marketplace is causing a softening of barriers between alternative investment categories. No longer can alternative investments be generalized by their historical asset-class tendencies. Therefore, a more dynamic approach is called for to evaluate the multiple strategies that may be employed by an alternative investment manager. The inclusion of factor analysis in order to more accurately appraise both the independent and the interrelated attributes of all traditional and alternative investments helps to move beyond the definition of asset class and its rigidity. The approach for most investors engaged in portfolio construction begins with an optimization of asset classes. The premise for this tactic is the existence and fairly well-formed criteria that define asset classes. However, the criteria for asset-class demarcation tend to be strict and not well tailored to the characteristics of alternative investments.

This chapter identifies quantitative factors as components of alternative investments through multiple linear regression analyses. Quantitative factor analysis across all alternative investments enables an investor to optimize a set of factors, rather than asset classes. Meanwhile, qualitative factors, such as illiquidity and counterparty risks, also are defined as characteristics that affect many alternative investments regardless of their structure. Qualitative factor analysis enables a judgmental overlay in creating portfolios of alternative investments.

One tenet for being considered as an asset class is having low historical correlation versus other asset classes. However, some alternative investment strategies exhibit correlation, and therefore may not be utilized jointly in a portfolio that may be optimized. In reality, this correlation may be spurious. Spuriously correlated investment strategies have similar return and volatility characteristics, but achieve their returns through exposure to separate independent return drivers or factors. An example is the potential for high correlation between an investment in timber and one in private investment in public entities (PIPE) transactions. Potential correlation between these strategies at certain points in time can relate to the serial correlation within their individual return strings, which may be caused by the infrequent or accrual pricing of these investments. Although some alternative strategies may at times be correlated, their returns tend to be driven by unique factors (e.g., the fact that tree growth can account for a majority of the returns from an investment in timber differs from the return for a PIPE transaction, which is dependent on the size of the discount from market paid for the securities.)

Once most relevant factors are identified, an investor is free to invest a portfolio across all factors in some form of optimization. The entire concept of traditional versus alternative investment classes changes. Defining asset classes becomes less relevant, as does the importance of style analysis within asset classes, which often are thinner slices of the same factors. It becomes apparent that a more effective and efficient way in which to construct portfolios is through assembling diversified factor exposures. The migration from asset class and style analysis to factor identification and optimization provides for a more robust portfolio. Once the rationale for this approach is fully discussed, the identification and measurement of factors that exist and may be used in portfolio construction is the work that is conducted in Chapter 11.

MARKETPLACE CHANGES THAT WARRANT FACTOR ANALYSIS

Changes in the marketplace are forcing all investors to consider a new lexicon for explaining alternative investments. The evolution of alternative investments has created some of the following trends: a merging among investment styles, a more competitive landscape leading to a wider-ranging search for investments with attractive returns, a movement toward less liquid investing styles, and changes in regulations. All of these trends render prior investment-class generalizations less useful and require the more exacting approach to alternative investment examination that factor analysis provides.

The merging among investment styles that has occurred throughout the alternative investment arena is perhaps no better exemplified than by hedge funds. These open architecture funds are perhaps far less constrained in their mandate than funds in the other alternative investment disciplines, such as real estate or private equity funds. Since their investment documents allow them to forage through the entire investable universe for their returns, hedge funds have increasingly taken on allocations to the other strategies in the broad alternative investment universe. The advent of multistrategy hedge funds also encourages the use of many investment strategies enables an improvement in diversification, and facilitates a reduction in volatility.

The result is that not only are the hedge funds in this mode less predictable and more difficult to evaluate, but they present benchmarking problems, style drift issues, and competition with the funds in the strategies that they are invading. Increasingly, hybrid benchmarks are warranted in the evaluation of hedge funds that are taking this tack. Additionally, the issue of style drift has become a more complex one for evaluators of these funds. Whereas historical sensibilities might dictate a less favorable view of style drift, if it is accompanied by skill in the new areas of investment, then it is more palatable. Furthermore, hedge funds drifting into the other alternative asset classes have different return and duration objectives than the resident funds in those strategies. For example, a private equity fund may have a return objective of 20 percent to 40 percent compounded annually for a buyout investment over a 5- to 10-year period, while a hedge fund may be seeking only 20 percent compounded over one third to one half of that time frame. In this instance, the hedge fund could afford to pay more for a target acquisition or control position than the private equity firm, thus creating competition for deals and lower returns for the private equity investor. (For more on this and related trends, see Chapter 7.)

There also is a trend of less liquid investments being made across the alternatives investment marketplace. This decline in liquidity has a couple of collateral effects. For example, many hedge funds are addressing a mismatch they have between the liquidity they offer to their investors and the increasing duration of the investments in their funds. Some are addressing this by extending lockup or liquidity terms for new investors or for all investors. Another effect is that less liquid investments provide for less frequent pricing of these investments, which in turn enables a smoothing of returns for these funds. This also raises a concern over the accuracy of pricing for these types of investments.

Regulatory changes are aiding this convergence among alternative investments. In an effort to be exempt from regulation by the Securities and Exchange Commission in the United States, hedge funds increasingly have extended the terms of liquidity that they offer to their investors. The less liquid terms encourage hedge funds to invest more like private equity funds. Although hedge funds tend to invest in more liquid securities than private equity funds, their increasingly long lockup terms forestall overt regulation. More restrictive liquidity terms encourage the funds to seek returns through less liquid investments.

THE ASSET-CLASS CONCEPT

The importance of garnering the imprimatur of asset class for an investment relates to granting entitlement to participate in the traditional approach to asset optimization during portfolio construction. Investments are defined as asset classes based on essentially eight criteria:

1. There must be enough depth of capacity in the asset class to consider it widely investable and it must have estimable intrinsic value.
2. The asset class must be investable and have adequate liquidity.
3. Low correlation should exist between the asset class and all other asset classes.
4. Members of the asset class must in some fashion be considered homogeneous.
5. The risk or standard deviation of returns for the asset class should be estimable.
6. The structure of the asset class and the regulation to which it must adhere should not be significant impediments for investment.
7. There should be a pool of talented managers from which to choose in order to gain access to the asset class.
8. An investable passive benchmark should exist.[1]

Characteristics of Asset Classes

Although one might argue how well certain alternative investments fit with all of the asset-class criteria, these types of criteria define the basic concept of asset class for many investors. Asset-class definition is a starting point for considering all investments in portfolio construction. However, as described more fully in this chapter, other techniques such as factor analysis move beyond this scope. To be considered as an asset class, many of the following characteristics must be present in the investment under consideration.

Estimable Intrinsic Value   An investment that possesses intrinsic value often is defined as an asset that provides a return that is calculable and not speculative. For instance, real estate has a return on investment through the rental receipts on the property. A value for the property can be calculated as a function of the present value of the future cash flows from the property. An expected return derived from this method is different than an implied return on investment due to capital appreciation from perhaps a reduction in interest rates, a change in macroeconomic variables, or an improvement in local occupancy rates. This criterion for an investment to be considered an asset class is one of the more challenging from the perspective of alternative investments.

In the classical sense, currency, for example, has no intrinsic value, except that it is backed by the financial solvency of government issuers. Currency may be considered simply a transfer mechanism or method of conveyance, not an asset or investment. It is merely a unit value with no specific return on investment other than a change in price determined by speculative buyers and sellers. The value of currency is simply the fact that one party on any given day may be willing to pay more for it than on another day or a value that is derived from purchasing power parity or short-term supply-and-demand considerations. Nevertheless, currency trading can be a very attractive opportunity that offers embedded inefficiencies that can provide uncorrelated returns.

Adequate Liquidity   A liquidity feature is required for an investment to be considered as asset class. The purpose of this characteristic is a threshold for measuring broad acceptance and ability to initiate and rebalance an asset in a diversified portfolio. Typically, acceptance of an asset under this criterion is done on a relative basis, such as answering the question of whether a contemplated asset class is large enough to be employed in all pension plans in the United States. However, this asset-class criterion does not allow inclusion of an illiquidity risk premium, which some alternative investments offer. As such, this definition is limiting to the detriment of investors.

Low Correlation with Other Asset Classes   Low correlation is a core value that new assets bring to a portfolio. A combination of assets with attractive covariance features enables compound returns for a portfolio to rise owing to a reduction in overall volatility. As the investment world has become more complex and sophisticated, the identification of assets with low correlation to recognized traditional asset classes is very appealing. The logic for using alternative investments in portfolio construction finds its cornerstone in the uncorrelated nature of these assets and the additional diversification that they can provide to a portfolio of traditional asset classes. However, a significant problem with the justification of an investment as an asset class is that although it may have attractive low correlation, it may fail other asset class tests. In this event, the traditional approach is simply to abandon the investment during an asset allocation process, or sequester it in an "other" bucket that is a parking place for a grab-bag of attractive low-correlation assets that do not fit the traditional definition of asset classes.

This conundrum has given birth to the far more meaningful analysis of factor determinants of asset-class returns and construction of portfolios based on factor combinations. Indeed, part of the potential for success in adopting this new approach is that many asset-class portfolio constructors have not yet done this. Therefore, there may still be robust returns from factor allocation as well as from the inclusion of nontraditional assets. These returns are available at the expense of traditional investors who effectively sell alpha in order to maintain antiquated methodologies. Investors in long-only asset classes tend to maintain low tracking errors to benchmarks at all costs, even if those costs equate to having low tracking errors to negatively returning benchmarks.

Members of the Asset Class Are Homogeneous   Homogeneity is a core element of consistency for an asset class that provides the ability to generate a normal distribution of returns for participants in the asset class. It furthermore enables intrinsic value and risk to be estimated in a mean sense. It also allows a benchmark to be created that is comprised of the asset-class elements. In essence, homogeneity is measured by low benchmark tracking error for any sample of the asset-class participants. For example, homogeneous U.S. large-capitalization equities in total comprise a benchmark such as the Standard and Poor's (S&P) 500. An investment manager operating in this asset class would be measured against this benchmark and should have a fairly reasonable tracking error to it.

In contrast, hedge funds often are not considered an asset class, since there are so many strategies and securities employed by hedge funds, such that they broadly are not homogeneous. Nevertheless, participants in certain hedge strategies are more homogeneous by their nature and may be measured against some traditional and nontraditional benchmarks.

Risk Is Estimable   If asset classes have estimable intrinsic value, then they usually have estimable risk. Risk is a measure of implied volatility. Often, estimated risk is derived from the standard deviation of an investment's historical returns. Granted, one could debate the veracity of using historical volatility to derive expected future volatility, but this often is what is done for traditional asset classes. For traditional asset classes, this approach may be consistently applied, because of the long historical data sets available. Such lengthy track records are rarely available for alternative investments. This often renders them difficult to use from a historical perspective for the development of estimated future risks. Furthermore, the basis for this asset test criterion is the desire to use estimated risk in a mean-variance portfolio optimization exercise. However, when applying it to nontraditional assets that have short track records and unique drivers of return and risk, the methodology comes into question. Risk is difficult to estimate for alternative investments because of their tendency to exhibit non-normally distributed returns. Therefore, the use of alternative investments with no constraints on their allocation in a mean-variance optimization (MVO) can offer faulty results.

Mean-variance analysis can be used as a tool for the initial constrained allocation to alternative investments, augmented by the subsequent use of regression analysis to determine the underlying factor drivers of return and risk for the investments. Indeed, if it is independent factors that determine the returns of certain alternative investments, then shouldn't the goal be to predict the movement and volatility of these factors? The task of factor prediction is different from the estimation of the volatility of returns for an investment. The returns and volatility of returns associated with an investment is the cumulative expression of the return and volatility of the investment's determinant factors. The analysis of factors that determine the risk exposures of a portfolio of assets is more directly related to enabling a risk manager to conduct stress tests for a portfolio, rather than conducting MVO of asset classes. However, a portfolio of alternative asset factors can be optimized, based on forward-looking estimates of return and volatility for those factors.

Structure and Regulation Are Not Impediments to Investing   The point of this criterion is related to the criteria for liquidity and sufficient number of asset managers from which to choose, which relate to having adequate size and depth of the potential asset class in order to have an economic impact on a broad array of investors. Structure of an asset refers to its legal configuration. Regulatory impediments can include lack of registration for an investment or an investment strategy that is restricted in its prevalence by banking, insurance, or brokerage regulations. Both structure and regulation can be impediments to investing and therefore can curtail liquidity and the number of market participants, thereby diminishing availability to a broader investor base. As this criterion pertains to alternative investments, the premise is still correct that difficult structure or regulatory characteristics can impede the wider adoption of these investments.

Nevertheless, there is a significant return factor that can be a cornerstone for some alternative investments, and that is illiquidity. Some investment strategies are illiquid partly because of structural and regulatory impediments. For example, investing in unregistered securities, which from a regulatory perspective does not fit traditional asset-class investing, can provide potentially handsome returns stemming from an illiquidity risk and return factor. These types of investments can represent inefficient niches with attractive returns. Illiquidity is a factor that represents a source of this return. This notion is at odds with the facility of structure and regulation being a prerequisite for an investment to be considered an asset class. If an investment is not deemed an asset class, then most traditional investors exclude the

investment from a mean variance–based portfolio optimization. The investment therefore simply does not exist in some traditional investor portfolios.

How can two approaches to investment, traditional and alternative,
be so diametrically opposed? It is this contradiction that helps to create
alpha for alternative investments, often through buying unconventional
investments for which there is less investor demand. The majority of
investors do not want investments with difficult structural or regulatory
traits. The structure and regulation pertaining to alternative investments
include the nature of private partnerships, lockups of investor capital, and
offshore investment vehicles with foreign domiciles and regulatory regimes.
Therefore, this criterion for asset-class definition is another example that
does not fit well with alternative investments.

A Large Pool of Talented Managers from Which to Choose   The importance
in depth of managers from which to choose is a key element for active
asset-class construction. Active management is an alternative to investing in
passive benchmarks. Active management can provide positive or negative
incremental returns for certain asset classes versus their benchmarks. It is
more difficult to generate incremental return through active management in
liquid and efficient asset classes than it is in less liquid and inefficient asset
classes. In the realm of alternative investments, active versus passive returns
can be difficult to separate. Alternative investments are new forms of assets
that often have unique drivers of return. As such, there can be a limited
number of investment managers that provide robust access to these unique
returns. Manager selection is important in alternative investments because
of a wide variation of performance among managers. Therefore, having a
large pool of active managers in alternative investments is less relevant than
having access to the most competent managers.

One might posit that the unique low correlation and attractive return
attributes of alternative investments are more robust to the extent that there
are few managers operating in areas of the realm. This is diametrically
opposed to the essence of the asset-class criterion of requiring a pool of
talented managers. Furthermore, this criterion assumes that the asset-class
exposure is accomplished through an active investment manager, rather
than the direct ownership of securities or through investment in a passive
benchmark. In the event that an asset class becomes very efficient, passive
investment might represent a more efficient route. This may already be the
case for some traditional asset classes. In this event, having a sufficient
number of active investment managers from which to choose is superfluous.

A Passive Benchmark in Which to Invest   Having a passive benchmark in
which to invest is a cornerstone to traditional asset-class declaration. The

best benchmark is the accumulation of all the securities and investment instruments used to comprise the investable universe that is the asset class. For example, the United States fixed-income asset class often uses as its passive benchmark the Lehman Aggregate Index, which is comprised of a large number of publicly traded fixed-income securities available in the U.S. markets. The reason for having a passive benchmark is the ability to measure active manager returns and volatility. However, the concept of having a benchmark is based on relative comparison for active management, including returns, volatility, correlation, and tracking error. To the extent that a portfolio is constructed with alternative investments, absolute performance becomes as important as relative performance versus a passive benchmark. Nevertheless, passive beta and alpha benchmarks can be derived in many instances for alternative investments.

ALTERNATIVE INVESTMENTS AND FACTOR ANALYSIS

The use of traditional asset classes in portfolio construction depends on these asset classes having relatively low correlation with each other. The lack of correlation enables a reduction in overall portfolio risk. However, one irony in this notion is that the correlations among traditional asset classes can be higher than their correlation to some alternative investments. This being the case, it is disappointing that the rigidity of asset-class criteria definitions do not seem to allow the inclusion of some alternative investments as asset classes. In most traditional approaches to portfolio construction, it is style analysis among traditional asset classes that plays a significant role in asset-class diversification. For instance, small-capitalization U.S. equity often is considered an asset class alongside large-capitalization U.S. equity, even though the correlation between these two assets is very high.

How is it that separate allocations to these two asset classes can occur, and an investment such as oil and gas is not considered an independent asset class? The answer to this type of question often is found in the following rationale: An investment that has no implicit rate of return cannot be considered an asset class. This relates to the asset-class criterion for the necessity of intrinsic value that is estimable. For instance, consider equities in general. The theoretical value of an equity may be found through the discounted present value of its expected future dividends and related growth rate. The value of a fixed-income instrument may be calculated through the expected return of its par value and the discounted present value of its expected future interest payments. In contrast, some alternative investments have no such estimable metrics. Therefore, it is easier for many investors to use different styles of existing traditional asset classes that have widely accepted intrinsic return features than it is to implement alternative investments that may have more beneficial correlation attributes than asset-class styles but more difficult-to-decipher intrinsic return traits.

Further difficulty in using alternative investments in most traditional approaches to portfolio construction is that the indexes that represent alternative investments typically are based on returns from funds, rather than compilations of market-wide securities. For instance, U.S. equity might be defined by the S&P 500, which is a broad-based basket of stocks that can be replicated in a passive investable form. In contrast, private equity indexes, for example, are measured by all reporting private equity funds, which cannot be replicated as a passive investment. The case for hedge funds is even more complex, since the degree of homogeneity among these vehicles is dubious. Alternative investments must be grouped in such a way as to be able to meet the tenor of traditional asset-class passive index purity. Even alternative investment indexes based on funds or peer groups, as long as they represent an investor's investable opportunity set, can be used for portfolio modeling purposes. Most investors utilize noninvestable indexes to replicate alternative investments in modeling portfolio allocations.

Although this approach has improved with the advent of dealer-provided derivatives on some of these indexes, a more exacting approach may be through factor identification and passive replication. The goal is to create sound processes for statistical modeling while including as many investments as possible and keeping fidelity to the goals of diversification, portfolio volatility reduction, and performance enhancement.

One helpful tool is factor analysis, which is the identification of underlying drivers of return and risk in an investment strategy. Some alternative investments can be partially described by traditional asset classes as well as other more exotic variables, such as liquidity and volatility. Not all of the return and risk in an alternative investments strategy can be described by investable factors. Some of the return is unique, which in fact can be a significant source of noncorrelated returns that these strategies have with traditional asset classes. This unique return represents the alpha term in a regression analysis. Regression analyses also determine the independent factors to which an alternative investment strategy is dependent.

The ability to identify factor sensitivities for alternative investments does not render risk budgeting among asset classes antiquated theory. Although there are caveats to be aware of when conducting an asset optimization that includes alternative assets, the process itself still is useful (see Chapter 11). The ability to model factors should encourage investors to perfect forward-looking expectations for all asset classes and factors. While using historical data for modeling portfolios is instructive, it is less conclusive when attempting to determine the likely future performance, volatility, and correlation of alternative investments. The ability to create better forward-looking asset-class and factor estimates, based on the detail that factor analysis provides, does not necessary guarantee that estimates will be more accurate. But, clearly, the ability to strive toward this end is improved. Once an investor considers the range of traditional and esoteric factor betas available for investment and seeks to build a portfolio populated with these risk premiums, the prior limitations associated with traditional portfolios construction become apparent.

PROBLEMS WITH SELECTING VEHICLES FOR ALTERNATIVE INVESTMENT PORTFOLIO CONSTRUCTION

The assumption for the techniques used to construct portfolios that use alternative investments is that the investments are achieved through private partnerships. A different approach is that the exposure to alternative investments is accomplished through the direct investment in stocks, bonds, real estate, private securities, private companies, and commodities. A direct investment approach has management complexities, but it also has the ability to customize portfolio exposures and engage more readily in tactical asset rebalancing. Investors with significant assets and investment staff are able to accomplish this. Moreover, some are able to add value through short-term tactical rebalancing. A large asset base is required to efficiently execute this approach when dealing with multiple alternative investments and hedging techniques. A large asset base also implies a budget that is significant enough to afford an in-house staff with requisite experience and sophistication to manage such an articulated portfolio.

Alternatively, an entire portfolio could simply be allocated in its entirety to tactical asset allocation investment managers, who focus on traditional as well as alternative investments either through direct investments or through commingled funds. In this event, an investor would have certain benefits and issues. Benefits include economies of scale that an investment manager could provide through marshaling a larger amount of capital, some potential investment management fee savings through this economy of scale, and a consolidated risk management and reporting functionality. The potential negative issues associated with such a consolidated approach to asset management include having concentrated manager-specific risk by having fewer investment managers controlling more assets and a requirement that the managers have investment and geographic expertise across many asset classes and strategies.

Investment through partnerships versus the direct purchase of securities are not mutually exclusive approaches. An investor can use both of these tactics in the expression of exposures in portfolio construction. The use of direct securities can generate fewer fees than investing through fund partnerships, which is analogous to investing in direct funds rather than funds of funds. Although in each case there is a savings in management and performance fees, there also is value-added skill that is forgone by not using investment managers in the implementation of portfolios. The issue boils down to whether the investor has the staff or consultative support to pursue one course of action over the other. Additionally, within the context of a diversified portfolio that employs an investment in both direct securities and funds, a program of asset-class rebalancing through the use of futures, swaps, or exchange-traded funds (ETFs) can be employed (see Chapter 8).

Defining alternative investments through direct investment in securities versus fund products is relevant in deciding how to build factor models. Should factor models be based on indexes, funds, funds of funds, or specific securities? What are the appropriate types of vehicles to use when trying to create passive proxies for alternative investments? The answers to these implementation questions may vary based on the type of alternative investment that is being considered and the quality, reliability, and investability of the indexes and other aggregate information available for each. From a practical perspective, it is far easier and less idiosyncratic to use index results where available for study purposes. Nevertheless, investors who re-create this methodology may choose other approaches that are better tailored to their specific circumstances and that might entail the use of custom peer groups or individual alternative investment securities.

QUANTITATIVE BUILDING BLOCKS

Factor analysis can be used in a more complete analysis of alternative investments and the identification of their sources of return and risk. It is helpful to conduct a brief review of the quantitative building blocks that underpin factor analysis. There is a progression in these building blocks and linkage among the following theories, beginning with the capital asset pricing model.

Capital Asset Pricing Model (CAPM)

The capital asset pricing model lays the foundation for factor analysis. However, the CAPM is based only on a single-market factor concept. The CAPM is a linear equation that solves the expected return for an asset based on that asset's beta to a market. Beta is a measure of the sensitivity of an asset to its market, and therefore it is a measure of an asset's risk versus its market. For example, an asset with a beta greater than 1.0 has systemic risk greater than its associated market.[2] The premise for the CAPM is that markets are efficient.[3] Therefore, the entire expected return for an asset is explained by its market and the risk-free rate. The CAPM equation is represented by:

$$E(r_p) = r_f + \beta_p(E(r_m) - r_f)$$

where $E(r_p)$ = the expected return for asset p
r_f = the risk free rate of return
β_p = beta, or the sensitivity of the asset to its market
$E(r_m)$ = the expected return for the market

and

$$B_p = \frac{Cov(r_p, r_m)}{Var(r_m)} = \frac{Cov(r_p, r_m)}{\sigma_m^2}$$

where r_p = the return for asset p
r_m = the return for the market

The expected return for a market above the risk-free rate is also considered to be the risk premium in a market and can be expressed as λ, such that:

$$E(r_m) - r_f = \lambda_m$$

Arbitrage Pricing Theory (APT)

Arbitrage pricing theory is an expansion of the CAPM to include multiple factors. The APT holds that the expected return for an asset is a function of the returns from multiple factors. The theory also maintains that asset-specific risk may be eliminated through diversification. The multifactor APT is expressed as:

$$E(r_p) = r_f + \beta_{p,1}(E(r_1) - r_f) + \beta_{p,2}(E(r_2) - r_f) + \cdots + \beta_{p,k}(E(r_k) - r_f)$$

where $E(r_p)$ = the expected return for asset p

r_f = the risk-free rate of return
$\beta_{p,k}$ = beta, or sensitivity of asset p to factor k
$E(r_k)$ = the expected return for factor k
$(E(r_k) - r_f)$ = the risk premium for factor k

The expected return for a factor above the risk-free rate is also considered to be the risk premium for the factor and can be expressed as λ, such that:

$$E(r_k) - r_f = \lambda_k$$

The APT can be simplified as:

$$E(r_p) = r_f + \beta_{p,1}\lambda_1 + \beta_{p,2}\lambda_2 + \cdots + \beta_{p,k}\lambda_k$$

The APT assumes that ultimately there is no room in the markets for arbitrage and that markets are in a state of equilibrium. Both the APT and the CAPM assume that the only alpha that exists is the risk-free rate. Under this framework, the only available trade-offs for an investor are factor or market betas and the risk-free rate of return. An investor may weight exposures to numerous factors and to the risk-free return.

Multiple Factor Models (MFMs)

The APT model is a multiple factor model. The basic equation for a MFM is

$$r_p = \alpha_p + \beta_{p,1}(r_1) + \beta_{p,2}(r_2) + \cdots + \beta_{p,k}(r_k)$$

where r_p = the expected return for asset p
α_p = the expected exogenous return for asset p
$\beta_{p,k}$ = the beta or sensitivity of asset p to factor k
r_k = the expected return from independent factor k

The migration from the CAPM to the APT to the more generalized MFM allows more flexibility to include various determinants of returns for assets, including the term alpha, or α, which is used here. Furthermore, alpha is presumed to be uncorrelated[4] to the variables in the model. MFMs tend to be based on historical data. The analysis uses the historical relationships among variables to project these sensitivities into the future. As such, a main use for MFMs is to project risk. Three examples of MFMs are macroeconomic, fundamental, and statistical.

Macroeconomic MFMs may be based on macroeconomic independent factors. In this fashion, an asset's return or sensitivity to these factors may be determined. Indeed, there are very complex econometric models based on this approach to MFMs. Often, these independent variables are divided into their actual versus their projected figures. In this sense, sensitivities can be determined as they relate to historical versus estimated relationships.[5]

Fundamental   Fundamental factor models focus on the minutia of securities analysis. These models often use ratios as their independent variables, such a price-to-book value, price/earnings ratio, and leverage ratios. They also may use style and sector analysis, such as sensitivities to industry sector, market capitalization, and growth versus value characterizations. MFMs using a fundamental perspective attempt to determine the sensitivities of a security or portfolio of securities to a series of fundamental factors.

Statistical   The third form of MFM is based on statistical factors. This approach takes time series from a wide range of independent factors and generates sensitivities to these factors for a dependent variable. However, the analysis is not dependent on a qualitative recognition of the likely relationship between the dependent variable and its independent factors. Inherently unrelated variables may exhibit correlation during certain periods of time. The analyst in this instance is only interested in the statistical relationship between the variables, not the rationale behind the relationships.

Principal Component Analysis (PCA)

An adjunct to the statistical approach to multiple factor models is principal component analysis. Once a regression analysis is performed on factors identified through statistical MFM, PCA is a technique for determining the principal components of error terms generated in the regression. This results in the creation of a set of component factors with back-tested efficacy and predictive power for that error term over a specified period of time. Essentially, in PCA the analysis is to determine a group of unidentified factors that best explain a dependent variable's historical return variances. This group can change over time and therefore continually will have strong explanatory power.[6]

Simple Linear Regression Model

The simple linear regression model assumes that a dependent variable is explained by three elements: a constant, an independent variable or regressor, and an error term. The formula for a simple linear regression model is altered from the pure explanatory powers of the CAPM, APT, or MFM. Not only do simple and multiple linear regression models include an alpha, or α term, but they also include a specific error, or ε term. Typically, in computer-modeled simple and multiple linear regressions, the error term is assumed to be normally distributed with a mean of zero. The simple linear regression equation is represented by:

$$y = \alpha + \beta x + \varepsilon$$

where y = a dependent variable
  x = an independent variable
  α = alpha, or an exogenous constant
  β = beta, or the regression coefficient of the independent variable
  ε = an error term

Multiple Linear Regression Model

An expansion of the concept of simple linear regression models is the use of multiple independent variables, which becomes the multiple linear regression model. In this instance, the multiple independent variables have individual associated regression coefficients. For instance, β_1 is the expected change in dependent variable y per unit change in independent variable x_1 when all other independent variables x_n are held constant. One of the interesting features of a multiple linear regression model is that as more independent variables are added to the model, assuming that they are statistically significant in their impact on the dependent variable and relatively uncorrelated to each other, the alpha and error terms have the capability of declining in relative importance. This fact is important when considering alternative investments and their various beta sensitivities. As more factor betas are identified, alpha and the error term may become less distinguishable from one another in terms of their importance and statistically indistinguishable from zero. Effectively, multiple linear regression models are MFMs and can be represented by the equation:

$$y = \alpha + \beta_1 x_1 + \beta_2 x_2 + \beta_n x_n + \varepsilon$$

where y = the return on the dependent investment
  x_n = any independent variable
  α = alpha, or an exogenous constant return
  β_n = beta, or the regression coefficient of any independent variable
  ε = an error term with a mean of zero and uncorrelated with the independent variables

(For more information on statistical tests on the validity of regression results, see Chapter 11.)

RISK BUDGETING USING FACTORS

A main use of MFMs is to conduct attribution analysis and in the case of investments to forecast returns and volatility of returns. This focus on returns and risk sensitivities is critical in understanding factor exposures of a single investment or a portfolio of investments. There is a linkage of MFMs based on historical time series and the monitoring of portfolios and identification of their factor sensitivities. Of course, much of this bridging between historical factor sensitivities and current portfolio exposures depends on historical correlations repeating themselves. This reliance is a significant shortcoming. Indeed, multiple factor analysis may provide a false sense of security, because of the risk of these models performing poorly out of sample. In this event, risk will have been underestimated.

The use of scenario analysis and stress testing has become a key method for solving an overreliance on historical sensitivities. Nevertheless, this too is an imperfect solution, since by its very nature, a crisis is not predictable. Only ex-post can a crisis event be appropriately analyzed for its correlation properties. Therefore, predicting the precise impact of an unknown crisis event on the return and volatility of certain assets is difficult. Furthermore, protection against every negative scenario and extreme stress test typically produces a drag on portfolio performance. This is the opportunity cost associated with buying securities that protects against extreme market movements. During periods of normally distributed returns, this expense will diminish returns for a portfolio of investments.

A Word about the Validity of Historical Covariance Matrixes

Correlation among investments is highly dependent on periodicity. Certain factors may have very strong influences that cause investments to be correlated over very short time frames, and others cause correlation over longer-term time frames. The more consistent variables of influence tend to be ones that impact investments over longer-term time frames. These factors are inclined to be the more predictive and repeatable ones. Longer-term factors are likely to be macroeconomic, while shorter-term factors may be driven more by sentiment and market reactions rather than economic outcomes. Moreover, predicting short-term outcomes of certain dependent variables assumes that their covariance with independent variables holds constant. In light of the wider range of independent variables that may influence dependent variables over short stretches, the fidelity of the variables to their historic correlations is less certain. This weakness is at the root of the limitation of the predictive power of value-at-risk models, which assume that correlations among assets and their determinant factors remain constant even during short time frames.

The entire concept of modeling short time frame covariance and volatility figures is at the heart of short-term trading strategies. Such strategies include trend-following commodity trading advisers, statistical arbitrage hedge funds, and leveraged quantitative global tactical trading funds. Each of these examples may use rapid-fire trades that rely on the maintenance of certain correlation assumptions. Many of these styles are based on the supposition that recent historical short-term relationships between securities and markets will continue over the short term. In part, the predictive power of these strategies is based on the fact that there are numerous market participants who use them. Systematic and technical analyses can become self-fulfilling because a certain amount of short-term activity in the market is based on them. However, when the reliability of these models stops, it often is because of new unforeseen short-term influences, such as disease, storms, or geopolitical events.

In addition to these influences that can fracture the reliability of short-term correlations among assets and assumed volatilities, over the long term these short-term models will yield to longer-term influences from changes in macroeconomic variables. Therefore, it appears that the more reliable way to study these codependent variables is through a longer-term vantage point. Otherwise, the accuracy of shorter-term models may become less trustworthy. While critics of this approach might say that longer-term models are just as vulnerable to short-term changes in historically derived covariances and assumed volatilities, over the longer term these short-term mismatches tend to be diluted by large time series.

BEYOND TRADITIONAL ASSET CLASS RISK BUDGETING

In addition to asset class and alternative investment strategy risk budgeting through mean-variance optimization that may be augmented by regression analysis, investors should include other approaches to risk budgeting, such as investment manager–specific risk budgeting, systemic risk budgeting, and organizational risk budgeting. Factor modeling is an important tool that can be used to assist in all of these risk-budgeting exercises. Factor analysis reveals sensitivities of funds or investments to a range of types of factors. Some of these factors are quantitative and can be measured, while others are qualitative factors, such as counterparty risk and due diligence risk. However, both quantitative and qualitative factor measurement depend on having portfolio and organizational transparency.

Security Transparency for Factor Analysis

Most regression analysis is based on historical data, not only as it pertains to investment returns but also for performance of the independent variables or factors that are used. The obvious problem that develops from this approach is that there is a temptation to believe that historical relationships between these variables will hold true in the future.

One approach used to skirt this issue is to employ security-level transparency in conducting this type of analysis. Once a portfolio of securities is attained, the factor sensitivities of the underlying securities can be measured, based on a series of groupings of these securities into their strategy and security types. The benefit of this approach is that although it is sensitive to the assumption that historical factor relationships still will hold true in the future, it is more accurate in determining a true current picture of a portfolio, rather than assuming that the future performance of a portfolio simply will mirror its historical performance sensitivities.

Security-level analysis improves what is still an imperfect quantitative approach to predicting future investment performance. This improvement is important in that it addresses the tendency for alternative investment funds to become increasingly blurred in their use of investment strategies.

Manager-Specific Risk Budgeting

Manager-specific risk budgeting relies on setting expectations for return and volatility of returns and marrying these guidelines with a level of conviction in the manager held by the investor. Larger allocation weights are placed on higher-conviction managers than lower-conviction managers, assuming equal expected returns and volatility. Conviction can be based on the qualitative merits of one manager's skill versus another. This type of measurement can be very subjective on the part of the investor. However, manager-specific risk budgeting also can be based on the evaluation of due diligence and portfolio risk considerations. Such risks can relate to counterparty exposure, illiquidity, and position concentration, all of which become far more pronounced risks during periods of market stress or crisis. In order to render opinions on these risks, transparency is required of an investment manager's organization and portfolio. Furthermore, this transparency must be provided readily and not selectively, such that a full disclosure is made.

The fact that each risk premium that an investor faces should have an expected level of return has two implications for investors. First, investors should be cognizant of the relationship between assuming a risk and expecting a return from that risk assumption. Acceding to a risk premium should not be done with ambivalent return expectations. Risk should be accepted consciously and with a very definite expectation of return. Second, investors should not consider in isolation one fund that offers a specific type of risk premium. Each purchase by an investor of a risk premium being sold by a fund should be considered not only relative to other fund opportunities in the strategy, but importantly also across all other alternative investment strategies.

For instance, a hedge fund that makes private investments in public equities (PIPEs) should be compared not only against other hedge funds that do the same type of investing but also against certain private equity firms. Conducting this sort of cross-strategy comparison enables a more appropriate comparison of expected returns. If the hedge fund in this example holds its PIPE investments for an average of two years, then this portion of its portfolio should have the same return and volatility comparison as a private equity firm making late-stage investments with similar maturities. Doing this comparison enables the investor to compare the expected return, volatility, and illiquidity of the potential investment. It could be that the investment in the hedge fund offers equal gross returns to the private equity investment, but with much more attractive liquidity terms (e.g., a 1-year lockup for the hedge fund versus a 10-year lockup for the private equity fund).

Alternatively, the private equity fund in this example may have a much more attractive fee schedule than the hedge fund, so the investor might decide to accept the longer lockup of the private equity fund in exchange for the prospect of higher returns net of fees. Furthermore, this process of cross-strategy analysis focuses the debate for an investor on whether the investment is being made in order to maximize Sharpe ratio, achieve an absolute return regardless of volatility, or accomplish a certain internal rate of return over a defined time period.

This type of debate transcends the typical investment decision, which usually is simply associated with filling an allocation to an asset class as the major consideration. Cross-strategy analysis can also be applied to risks associated with due diligence, counterparty exposure, portfolio leverage, and position concentration. Cross-strategy analysis enables the investor to better match manager-specific risk budgeting to an overall asset allocation risk budget.

Systemic Risk Budgeting

Another area of risk budgeting relates to systemic risk. Alternative investments often deal in visible traditional risks, such as leverage, but they also have more opaque risks, such as notional leverage through the use of derivatives, illiquidity, and counterparty risk. Opaque risks provide an entirely new set of concerns for all investors. Although opaque risks often are associated with alternative investments, these risks are far reaching and in their fruition could negatively impact investors with no direct exposure to alternative investments. For instance, counterparty risk is an area that could touch areas as simple as commercial checking accounts as easily as it could affect a buyer of derivative contracts. This is because of the concentration of many types of risks in large banks with diversified lines of business. Although alternative investment managers have assisted in the proliferation of opaque risks that could have systemic impacts, all financial participants have exposure in the event of a systemic incident. Both obvious and opaque risks force investors to contemplate how well they are positioned for systemic risk, not only in terms of protecting against the unknown manifestation of systemic risk, but also in recouping some of the potential loss through more dynamic investments that might be able to take advantage of systemic volatility. Alternative investments paradoxically may be able to provide an area of shelter from a risk that they exacerbate. The low correlation benefits and tactical nimbleness of some alternative investments are attributes that could provide some protection from systemic risk.

Organizational Risk Budgeting

Another unconventional area to consider within the context of overall risk budgeting pertains to organizational risk. It could be that an investor already is exposed to significant risk in its normal business or income generating endeavors. This may suggest that having a very conservatively managed portfolio is appropriate, with more actual risk being taken at the organization's operations. Investors should consider risk budgeting inclusive of their organizational balance sheet and income statement. An organization may already have a large amount of debt, or it may be a significant user of derivatives in its operating activities. Therefore, risk budgeting must be considered not only in light of an investment portfolio, but also in terms of risk that the entity is taking in other areas of its organization. A risky enterprise should not necessarily have the same portfolio risk budgeting process as a more creditworthy investor.

QUALITATIVE INDEPENDENT VARIABLES

Both qualitative and quantitative factors are common among alternative investments. Qualitative elements that determine the outcome of alternative investments include at least two significant factors: counterparty risk and illiquidity. (Quantitative independent variables and their analysis through regression is the subject of Chapter 11.) In some cases, qualitative factors are unique to alternative investments and not found in traditional investments. It is difficult to measure counterparty risk and illiquidity, much less ensure that the investor is being compensated for accepting them. Furthermore, qualitative factors also are not easily modeled or optimized. The benefit from creating an objective methodology to compare qualitative factors is to have a uniform approach for producing a level playing field for appraisal. Such an approach enables a comparison across a range of alternative investments in order to measure the relative return being offered in the marketplace for exposure to qualitative factors. This ability is increasingly becoming an important cornerstone for investors' ability to evaluate a range of alternative investments.

Counterparty Risk

Commercial banks, investment banks, traditional insurance companies, and large fixed-income investment managers have acquired significant counterparty risk with alternative investment managers. Although one could argue whether the concentration of counterparty risk is actually among these traditional market participants rather than the emerging alternative investment participants, the risk in counterparty failure is twofold. First, there is the local impact from failure of a single market participant and the devastating ramifications this can have on the failed entity's specific counterparties when it occurs. Second, there could be a systemic impact that potentially causes catastrophic and widespread losses, which could occur through the failure of a global counterparty that has a large market footprint, as do many of the traditional market participants. In this case, a counterparty failure could cause a particular marketplace to seize. These two concepts really are divided by size of participants. However, even a small-sized market participant that uses large amounts of leverage and derivatives could have a negative affect on larger-sized players.

No matter who would be to blame as the source of a market dislocation, the growth in the use of derivatives in all markets has concentrated counterparty risk among the large dealers of these securities. Generally speaking, hedge funds have spurred the use of derivatives and leverage. But these tools are supplied to the hedge funds by the major market dealers, who have therefore become the primary counterparties for the hedge fund industry. Furthermore, the hedge fund industry, while its growth in assets has been robust, still is in the early years of creating robust back-office support and clearing functions. Therefore, does the symbiotic relationship between hedge funds and traditional financial service firms now render the established market dealer community just as risky as the hedge fund industry? Perhaps hedge funds have more idiosyncratic risk, but traditional financial trading parties are the source of more potential systemic risk, due to their market share concentrations.

Ironically, the purchase of credit default swaps (CDSs) has enabled hedge funds to become more risk averse, since these instruments act like put options on bonds. However, hedge funds have become such voracious users of CDSs and with such complicity on the part of traditional financial counterparties that new and uncertain systemic risks have emerged that affect all corners of the investment world. Furthermore, an investor's risk exposure to a counterparty may be compounded by the investor's normal course of business. For example, a corporate pension plan that is invested in a hedge fund that has significant counterparty risk with a large market dealer may have exposure to the same dealer in the corporation's treasury through purchase of interest rate or currency derivatives to sustain its ongoing business operations. Risk budgeting of counterparty exposure must be considered not only within the context of overlapping risks in an investment portfolio but also in an investor's operating areas.

There are few ways to quantify counterparty risk so it can be uniformly measured across alternative investments. One way is through the CDS market. Not only has the CDS market created much of the counterparty risk that exists among derivatives dealers, but it also prices this risk through CDSs whose reference entities are the dealers themselves. Although the CDS market is an effective way to price credit risk among major financial dealers, this market typically does not have securities prices on hedge fund credits. However, some credit rating agencies have begun to rate hedge funds from a credit and a counterparty perspective. The more transparent that hedge funds become, the easier it will be for a variety of these services to price the counterparty risk that is associated with hedge funds. A regular review of credit ratings on counterparties that are issued by credit rating agencies is an appropriate course of action. Nevertheless, there are few credit ratings that occur for private equity firms or funds. Counterparty risk pertains more to hedge funds than other types of alternative investments because of the prevalence of derivatives and the associated notional leverage among these funds.

ILLIQUIDITY FACTOR

An additional factor that can contribute return to a wide range of investments is the concept of illiquidity. The return from illiquidity is fundamental to the pricing of alternative investments. An interesting question is how can one make an investment in illiquidity from a passive perspective and therefore create a metric by which to measure illiquidity when it is cheap or expensive? There is not an obvious solution for a benchmark to be able to passively index illiquidity. Although illiquidity is a return factor that is valuable and can be assigned an expected risk premium, it may be easier to do so on a qualitative rather than quantitative basis. In spite of its enigmatic character, an illiquidity factor may be teased out of many alternative investments so that a comparison of risk premiums across assets can be made. One approach to doing this across alternative investments is by assigning a measure of illiquidity based on the magnitude of historical serial correlation of returns for various types of funds.

Illiquidity is a tricky qualitative factor to quantify and map. However, it is one of the most important factors for an investor in alternative investors to contemplate. This is particularly true as alternative investment funds continue to overlap in their investment styles, including private equity, real estate, and corporate control positions. The salience for an investor is to ensure that the illiquidity risk premium is being properly measured and compared across the various alternative investment categories to which access is available. Once an illiquidity risk premium can be quantified and measured, the investor can gauge the expected return on the investment attributable to the illiquidity risk. For that matter, the investor also can measure whether the expected return for illiquidity is priced expensively or cheaply for an investment being considered, relative to other illiquid investments being offered in the marketplace. Although the examples in this chapter focus on identifiable illiquidity characteristics of various investments, it does not account for exaggerated illiquidity during market shocks. Indeed, market shocks can trigger structural factors in partnership agreements (such as gating mechanisms) that restrict redemptions as well as limit market liquidity.

Illiquidity Factor Examples

When attempting to define the illiquidity risk premium, one approach is to observe market pricing for this risk through examples in various alternative investment areas. In doing so, there are several examples where illiquidity is actively priced and sometimes even arbitraged by investors in alternative investments. The following market examples provide illustrations.

Illiquidity Example 1: Private Equity Interests in the Secondary Market   One example of illiquidity's being valued and traded is the secondary market for limited partnership interests in private equity funds. For various reasons, occasionally the initial investors in limited partnership interests in private equity funds find themselves in need of monetizing these investments prior to the end of the life of the funds (for more detail on this, see Chapter 8).

Supply and demand in this secondary market can be cyclical, which affects the spread between the stated net asset value (NAV) of a partnership and the price that buyers are willing to pay in the secondary market. In effect, this spread represents the price for liquidity in these otherwise illiquid investments. In addition to the cyclical forces at work that have an impact on spreads, another element that affects pricing is the length of time required prior to the expected maturity of the partnership, in terms of both its underlying investments and the stated life of the fund inclusive of extensions. This pricing factor is a measurement of duration for the expected payment of principal and cash flows.

An additional spread determinant is the fundamental appraisal of the private equity portfolio, which is a measurement of the veracity of the NAV compared with a current appraisal of the underlying investments and expected future value of the investments. A rule of thumb for the discount that this secondary market commands is 5 percent to 15 percent from the most recent audited NAV of the partnership. Nevertheless, depending on cyclical factors and a buyer's analysis of a portfolio under consideration, this discount can at times be higher or much lower.

Illiquidity Example 2: Hedge Fund Lockups A lockup for a hedge fund is an initial period of investment when an investor may not redeem the investment, unless perhaps a penalty is paid. Initial lockups and subsequent redemption periods offered to investors in hedge funds also provide mileposts for measuring the way in which alternative investments price illiquidity. Many hedge funds offer multiple series of investment classes that have varying degrees of liquidity. Some investors are willing to accept less liquid redemption terms. Each series or class also often has a fee structure that scales with the liquidity terms that are offered. For example, while a hedge fund might put forward a basic fee structure of a 2 percent management fee plus a 20 percent performance fee with an initial one-year lockup and quarterly redemption privileges thereafter, it might also have a separate series of investment class with a management fee of 1.5 percent and performance fee of 20 percent with a two-year lockup, or it may have a class with a 2 percent management fee and an 18 percent performance fee with a two-year lockup period. In these alternative offerings, pricing a 50-basis-point management fee savings or a 200-basis-point performance fee reduction are directly associated with accepting less liquidity. The ultimate dollar savings to the investor for accepting one or another of these proposals depends on the amount of capital invested and the performance of the investment over the lockup time period.

Whereas the example of the secondary market price spread for private equity partnership interests is easier to calculate as a discount from an

NAV price, the case of fee reductions for hedge funds is more difficult to price, since it is a function of the present value of future fee payments, some of which depends on the fund's future performance. For example, if one assumes a 10 percent gross hedge fund performance figure, then a 200-basis-point performance fee concession amounts to a 16-basis-point discount (i.e., 10 percent gross performance minus 2 percent management fee times 200 basis points equals 16 basis points). As illustrated in Table 10.1, the performance fee discount for this example as a percentage of net returns is 2.5 percent. This 2.5 percent illiquidity discount recurs regardless of the magnitude of the gross performance.

However, the illiquidity discount that results from a management fee discount is more variable than the illiquidity discount that results from a performance fee discount. This is ironic, since the savings from a management fee discount is an absolute figure and the savings from a performance fee discount depends on performance. (These concepts are depicted in Table 10.1.) Illiquidity discounts resulting from management fee discounts are particularly sensitive to gross performance. When gross performance is low, the illiquidity discount can be sizable. One could make the case that in a low risk-free interest rate environment, which is assumed to be a low-return environment for hedge funds, the illiquidity discount generated through a management fee discount can be enormous.

Example 3: PIPE Transaction Discounts   Private investments in public equities are often referred to as PIPE transactions. These deals are sold to investors willing to accept unregistered securities with the promise that a registration statement will be filed for the securities, thereby making them salable. Often, these securities will remain unregistered for a period of 45 to 90 days or longer during the period prior to the registration statement's becoming effective with the relevant regulatory body. The corporate issuers of these securities offer a price discount to buyers as an inducement to assume the illiquidity and the risk of price change that can occur between the time that the unregistered securities are purchased and the time that they become effectively registered and freely tradable. In most cases, this inducement is in the form of a spread between the purchase price of the unregistered securities and the market price of the comparable public securities at the time of the transaction. However, the inducement can also include the granting of warrants to purchase additional unregistered securities, or it can include a sliding scale for the ratio of securities to be issued that associates the purchase price with the ultimate market price realized for the securities when sold. In any event, a simple price discount in the range of 10 percent to 20 percent is not uncommon for these transactions. This discount is expected to be monetized by the PIPE buyer over a very short

TABLE 10.1 Matrix of Sample Hedge Fund Fee Discounts for Accepting Illiquidity Terms

	Gross Return %	Management Fee %	Return Net of Management %	Performance Fee %	Net Return %	Illiquidity Spread %	Illiquidity Discount as % of Net Return
No discount	20.0	2.0	18.0	20.0	14.40	0.00	0.0
Management fee discount	20.0	1.5	18.5	20.0	14.80	0.40	2.8
Performance fee discount	20.0	2.0	18.0	18.0	14.76	0.36	2.5
No discount	15.0	2.0	13.0	20.0	10.40	0.00	0.0
Management fee discount	15.0	1.5	13.5	20.0	10.80	0.40	3.8
Performance fee discount	15.0	2.0	13.0	18.0	10.66	0.26	2.5
No discount	10.0	2.0	8.0	20.0	6.40	0.00	0.0
Management fee discount	10.0	1.5	8.5	20.0	6.80	0.40	6.3
Performance fee discount	10.0	2.0	8.0	18.0	6.56	0.16	2.5
No discount	5.0	2.0	3.0	20.0	2.40	0.00	0.0
Management fee discount	5.0	1.5	3.5	20.0	2.80	0.40	16.7
Performance fee discount	5.0	2.0	3.0	18.0	2.46	0.06	2.5

period of time, usually less than one quarter of a year. However, the risk embedded in these transactions is higher than one might think. Once news of a PIPE transaction becomes public, the market price of the securities may decline toward the discounted price at which the PIPE securities were sold. Therefore, although the PIPE discount initially seems larger than other forms of illiquidity pricing, there is vulnerability for the public and private securities to partially converge during the period of time prior to the unregistered securities' becoming registered.

PIPE deals can have other risks associated with them. For example, the accounting for and valuation of these securities can be questionable. In most cases, the gain implied by the discount between the price of the PIPE transaction and the market price is accrued by the buyer over time. For instance, a hedge fund that purchases a security through a PIPE deal at a 15 percent discount from the then market price of the security might accrue the implied gain up until the point of liquidity for the security, which may be separate from the carrying value of the market price of the security. Another issue surrounding PIPEs is the hedging of the underlying security. Buyers of PIPE transactions are not allowed to sell the underlying security until it has been registered for trading with the appropriate regulatory body. However, investors sometimes circumvent this rule from a risk or economic perspective through purchasing swaps, shorting similar securities such as ETFs, or improperly circumventing the law all together. Finally, the PIPE strategy may represent only a periodic strategy that is available either in very poor markets when capital is not widely available, or in very good markets when capital is too widely available for lower quality corporate credits. Therefore, drawing a conclusion about the veracity of illiquidity pricing from PIPE transactions may incorrectly rely on a highly idiosyncratic or fleeting investment style.

Example 4: Initial Public Offering (IPO) Transactions   The purchase of IPOs is not an alternative investment per se, but an example of the market's pricing of illiquidity. Furthermore, both private equity funds and hedge funds are involved in this junction in the capital markets landscape. During IPOs of equity securities, it is common practice for the underwriting firms to be paid a selling concession. However, in the event that an IPO deal is not considered hot and it opens flat relative to its offering price, initial purchasers of IPO shares who decide to sell may only receive their purchase price minus the underwriters' selling concession. This discount paid to the investor manifests itself in the form of a penalty bid set by the underwriters at a discount to the IPO price. This convention used for IPOs that do not perform well in their initial debuts represents a form of illiquidity discount that the initial IPO purchaser is paying in order to exit the investment.

The underwriter actually makes a profit in this instance, since typically IPOs are oversold and the underwriters possess a short position at the IPO price.

The interesting aspect of this illiquidity risk premium is that the buyers of the IPO are able to "put" their shares to the underwriters at a cost equal to immediate liquidity. This is similar to a seller of a private equity partnership in the secondary market putting its partnership interest to a buyer at a cost, which equals liquidity. Even though it would not be surprising to see the cost of liquidity in the IPO example being smaller than that in the private equity example, because the speed of sale in the IPO example is far faster than in the private equity example and the counterparty in the IPO example really has no risk, this is true on a simple but not annualized return basis. As illustrated in Table 10.2, the initial discount in the IPO example is captured immediately, while the secondary private equity partnership discount is not monetized until its cash flows are realized or until the end of the life of the fund. On a duration-adjusted basis, the implied IPO liquidity discount is very large and larger than the secondary private equity partnership discount.

Example 5: Life Settlements   Life settlements represent the secondary market for life insurance policies. This niche market often involves the purchase of whole-life insurance policies at prices above the policies' guaranteed cash values. The rationale for these transactions is that the guaranteed cash values of insurance policies with short expected maturities often are underpriced relative to the present value of the principal value of the insurance contract. This mispricing develops from changing life expectancies of insured parties over a period of time following the initial date of issuance of policies. Frequently, the life insurance companies that write these policies do not adjust the scale that calculates the periodic guaranteed cash values of the policies, even if the initial assumptions for the length of the life expectancy of the insured parties begins to shorten. Specialty investment firms have developed to fill this inefficiency and offer the insured parties purchase prices for these life insurance policies that are higher than the guaranteed cash values. These secondary market purchasers then hold the policies until maturity, which equates to the death of the insured.

There are several elements that contribute to the pricing of these transactions. In the secondary purchase of a life insurance policy, the buyer is required to make assumptions about the insured's life expectancy, which is typically achieved through a thorough medical review. Most of the insured parties in these situations have an illness of one sort or another that limits their life expectancy, and they seek to monetize their insurance at the highest possible price in order to use the proceeds during their remaining lives. The most liquid part of the secondary market for these policies relates to insured parties who have life expectancies of five to eight years. Buyers of the policies

TABLE 10.2 Examples of Discounts in Market Pricing for Liquidity

Example	Specifics	Visibility, Certainty, and Quality of Credit	Time to Maturity (a)	Discount (b)	Annualized Discount (c)	Annualized Spread (d)
Risk free	U.S. Treasury zero-coupon bond	Very high	1 year	5.3%	5.3%	0.0%
1	Private equity secondary market	Low	7 years	10.0%	1.4%	−3.9%
2	Hedge fund lockup (e)	Medium	2 years	1.0%	0.5%	−4.8%
3	PIPE transaction	Medium/low	90 days	15.0%	60.0%	54.7%
4	IPO penalty bid	High	1 day	5.0%	1,825%	1,820%
5	Life settlements	High	6.5 years	10.0%	10.0%	4.7%
6a	Merger arbitrage—cash deal	High/medium	85 days	2.1%	10.0%	4.7%
6b	Merger arbitrage—stock deal	High	95 days	2.3%	8.0%	2.7%
7	Revolving credit commitment fees	High/medium	1 year	1.25%	1.25%	−4.1%

(a) The duration in each instance is assumed to equal the maturity of the transaction, with the assumption that there are zero cash flows prior to maturity.

(b) Stated as a percentage of the current principal value of the transaction. Midpoint taken where examples have indicated ranges as of 2006.

(c) All transactions are adjusted to have equal durations. Simple, not compounded.

(d) The market price minus the risk-free rate. The concept here is that the risk-free rate is a subcomponent of the discount in each example. In theory, if the market for liquidity is priced correctly, transactions with higher risk should have higher spreads. However, this is not always the case for the examples cited.

(e) This example refers to a 50-basis-point savings per year for an investor accepting a two-year lockup provision, therefore indicating a 100-basis-point savings on initial invested capital.

price them according to a required internal rate of return (IRR) calculation, often amounting to 10 percent per year. The IRR calculation is based on the purchase price, the terminal or face value of the policy, and negative cash flow in the form of insurance premiums that the buyer still is required to pay on the policy during the remainder of its term. Since the expected return from these investments is based on an IRR calculation, the assumption for the maturity of the investment is important. A misestimation of life expectancy can cause a lower-than-expected IRR (if the life expectancy is materially longer than expected), or a higher-than-expected IRR (if the life expectancy is materially shorter than expected). Additional risks must be evaluated, such as the credit quality of the insurance company that issued the policy, the regulatory risks associated with possible restrictions on this investment strategy, and state insurance board regulation since each of these transactions typically undergoes unique state-specific filings. Additionally, buyers of life insurance policies must be aware of maintaining policy diversification by varying exposures to life expectancy, illness type, geography, and regulatory risk.

Meanwhile, the sellers of the life insurance policies receive a premium to a policy's guaranteed cash value. The spread that a seller receives is unique and characterized by the inefficiencies of this illiquid market. In this example, the seller is avoiding an illiquidity discount that it would receive (i.e., from the insurance company willing to pay only the guaranteed cash value) by securing a higher price from the open market (i.e., from the secondary purchaser of the policy). A range of possible premiums that the seller may encounter in these transactions is 3 percent to 13 percent. This relatively large range is explained by the inefficient and illiquid nature of this market. However, participants in this market often cite a premium of about 5 percent received by sellers in many transactions.

Assuming that the life expectancy of the insured is calculated accurately and all other credit risk premiums are correctly appraised, the estimated 10 percent IRR being paid to the buyers of the policies include a risk-free rate and a risk premium associated with providing liquidity to the seller. Therefore, there are two sides of the illiquidity equation in this transaction. One relates to an illiquidity cost that the seller is avoiding by finding a secondary buyer. The other is a remaining illiquidity risk premium that the buyer is assuming through ownership of the life insurance policy. Table 10.2 indicates the annual IRR that the buyer is expecting, which includes an illiquidity risk premium it is being paid and a risk-free rate.

Example 6: Merger Arbitrage Merger arbitrage often has been likened to a form of insurance. Its essence in this sense is one investor relieving another of the risk associated with the final expected return from the completion of an announced acquisition. In return for assuming this risk, the merger arbitrageur is paid the final return on a security upon the successful acquisition of its issuer. Of course, as is the case with any insurance, a merger arbitrageur is assuming the risk that a deal does not close. A broken deal can lead to substantial losses for the provider of insurance, exacerbated by the probable use of leverage by managers operating in this strategy. The merger arbitrageur also has an upside to its investment in the form of the materialization of a higher than expected purchase price ultimately being paid. The ultimate ability for a merger arbitrageur to be successful in this strategy depends on deal diversification, the fact that deal duration often is short and capital therefore is turned over multiple times in a year, and the use of leverage.

This form of insurance also can be considered as a measurable type of illiquidity risk premium. The seller of the securities to the merger arbitrageur can actually calculate what is being forgone in order to purchase liquidity prior to the completion of the deal. Often, merger arbitrage rates of return are quite small, given the liquid nature of these securities as being publicly traded and the short durations involved prior to transactions closing. The returns often are cited on an annualized basis, since many of the transactions close in a matter of months, and thereafter capital is recycled into other transactions during a 12-month period.

Furthermore, deal spreads can be widely divergent over the course of an interest rate cycle. The risk-free interest rate is the starting point to which risk premiums are added in order to set a desired annualized rate of return on a merger arbitrage trade. Spreads may tighten very close to this risk-free rate when the merger arbitrage strategy is flush with capital and there are a large number of investment managers using the strategy. Investment manager returns are influenced by the number of investment managers utilizing the strategy, the amount of leverage used by managers in the strategy, and the overall amount of equity capital being managed by managers in the strategy. The absolute rate of return on the transactions will migrate over time along with the general level of market volatility, which can cause a cluster of merger arbitrage transactions to collapse. At times, spreads in merger arbitrage are influenced not only by demand, the risk-free interest rate, and the credit quality of specific merger arbitrage transactions, but also by a size factor. Larger-sized transactions have greater liquidity than smaller-sized transactions. Large merger arbitrage deals often have tighter spreads than smaller-sized transactions. The size influence also affects merger arbitrage liquidity, which is analogous to the size influence on liquidity and pricing in the fixed-income market.[7]

Thus, there are many risk premiums implied in merger arbitrage spreads over the risk-free rate. However, for the purposes of the examples in

Table 10.2, the entire arbitrage spread is considered to arise from the fundamental role of seller of liquidity and assumer of illiquidity risk that the arbitrageur is providing to the marketplace. Examples in the merger arbitrage realm include (1) a merger arbitrage spread of an annualized 10 percent for an all-cash acquisition with an expected maturity of 85 days and (2) an 8 percent annualized return for an all-stock merger with an expected maturity of 95 days. The price being paid by the original shareholder to the merger arbitrageur for liquidity is 2.3 percent over 85 days in the case of the cash acquisition and 2.1 percent over 95 days in the case of the stock transaction. The difference between cash and stock transactions is that the acquirers are paying cash to shareholders in the cash deals, and they are paying acquirers' stock to shareholders in the stock transactions. The implied inverted yield curve between these two different duration transactions relates to the lack of inherent hedging in cash transactions rendering them somewhat more risky, whereas stock transactions are naturally hedged with a short sale position in the stock of the acquirer. Furthermore, cash transactions offer an additional element of risk associated with the acquirer's securing and maintaining to fruition the financing for such a transaction.

Example 7: Revolving Credit Commitment Fees Revolving credit agreements are lines of credit usually offered by banks to corporate borrowers. However, there is a secondary market for these instruments. Often, a revolving credit agreement has nothing drawn on it, but the would-be borrower still pays, for example, 1 percent to 3 percent per year on the value of the commitment for the benefit of having liquidity made available. The size of this fee is a function of the borrower's credit quality at the time the facility is created. However, the market price for revolving credit facilities in the secondary market can change (decline) as the credit quality of the borrowers declines and as it appears more likely that the borrowers may draw funds on the committed lines of capital. Typically, revolvers have one-year terms, and they can be renewed for subsequent annual terms thereafter.

There is considerable difference between a bank's selling a stressed or impaired credit versus selling a revolving credit agreement that is of a higher credit quality. Generally, higher-quality credits receive smaller market discounts and have a larger pool of potential buyers. However, there are some concrete reasons why secondary buyers of revolving credit lines may be less willing to purchase these instruments, compared with purchasing term loans with the same borrower or one of similar credit quality. Revolving loans have at least two mechanical features that make them less attractive from a structural or servicing perspective. For instance, the buyer of an existing revolving credit agreement often is required to post collateral against the unused portion of the credit line. Another issue is that the borrower may desire to increase or decrease the amount drawn on the revolving credit line throughout the life of the agreement. Servicing this need can be a back-office problem for some secondary buyers of these credit lines. Issues such as these reduce the pool of potential secondary buyers of revolving credit agreements, compared with the number of potential buyers of term loans in the secondary market. This winnowing of prospective buyers decreases the relative liquidity of revolving credit agreements in the secondary market, compared with a similar credit quality term loan. This illiquidity risk premium often is in the 10 percent area from an IRR perspective. In other words, if the standard desired rate of return for the purchaser of a secondary loan is 10 percent, a revolver would have an implied IRR of 100 to 150 basis points wider than this (i.e., 11 percent to 11.5 percent).

Illiquidity Pricing Methodology

Using the observations of the aforementioned examples of pricing and the implied expected returns associated with illiquidity, this factor can be modeled. There are at least three influences that affect the pricing of illiquidity: credit, interest rates, and duration. For example, credit reflects the quality of the investment or fund to which an investor is considering committing capital; the expected risk-free interest rate is the starting point to which an illiquidity risk premium is added; and duration reflects the length of time that the investor will be asked to relinquish liquidity.

If one extends this notion of pricing to the illiquidity of alternative investments, the same types of factors are at play: a discount rate, time to maturity, and the credit quality of the issuer. For instance, a private equity partnership purchased in the secondary market at a discount should be priced based on these three factors. Moreover, the cheapness or expensiveness of the pricing for such a sale can be measured versus the risk-free rate with the same maturity. In other words, the pricing can be considered as a spread over comparable zero-coupon bonds issued by the U.S. Treasury. Although the U.S. Treasury may not have issued and in circulation any zero-coupon bonds with a maturity that matches the maturity of an alternative investment at any point in time, a theoretical risk-free security can be modeled nonetheless. This process is assisted by market pricing for U.S. Treasury principal strips, which are created by dealers in the market by separating the principal from the coupon payments of U.S. Treasury securities. Additionally, given the fact that several liquidity discounts measured in the marketplace have relatively short durations, in some cases measured as short as 3 to 12 months, a comparison with U.S. Treasury bills is straightforward. In their purest form, U.S. Treasury bills are a form of zero-coupon bond since they are issued at a discount.

Receiving the par value of a bond depends on the creditworthiness of the issuer. For instance, a zero-coupon bond issued by the U.S. Treasury might be expected to have a very high credit score and virtually no credit risk, whereas a corporate issuer of a zero-coupon bond may have some element of credit risk. The duration of a bond equals the amount of time required for the purchase price of the bond to be repaid through its internal cash flows. Furthermore, the duration of a bond is a measure of its volatility. Bonds with long durations and long maturities are more volatile in response to changes in interest rates than is the case for bonds with short durations and short maturities. Duration also calculates the expected price change of a bond resulting from a change in interest rates. This excludes the valid notion of convexity as a determinant and influence of bond pricing. The duration of a zero-coupon bond essentially is equal to its maturity, because the only cash flow from the bond occurs at its maturity. Thus, the premise for considering zero-coupon bond pricing to value illiquidity as a return factor relies on the notion that the price paid for buying illiquidity is only recaptured upon the maturity of the investment. More specifically, the maturity of an alternative investment is assumed to equal the next period when its natural terms allow for its liquidation.

A standard valuation technique for a zero-coupon bond is represented by the following formula:

$$P = \frac{FV}{(1+i)^{t \times 2}}$$

where $P =$ the present value or current price of the bond
$FV =$ the maturity value of the bond, or its par value
$i =$ the discount rate expressed on a semiannual basis
$t =$ the number of years to maturity

For example, a zero-coupon bond with the following characteristics would be valued accordingly:

$$FV = \$1{,}000$$
if $i = 3.5\% = 0.035$
$t = 5$

then $P = \dfrac{\$1{,}000}{(1+0.035)^{5 \times 2}} = \$708.92$

Therefore, the buyer of this sort of instrument is being paid the maturity value of the bond minus the current price in order to accept the bond's various risk premiums until maturity. The zero-coupon bond discount, of which the illiquidity risk premium is a part, can be expressed in the following formula:

$$D = FV - P$$

where   D = the bond discount
          P = the present value or current price of the bond
          FV = the maturity value of the bond, or its par value

However, the bond discount term is comprised of component pieces, including a risk-free interest rate, a credit component, an illiquidity risk premium, and duration. One way to consider illiquidity across investments is to measure liquidity discounts and durations using the zero-coupon bond pricing methodology. In this way, disparate assets can be compared on a relative basis, on an adjusted basis by adjusting all durations to one year for example, and on a spread basis relative to a risk-free rate. Table 10.2 illustrates this approach in conjunction with Examples 1 through 7, including a comparison of the examples with a risk-free U.S. Treasury zero-coupon security. Table 10.2 is eye opening in its illustration of the comparative pricing of the various liquidity discounts in the market and their spreads versus the risk-free rate. When these discounts are adjusted to the same one-year maturity, they can be compared equally on an annualized basis. Taking the annualized liquidity discounts and subtracting the risk-free rate from them provides annualized spreads above the risk-free rate for each type of liquidity discount.

This illustration provides an approach for investors seeking to sell or buy liquidity. The inefficiency of the pricing for liquidity is apparent from this comparison. As it pertains to alternative investments, one can see from Table 10.2 where an attractive annualized return can be generated by accepting illiquidity and alternatively where pricing is relatively unattractive on a spread basis versus the risk-free rate.

One initial observation about these spreads is that the liquidity discounts offered for some alternative investments are close in comparisons (e.g., Examples 1 and 2) but show a negative spread versus the risk-free rate. For example, given the uncertain credit for hedge funds in Example 2, why would an investor accept less than the risk-free rate in locking up capital in the illiquid version of this alternative investment vehicle? (The alternative for Example 2 was not accepting the illiquid terms, but not receiving the fee discount either.) The answer probably lies in the inefficiency with which the market for illiquidity is measured and priced and the large amount of capital in these markets willing to accept less-than-optimal terms. In Example 2, an investor may be willing to accept a longer-lockup hedge fund in spite of the discount possibly being mispriced, because of valuing the access being granted to the hedge fund. In this case, a token fee discount is better than no fee discount at all.

In Table 10.2, Examples 3 and 4 are more in line with the type of high-risk premium that one would expect to see in return for accepting illiquidity. In Example 3, which illustrates the discount associated with a PIPE transaction, the annualized return and spread over the risk-free rate seem more in line with the level of uncertainty associated with an investor's ability to see a return of capital and potential profit from this type of transaction. Similarly, in Example 4, which shows IPO penalty bid pricing, the premium associated with immediate liquidity in an IPO with poor initial price performance is probably correlated to the degree of panic and general angst possessed by the seller.

Example 5 depicts the return to the provider of liquidity from sellers of life insurance policies. This example represents the recapture of an illiquidity risk premium over an unknown but generally predictable duration. The magnitude of this premium, as illustrated in Table 10.2, is robust on an absolute basis compared with the other examples, but it also is based on a longer recapture period than some others. The central uncertainty for this type of transaction is the predictability of duration, which will determine the annualized return as this illiquidity risk premium ultimately is monetized.

Examples 6a and 6b, which pertain to the merger arbitrage world, may be the most efficiently price among these examples. Indeed, the participants in these markets intentionally use the risk-free rate as a starting point for their expected return on capital invested. Merger arbitrageurs would be unlikely to withdraw capital from cash accounts earning the risk-free rate unless they expected to be rewarded with a spread above the risk-free rate. The merger arbitrage risk premium above the risk-free rate is annualized at 270 to 470 basis points in the examples. Presumably, risk arbitrageurs would add leverage to this return to increase it further.

Example 7 also is curious in its negative annualized spread to the risk-free rate. Many revolving credit agreements purchased in the secondary market have annual exit clauses. Therefore, the risk that the purchaser of this instrument has associated with deploying additional capital to the borrower is limited to successive annual terms. It is likely that the risk-free rate is already captured in the interest rate of the revolving credit agreement. Therefore, the enhancement to total return from the higher implied interest rate for purchasing these instruments in the secondary market is not expected to track the risk-free rate.

Although illiquidity discounts often represent only one-time events, in some cases the discount is a multiyear benefit that accrues to the buyer for accepting illiquidity. However, the validity of this accrual depends on the ability of the investor to reap the spread between the discounted price and the true NAV of the asset. For example, this is the case for the secondary purchase of private equity partnerships, where the illiquidity discount at the time of purchase is not fully realized until the individual investments in the partnership mature and are sold or until the total partnership runs the course of its life and matures. In the private equity example, the entire discount is received at the initiation of the transaction, but the investor cannot actually monetize that discount until a number of years has passed. The hedge fund example also can be highly dependent on the gross return generated by the fund in any one year, as illustrated in Table 10.1.

As with zero-coupon bonds, volatility and length of duration should be linked when examining illiquidity risk premiums. A longer duration accepted for an illiquid investment should equate to a larger standard deviation of expected returns. Other elements, such as credit quality, also determine the ultimate range of possible return outcomes when investing in an illiquid asset. The previously mentioned examples regarding illiquidity do not specifically identify the level of expected volatility associated with a certain length of duration for the illiquid investment. Nevertheless, one can surmise that the association of long duration with high potential volatility is likely to be present for these investments as well.

Possible Passive Benchmark for Illiquidity

Once characteristics are determined for a low-credit-risk zero-coupon bond, such as one issued by the U.S. Treasury, this security can be used as a baseline proxy for pricing illiquidity in the marketplace for alternative investments. The key importance of creating a benchmark for measuring the market pricing of illiquidity is to be able to gauge passive versus active portions of a liquidity discount. The expected return from illiquidity in a specific alternative investment should be comprised of a risk-free rate (passive) and an investment-specific rate (active). Having a risk-free benchmark enables an investor to measure an illiquidity beta and alpha associated with the investment opportunity. This furthermore enables the investor to generalize about the expected return due to illiquidity in certain alternative investment strategies, as well as measuring this return characteristic across alternative investment strategies.

This approach to measuring the illiquidity risk premium enables an investor to place all alternative investments on an equal footing to gauge their expected and actual returns associated with a uniform definition of illiquidity. An approach such as this is becoming a central tool for investors as managers of alternative investment funds become more defined by their structure and lockups than by their strategies and types of assets used to construct portfolios.

Problems with Modeling Illiquidity

A number of problems emanate from attempting to use zero-coupon bond pricing to model illiquidity in alternative investments. The central issue is that the liquidity discount associated with these investments often includes credit, duration, and illiquidity components. For instance, it is difficult to set an appropriate discount rate to appropriately value the credit quality of the investments underlying a private equity partnership. While time to maturity is fairly estimable in this example, the terminal value for the partnership is not. It also is difficult to create a uniform system for the measurement of the credit risk associated with each type of alternative investment. A wide range of systems to evaluate credit risk will likely generate a wide range of discount rates and spreads above a risk-free zero-coupon bonds when valuing illiquidity for these investments. Although various avenues exist for using single systems for valuing specific types of alternative investments, there are no apparent unified systems available to consider the credit risk associated with all types of alternative investments. Therefore, while an assigned return can be placed on the credit element of each type of alternative investment, the basis for this calculation will not likely be uniformed.

Also problematic are the cash flows from and to the private partnerships. Irregular cash flows represent another problem in using zero-coupon bonds as a passive illiquidity benchmark. The value and timing of alternative investment cash flows may render the zero-coupon bond methodology inappropriate. Furthermore, few bond-pricing formulas ever contemplate negative cash flows from a bond, as would be the analogous case for capital calls from a private equity partnership. Nevertheless, one could naively assume that the cash flows from such a partnership would be zero on a net basis, or take the point of view that since the partnership was being purchased after most of its capital calls have been made, subsequent cash flows have a high probability of being positive on a net basis.

SUMMARY

Presently, most traditional investors categorize investments by asset class, investment style, or quantitative factor exposure. However, the vast majority of this occurs post the initial categorization of an investment by asset class.

The trouble in doing this with alternative investments is the inability to consider return drivers that may overlap one alternative investment strategy and another. For instance, how does an investor evaluate a three-year lockup hedge fund that is 50 percent invested in private or illiquid transactions? Since such an investment falls between typical hedge fund and private equity generalizations, it often may be mispriced in terms of required risk-adjusted returns relative to other types alternative investments.

Alternatively, an investor's inability to grapple with an alternative investment that does not fit neatly into preconceived and rigid asset classes may lead to very attractive opportunities simply being neglected. As alternative investment strategies blur and overlap, an ability to compare identical return drivers across disparate strategies is critical for an investor's success and ability to construct an efficient portfolio of alternative investments. This ability can be rendered through the analysis of quantitative and qualitative factors that derive the return and risk for alternative investments.

Furthermore, traditional risk budgeting techniques used by investors can be expanded into risk budgeting for manager-specific risks, systematic risk, and organizational risk. Risk budgeting also can be extended into the budgeting of factors that are identified through factor analysis.

CHAPTER 11

Factor Analysis: The Findings and Discovering Active Alpha

T his chapter provides a portfolio construction methodology for investors implementing alternative investments, thereby enabling them to measure the sources of return and risk in their investment allocations. Initial portfolio allocations determined through optimization are used in conjunction with regression analysis to identify factor exposures. Then the independent factors that drive returns and risks in alternative investments are reapplied in a risk budgeting context. The resulting optimized factor portfolios provide a clearer depiction of exposures in a diversified portfolio that uses both traditional and alternative investments. In doing so, the unexplained return from alternative investments also is identified. The alpha characteristic is broken into its passive risk-free component and its active return. This approach to factor identification aids in the creation of passive benchmarks for alternative investment portfolios. These passive benchmarks also may be investable, thereby potentially offering synthetically created alternative investment portfolios. This process concludes with the ability to conduct factor measurement for risk monitoring and portfolio rebalancing.

TIME SERIES DELINEATION AND ISSUES

In selecting data sets for the quantitative factor analysis of traditional and alternative investments, choices include historical time series, historical points in time, and the creation of future expectations. Although not without its own group of problems, one accepted approach is the use of historical time series. The use of forward-looking expectations requires a methodology for substantiating these assumptions. Depending on the methodology chosen for forward-looking expectations, a wide range of results can be generated. In this chapter, the process of mean-variance optimization (MVO) is conducted through the use of historical time series and the generation of mean results, standard deviations, and correlations. The next step of the analysis using regressions employs the same historical time series and expands the data set to include historical time series for independent factors. The final step of applying the initial MVO portfolio allocations to the independent factors identified through regressions for each dependent variable also uses historical data strings. (The appendix to this chapter contains a description of the data used in this analysis, its source, and its frequency.) An implication from this work is that investors can use the historical relationships among dependent and independent factors to inform forward-looking estimates for both of them. Projections for the direction and magnitude of movements in independent factors provide guidance for the likely movements of the dependent factors, which are represented by the alternative investments categories. Projections of independent factors can be accomplished through econometric modeling, which then can be used to estimate the future performance of alternative investments, such as private equity, hedge fund strategies, and real estate. This chapter does not delve into the process of econometric modeling to create forecasts of future performance of alternative investments based on forecasts of their independent factor sensitivities, but it frames the ability to identify these relationships through the use of historical data.

There are numerous shortcomings to an analysis of alternative assets based on historical time series. Problems with this analysis are focused on the quality of the data used. Typical data issues relate to the veracity of the performance represented by indexes, including the following: survivor bias, backfill bias, and incomplete representation. Survivor bias implies that index data may be vulnerable to unsuccessful funds dropping out of time series, in which case the performance of the index may be artificially elevated above what an investor might hope to achieve on average. Backfill bias also can inflate a time series through the inclusion of historical data from successful funds that belatedly are included in a time series once the funds have achieved confidence in sharing their performance results to indexes. Both survivor bias and backfill bias reflect selectivity in the ability of funds to report or not report to index providers. Incomplete representation is another form of subjective fund reporting. Some funds choose not to report to index providers at all, thereby questioning whether an index truly is representative of the average experience being realized by investors in a strategy. Indeed, some of the best-performing and largest hedge funds do not report to and do not wish to be included in indexes, because of their desire to keep this information confidential. This phenomenon of fund-dependent reporting for index creation, which is commonplace among alternative investments, is quite different from traditional assets, which tend to be defined from an index perspective by an all-inclusive, objective list of public securities.

Another group of data problems relating to alternative investments and their representation by indexes is focused on implementation. The question of whether a mean index result for an asset can be replicated by an investor is subject to the following topics: dispersion of all index components around the mean index result, dollar versus equal weighting of index components, investability of indexes, and tracking error to indexes. Dispersion is the concept of having a wide standard deviation of results around a mean. Dispersion tends to be higher for funds operating in alternative investments than is the case for traditional investments. The reasons for higher dispersion can relate to leverage, the use of derivatives and the related notional leverage that they imply, shorting of securities, a potential lack of diversification of securities, and the use of illiquid securities. These techniques can cause volatility in returns, and in comparison they typically are not present in traditional asset classes, such as U.S. equity or fixed income. The problem with dispersion for an investor is the risk that an investor winds up investing, for example, in a fourth-quartile fund that has a materially different performance outcome relative to the average performance of the strategy. In contrast, a fourth-quartile performance for a traditional asset class might not be that different on an absolute basis from the average performance because of generally tighter dispersions of returns between the first and fourth quartiles. Another issue pertaining to index configuration is the use of dollar versus equal-weighted fund performance. Dollar-weighted indexes use heavier weights for funds with larger assets under management. Equal-weighted indexes employ equal weights for all funds in an index regardless of size. Depending on an investor's actual fund selection, either dollar-weighted or equal-weighted indexes may be most representative of the investor's realized performance. This issue is less one of comparing active versus passive management. It is more one of the structural difficulty for an investor to replicate the experience of an alternative investment index. Many alternative investment indexes are not investable. Although clearly there are investable indexes in certain alternative investments areas, most tend not to be all-encompassing of the experience of the total strategy that they seek to replicate. Because of the difficulty in accurately replicating the experience of all alternative investments from a passive perspective, investors often will experience some sort of tracking error to the available indexes. Indexes tend to understate risk in comparison with single-fund investments, because of the reduction in index volatility that occurs through diversification with the use of many funds.

Length of Time Series

A problem with both the MVO and regression analysis approaches is that the length of time series used can be relatively short. The return data for alternative investments in general does not have the number of observations that is experienced in more traditional assets classes. Therefore, the veracity of an analysis based on relatively short data sets may be questioned. Although the data used in the examples contained in this chapter covers a span of approximately 10 years, this is not considered a long period of time in the investment world. Furthermore, a decade-long period is subject to the vicissitudes of business, market, and investment climates that may reign during this period. A longer data set spread over many decades and many economic environments will likely provide a more balanced source of data from which to draw conclusions.

Commonality of Length of Time Series

The different starting points for various individual alternative investment strategies limit an analysis across these investments to the time series with the shortest length. This commonality enables the use of as many individual time series as possible, but can disregard an enormous amount of data for more mature time series. Furthermore, forcing the analysis to the shortest common time period can limit the veracity of covariance estimates created from the historical data. The implication from using data series that are truncated and that yield return, volatility, and correlation information that may be inaccurate over longer periods of times is the risk of constructing optimized portfolios that are less than optimal over longer time frames.[1] In turn, faulty correlation assumptions can lead to the construction of a portfolio that is too concentrated in its allocations to similar investments with perhaps similar factor dependencies.

End-Period Dependence

Another issue related to using short data sets is end-period vulnerability. Measuring performance data using short data sets creates pronounced sensitivity to beginning and ending points. Short sections within any data set may have very different characteristics than the data set as a whole. Furthermore, not all alternative investment performance time series have the same periodicity. This can be said about the frequency of the data observations as well as the length of the time series. A problem in MVO analysis is the reliance on historical data and the time periods used for the data sets.

Data Frequency

The frequency of data for some alternative investments is quarterly, while for others it is monthly. Because of the proclivity of some alternative investments to be illiquid, the pricing of these investments often is infrequent and represented by appraisals rather than actual transactions. The mismatch of data frequency can make an analysis of this data difficult. For the regression analyses performed in this chapter, dependent variables that only have data with quarterly frequency were regressed against independent variables whose data frequency was adjusted to quarterly from monthly.

Data Smoothing

Data smoothing is related to data frequency. Some alternative investments are priced through appraisals or estimates. Examples of these investments include real estate and private equity. This process can have the effect of smoothing the value of the investments over long periods of time. It also can afford the managers of the investments the ability to selectively reprice certain portfolio investments at opportunistic times, which helps to smooth overall results by matching portfolio investments that require upward valuations with other investments that require downward valuations. The problem with smoothing of investment performance is the effect is has on smoothing volatility and possibly altering correlations with other types of assets. Smoothed volatility and altered correlations of smoothed assets can result in unsmoothed assets receiving smaller allocations during the optimization of portfolios. Some critics attempt to unsmooth returns from infrequently pricing alternative investments in order to achieve their perception of more realistic volatilities and correlations, which results in lower allocations to alternative assets in portfolio optimizations.[2] However, a problem pertaining to unsmoothing is that it tends to result in suboptimal portfolios that perform worse in most market environments than portfolios that do not use this technique. The opportunity cost for using unsmoothed return strings may outweigh the benefit of achieving lower overall portfolio volatility in the infrequent instances of events that cause high correlations among many asset classes. Furthermore, the presumption that unsmoothed data equates to more realistic data in terms of volatility and correlations assumes that the infrequent pricing of alternative investments is a convention that will change in the future. More likely, the prevalence of illiquid alternative investments, along with their infrequent pricing and appraisal methodology, will increase in the future.

MEAN-VARIANCE OPTIMIZATION[3]

MVO based on resampling of data provides a methodology for portfolio construction. However, there are significant problems in doing so when using alternative investments, which are discussed later in this chapter. MVO creates an efficient frontier of portfolio allocations, based on asset correlations and a trade-off between risk and return for each asset. The return for each asset is described by its mean historical or expected future return, and its risk is described by the standard deviation (or the square root of the variance) of its returns. The addition of multiple assets with correlations less than 1.0 to each other provides diversification, which reduces the overall standard deviation of returns for the portfolio in total. Each point along the efficient frontier represents the most optimal return per unit of risk assumed in the portfolio assemblage. However, the optimal point on the efficient frontier may be represented by the highest Sharpe ratio point on the curve.

Constraints

Many practitioners who use the MVO approach to portfolio construction often employ artificial constraints, which restrict the amount of allocation to any one asset. The optimizations included in this chapter use a variety of asset allocation constraints. Constrained models are compared with unconstrained models as well. However, in both cases, the MVOs are used for illustrative purposes. The analysis does not purport to provide an optimal all-weather portfolio of traditional and alternative assets. Rather, it is a standard approach to allocation that enables an investor to take the results and divine their factor drivers of return through subsequent regression analysis.

A convention used in the mean-variance optimizations included in this chapter is the allowance only for positive allocations to assets. Negative allocations, or the ability to sell short the traditional and alternative assets, have been constrained. The rationale for this constraint is the difficulty in replicating short positions for certain alternative assets in the real world. For instance, short selling venture capital or leveraged buyouts (LBOs) is not easy to replicate in investment applications, even though this might be achievable through derivatives or swap agreements.

Approach and Observations

The approach taken to MVO begins with traditional asset classes and adds alternative investments to this construct. The utilized data is historical, and it is based on various indexes. This approach serves to demonstrate the change in an investor's portfolio as alternative investments are added. This is a quantitative approach that creates initial optimized allocations to all assets in a portfolio. It is illustrative in nature, because it is based on historical data, and index data has numerous shortcomings. In spite of the vulnerability to potential data problems and the limitation of MVO in its use of alternative investments, this approach is far better than a purely qualitative approach to portfolio construction using alternative investments, which can characterize many investors. This approach begins to move beyond the simple token allocations to alternative investments that are made by most investors with little regard to sound quantitative underpinnings or portfolio construction regimen, and is a reference for subsequent factor analysis.

Unconstrained Traditional Asset Portfolio   Figure 11.1 depicts a portfolio allocated only to traditional asset classes with no constraints on the amount of allocation to each investment. The optimization is based on historical data and essentially reflects perfection with the benefit of hindsight knowing the exact historical performance, volatility, and correlations for these asset classes. Each point along the efficient frontier represents the highest return per unit of associated risk. The optimal point represents portfolio with the highest Sharpe ratio[4] along the efficient frontier. The purpose of including the illustration in Figure 11.1 is to represent a base case performance for portfolio asset allocation in a classical sense.

Traditional Portfolio Constrained by 25 Percent   From Figure 11.1, the next iteration for most investors is to include constraints on the amount of allocation available to any one traditional asset class. The point of doing this is to guard against investing too heavily in one asset class and being imprudent in doing so. Of course, the illustration in Figure 11.1 represents an environment where the portfolio was perfectly constructed. Since this is an unusual circumstance, most investors include certain constraints on asset allocations knowing that the probability of being perfect in any strategic or tactical asset allocation endeavor is likely to be low. Thus, the optimization depicted in Figure 11.2 shows a 25 percent constraint on the ability to allocate to any one traditional asset class. The resulting efficient frontier has a materially truncated risk-and-return profile, compared with the unconstrained model in Figure 11.1. Thus, Figure 11.2 illustrates the potential through the use of constraints to somewhat reduce fiduciary risk associated with an unconstrained portfolio allocation.

Portfolio Constrained 25 Percent to Traditional and 5 Percent to Alternative
The next step in the migration of a typical investor is the tepid inclusion of alternative investments into a portfolio that otherwise is populated with only traditional asset classes. Typically, this occurs in an environment that already uses constraints in allocations made to traditional asset classes. The affinity for constraining asset allocations usually is extended to the initial foray into alternative investments. Figure 11.3 illustrates an investment

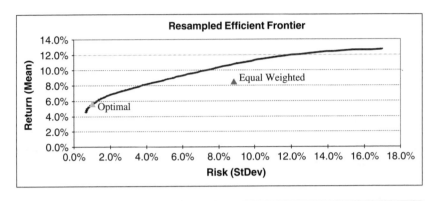

	Optimal Portfolio	Equal Portfolio	Optimal Portfolios -- by Rank					
			1	11	21	31	41	51
Short Term	36.0%	10.0%	73.5%	10.2%	1.3%	0.1%	0.0%	0.0%
Core FI	17.5%	10.0%	3.3%	23.6%	20.6%	13.5%	6.0%	0.6%
US ILBs	7.5%	10.0%	5.6%	12.4%	28.2%	27.7%	14.5%	2.1%
High-Yield	0.5%	10.0%	0.7%	0.8%	2.0%	2.5%	1.7%	0.1%
US EQ	0.1%	10.0%	0.0%	0.6%	3.3%	4.9%	6.3%	8.4%
Unhdgd Intl EQ	0.0%	10.0%	0.0%	0.1%	1.0%	1.7%	1.8%	1.8%
100% Hdgd Intl EQ	0.0%	10.0%	0.0%	0.3%	1.3%	1.4%	1.5%	0.9%
Emrg EQ	0.0%	10.0%	0.0%	0.2%	2.5%	5.4%	12.0%	40.6%
Emrg Debt	0.4%	10.0%	0.0%	2.7%	16.6%	36.5%	54.5%	45.6%
Dev.Non U.S. FI (Hedged)	38.0%	10.0%	16.9%	49.0%	23.1%	6.3%	1.5%	0.0%
Total	100.0%	100.0%	100.0%	100.0%	100.0%	100.0%	100.0%	100.0%
Average Annual Return	5.6%	8.5%	4.5%	6.5%	8.0%	9.8%	11.5%	12.7%
Standard Deviation	1.0%	8.8%	0.7%	1.7%	3.8%	6.8%	10.6%	16.9%

FIGURE 11.1 Portfolio Optimization of Traditional Asset Classes (Unconstrained)
Note: Model is unconstrained. Data is 1996 through June 2006.
Source: RogersCasey; Resampled Efficient Frontier™ provided by New Frontier Advisors, LLC.

portfolio that already is constrained by 25 percent to any one traditional asset class (similar to the concept in Figure 11.2), and it includes alternative investments that are constrained by 5 percent to any one asset. This model simulates the typical nominal allocations to alternative investment that are used by most investors who have no other way of refining these allocations and no ability to convey an approach for doing so to their constituents.

A comparison of the results in Figure 11.3 and Figure 11.2 reveals an improvement both in the return and the risk spectrum of available portfolios. This type of analysis and comparison generally is considered as a validation for the inclusion of alternative investments into a portfolio that otherwise only uses traditional asset classes. Of course, as mentioned, the data is based on historical results and includes indexes that for alternative investments may be difficult to duplicate. Nonetheless, the basic notion for

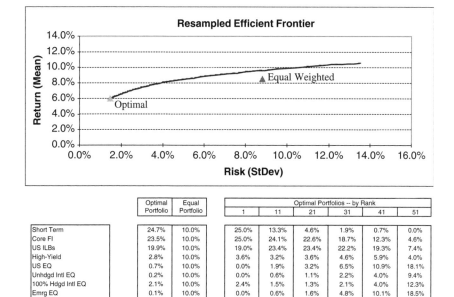

FIGURE 11.2 Portfolio Optimization of Traditional Asset Classes Constrained at 25 Percent

Note: Model allows for a maximum of 25 percent allocation to any one investment class. Data is 1996 through June 2006.

Source: RogersCasey; Resampled Efficient Frontier™ provided by New Frontier Advisors, LLC.

including alternative investments in a portfolio of traditional asset classes appears to have appeal.

Portfolio Constrained 25 Percent to Traditional and 25 Percent to Alternative

It is encouraging that the inclusion of alternative investments represented in Figure 11.3, albeit constrained at a much lower level per asset type than the constraints applied to traditional assets, represents an improvement over the model in Figure 11.2, which excludes alternative investments. However, the improvement also questions the rationale for placing a low constraint (i.e., high restriction) on the use of alternative investments. Why do traditional assets deserve a relatively larger allocation than alternative investments? The answer to this question appears to be grounded more in

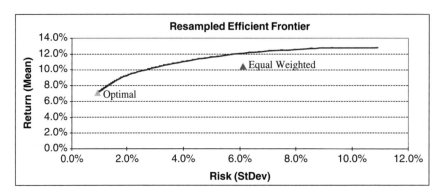

	Optimal Portfolio	Equal Portfolio	Optimal Portfolios -- by Rank					
			1	11	21	31	41	51
Short Term	24.9%	3.6%	25.0%	13.0%	1.9%	0.1%	0.0%	0.0%
Core FI	19.5%	3.6%	21.4%	20.3%	15.6%	9.4%	4.6%	0.6%
US ILBs	2.0%	3.6%	2.1%	3.0%	7.4%	11.0%	8.5%	1.8%
Real Est	5.0%	3.6%	5.0%	5.0%	5.0%	5.0%	5.0%	2.9%
High-Yield	0.1%	3.6%	0.1%	0.4%	0.9%	1.3%	1.1%	0.4%
US EQ	0.0%	3.6%	0.0%	0.0%	0.5%	1.3%	3.1%	11.2%
Unhdgd Intl EQ	0.0%	3.5%	0.0%	0.0%	0.1%	0.4%	0.9%	4.2%
100% Hdgd Intl EQ	0.0%	3.5%	0.0%	0.0%	0.1%	0.3%	0.7%	4.4%
Emrg EQ	0.0%	3.5%	0.0%	0.0%	0.4%	1.4%	4.1%	15.3%
Emrg Debt	0.0%	3.5%	0.0%	0.0%	1.3%	6.7%	15.0%	20.1%
All REITs	0.0%	3.5%	0.0%	0.0%	1.1%	2.8%	3.9%	4.1%
Commod	0.0%	3.5%	0.0%	0.0%	0.0%	0.3%	0.9%	1.5%
Private Equity	1.5%	3.5%	0.8%	3.1%	4.3%	4.7%	4.8%	4.2%
Dev.Non U.S. FI (Hedged)	25.0%	3.5%	25.0%	24.5%	20.2%	7.6%	1.1%	0.0%
Currency	0.1%	3.6%	0.0%	0.4%	1.1%	1.6%	1.4%	0.4%
Oil and Gas	0.5%	3.6%	0.0%	2.8%	4.4%	4.9%	5.0%	4.4%
Equity Market Neutral	4.4%	3.6%	4.4%	4.6%	4.4%	4.0%	2.8%	0.4%
Equity Hedge	0.1%	3.6%	0.0%	1.1%	3.3%	4.5%	4.7%	3.8%
Short Selling	0.0%	3.6%	0.0%	0.0%	0.0%	0.0%	0.0%	0.2%
Event Driven	5.0%	3.6%	5.0%	5.0%	5.0%	5.0%	5.0%	3.2%
Merger Arbitrage	1.5%	3.6%	0.9%	2.5%	3.3%	3.7%	2.9%	0.7%
Distressed Securities	0.2%	3.6%	0.0%	1.6%	3.5%	4.4%	4.6%	3.4%
Relative Value	5.0%	3.6%	5.0%	5.0%	5.0%	4.9%	4.2%	1.2%
Convertible Arbitrage	0.2%	3.6%	0.1%	0.9%	2.2%	3.3%	3.3%	1.2%
Macro	0.5%	3.6%	0.2%	1.5%	2.6%	3.5%	3.5%	1.6%
Venture	0.0%	3.6%	0.0%	0.0%	0.2%	1.3%	2.8%	4.4%
Buyout	1.4%	3.6%	0.5%	3.3%	4.2%	4.6%	4.7%	4.3%
Timber	3.2%	3.6%	4.5%	1.8%	1.8%	1.9%	1.4%	0.3%
Total	100.0%	100.0%	100.0%	100.0%	100.0%	100.0%	100.0%	100.0%
Average Annual Return	7.1%	10.4%	6.8%	8.2%	9.5%	10.7%	11.8%	12.8%
Standard Deviation	0.9%	6.1%	0.9%	1.4%	2.2%	3.5%	5.5%	10.9%

FIGURE 11.3 Portfolio Optimization Constrained at 25 Percent to Traditional Assets and 5 Percent to Alternative Assets

Notes: Model allows for a maximum allocation of 25 percent to any one traditional asset class and 5 percent to any one alternative investment. Data is 1996 through June 2006. Data for private equity, venture capital, and buyouts ends March 2006.

Source: RogersCasey; Resampled Efficient Frontier™ provided by New Frontier Advisors, LLC.

accepted convention rather than historical returns and risk. It is the basic resistance to alternative investments that is the cause of low allocations to alternative investments, rather than in a high degree of affinity for traditional investments. The predisposition to utilizing traditional investments is more grounded in human nature and comfort found in historical norms, rather than in a rational comparison of statistics. Many traditional asset classes have demonstrated less attractive historical volatility and return statistics than alternative investments.

A more enlightened approach to optimizing a portfolio loosens the restriction on the use of alternative investments. In this regard, Figure 11.4 depicts an optimization that has a 25 percent constraint on the use of any one traditional asset class or alternative investment. The concept behind this model is to allow the optimization to be more liberal in the use of the available asset choices, without regard to investor prejudice or preference. The results of this model are illuminating for several reasons. First, Figure 11.4 illustrates an improvement in the return-and-risk trade-off versus Figure 11.3, which models a 25 percent constraint to traditional assets and a 5 percent constraint to alternative investments. Second, the efficient frontier is steeper at lower levels of risk than is the case for Figure 11.3. The implication of this steepness is that the benefit to returns from the inclusion of higher allocations to alternative investments is accomplished even at very low risk levels. Third, the efficient frontier has a truncated risk spectrum, compared with the degree of volatility depicted in Figure 11.3. This is another sign that the low correlation benefits of alternative investments blended with traditional asset classes reduces total portfolio risk.

Although it is statistically apparent that the increasing use of alternative investments reduces overall portfolio risk, most investors who are new to this field might find this to be counterintuitive. Of course, there is a limit to this benefit and a point at which too much use of any one traditional asset class or alternative investment can increase total portfolio risk, because of a reduction in diversification. An investor might note that the portfolios depicted in Figure 11.4 are substantially laden with alternative investments. Although the model in Figure 11.4 restricts an investment to an allocation of no more than 25 percent, as a group the alternative investments represent a majority of each portfolio. Figure 11.5 depicts the total allocation to alternative investments versus traditional asset classes that are associated with the portfolios in Figure 11.4. Such a substantial migration to alternative investments from traditional asset classes has ramifications for liquidity, manager fees, and the general comfort level of investors pursuing this path. Nevertheless, this depiction is altered once alternative investments are better divided between their alpha and factor betas, as is depicted in Figure 11.8

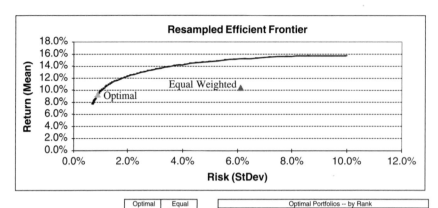

	Optimal Portfolio	Equal Portfolio	Optimal Portfolios -- by Rank					
			1	11	21	31	41	51
Short-Term	7.9%	3.6%	25.0%	2.3%	0.0%	0.0%	0.0%	0.0%
Core FI	8.2%	3.6%	10.4%	7.0%	1.9%	0.3%	0.0%	0.0%
US ILBs	2.8%	3.6%	2.5%	3.3%	2.0%	0.3%	0.0%	0.0%
Real Est	24.9%	3.6%	20.1%	25.0%	25.0%	22.1%	10.4%	0.4%
High-Yield	0.2%	3.6%	0.2%	0.2%	0.4%	0.3%	0.1%	0.0%
US EQ	1.1%	3.6%	0.0%	2.1%	3.0%	1.8%	1.1%	2.5%
Unhdgd Intl EQ	0.0%	3.5%	0.0%	0.0%	0.0%	0.1%	0.1%	0.7%
100% Hdgd Intl EQ	0.0%	3.5%	0.0%	0.0%	0.0%	0.0%	0.1%	0.8%
Emrg EQ	0.0%	3.5%	0.0%	0.1%	1.2%	1.8%	2.5%	8.0%
Emrg Debt	0.0%	3.5%	0.0%	0.2%	1.3%	3.1%	4.0%	5.0%
All REITs	0.0%	3.5%	0.0%	0.0%	0.8%	3.3%	6.2%	10.6%
Commod	0.0%	3.5%	0.0%	0.0%	0.0%	0.0%	0.0%	0.4%
Private Equity	0.4%	3.5%	0.3%	0.6%	2.8%	7.0%	12.6%	14.9%
Dev.Non U.S. FI (Hedged)	23.9%	3.5%	24.9%	21.7%	4.3%	0.1%	0.0%	0.0%
Currency	0.1%	3.6%	0.0%	0.2%	0.2%	0.1%	0.0%	0.0%
Oil and Gas	0.1%	3.6%	0.0%	0.3%	3.8%	9.9%	15.7%	15.8%
Equity Market Neutral	0.9%	3.6%	0.4%	1.3%	2.5%	1.0%	0.1%	0.0%
Equity Hedge	0.0%	3.6%	0.0%	0.0%	0.6%	2.8%	6.9%	7.7%
Short Selling	0.0%	3.6%	0.0%	0.0%	0.0%	0.0%	0.0%	0.1%
Event Driven	14.3%	3.6%	7.5%	18.2%	24.8%	24.3%	20.2%	5.8%
Merger Arbitrage	0.0%	3.6%	0.0%	0.0%	0.1%	0.0%	0.0%	0.0%
Distressed Securities	0.0%	3.6%	0.0%	0.0%	0.7%	1.9%	1.9%	0.4%
Relative Value	11.3%	3.6%	8.1%	12.6%	14.6%	5.3%	0.4%	0.0%
Convertible Arbitrage	0.0%	3.6%	0.0%	0.0%	0.0%	0.0%	0.0%	0.0%
Macro	1.0%	3.6%	0.2%	1.2%	1.6%	1.3%	0.5%	0.0%
Venture	0.0%	3.6%	0.0%	0.0%	0.2%	1.1%	4.1%	17.3%
Buyout	2.6%	3.6%	0.4%	3.8%	8.1%	12.0%	13.1%	9.4%
Timber	0.0%	3.6%	0.0%	0.0%	0.0%	0.0%	0.0%	0.0%
Total	100.0%	100.0%	100.0%	100.0%	100.0%	100.0%	100.0%	100.0%
Average Annual Return	9.3%	10.4%	7.7%	9.9%	11.8%	13.4%	14.7%	15.7%
Standard Deviation	0.9%	6.1%	0.7%	1.0%	1.7%	2.9%	4.7%	10.0%

FIGURE 11.4 Portfolio Optimization of Traditional and Alternative Assets Both Constrained at 25 Percent

Notes: Model allows for a maximum of 25 percent allocation to any one investment class.

Data is 1996 through June 2006. Data for private equity, venture capital, and buyouts ends March 2006.

Source: RogersCasey; Resampled Efficient FrontierTM provided by New Frontier Advisors, LLC.

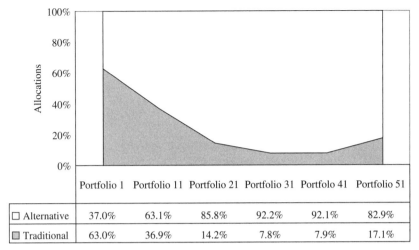

	Portfolio 1	Portfolio 11	Portfolio 21	Portfolo 31	Portfolio 41	Portfolio 51
☐ Alternative	37.0%	63.1%	85.8%	92.2%	92.1%	82.9%
▨ Traditional	63.0%	36.9%	14.2%	7.8%	7.9%	17.1%

Efficient Frontier Portfolios

FIGURE 11.5 Aggregated Allocations to Traditional Assets versus Alternative Investments (Constrained at 25 percent)
Notes: Model allows for a maximum of 25 percent allocation to any one investment type.
Data is 1996 through June 2006. Data for private equity, venture capital, and buyouts ends March 2006.
Source: RogersCasey.

later in this chapter. Many of the betas to which the alternative investments are sensitive simply are traditional asset classes.

Portfolio with Unconstrained Allocations to Traditional and Alternative   To take this notion a step further, Figure 11.6 illustrates an optimized portfolio of investments where the available allocations to traditional asset classes and alternative investments are unconstrained. Rather than limiting the potential allocations to any one asset to 25 percent of the total portfolio, which is the case in Figure 11.4, Figure 11.6 enables acute portfolio allocations. This freedom generates a spectrum of both higher and lower extremes for risk and returns. Ostensibly, this ability to go for broke does have the appeal of exposing an investor to a range of possible return results that on an absolute basis are higher than the range of potential results that are available under the circumstances in Figure 11.4, where constraints are used on the magnitude of allocation to any one asset. However, the downside to this lack of constraints is that it also generates a range of potentially lower absolute returns than is the case in Figure 11.4.

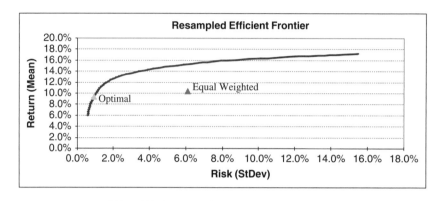

	Optimal Portfolio	Equal Portfolio	Optimal Portfolios -- by Rank					
			1	11	21	31	41	51
Short -Term	9.2%	3.6%	55.2%	9.2%	0.1%	0.0%	0.0%	0.0%
Core FI	6.4%	3.6%	3.6%	6.4%	1.0%	0.0%	0.0%	0.0%
US ILBs	2.9%	3.6%	3.6%	2.9%	1.5%	0.1%	0.0%	0.0%
Real Est	32.2%	3.6%	8.9%	32.2%	41.1%	16.5%	1.3%	0.0%
High-Yield	0.2%	3.6%	0.6%	0.2%	0.2%	0.0%	0.0%	0.0%
US EQ	0.6%	3.6%	0.0%	0.6%	2.0%	1.8%	0.7%	0.3%
Unhdgd Intl EQ	0.0%	3.5%	0.0%	0.0%	0.0%	0.1%	0.1%	0.1%
100% Hdgd Intl EQ	0.0%	3.5%	0.0%	0.0%	0.0%	0.0%	0.0%	0.0%
Emrg EQ	0.2%	3.5%	0.0%	0.2%	2.0%	2.7%	3.4%	7.4%
Emrg Debt	0.1%	3.5%	0.0%	0.1%	2.1%	3.7%	3.0%	0.9%
All REITs	0.0%	3.5%	0.0%	0.0%	1.2%	4.4%	7.0%	6.6%
Commod	0.0%	3.5%	0.0%	0.0%	0.0%	0.0%	0.0%	0.0%
Private Equity	0.6%	3.5%	0.2%	0.6%	2.8%	8.6%	17.0%	20.0%
Dev.Non U.S. FI (Hedged)	21.7%	3.5%	19.5%	21.7%	3.6%	0.0%	0.0%	0.0%
Currency	0.1%	3.6%	0.0%	0.1%	0.0%	0.0%	0.0%	0.0%
Oil and Gas	0.2%	3.6%	0.0%	0.2%	3.3%	11.8%	19.9%	12.8%
Equity Market Neutral	0.7%	3.6%	0.0%	0.7%	0.5%	0.0%	0.0%	0.0%
Equity Hedge	0.0%	3.6%	0.0%	0.0%	0.6%	3.7%	6.0%	4.0%
Short Selling	0.0%	3.6%	0.0%	0.0%	0.0%	0.0%	0.0%	0.0%
Event Driven	12.0%	3.6%	4.6%	12.0%	23.0%	28.1%	16.4%	1.7%
Merger Arbitrage	0.0%	3.6%	0.0%	0.0%	0.0%	0.0%	0.0%	0.0%
Distressed Securities	0.0%	3.6%	0.0%	0.0%	0.3%	0.8%	0.5%	0.0%
Relative Value	9.3%	3.6%	3.8%	9.3%	5.4%	0.5%	0.0%	0.0%
Convertible Arbitrage	0.0%	3.6%	0.0%	0.0%	0.0%	0.0%	0.0%	0.0%
Macro	1.8%	3.6%	0.0%	1.8%	2.2%	0.5%	0.0%	0.0%
Venture	0.0%	3.6%	0.0%	0.0%	1.1%	3.7%	12.2%	42.1%
Buyout	1.8%	3.6%	0.0%	1.8%	6.2%	12.9%	12.4%	4.2%
Timber	0.0%	3.6%	0.0%	0.0%	0.0%	0.0%	0.0%	0.0%
Total	100.0%	100.0%	100.0%	100.0%	100.0%	100.0%	100.0%	100.0%
Average Annual Return	9.4%	10.4%	5.9%	9.4%	12.2%	14.2%	15.7%	17.3%
Standard Deviation	0.9%	6.1%	0.6%	0.9%	1.7%	3.7%	7.2%	15.5%

FIGURE 11.6 Portfolio Optimization of Traditional and Alternative Assets (Unconstrained)

Note: Model is unconstrained. Data is 1996 through June 2006. Data for private equity, venture capital, and buyouts ends March 2006.

Source: RogersCasey; Resampled Efficient Frontier™ provided by New Frontier Advisors, LLC.

Not surprisingly, the ability to achieve higher and lower extreme returns also results in extreme volatility in this optimization. The extended tails in Figure 11.6 indicate the occurrence of both higher and lower extreme standard deviation events that are coincident with the extreme maximum and minimum returns. The concept of constraints used in Figure 11.4 is employed in order to limit the occurrence of these tails. Another finding in Figure 11.6 is an optimal portfolio (highest Sharpe ratio) with a faintly higher return. However, for most investors, this minor improvement in the optimal return very likely is not worth the inclusion of higher potential volatility (by approximately 550 basis points at maximum return levels) and lower potential absolute returns (by approximately 200 basis points at minimum volatility levels).

An important conclusion that can be drawn from a comparison of Figure 11.6 and Figure 11.4 is that it is not the sole fact that alternative investments are included in the optimization that benefits the investor. The inclusion of different types of assets in a portfolio is beneficial, but it has the potential for less extreme outcomes if done with constraints. The improvement that a portfolio can generate with the help of alternative investments is a function of the return and volatility traits of these investments as well as their low correlation attributes. The use of constraints is important to safeguard these benefits and ensure that anticipated diversification actually happens. Were it not for constraints, a concentrated portfolio of high Sharpe ratio assets could result in extreme results that may be undesirable. Although both Figure 11.6 (traditional and alternative assets both unconstrained) and Figure 11.4 (traditional and alternative assets both constrained at 25 percent) depict an improvement in returns and reduction in volatility versus Figure 11.1 (only traditional assets unconstrained), the points on the efficient frontier for Figure 11.4 generally have higher information ratios than the points on the efficient frontier for Figure 11.6. This illustrates the fact that it is not just the inclusion of alternative investments that improves a portfolio, but it also is the use of constraints to all investments that improves risk-adjusted returns.

The importance of constraints can be highlighted whether alternative investments are used with traditional asset classes or not. Figure 11.6 and Figure 11.1, which are both unconstrained, have similarly long tails from a risk perspective than do the constrained models represented by Figures 11.4 and 11.2. The unconstrained traditional asset class model (Figure 11.1) and that same model with the inclusion of unconstrained alternative investments (Figure 11.6) leads to the possibility of undesirable extreme risk results. Although the inclusion of alternative investments with their higher historical results improves the efficient frontier returns of Figure 11.6 versus Figure 11.1, the lack of guarantee that historical returns will be repeated is an important caveat. A more reliable assumption is that the tail truncation of risk that occurs through the inclusion of more types of assets (in this case alternative investments) will be repeatable and represents a structural improvement to a potential portfolio of assets. This improvement is reliant on constraints being used on the asset classes employed as well as stability of correlations.

Constraints may be more important in the use of portfolio construction than either the isolated use of traditional or alternative investments. However, the use of artificially low constraints in the implementation of alternative investments does not appear to be warranted. The magnitude of constraints can be developed by replicating the market capacity of each asset, which often is referred to as the equilibrium approach. (When applied to alternative investments, this approach has certain difficulties, which are discussed later in this chapter.) Or it can be based on general thresholds. For instance, the use of a 25 percent constraint for any one asset in a portfolio is large enough to provide significant allocations to better-performing assets. The combination of more generous constraints and the inclusion of a greater number of low-correlation assets from which to choose provides an improvement in the efficient frontier of portfolio opportunities.

How High or Low to Set Constraints?

The addition of low-correlated assets to a portfolio reduces the overall risk in the portfolio.[5] However, what maximum or minimum weight of these assets tampers with the benefit of diversification? Much of this question lies in the degree of correlation among the assets used in the portfolio. A lower correlation among assets equates to the potential to have a higher weight per asset while still maintaining diversification. A high correlation among assets implies that smaller weights to each asset must be used in order to eke out the available benefit from diversification that is present. Each portfolio of assets may be tested with various maximum and minimum constraints in order to determine the most optimal efficient frontier. Alternative investment portfolios should not be limited to low constraints, because of their generally low correlation over long time frames to traditional assets.

Historical Performance and Standard Deviation

The performance and standard deviation of returns for traditional assets and alternative investments are listed in Table 11.1. (The description of these assets is listed in Table 11.5 in the appendix of this chapter.) This information is supplied for roughly a 10-year period that included a fairly significant bubble at the turn of the century that affected both traditional

TABLE 11.1 Traditional versus Alternative Investment Historical Returns and Risk

Asset Type	Average Annual Return	Standard Deviation	Compound Return
Traditional Asset Class Return and Risk (1996–2006 Q2)			
Cash	3.77%	0.93%	3.77%
Core fixed income	6.00%	3.61%	5.94%
Inflation-linked bonds (TIPS)	6.74%	4.30%	6.65%
High-yield	6.99%	7.77%	6.70%
U.S. equity	10.74%	17.79%	9.30%
International equity (unhedged)	8.46%	18.62%	6.85%
International equity (hedged)	8.99%	17.99%	7.49%
Emerging markets equity	12.69%	27.82%	9.20%
Emerging markets debt	13.69%	13.07%	12.94%
Developed market non-U.S. fixed income (hedged)	6.80%	2.92%	6.76%
Alternative Investment Return and Risk (1996–2006 Q2)			
Real estate	11.67%	2.11%	11.65%
Real estate investment trusts (REITs)	15.24%	14.85%	14.28%
Commodities	9.20%	14.02%	8.30%
Private equity*	16.76%	15.73%	15.70%
Currency	5.75%	7.16%	5.50%
Oil and gas	16.93%	13.05%	16.20%
Equity market neutral	7.65%	3.31%	7.60%
Equity hedge	14.37%	11.09%	13.83%
Short selling	3.65%	23.22%	1.02%
Event-driven	13.01%	8.08%	12.73%
Merger arbitrage	9.31%	4.69%	9.21%
Distressed securities	12.27%	7.49%	12.02%
Relative value	9.58%	4.07%	9.50%
Convertible arbitrage	9.45%	4.72%	9.35%
Macro	9.78%	6.06%	9.61%
Venture capital*	19.53%	29.13%	15.93%
Leveraged buyout (LBO)*	15.12%	12.27%	14.47%
Timber	8.27%	5.76%	8.12%

*The strategies' ending data point is 2006 Q1.
Source: RogersCasey.

and alternative investments. Prima facie, this data implies that historically there has been reason to consider using alternative investments alongside traditional investments in the context of a diversified portfolio. Not only have there been some attractive returns supplied from certain alternative investments, but there also have been low volatilities of returns from some as well. The implication is that there are higher Sharpe ratios and information ratios that can be derived from certain alternative investments than is the case for some traditional assets. However, a sole reliance on these ratios for the selection of alternative investments ignores the potential for extreme events of volatility that may occur. The risk in simply picking high-risk adjusted returns that are based on mean performance results and smoothed standard deviations is the underestimation of volatility that can occur during short periods. The susceptibility to events associated with kurtosis is more pronounced with alternative investments, because of the leverage, derivatives, illiquidity, and shorting that they employ.

Historical Correlations

The historical correlations contained in Table 11.2 indicate a broad range of traditional assets and alternative investments with correlations of less than 1.0 to each other. The implication from these figures is that there are diversification benefits to be gained from the inclusion of combinations of these assets in a portfolio. This premise must be accepted for an investor to embark on a path of portfolio optimization. The MVO process is dependent on the identification of correlations between assets. The simple concept of a two-asset-class portfolio is grounded in the notion that risk reduction benefits will be derived from diversification based on correlation between the assets that is less than 1.0. The data used in the MVO analyses in this chapter is historical. Rolling correlations, which illustrate a change in correlations over periods of time, also should be considered. In the event that forward-looking estimates are used in an MVO analysis, anticipated future correlations between assets may be required to be forecasted.

Shaded regions in Table 11.2 indicate where the correlation between alternative investments and traditional asset classes is greater than 0.5. There are several observations associated with this demarcation. The first is that there are quite a number of instances where there is less than a 0.5 correlation between alternative and traditional assets. Even correlations higher than 0.5 still are acceptable in terms of providing diversification to a portfolio. Nevertheless, it is illustrative to note the large number of observations below a 0.5 correlation among these pairs, which indicates the potential for a fairly robust diversification benefit from the inclusion of a number of these alternative investments alongside traditional investments

TABLE 11.2 Correlation Matrix (1996–2006 Q2)

	Cash	Core FI	ILBs	Real Estate	High Yield	U.S. EQ	Dev EQ (unhdgd)	Dev EQ (hdgd)	EMD	REITs	Commo-dities	PE	Emrg Mkt EQ	Dev FI (hdgd)	Currency	Oil & Gas	EMN	EQH	SS	ED	MA	DS	RV	CA	MI	Venture	LBO	Timber
Cash	1.00																											
Core Fixed Income	0.20	1.00																										
Inflation Linked Bonds (TIPs)	-0.06	0.73	1.00																									
Real Estate	0.19	-0.02	-0.20	1.00																								
High Yield	-0.25	-0.16	-0.20	-0.05	1.00																							
U.S. Equity	-0.04	-0.41	-0.49	0.14	0.60	1.00																						
Developed Mkt. Equity (Unhedged)	-0.21	-0.45	-0.46	0.17	0.45	0.85	1.00																					
Developed Mkt. Equity (Hedged)	-0.06	-0.57	-0.57	0.24	0.49	0.89	0.91	1.00																				
Emerging Market Debt	-0.08	-0.15	-0.02	-0.12	0.59	0.59	0.51	0.55	1.00																			
REITs	-0.16	0.09	-0.01	0.38	0.30	0.37	0.30	0.51	0.29	1.00																		
Commodities	-0.19	-0.18	0.16	-0.09	-0.04	0.01	0.14	0.01	0.00	0.10	1.00																	
Private Equity	0.13	-0.40	-0.21	0.27	0.25	0.71	0.64	0.80	0.50	0.18	0.04	1.00																
Emerging Market Equity	-0.35	-0.55	-0.33	-0.10	-0.10	0.71	0.77	0.80	0.58	0.38	0.14	0.53	1.00															
Developed Mkt. FI (Hedged)	0.42	0.76	0.55	0.12	0.04	0.03	0.10	-0.03	0.02	-0.07	-0.09	-0.20	0.35	1.00														
Currency	0.13	0.26	0.26	0.01	0.04	0.02	-0.14	-0.10	0.25	0.27	-0.19	-0.02	-0.01	0.16	1.00													
Oil & Gas	0.06	0.31	0.31	-0.10	0.41	0.16	0.14	0.16	0.02	0.50	0.11	-0.21	-0.02	0.14	0.02	1.00												
Equity Market Neutral	0.59	0.16	-0.04	0.20	-0.04	0.03	0.02	0.16	0.60	0.18	0.00	0.30	-0.16	0.08	0.01	0.14	1.00											
Equity Hedge	0.11	-0.39	-0.34	0.05	0.36	0.83	0.72	0.80	0.60	0.26	0.08	0.87	0.69	-0.24	0.13	-0.09	0.26	1.00										
Short Selling	0.20	0.44	0.34	0.02	-0.46	-0.86	-0.74	-0.77	-0.60	-0.27	0.02	-0.74	-0.74	0.35	0.07	0.07	0.03	-0.85	1.00									
Event Driven	0.00	-0.26	-0.34	-0.02	0.63	0.81	0.70	0.77	0.70	0.51	0.02	0.66	0.72	-0.36	0.06	0.27	0.30	0.79	-0.71	1.00								
Merger Arbitrage	0.39	-0.43	-0.19	0.20	0.34	0.62	0.51	0.61	0.53	0.41	0.12	0.58	0.37	-0.21	0.05	0.19	0.07	0.64	-0.42	0.75	1.00							
Distressed Securities	-0.25	-0.17	-0.12	-0.13	0.54	0.59	0.55	0.59	0.65	0.52	0.14	0.49	0.60	-0.44	0.01	0.30	0.62	0.59	-0.59	0.87	0.51	1.00						
Relative Value	0.25	-0.08	0.00	-0.05	0.39	0.45	0.46	0.46	0.61	0.38	0.22	0.51	0.34	-0.20	-0.11	0.29	0.10	0.57	-0.37	0.74	0.75	0.72	1.00					
Convertible Arb.	0.35	-0.08	-0.01	-0.28	0.35	0.30	0.18	0.22	0.50	0.22	0.09	0.29	0.22	-0.13	0.35	0.26	0.48	0.43	-0.25	0.56	0.59	0.53	0.82	1.00				
Macro Investing	-0.06	-0.06	-0.25	-0.10	0.32	0.52	0.57	0.54	0.45	0.35	0.04	0.48	0.56	-0.07	0.01	0.01	0.35	0.67	-0.48	0.61	0.36	0.53	0.43	0.29	1.00			
Venture Capital	0.26	-0.33	-0.25	0.16	0.09	0.53	0.46	0.56	0.41	0.01	0.08	0.93	0.41	-0.13	0.35	-0.27	0.23	0.81	-0.62	0.49	0.47	0.31	0.43	0.29	0.41	1.00		
Leveraged Buyouts	-0.08	-0.42	-0.32	0.39	0.42	0.79	0.74	0.76	0.51	0.36	-0.04	0.83	0.57	-0.24	0.12	-0.10	0.32	0.73	-0.71	0.73	0.60	0.61	0.49	0.25	0.46	0.57	1.00	
Timber	0.09	0.01	-0.09	0.64	0.06	0.18	0.17	0.19	0.11	0.09	-0.09	0.45	-0.01	0.07	0.11	-0.21	0.20	0.17	-0.10	0.12	0.22	0.05	0.11	-0.07	0.16	0.32	0.52	1.00

Note: Shaded regions indicate relatively high correlations of greater than 0.5 between alternative and traditional assets. This shading excludes high correlations between alternative investments and between traditional investments. Descriptions of each asset may be found in the appendix to this chapter. Data for private equity, venture capital, and leveraged buyouts ends March 2006.

Source: RogersCasey.

in a portfolio at least from an historical perspective. Second, it is likely from an intuitive perspective that many of the alternative and traditional assets that have correlations greater than 0.5 also have similar factors that ultimately determine their performance and volatility. Factor overlaps are explored more fully in the regression analysis section of this chapter. Third, the fact that some alternative investments may overlap traditional asset classes from a factor perspective does not necessarily mean that those alternative investments should be discarded. It may be that some alternative investments with high correlations to traditional asset classes actually are the preferred way to express exposure to a factor.

Rather than excluding an alternative investment where there is high correlation to a traditional investment, an investor might replace the traditional asset-class allocation with the alternative investment in order to achieve a more advantageous representation of a factor. For instance, there may be a perspective that the alternative investment structure offers more flexibility in moderating an exposure to the factor, or some belief that the managers from which to choose in the alternative investment arena are more capable or more nimble. Another example is that an investor may hold the belief that a long/short equity allocation through hedged equity is a less volatile approach to establishing an exposure to the equity markets than a long-only equity investment through U.S. equity. These two assets had a correlation of 0.83 from an historical perspective over the 10-year period ended the second quarter of 2006, as depicted in Table 11.2. However, as noted in Table 11.1, hedged equity generated a higher return with lower volatility than long-only U.S. equity during the same time period. As such, the potential utilization of hedged equity rather than long-only equity could have resulted in a better risk-adjusted return with a similar factor dependency. Of course, implementation of this in the real world has its risks as well. The historical data upon which this is based can be vulnerable to biases, and the implementation of such a trade-off has the risk of manager selection. Manager selection risk is generally higher for hedged equity relative to long-only U.S. equity, because of a relatively higher dispersion of returns among hedged equity managers.

There are additional issues in relying upon historical covariance matrixes. The implied covariances may be too high. Survivor bias, which can lead to inflated performance and positive serial correlation for funds that report to indexes used in the analysis, may cause spurious correlation among alternative investments, thereby overstating the correlations among the alternative investments used in the matrix. Alternatively, the correlations between assets on a historical basis may be too low. The time frame used of approximately 10 years is truncated by the availability of data from all the alternative investments. This time frame is short relative to the available data for traditional assets. Furthermore, even a 10-year time frame obscures short periods of asset correlation. Short-term spikes in correlation can relate to market shocks, which can cause a lack of liquidity in otherwise liquid assets and can lead to coincident falling prices.

Equilibrium Approach

In equilibrium, a passive portfolio's allocation to assets should replicate the magnitude of the worldwide opportunity for each asset class. Adjustments to equilibrium can then be made based on levels of conviction. The equilibrium approach characterized by the Black-Litterman model can be difficult to deploy for the alternative investment universe. Not only is the size of the investable opportunity sets for certain assets (such as real estate) difficult to accurately measure, but the true availability of some assets is not uniform for all investors. For instance, certain hedge funds and venture capital funds are closed to new investors but open to their existing investors who may wish to add more capital. Moreover, these soft-closed funds can represent a large amount of the investable universe, or they can represent a significant share of the top quartile of performance. The absence of the availability of these funds may materially alter the market size for these alternative investments, thereby undercutting the validity of an equilibrium position.

Indeed, a drawback of the equilibrium approach is that in some cases the investable universe may be vague. Another example occurs when considering timber as an investable asset class. Should one deem the available market opportunity to equal the amount of institutional assets invested in timber funds, or all corporate timber operating assets that may be available for sale to these funds, or these two amounts plus all international country-owned timber tracts that are available for lease to loggers and potentially under the right circumstances available for sale? In the last case, the investable universe could dwarf many other alternative investment strategies, but not accurately reflect the current opportunity set.

These issues highlight the subjective nature of determining the equilibrium position. They have deeper meaning than just not being able to use the equilibrium approach with uniformed accuracy. The implications include potential problems in using historical performance statistics for certain alternative assets when conducting an MVO. For instance, it questions whether the mean performance of an alternative investment truly is reflective of an investor's opportunity in the area. This further highlights the need to create more accurate forward-looking expectations for the return, volatility, and correlation statistics of alternative investments possibly with the aid of factor analysis.

PROBLEMS USING MEAN-VARIANCE OPTIMIZATION WITH ALTERNATIVE INVESTMENTS[6]

There are problems when using MVO with alternative investments in a diversified portfolio. A chief concern is the assumption that the returns from alternative investments are normal in their distribution and do not exhibit kurtosis. Kurtosis is represented by a distribution of returns that may be symmetrical in shape around its mean but has more frequent than expected observations in the tails of the distribution. Skewed return distributions or symmetric distributions with the presence of kurtosis can understate risk. Risk is depicted by the standard deviation of returns, which is one of the foundation statistics used in conducting the MVO analysis. The typical manifestation of this understated risk is negative performance of an alternative investment, which may be exacerbated by leveraged and market crisis events.

Most MVOs make large allocations to assets that have a combination of high returns, low standard deviation of these returns, and low correlation to other assets used in the portfolio. As a result, an unconstrained MVO process tends to include ample allocations to alternative investments that have these characteristics. Some alternative investments have low standard deviation of returns because of their illiquid nature. Their infrequent portfolio revaluations result in smoothed returns. Most practitioners who use MVO employ constraints on allocations made to assets, in order to limit allocations to any one asset and defend against this notion of understated risk. However, this constraining process often can be arbitrary in determination of magnitude. One approach to providing for a less arbitrary system of constraints is the Black-Litterman model, which bases initial allocations on an equilibrium base case of asset-class sizes. Another approach is to unsmooth returns from alternative investments in order to artificially increase their standard deviations and resulting correlations to other assets.

REGRESSION ANALYSIS WITH ALTERNATIVE INVESTMENT FACTORS

Regression analysis can be used to determine the factor sensitivities of alternative investments. Using this approach, only independent factors that are investable have been employed. The goal for this type of analysis is to identify independent factors that explain with some significance the performance of the various dependent alternative investment variables. This modeling does not seek to explain as fully as possible the results of each dependent time series, in which case a range of additional noninvestable factors might have been included. Indeed, the affect of certain independent noninvestable factors on alternative investments can be pronounced. An example of this is the influence that regional employment can play on the returns for real estate. These types of factors, which are not investable per se, can be more important than the investable factors that might also be considered, such as interest rates. However, limiting the analysis to investable factors simply is in order to highlight the potential for re-creating alternative investments through passive investment in investable independent factors. Furthermore, the data utilized here only is in an effort to provide examples. These relationships change with time and with the addition of new data. Therefore, the usefulness of the analysis is temporal in nature. The analysis should be considered in the context of observing the influence of independent factors on the outcome of alternative investments and how these factors can be present in many different alternative investments.

Once allocations to traditional and alternative investments have been determined through MVO and evaluated, despite the limitation of that approach, a separate step represented by regression analysis can be conducted. Running regressions using alternative investments as dependent factors enables the identification of independent factors that have significance in the determination of returns and the volatility of returns for these assets. The independent factors utilized for the regressions in this chapter generally are investable, either through indexes or through the availability of counterparties that engage in swap agreements. The independent factors include major traditional asset classes. In doing so, the concept is to determine the existence of overlap between traditional asset classes and alternative investments. With this information, an investor is armed with more accurate data in structuring a diversified portfolio. The regressions also identify the betas that are associated with the traditional asset-class independent factors, thereby giving the investor revealing information about the degree of overlap with alternative investments. An implication from the identification of traditional asset classes that underlie alternative investments relates to fees for active management. If part of the return derived from alternative investments can be replicated by traditional asset classes, then the investor may wish to attempt this replication in a lower-fee environment than is the case for alternative investments. Perhaps a two-tiered fee structure could be presented to investment managers in some instances, whereby the investor pays an adjusted fee on traditional asset class factor returns and a higher fee on the portion of returns from alternative investments that cannot be attributed to traditional asset-class factors.

REGRESSION ANALYSIS RESULTS AND OBSERVATIONS

The regression analyses conducted in this chapter are meant to be illustrative of the type of approach that is available to all investors. The methodology informs the construction process for diversified portfolios that use all types of investments. The identification of traditional asset-class factors that underlie alternative investments enables the investor to avoid duplicative factor bets when using alternative investments in conjunction with traditional investments. Put in a different light, elucidation of the traditional asset-class exposures that are incorporated as independent factors in alternative investments potentially should cause an investor to reduce direct allocations to traditional investments. Constructing portfolios through a more precise measurement of factor exposures holds the potential benefit of enabling an investor to assemble a more accurate portfolio for the type of factor diversification that is trying to be achieved through the use of alternative investments.

The regression results for each alternative investment considered are contained in the appendix to this chapter (Tables 11.6 through 11.22), as are related correlation matrixes (Tables 11.23 and 11.24). The summary of the results for each regression is contained in Table 11.3. Table 11.5 in the appendix of this chapter lists the dependent and independent factors used in the MVO and regression analyses along with the data acronyms, descriptions, frequencies, and sources. There is a range of statistical significance and explanatory power that emits from the regression results, as is illustrated by the t-statistics and adjusted R-squareds generated for each regression, as well as positive and negative serial correlation sensitivity for some data that is identified through the Durbin-Watson (D-W) statistic. Various regression runs were used for each dependent factor, thereby generating the best fit for the data used, which is summarized in Table 11.3.

A larger group of independent variables could have been used. This list could have included substyles of traditional asset classes (e.g., growth versus value), noninvestable variables (e.g., unemployment rate), and potential qualitative factors (e.g., illiquidity). However, in an effort to provide a simplified example, the broad traditional asset classes were used along with measurements for volatility, which can be replicated through indexes or swaps. Only investable factors were included in an effort to enable an investor to re-create the portfolio. For instance, while the unemployment rate or gross domestic product might have made a better fit than the Russell 2000 in some instances, it is the Russell 2000 that is an investable factor. As discussed in Chapter 10, although there are some qualitative factors that might be quantified, there is difficulty in doing this and including all qualitative factors. Therefore, the qualitative factor of

TABLE 11.3 Summary Regression Results

Factors	Event Driven			Long/Short Equity		Tactical Trading	Relative Value			Private Equity			Real Estate		Commodities, Currencies, Oil & Gas, Timber			
	Event Driven	Merger Arbitrage	Distressed Securities	Equity Hedge	Short Selling	Macro Index	Convert-ible Arbitrage	Equity Market Neutral	Relative Value Arbitrage	Venture	Leveraged Buyout	All Private Equity	NCREIF	NAREIT	DJ-AIG Commod-ities	Currency	Oil and Gas	Timber
Intercept (Alpha)	0.858	0.710	0.892	0.689	1.256	0.387	0.791	0.537	0.754	2.767	2.709	2.643	3.059	0.597	0.319	NA	0.861	1.953
	(9.68)***	(9.52)***	(8.77)***	(5.98)***	(4.35)***	(2.39)***	(9.69)***	(6.26)***	(11.77)***	(1.41)	(4.25)***	(2.94)***	(15.56)***	(1.86)*	(0.88)		(2.41)**	(4.58)***
1) VIX Index				0.026														
				(2.98)***														
2) MOVE Index	-0.022	-0.016	-0.030				-0.013		-0.019									
	(-3.58)***	(-2.95)***	(-4.18)***				(-2.27)**		(-4.20)***									
3) LB Aggregate						0.582		0.180										
						(4.49)***		(2.63)***										
4) LB TIPS													-0.118	0.531	0.488		0.629	
													(-1.72)*	(2.56)**	(2.08)**		(2.66)***	
5) Russell 3000				0.155	-0.331					0.879		0.627						0.281
				(3.50)***	(-3.10)***					(4.12)***		(6.41)***						(2.54)**
6) Russell 2000	0.267	0.109	0.157	0.360	-0.719	0.196	0.055	0.045	0.077					0.336	0.170		0.222	-0.196
	(16.85)***	(8.21)***	(8.64)***	(11.27)***	(-8.73)***	(7.78)***	(3.76)***	(3.35)***	(6.74)***					(6.49)***	(2.91)***		(3.87)***	(-2.17)**
7) MSCI World											0.563							
											(7.65)***							
Significant Factors	2, 6	2, 6	2, 6	1, 5, 6	5, 6	3, 6	2, 6	3, 6	2, 6	5	7	5	4	4, 6	4, 6	NA	4, 6	5, 6
Common Factors		6		6		6		6			4		4			6		
Adj. R-Squared	71.3	39.5	44.9	77.7	72.0	34.6	13.9	9.5	36.1	27.0	57.2	48.3	4.2	24.1	6.4	NA	12.2	9.4
Durbin Watson Stat	1.52	1.52	1.16	1.50	1.91	1.70	0.94	1.79	1.36	0.88	1.81	0.90	0.66	2.27	1.85	NA	2.09	1.81

Note: Data strings are used from January 1995 to March 2006. NA, currency exhibited no correlation with any statistical significance to the independent factors used. T-statistic in parentheses.
***Significant at 1 percent.
**Significant at 5 percent.
*Significant at 10 percent.
Source: RogersCasey.

liquidity was excluded from the regressions, which did not attempt to create it. The analysis is not intended to be a definitive piece on the specific factors that hold relevance for alternative investments, as much as it describes a methodology for understanding and identifying factor sensitivities, which will change over different time frames and may require other traditional independent variables to be used.

Also, it should be noted that T-bills or the London Interbank Offered Rate (LIBOR) has not been used as an independent variable in the regressions. Many hedge strategies have the risk-free rate as a component of their spread returns and therefore a starting point of targeted returns. Also, real estate can be sensitive to short-term interest rates, particularly relative to their impact on mortgage rates. Nevertheless, the use of the risk-free rate as an independent variable in regressions for alternative investments often causes it to draw an overwhelming majority of the explanatory power. The rationale for this may be the serial correlation in some alternative investments, which has similar characteristics to the low volatility and only positive results for risk-free instruments. When the risk-free rate is removed as an independent variable in these regressions, the remaining independent variables assume far greater importance and the statistical significance of the results remains valid. Furthermore, once independent factors are identified and used in a subsequent factor optimization exercise, the absence of the use of the risk-free rate as an independent factor allows for improved diagnosis. However, a risk for excluding cash from the regression analysis is that the sensitivities to the remaining independent variables become overstated. This may be an inherent drawback in the analysis. Alternatively, cash and leverage can be explained as ways to moderate or increase the exposures to risk premiums in a portfolio, respectively, rather than as return drivers.

Hedge Strategy Regression Results

An observation from the summarized regression data for hedge strategies is the frequent existence of betas to equity independent variables. The sensitivity of many strategies to the equity market, whether in small order or of a higher magnitude especially during periods of volatility, is not something to be forgotten by investors in alternative investments. On one hand, an equity orientation, to the extent that it represents a growth posture, may be deemed a positive portfolio positioning. On the other hand, given the high fee structure and long lockup nature of alternative investments, the expected return from these investments should incorporate an absolute return element regardless of equity market sensitivity. Also, there are some negative betas to bond volatility. Although these negative betas are not large in size, they tend to be corroborated by the correlation information contained in Tables 11.23 and 11.24. Another observation is positive betas to the bond market for the macro and equity market-neutral hedge strategies. Positive betas to bonds for these substrategies are consistent with the fixed-income securities that generally are traded in the macro strategy and the low volatility characteristic of the market-neutral equity approach. In a broad sense, it is not surprising that some hedge strategies exhibit positive betas to both equities and bonds. It is the blend between equity and bond characteristics that often is cited as the key appeal for investors in hedge funds and the strategies that they employ. Nevertheless, by virtue of D-W statistics that are less than 1.5, there is serial correlation present in distressed debt, convertible arbitrage, and relative value arbitrage.

Private Equity Regression Results

The infrequent pricing of private equity funds and the tendency toward serial correlation of all private equity and venture capital index returns is problematic. By virtue of D-W statistics that are less than 1.5, there is serial correlation present in the venture capital and the all-private equity areas. Nevertheless, the only real beta sensitivities to the independent factors used in the regressions are equity oriented. In concept, this is not surprising, given the dependence that the private equity world has on the public equity markets for much of the liquidity that is required to exit transactions. Furthermore, the regression results for all-private equity and for venture capital indicate sensitivity to equity inclusive of all capitalization issues as is characterized by the Russell 3000. Indeed, the beta coefficient to equity inclusive of all capitalization for private equity, in particular for venture capital, is positive and higher than it is for any of the other regression results for the alternative investments. All-private equity includes venture capital, LBOs, mezzanine debt, and other ancillary strategies. It is interesting that the regression results for all-private equity indicate a greater response to the Russell 3000 than the Russell 2000. The basis for a stronger reaction to an index that includes a smaller amount of small-capitalization issues versus a somewhat smaller-capitalization index may relate to the volatility of returns that are apparent in smaller-capitalization stocks versus larger-capitalization stocks. Although volatility is consistent with the higher standard deviation of returns that is characteristic of venture capital in particular and all-private equity in general, venture capital is not the majority of the all-private equity index, and its influence in this broader index may be reduced. The LBO area exhibits sensitivity to international stocks through the MSCI World Index. It is not surprising to see a greater influence from international exposure in the LBO area versus venture capital, since a large portion of venture capital is conducted in the United States, while LBOs tend to include more international deals. Another observation about the regression results for private equity is the presence of relatively high alpha across each of the private equity categories. Furthermore, these high alphas are generally associated with acceptable adjusted R-squareds. These alphas may be associated with the high absolute historical returns that have been generated from these strategies compared with the other alternative investments.

Real Estate Regression Results

The regression results for real estate indicate some sensitivity to inflation-protected bonds, or TIPS. It is understandable that real estate is sensitive to inflation-linked securities, since inflation protection often is cited as an attribute of real estate. Indeed, real estate as a hard asset often will change in value based on inflationary considerations. A general positive correlation to inflation would be expected. However, a reading of negative beta to TIPS is found for the National Council of Real Estate Investment Fiduciaries (NCREIF) index. This is unexpected but should not be emphasized because of the very low associated adjusted R-squared and relatively less significant t-statistic. Nevertheless, it is also worth noting the existence of negative correlation that the NCREIF real estate index has to TIPS and commodities illustrated in Table 11.24. Reasons for this negative correlation may include a one-quarter lagged reporting for the NCREIF index, the fact that TIPS are driven by inflation expectations as well as real yields, and the TIPS market still is somewhat immature and during its early use has to some extent been driven by market technicals and less so by fundamentals. By virtue of a D-W statistic that is less than 1.5, there is serial correlation present in the NCREIF real estate strategy.

Meanwhile, the National Association of Real Estate Investment Trusts (NAREIT) index of publicly traded real estate investment trusts indicates a fairly strong positive beta to TIPS. Interestingly, the NAREIT index exhibits positive correlation to TIPS on a monthly basis in Table 11.23 and a negative correlation to TIPS on a quarterly basis in Table 11.24. This further highlights the fact that market forces may be influencing the purity of expected correlations between TIPS and either the NCREIF or the NAREIT. Nevertheless, the model indicates that 53 percent of the monthly movement in the NAREIT is explained by the monthly movement in TIPS. There also appears to be some sensitivity of REITs to equity. This also is a positive beta indicating that 33.6 percent of the monthly movement in the NAREIT is determined by the monthly movement in the Russell 2000. This also might be intuitive, because of the fact that REIT securities are traded in the public equity markets.

Commodities, Oil and Gas, Currency, and Timber Regression Results

The results for commodities, as represented by the Dow Jones-AIG (DJ-AIG) commodity index, are fairly inconclusive owing to the generation of a low adjusted R-squared and the presence of multicollinearity, which is exhibited through the negative beta to bonds and the positive beta to TIPS that is illustrated in some of the commodities regressions in the appendix. TIPS and bonds are expected to have similar signed betas, since they exhibit very high correlation to each other, which is confirmed in the correlation matrix in Table 11.2. The elimination of multicollinearity results in the isolation of a positive beta for commodities to TIPS being the more relevant observation. Nevertheless, even this elimination does not change the lack of relevance of the selected model, as witnessed by its low adjusted R-squared. Although the results intuitively are correct, the low adjusted R-squared renders the regression of low statistical significance. Some beta to equity also is present in the model.

Oil and gas appear to have a relatively high positive beta to TIPS and a somewhat lower positive beta to the equity market. The adjusted R-squared for the model of 12.2 indicates that the regression is only of minor statistical importance. This suspicion seems to be confirmed by the relatively low correlations indicated in Tables 11.23 and 11.24 between TIPS and oil and gas. Nevertheless, the notion of a high beta between this hard asset and inflation-protected bonds may be intuitive. Although a proxy on high-yield bonds was not used in the regression, it is perhaps more relevant to note the interesting correlation between oil and gas and high yield in Table 11.2. This may result from the fact that the majority of returns from oil and gas typically are associated with cash flow from producing properties. In effect, these investments are yield oriented, as are high-yield bonds. The covariance matrix (Table 11.2) also reveals an even higher correlation between two alternative investments: oil and gas and REITs. REITs, because of their yield-dominant characteristics, are also expected to correlate to oil and gas investments.

Currencies as an alternative investment exhibit no regression sensitivity to the independent factors used. The currency regressions that were attempted in the analysis are excluded from the appendix, because none showed any relevance. Therefore, currencies are not depicted in Table 11.3 with any independent factor betas. An observation to be drawn from this is the relative independence of the returns that historically have been generated from the currency index that was utilized. With little apparent beta sensitivity to the independent variables used in the analysis, a conclusion might be that currencies could make an appealing absolute return investment in a diversified investment program, because of the insignificant dependence on traditional asset classes. This lack of correlation of the currency index both to traditional asset classes and to other alternative investments appears to be confirmed in the covariance matrix illustrated in Table 11.2.

The regression results for timber are very inconclusive because of the low adjusted R-squareds generated as well as the presence of multicollinearity. There is evidence of multicollinearity being present by virtue of the conflicting coefficient signs in the regression for the independent variables, which have high correlation to each other. Timber often is placed as a subset of real estate in the groupings of alternative assets. Indeed, the high historical correlation of returns for timber and real estate of 0.64, as depicted in Table 11.2, would lead an investor to believe that this is true. Nevertheless, the regression results and lack of statistical confirmation indicate that there likely is more at work in the defining of returns from timber. It may be that the natural growth in trees as a significant component of return in timber is a source of this differentiation. In any event, it appears that there may be unique sources of return in timber that render it apart from real estate and enable it to be a diversifier in a portfolio of alternative investments. Another observation about the timber regression results is the generation of relatively high alpha. Although a high alpha would be consistent with the notion of the presence of a statistically difficult to regress independent factor such as tree growth, the low adjusted R-squared in this specific regression may make this reading unreliable.

PROBLEMS WITH CONDUCTING REGRESSION ANALYSIS ON ALTERNATIVE INVESTMENTS

There are many observations that can be drawn from the summary in Table 11.3 and the individual regressions that underlie it. However, it is the methodology that is more relevant than the specific results that occur during any one period of time. Regression analysis can be used to evaluate the recommendations that emit from mean-variance optimization. However, regression analysis can yield different results depending on the times frames and the dependent and independent variables that are used. The particular relationships and correlations among variables may vary over specific time periods. Using regression analysis in conjunction with optimization techniques enables a better understanding of the true sensitivities of investments in a diversified portfolio. A look-through to the factor sensitivities of alternative investments provided by regressions is alluring for its apparent transparency. Nevertheless, problems exist with conducting regressions and include the following: regressions are time-period sensitive and can generate statistically ambiguous results; there is a lack of differentiation among alternative investment strategies pertaining to leverage and the impact it has on returns and risk; index data is based on historical time series rather than an evaluation of current-day sensitivities for securities that underlie funds contained in the indexes; and the presumption in the regressions is that the error term is equal to zero, and if it is not, a portion of alpha can be attributed to the error term.

There are numerous tests to measure the statistical significance of regression results. These include beta coefficients, t-statistics, adjusted R-squared, and Durbin-Watson statistics. There may be regressions results that are associated with very low adjusted R-squareds, thereby indicating that the identified independent variables explain only a very small portion of the results for the dependent variables. On one hand, this is disappointing for an investor seeking to explain a large portion of returns from an alternative investment that can be derived from traditional investments. On the other hand, this result is reinforcing for an investor who is operating under the presumption that the source of returns from some alternative investments is unique and uncorrelated with traditional asset classes. (The appendix to this chapter discusses these statistical tests in more depth.)

A problem in using regression analysis with alternative investment indexes is the lack of differentiation in terms of which fund members of an index are assisted through leverage. In other words, some of the return and risk attributes of an index are a function of index members using variable amounts of leverage that is applied to factor betas. The impact from this on one hand is that some strategies that generate their returns from the same factor drivers as another strategy will perform better, all other things being equal, because of greater leverage used. On the other hand, some strategies are reliant on leverage in order to execute their strategies. For example, a hedge fund strategy that employs futures contracts to replicate exposure to interest rates in a certain country may have the same factor beta exposure as a leveraged buyout fund engaged in the purchase of a bank in that country. Both of these investments likely will be influenced by the movement in interest rates in the county in which they are invested. However, the futures strategy may employ tenfold notional leverage and the LBO investment perhaps only three to five times leverage. The amount of leverage used cannot easily be separated from the structural aspects of how each strategy is conducted. All other things being equal, the more leveraged strategy may perform better than the less leveraged strategy. However, this would be due to the leverage involved, assuming returns from both of these investments were completely explained by only one investment factor and no residual return contributors.

Regression analysis usually is based on historical index data, which often does not represent the specific characteristics of individual funds in which an investor may have an investment. Therefore, it may be more accurate for an investor to utilize historical data for their investment managers rather than index returns. Moreover, a better approach may be to consider the historical factor sensitivities of a manager's returns and the factor betas in the investment manager's current portfolio. This approach requires transparency of the investment portfolio. It also requires a system to assign factor betas to the securities in a portfolio, through which value at risk and stress tests can be conducted. This approach is described more fully in the section of this chapter entitled "Factor Measurement and Risk Monitoring."

FACTOR OPTIMIZATION

Once an asset optimization has occurred and factor sensitivities are determined through regression analysis, factors themselves can be optimized. Factor optimization represents the act taking the factor betas that have been identified for alternative investments through regression analysis and applying them to the optimized portfolio allocations. Traditional assets are unchanged in their allocations; however, they are increased to the extent that some of the alternative investments have traditional asset betas that must be represented. The chief benefits from this exercise are: (1) the separation of traditional asset class betas from alternative investments, (2) the division of skill-based versus market-based returns from an alternative investment and resulting fee bifurcation that may occur, and (3) the identification of alpha as a discrete source of return that varies from the risk-free rate of return. None of these specifically relates to the qualitative aspects of the factor analysis, which may be as important as the quantitative aspects. Thus, the analysis should be considered in this light.

Table 11.4 and Figure 11.7 illustrate the same portfolio optimization utilized in Figure 11.4, which represents a 25 percent constraint to any one traditional asset class or alternative investment. However, Table 11.4 and Figure 11.7 utilize the following: (1) the same traditional asset class allocations used in Figure 11.4 and (2) the alphas and independent factor betas that were determined through regression analysis for the alternative investments and summarized in Table 11.3 applied to the alternative investment allocations that were determined in Figure 11.4. The independent factors used in the analysis were intentionally those that are investable. Although some of these factors represent traditional asset classes that can be replicated passively through indexes, other factors such as equity and bond volatility may also be replicated in an investable form through the use of swap contracts with counterparties. The results in Table 11.4 and Figure 11.7 include a significant weighting to T-bills. T-bills had some weighting in the original

TABLE 11.4 Factor Optimization based on Traditional Assets and Alternative Investments Constrained at 25 Percent

	VIX	Move	LB Agg	Tips	Russell 3000	Russell 2000	MSCI World	Cash	High Yield	Int'l Equity Unhedged	Int'l Equity Hedged	Emerging Market Equity	Emerging Market Debt	Developed Fixed Income	Currency
Portfolio 1	0.00%	−0.20%	10.45%	0.15%	0.19%	2.68%	0.20%	61.40%	0.19%	0.00%	0.00%	0.00%	0.00%	24.88%	0.04%
Portfolio 11	0.00%	0.05%	7.21%	0.53%	2.47%	6.19%	2.12%	59.05%	0.19%	0.00%	0.00%	0.14%	0.16%	21.73%	0.16%
Portfolio 21	0.02%	0.07%	2.32%	1.87%	4.99%	9.63%	4.55%	69.02%	0.44%	0.04%	0.01%	1.23%	1.33%	4.32%	0.17%
Portfolio 31	0.07%	0.08%	0.48%	5.65%	7.55%	11.83%	6.78%	62.02%	0.31%	0.08%	0.03%	1.84%	3.06%	0.12%	0.11%
Portfolio 41	0.18%	−0.25%	0.03%	11.94%	13.64%	13.86%	7.39%	46.39%	0.05%	0.13%	0.08%	2.52%	4.00%	0.00%	0.04%
Portfolio 51	0.20%	−0.11%	0.00%	15.72%	28.22%	11.49%	5.30%	24.52%	0.00%	0.75%	0.85%	7.99%	5.02%	0.00%	0.05%

Note: While the initial constraint is 25 percent to any one asset in the optimization, allocations may rise above this constraint as traditional asset class factors that underlie alternative investments are identified through regression analysis.

Note: For descriptions of each asset, refer to the appendix of this chapter.

Source: RogersCasey.

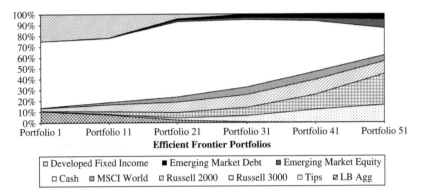

FIGURE 11.7   Asset Allocation: Using Factor Optimization Based on Traditional
Assets and Alternative Investments Constrained at 25 Percent
Note: Assets with less than 1 percent allocations indicated in Table 11.4 have been
removed from this figure.
Source: RogersCasey.

optimization and were used as a surrogate for the accumulated alpha
determined through the regressions for each of the optimized alternative
investments. The regressions yielded large amounts of alpha. This alpha may
be spurious, because of the innumerable factor betas that may exist and
may not have been used in the example analysis. Nevertheless, T-bills are
used to proxy alpha from a passive asset allocation perspective. This does
not resolve the potential use of leverage and its assistance in the amount of
alpha that alternative investments create.

There are many alternative investment alpha and beta influences that
have caused the shape of the factor allocations in Figure 11.7. One observation is the increase in the allocation to T-bills in the middle of the
efficient frontier. These middle portfolios have a higher allocation to hedge
strategies, which in the regression results have small factor betas and large
alphas. This trend dissipates as the efficient frontier extends and higher
allocations are made to private equity, venture capital, and REITs, which in
the regression results have high-equity factor betas. Alternative investments
with small factor betas tend to have high resulting proportions of returns
that can be attributable to alpha, and the opposite can be said for alternative
investments with high factor betas.

However, it should be noted that not all of the allocation to T-bills
in Figure 11.7 is attributable to alternative investment alpha. Some of it
relates to the original asset optimization (Figure 11.4), which included an
allocation to T-bills in the low risk efficient frontier portfolios. The division
between the allocation to T-bills that is from this original allocation versus

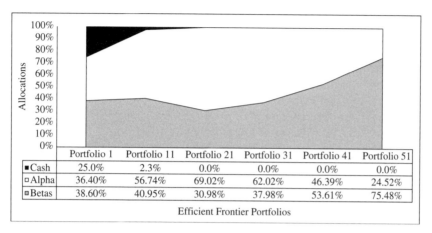

	Portfolio 1	Portfolio 11	Portfolio 21	Portfolio 31	Portfolio 41	Portfolio 51
■ Cash	25.0%	2.3%	0.0%	0.0%	0.0%	0.0%
□ Alpha	36.40%	56.74%	69.02%	62.02%	46.39%	24.52%
▫ Betas	38.60%	40.95%	30.98%	37.98%	53.61%	75.48%

Efficient Frontier Portfolios

FIGURE 11.8 Alpha versus Beta, Based on Optimization of Traditional Assets and Alternative Investments (Constrained at 25 Percent)
Note: Betas represent all identifiable traditional asset class betas and independent factor betas derived from alternative investments used for each portfolio.
Source: RogersCasey.

the allocation that occurred through the assignment of T-bills as a proxy for alpha from alternative investments is illustrated in Figure 11.8. Furthermore, the betas that are identified in Figure 11.7 can be simplified by summarizing all of the identified traditional asset classes and the identifiable independent factor betas generated from the alternative investment regressions, based on the efficient frontier that was generated by using a 25 percent constraint to any one traditional asset class or alternative investment (Figure 11.4). Thus, in Figure 11.8, the beta allocation includes all of the betas that were derived from alternative investments as well as the allocations to traditional asset classes generated through the original optimization. The amount of allocation to alternative investment alpha indicated in Figure 11.8 is less than the summarized optimization in Figure 11.5, because of the alternative investment factor betas that have been identified. This does not necessarily mean that the optimization summarized in Figures 11.4 and 11.5 are incorrect, but they are not so lopsided in their weighting toward alternative investments as one might think, once the underlying factor betas are revealed.

A Reconciliation of Factor Optimization with Asset Optimization

Once the factor optimization has been completed, a comparison of this work can be made with the performance and volatility characteristics of the original optimized portfolio (Figure 11.4). Indeed, the two models track each other well. Figure 11.9 illustrates a reconciliation of the factor optimization approach with the initial traditional asset class and alternative investment optimization that is constrained at a maximum of 25 percent to any one investment. Figure 11.9 depicts the quarterly performance of the original optimal investment portfolio compared with the optimal factor portfolio. (The other comparative portfolios constructed as a part of the efficient frontier for this analysis are located in the appendix to this chapter as Figures 11.12 through 11.17.) The performances of the two time series in Figure 11.9 are very similar and follow each other very closely. However, the return string for the optimal factor portfolio is fairly consistently lower relative to the return string for the optimal traditional asset class and alternative investments portfolio.

The chief reason that the optimal factor portfolio generates lower returns than the investment strategy optimal portfolio is the use of T-bills as a proxy for alpha in the factor approach. The factor optimization represents a passive investment allocation to traditional asset classes and alternative investments, while the investment strategy optimal portfolio represents a passive traditional asset-class allocation and effectively an active alternative investment allocation. However, there may be some additional influences at

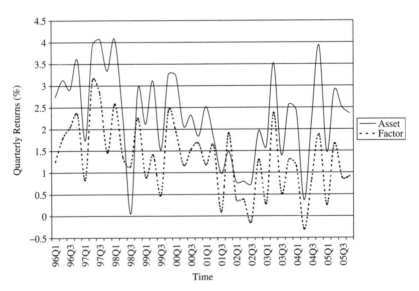

FIGURE 11.9 Quarterly Returns for Optimal Portfolio, Based on Optimized Traditional Assets and Alternative Investments (Constrained at 25 Percent) versus Optimized Factors

work that are more minor but still representative in their impact. Alternative investment alpha may be higher than factor alpha (T-bills) during negative beta periods (present in some of the portfolios illustrated in Figures 11.12 through 11.17), because of the cessation of performance fees being charged by alternative investment managers. Additionally, alternative investment alpha may be higher than factor alpha (T-bills) in positive beta periods, because of the presence of leverage in the active strategies. Furthermore, skill in security selection may exist and provide the alternative investment managers with an advantage over T-bill returns. Another issue may be that alternative investment managers employ tactical allocation to factor betas during interim periods. A tactical approach to factor allocations may be smoothed over long periods, but become more identifiable over shorter time frames, such as are illustrated in the quarterly data represented in Figure 11.9. This result is actually what might be expected from hedge fund short-term trading profits, which are the equivalent of the assignment to alpha of benefits from tactical allocations to beta factors. The analysis indicates that alternative investments generate a unique return that is not attributable to traditional asset classes, is above the risk-free rate, and is positive most of the time.

ACTIVE ALPHA VERSUS PASSIVE ALPHA

The concept of alternative investment alpha and the associate T-bill proxy can be described in terms of active alpha and passive alpha. While passive alpha is T-bills, active alpha is the difference between alternative investment alpha and T-bills (i.e., alternative investment alpha minus T-bills). Active alpha is the gap between the time series lines represented in Figure 11.9 and Figures 11.12 through 11.17. Active alpha may simply be undetermined factor betas, sometimes referred to as exotic betas. Or active alpha may be represented by unique value added or an edge in an investment manager's process, such as research or deal flow. The attribution of active alpha may also relate to tactical allocation to factor betas, not only reweighting among betas but also making negative and positive allocations to factors through shorting. Alpha also can include an error term, since the presumption in the regressions is that the error term is equal to zero. Where there is no identification of factor betas in the regression analyses, the risk-free rate is used to emulate alpha, as depicted in Figures 11.7 and 11.8. However, the returns from the alternative investments that are unexplained by factor betas are actually higher than the risk-free rate. Thus, the spread in performance depicted in Figures 11.9 and 11.12 through 11.17 represents the active alpha spread over the passive risk-free rate.

Figure 11.10 illustrates the concept of active alpha spread returns above the risk-free rate of return, based on the same set of data as used in Figures 11.9 and 11.12 through 11.17. Figure 11.10 represents active alpha spread that is associated with the efficient frontier results. The bars in this figure represent the maximum and minimum quarterly alpha spread above the risk-free rate, and not surprisingly their range expands as the efficient frontier extends into higher return and risk terrain. Figure 11.10 exposes several interesting trends. The first is that the average quarterly active alphas for the portfolios contained in the efficient frontier are all positive, even though the ranges do include negative active alpha observations. A second observation is that these average active alpha readings actually peak and then decline for the extreme portfolios farther out on the efficient frontier. The average active alpha across all of these portfolios is approximately 144 basis points per quarter. A third observation is that the volatility of the active alphas increases, as might be expected, for the more aggressive efficient frontier portfolios. In fact, the rising standard deviation for these more aggressive portfolios likely is a cause for the falling mean active alphas. This indicates that an investor is compensated less on average for assuming more risk in order to potentially achieve higher active alpha returns in these more aggressive portfolios. Accordingly the information ratio (returns divided by standard deviation) drops precipitously for these outlier portfolios.

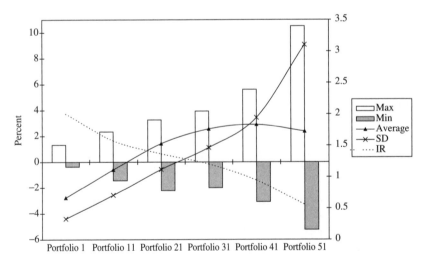

FIGURE 11.10 Active Alpha Quarterly Returns for Efficent Frontier Portfolios
Notes: Column scale is on the left; line scale is on the right. SD, standard deviation; IR, information ratio. Active alpha is alpha minus the risk-free rate. Data is quarterly 1996–2005.

Therefore, not only does active alpha decline on average for more aggressive portfolios on the efficient frontier (as illustrated in Figure 11.8), but it becomes very unstable and difficult to attain as seen through its sharply higher standard deviation and declining information ratio in Figure 11.10.

A possible conclusion that can be drawn from this analysis is that while it may be reasonable for an investor to make a significant allocation to alternative investments in order to generate results that are not aligned with factor betas, aggressive efficient frontier portfolios as less likely to achieve high active alpha. A more appealing segment of such an allocation is represented by portfolios that reside on the lower-risk spectrum of the efficient frontier. Another conclusion, based on the particular data set utilized, is that investing through active alternative investments rather than passive factor betas enables access to a premium return in the form of active alpha. This active alpha return, or alpha above the risk-free rate of return, approximates an average annual figure of 575 basis points across the efficient portfolios used in the example. However, in taking the active alpha approach, it does not appear to benefit an investor to reach too far into the risk spectrum to attain incremental active alpha, since it is more likely that this effort will meet with disappointment.

PROBLEMS WITH FACTOR OPTIMIZATION

Factor optimization should be considered a diagnostic approach that uses passive beta and alpha proxies, which may or may not match the experience that an investor has with active alternative investment managers. Reasons for this tracking error include variable amounts of manager-specific leverage and the potential for overstatement of alpha and understatement of beta. During an optimization of alternative investment strategies, one strategy may be favored over another during certain time periods, owing to the leverage that its underlying managers employ rather than any material difference in factor exposures. A more detailed view of leverage that may be embedded in passive factors and active alternative investment managers at various points in time must be developed in conjunction with any analysis. The concept of leverage and its influences on alternative investments is explained more fully in Chapter 9. Another problem with factor optimization is the two-pronged risk for overstating alpha and understating factor betas. Alpha is multifaceted and can include aspects of skill and competitive advantage, but it can also include factor betas that have not been properly identified and measured. A differentiation between these components of alpha is instrumental for setting expectations for returns, volatility, and correlations from alternative investments as well as conducting accurate attribution analysis of results from active alternative investment managers.

SYNTHETIC PORTFOLIOS OF ALTERNATIVE INVESTMENTS

The division of factor betas from alternative investments leads to the contemplation of "synthetic" funds, or portfolios of alternative investment factor betas. If investable factor betas can be sheared away from alternative investments, then they have the potential to be reconstituted into synthetic investment portfolios. These factor portfolios could be comprised of traditional investment factors as well as nontraditional factors such as volatility. Through the use of index products, swaps, and derivatives, it is possible to reconstitute these exposures in very liquid structures. Such an approach does not answer the question of where an investor could replicate the active alpha component of alternative investments. Indeed, active alpha comprised a much greater proportion of total returns than beta factors, based on the analysis that was conducted in this chapter using an optimization constrained 25 percent to any one traditional asset class or alternative investment (see Figures 11.4 and 11.11). Nevertheless, the large proportion of active alpha in total returns may be due to a limited dissection of alpha into its beta subcomponents. As the identification of factor betas becomes more robust and these betas are replicated through financial derivatives, they too will be able to be added to a synthetic alternative investment package of beta exposures. The division of alternative investment betas into investable

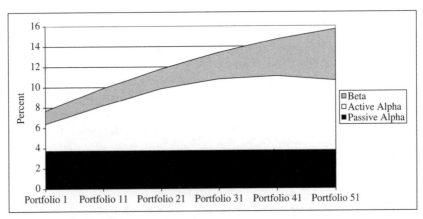

FIGURE 11.11 Efficent Frontier Attribution of Average Annual Returns from Active Alpha, Beta, and Passive Alpha (T-bills)
Note: Data is based on the efficient frontier of optimized traditional assets and alternative investments constrained at 25 percent. Betas are defined as traditional assets plus factor betas derived from alternative investments through regression.

products enables replication of this portion of returns in a vehicle that may have deeper capacity than individual alternative investment strategies and managers. Synthetic alternative investment products could represent passive substitutes for alternative investment factor betas, while also posing as suitable benchmarks for alternative investment returns.

An unanswered question associated with a synthetic approach to beta replication is who or what mechanism would determine the strategic or tactical allocation to the alternative investment factor betas? One solution could simply be to optimize using historical data, as was done in this chapter. However, a more elegant approach would be to base allocations on econometric models that create forecasts of returns, volatility, and correlation for these factors. Moreover, if a forecasting approach for factors is adopted, rather than having 5- to 10-year estimated returns for traditional asset classes, which is the norm for most asset liability modeling studies, the process potentially could be more accurate by setting new factor estimates far more frequently. This forecasting concept may be required as more capital enters alternative investments, as more factor betas are defined, and as truly unique alpha from alternative investments potentially shrinks in its proportional contribution to total returns. A shrinking alpha in the future would not be surprising, simply because of better identification of factor betas.

FACTOR MEASUREMENT AND RISK MONITORING

The revelation that alternative investments have factor betas that can be detected implies that fertile ground exists for monitoring these factor exposures on an ongoing basis. Indeed, there are numerous systems that have been developed for just such an application. Many of these systems, which depend on transparency of portfolio holdings, have been employed to analyze long-only equity, fixed income, and hedge fund portfolios. These types of investment strategies generally utilize publicly traded securities, which can be considered in terms of their asset class or factor sensitivities. For instance, a convertible bond arbitrage strategy can be monitored for its sensitivity to changes in equity volatility, credit spreads, and interest rates. Value-at-risk and scenario analysis can be employed to measure implied risks and calculate the probability for and magnitude of loss in the event of certain changes to factors. All of this points to the ability to expand the use of these tools and methods to monitor the risks and exposures for a broad based portfolio of alternative investments. Although the illiquidity features of some alternative investments may make acting on this information difficult in terms of adjusting specific allocations, contra investments could be initiated in a portfolio to neutralize perceived overweightings to certain risks. The use of factor overlays in such a fashion could enable an investor to better manage portfolio allocations to strategic targets.[7] They also could facilitate rebalancing even in the case of less liquid alternative investments. Undoubtedly, the use of factor measurement systems for risk management will become more broadly adopted by investors who seek to manage their portfolios with greater lucidity. However, conducting factor analysis through risk aggregation systems requires a certain level of underlying security transparency for alternative investments, which is not always information that is forthcoming from these managers.

SUMMARY

One clear understanding from the methodology and examples used in this chapter is the emergence of unexplained alpha that is associated with nonsystemic return and risk drivers. This alpha may be comprised of exotic betas, active alpha, passive alpha, and error elements. The attainment of this return, which is separated from traditional asset-class returns, is what investors seek in alternative investments. The ability to more accurately segregate investment returns by their sources provides a better representation of portfolio characteristics. Achieving this is increasingly important in a world where alternative investments overlap each other and traditional asset classes. Factor analysis provides a framework that enables an investor to measure alternative investments regardless of fund structure or depiction. This ability is not present when using only asset class descriptions. Factor analysis also can be deployed to respond to investment managers as they make dynamic changes in their allocations to all types of investment strategies.

The ability to benchmark and measure factor risks accurately is key to investors explaining these exposures in their portfolios, especially as it pertains to alternative investments. This enables a more articulate dialogue about the nature of a portfolio and its true underlying sources of return and risk. Often, investors who are increasing allocations to alternative investments have difficulty in garnering support from their constituents because of an inability to convey the true nature of these investments. The characteristics of alternative investments broken down to their alpha and beta components assists in bringing clarity to this discourse. The methodology described in this chapter provides a quantitative pathway for sizing, rebalancing, and explaining these investments. Many investors wish to emulate the success that large endowments have had through the use of alternative investments, but feel unable to re-create the unique investment skill that these organizations seem to possess. Measurement of factor exposures and their decomposition from alternative investments assists in explaining this skill. Capturing a greater number of independent investment factors and being able to measure portfolio exposures improves an investor's ability to attain true diversification. Greater clarity of decision making for rebalancing portfolios provides an important element of total risk control that token allocations to alternative investments does not fully achieve. Attaining these benefits reduces an investor's vulnerability to the cyclical peaks and valleys associated with investing in multiple asset class portfolios.

APPENDIX: REGRESSION METHODOLOGY[8]

The purpose of the regression examples in this chapter is to identify independent variables that underlie alternative investment strategies in order to build factor-based models. Multiple variations of regressions are conducted using different sets of explanatory variables, and this process is performed for each alternative investment strategy. The final aim of this process is to build a composite portfolio that is comprised of different independent factors based on the betas obtained from the multiple regression analyses. The multivariable regression analysis statistical technique is performed using the MINITAB 14 statistical software. A limited set of independent factors is used for illustration and modeling purposes to explain the dependent factors as represented by the alternative investment strategies. Independent factors are limited to investable variables, in an effort to be in a subsequent position to create investable passive benchmarks. The independent and dependent factors are listed and described in Table 11.5.

Why Was Multivariable Regression Analysis Selected for Building Factor Models?

Multivariable regression analysis is a common technique used in statistical analysis. There are also a number of readily available software packages available to conduct this process. The identification of factors that inform the dependent variables also lays the groundwork for developing future forecasts of the independent factors. Furthermore, using multiple regressions and multiple factors creates a more comprehensive mosaic for the dependent variables than would be the case for simple regressions using single independent variables. In general, multivariable regression allows the researcher to determine the best predictors of dependent variables. Such predictions can be based on short- or intermediate-term forecasts as well.

Steps in Regression Analysis

The major steps involved in the approach to multivariable regression analysis include formulating assumptions regarding the likely factor associations, developing a scatter plot with a least squares regression line, generating a correlation matrix for the variables involved in the analysis, setting a methodology for identifying and resolving multicollinearity, setting a methodology for identifying and resolving autocorrelation, running a full regression model with all explanatory variables that have been identified, and performing iterative runs to identify the most predictive explanatory variables.

Step 1: Assumptions   In order to build a factor model through regression modeling, a set of underlying assumptions must be crafted that enable the selection of variables to be used. The following are the assumptions for initiation of the model. However, each of these must be tested based on the regression results.

- The independent variables do not influence each other, and there is an absence of multicollinearity.
- There is no autocorrelation.
- The analysis is not biased toward particular explanatory variables.
- The regression coefficients associated with each of the independent factors that comprise the regression function are unknown.
- The data is costationary, meaning that its mean value and variance do not vary systematically over time and covariances between all factors also are stationary.
- The selected independent variables explain the dependent variable in a significant manner.
- The variables in each of the subpopulations are normally distributed about their means with stable standard deviations.
- The errors are assumed to be homoscedastic and each is normally distributed with a mean of zero.
- The factor data is reliable, accurate, relevant, consistent, and timely.

Step 2: Scatter Plot   The next step is to generate scatter plots with the lines of best fit individually between the selected dependent and independent variables. The benefit of considering scatter plots is the light that they shed on the nature of the relationships that exist between the independent and the dependent variables. This further helps in identifying the strength of the relationships and the predictive value of the variables.

Step 3: Correlation Matrix   The construction of a correlation matrix is achieved by computing the simple correlation coefficients for each combination of pairs of variables. The correlation matrix serves to identify the direction and strength of relationships that are present between the dependent and the independent variables. Correlation matrix analysis further helps in recognizing if there is presence of multicollinearity between the explanatory variables. The analysis of the correlation matrix is an important initial step in identifying potential problems involving multiple independent variables.

Step 4: Multicollinearity   Multicollinearity is one of the potential problems in building multivariable regression models. It often is referred to as intercorrelation among the independent variables. Multicollinearity occurs when the independent variables interfere with each other and render regression results meaningless. Resulting regression equations with the presence of multicollinearity may produce spurious coefficient results. Multicollinearity can be recognized through the following evidence.

- There is a strong correlation present among independent variables, which is indicated in the correlation matrix.
- The VIF (variance inflation factor) value is much greater than 1. If the VIF is 5 to 10, the regression coefficients are poorly estimated. The strength of the multicollinearity is measured by VIF. A VIF near 1 suggests that multicollinearity is not a serious problem for an independent variable and its estimated coefficient and that its t-value will not change much as other independent variables are added to and deleted from the regression equation. VIF is equal to $\frac{1}{1-R^2}$ and the standard error of the slope coefficient is directly proportional to the VIF.
- The t-statistics of the seemingly important explanatory variables are very low, due to which they might be considered insignificant and yet the F-test indicates the regression is significant.
- The estimated regression coefficient signs for each of the explanatory variables are opposite to what would logically be expected from them.

The following are possible solutions to the problem of multicollinearity.

- Identify and drop one of the highly correlated explanatory variables from the multivariable regression.
- The structure of the regression equation may be changed using one of the following methods.
  - Estimate the equation on a first-difference basis.
  - Introduce a new variable, which may be a combination of explanatory variables that are uncorrelated, and rerun the regression.
  - Divide the dependent and the independent variables by some series that will leave the basic economic logic but resolve multicollinearity.

Step 5: Autocorrelation Another potential problem associated with multiple regression analysis is autocorrelation, also called as serial correlation. When a variable is measured over time, the observations frequently are related or correlated during certain periods. This correlation is measured using the autocorrelation function. Autocorrelation can occur if the effect of a predictor variable on the dependent variable is distributed over time. Strong autocorrelation can make two unrelated variables appear to be related, and this helps to create spurious regression results. The presence of autocorrelation usually indicates that an important part of the dependent variable has not been explained by the explanatory variables. The presence of autocorrelation can be detected by using the Durbin-Watson (D-W) statistic. A D-W statistic value of 2.0 generally indicates the absence of autocorrelation. Generally speaking, the following table can also be used for modeling purposes.

D-W Statistic	Autocorrelation
Between 1.5 and 2.5	No autocorrelation
Below 1.5	Positive autocorrelation
Above 2.5	Negative autocorrelation

The major causes of autocorrelation include the following:

- One or more key independent variables have been omitted from the regression equation.[9]
- Variables that have a trend component have been included.
- The model has been created with improper specifications.
- The independent error terms are correlated over a period of time.

The following represent methods to minimize the problem of autocorrelation.

- A revised regression can be run on a simple differencing basis, in which the regression model is specified in terms of changes rather than levels.
- A new independent variable that has strong explanatory power can be added to the model.
- The regression can be performed using a log linear model rather than least squares model.
- Models can be run using ARCH (autoregressive conditional heteroscedasticity).

Step 6: Full Regression Model and Iterative Runs A full regression model involves performing regressions between dependent variables of particular interest and predetermined independent variables. The output of these regressions is associated with various statistics that can be used to evaluate the model, including the t-statistic, F-test, R-squared, adjusted R-squared, variance inflation factor, and D-W statistic. Based on the measurements of these statistics, iterative regressions can be run to improve the statistical significance of the regression results and to identify the best predictive explanatory variables. The final goal is to build a model that has strong explanatory power and can be used to create forecasts for dependent variables.

TABLE 11.5 Description of Traditional Assets, Alternative Investment, and Factors

ID	Series	Name	Source	Note	Frequency
			Traditional Asset Classes		
Cash	90-day T-bills	Short-term Treasury bills	U.S. Treasury	The risk-free rate of return	Monthly
Core FI	Lehman Brothers Aggregate Bond Index	Core fixed income	Lehman Brothers	This index includes U.S. government, corporate and mortgage-backed securities with maturities of at least one year	Monthly
US ILBs	LB U.S. Treasury: U.S. TIPS	U.S. inflation-linked bonds	Lehman Brothers	Inflation-protected U.S. Treasury bonds	Monthly
High-yield	Citigroup High Yield Index	High-yield bonds	Citigroup	U.S. high-yield bonds	Monthly
US EQ	Russell 3000	U.S. equity	Russell	A very broad measure of U.S. equity	Monthly
Unhedged Int'l EQ	MSCI EAFE (unhedged)	Unhedged international equity	MSCI	Developed market international equity, unhedged for currency	Monthly
100% Hedged Int'l EQ	MSCI EAFE (hedged)	100% hedged international equity	MSCI	Developed market international equity, hedged for currency	Monthly
Emrg EQ	MSCI Emerging Markets	Emerging market equity	MSCI	Emerging market equity	Monthly
Emrg debt	J.P. Morgan EMBI +	Emerging market debt	J.P. Morgan	Emerging market debt	Monthly
Dev. Non U.S. FI (Hedged)	Citigroup non-U.S. WGBI hedged	Developed market non-U.S. fixed income (hedged)	Citigroup	Developed market international debt, hedged for currency	Monthly

Alternative Investment–Dependent Variables

Hedge Fund Strategies

ED	Event-driven	HFRI Event-Driven Index	HFR, Inc.	Event-driven	Monthly
MA	Merger arbitrage	HFRI Merger Arbitrage Index	HFR, Inc.	Event-driven	Monthly
DS	Distressed	HFRI Distressed Securities Index	HFR, Inc.	Event-driven	Monthly
EQH	Equity hedge	HFRI Equity Hedge Index	HFR, Inc.	Long/short	Monthly
SS	Short selling	HFRI Short Selling Index	HFR, Inc.	Long/short	Monthly
MI	Macro	HFRI Macro Index	HFR, Inc.	Tactical trading	Monthly
CAI	Convertible arbitrage	HFRI Convertible Arbitrage Index	HFR, Inc.	Relative value	Monthly
EMN	Equity market neutral	HFRI Equity Market Neutral Index	HFR, Inc.	Relative value	Monthly
RV	Relative value	HFRI Relative Value Arbitrage Index	HFR, Inc.	Relative value	Monthly

Private Equity

Ven	Venture capital	Time-weighted pooled IRR, all venture capital	Venture Economics	Measures the performance of venture capital funds	Quarterly
Buyout	Buyouts	Time-weighted pooled IRR, all buyouts	Venture Economics	Measures the performance of buyout funds	Quarterly
AllPE	All-private equity	Time-weighted pooled IRR, all private equity	Venture Economics	Measures the performance of all private equity funds	Quarterly

(continued)

TABLE 11.5 (*Continued*)

ID	Series	Name	Source	Note	Frequency
Real Estate Data					
NCREIF	NCREIF	NCREIF Property Index	National Council of Real Estate Investment Fiduciaries	NCREIF Property Index (NPI) consists of both equity and leveraged properties, but the leveraged properties are reported on an unleveraged basis. So the index is completely unleveraged.	Quarterly
NAREIT	NAREIT	NAREIT-All REIT Index	National Association of Real Estate Investment Trusts, Inc.	Represents the full universe of publicly traded REITs, including those companies that do not meet minimum size, liquidity criteria, or free-float adjustments.	Monthly
Commodities, Currencies, Oil and Gas, Timber					
Com	Commodities Factors	DJ-AIG Commodity TR Index	Dow Jones	Includes 20 commodity futures contracts in 5 major commodity groups.	Monthly
Cur	Currency	Parker FX Index	Parker Global	A performance-based benchmark that measures both the reported and the risk-adjusted returns of global currency managers.	Monthly

O&G	Oil and gas	Alerian MLP Index	Alerian, Standard and Poor's	Measures the composite performance of the 50 most prominent energy master limited partnerships. Calculated by Standard and Poor's using a float-adjusted, capitalization-weighted methodology.	Monthly
TIM	Timber	NCREIF Timberland Index	The National Council of Real Estate Investment Fiduciaries	Timberland investment managers contribute information on appraised value, net income, capitalized expenses and any partial sales or purchases for every property in the United States they manage that satisfies the criteria for inclusion in the index. To qualify, a property must be held in a fiduciary environment and "marked-to-market" at least once per year.	Quarterly

Independent Variables

Volatility Factors

VIX	Equity volatility	VIX Volatility Index	Bloomberg	Measures market's expectation of 30-day volatility. It is constructed using the implied, forward-looking volatilities of a wide range of S&P 500 index options.	Monthly

(continued)

323

TABLE 11.5 (*Continued*)

ID	Series	Name	Source	Note	Frequency
MOVE	Bond volatility	Merrill Lynch MOVE Index	Merrill Lynch	Measures bond market volatility	Monthly
			Bond Factor		
LBAgg	Core fixed income	Lehman Brothers Aggregate Bond Index	Lehman Brothers	Includes U.S. government, corporate and mortgage-backed securities with maturities of at least one year.	Monthly
			Inflation Factor		
TIPS	Inflation-linked bonds (ILBs)	LB U.S. Treasury: U.S. TIPS	Lehman Brothers	Inflation-protected U.S. Treasury bonds	Monthly
			Equity Factors		
Rus 3000	Russell 3000	Russell 3000 Index	Russell	A very broad measure of U.S. equity	Monthly
Rus 2000	Russell 2000	Russell 2000 Index	Russell	A small cap measure of U.S. equity	Monthly
MSC	MSCI World	Morgan Stanley Capital International World Index	MSCI	Measures the performance of the developed country stock markets outside of the United States	Monthly

Source: RogersCasey.

TABLE 11.6 Regression Results: Event-Driven

	(1)	(2)
Constant	0.858 (9.68)***	0.560 (6.18)***
VIX		
MOVE	−0.022 (−3.58)***	−0.022 (−4.01)***
LBAgg		
TIPS		
Russell 3000		
Russell 2000	0.26671 (16.85)***	0.26712 (19.21)***
MSCI World		
LagED		0.253 (6.23)***
Adj R-sq	71.3	78.0
D-W Stat	1.52	2.14

Figures in parentheses are t-statistics.
***Significant at the 1 percent level.
**Significant at the 5 percent level.
*Significant at the 10 percent level.
ED = 0.86 − 0.02 MOVE + 0.27 Russell 2000
1. Regression Equation (1) was obtained by the full model in which all variables are being used.
2. There is a limitation to equation (2) as the series lagged event-driven is not investable. As such model (2), while producing a higher adjusted R-squared, shall not be used as the best-fit model.
Source: RogersCasey.

TABLE 11.7 Regression Results: Equity Hedge

	(1)	(2)	(3)	(4)
Constanty	0.689 (5.98)***	0.530 (4.46)***	0.718 (6.30)***	0.548 (4.64)***
VIX	0.026 (2.98)***	0.018 (2.11)**	0.023 (2.76)***	0.016 (1.95)*
MOVE				
LBAgg				
TIPS				
Russell 3000	0.155 (3.50)***	0.131 (3.07)***		
Russell 2000	0.360 (11.27)***	0.361 (11.76)***	0.372 (12.41)***	0.371 (12.95)***
MSCI World			0.146 (3.44)***	0.126 (3.08)***
LagEQH		0.151 (3.74)***		0.152 (3.78)***
Adj R-sq	77.7	79.7	77.60	79.7
D-W Stat	1.50	1.88	1.47	1.86

Figures in parentheses are t-statistics.
***Significant at the 1 percent level.
**Significant at the 5 percent level.
*Significant at the 10 percent level.
EQH = 0.69 + 0.03 VIX + 0.16 Russell 3000 + 0.36 Russell 2000
1. Regression Equation (1) was obtained by the full model in which all variables are being used.
2. There is a limitation to equation (2) as the series - lagged equity hedge is not investable. As such, model (2), while producing a higher adjusted R-squared, shall not be used as the best-fit model.
3. Models (3) and (4) are included to show that MSCI could also be used in modeling equity hedge returns. However, since model (3) results in a lower adjusted R-squared value, model (1) shall be used.
Source: RogersCasey.

TABLE 11.8 Regression Results: Equity Market Neutral

	(1)	(2)	(3)
Constant	0.537 (6.26)***	0.559 (6.37)***	0.512 (5.92)***
VIX			0.010 (1.74)*
MOVE			
LBAgg	0.180 (2.63)***	0.159 (2.29)**	0.175 (2.57)**
TIPS			
Russell 3000		0.039 (2.24)**	
Russell 2000	0.045 (3.35)***		0.061 (3.76)***
MSCI World			
LagEMN			
Adj R-sq	9.50	5.40	10.90
D-W Stat	1.79	1.92	1.82

Figures in parentheses are t-statistics.
***Significant at the 1 percent level.
**Significant at the 5 percent level.
*Significant at the 10 percent level.
EMN = 0.54 + 0.18 LBAgg + 0.05 Russell 2000
1. Regression Equation (1) was obtained by the full model in which all variables are being used.
2. Equation (2) is included to show how the model would change if the Russell 3000 is used instead of Russell 2000.
3. Model (3), while producing a higher adjusted R-squared, shall not be used as the best fit model because the coefficient on VIX is not significantly different from zero at a 5 percent level of significance.
4. Hence, model (1) has been chosen to best represent returns derived from equity market-neutral strategy for the given time frame.
Source: RogersCasey.

TABLE 11.9 Regression Results: Short Selling

	(1)	(2)	(3)
Constant	1.256 (4.35)***	1.217 (3.37)***	1.141 (3.86)***
VIX			
MOVE			
LBAgg			
TIPS			
Russell 3000	−0.331 (−3.10)***	−1.068 (−13.13)***	−0.921 (−17.78)***
Russell 2000	−0.719 (−8.73)***		
MSCI World			
LagSS			
Adj R-sq	72.00	56.10	70.20
D-W Stat	1.91	1.89	2.01

Figures in parentheses are t-statistics.
***Significant at the 1 percent level.
**Significant at the 5 percent level.
*Significant at the 10 percent level.
SS = 1.26 − 0.33 Russell 3000 − 0.72 Russell 2000
1. Regression Equation (1) was obtained by the full model in which all variables are being used.
2. Models (2) and (3) are included to illustrate the explanatory power for a single independent factor in describing the short selling strategy returns.
Source: RogersCasey.

TABLE 11.10 Regression Results: Merger Arbitrage

	(1)	(2)	(3)	(4)
Constant	0.710 (9.52)***	0.531 (5.90)***	0.702 (8.73)***	0.525 (5.43)***
VIX				
MOVE	−0.016 (−2.95)***	−0.014 (−2.73)***	−0.129 (−2.24)**	−0.011 (−2.05)**
TIPS				
Russell 3000			0.125 (6.61)***	0.123 (6.72)***
Russell 2000	0.109 (8.21)***	0.108 (8.40)***		
MSCI World				
LagMA		0.220 (3.34)***		0.221 (3.13)***
Adj R-sq	39.5	43.8	31.3	35.7
D-W Stat	1.52	2.08	1.71	2.25

Figures in parentheses are t-statistics.
***Significant at the 1 percent level.
**Significant at the 5 percent level.
*Significant at the 10 percent level.
MA = 0.71 − 0.02 MOVE + 0.11 Russell 2000
1. Regression Equation (1) was obtained by the full model in which all variables are being used.
2. A limitation to using equation (2) is that the series lagged merger arbitrage is not investable. As such model (2), while producing a higher adjusted R-squared, shall not be used as the best-fit model.
3. Models (3) and (4) are included to show that Russell 3000 could also be used to explain merger arbitrage returns, albeit more poorly compared to Russell 2000 Index. Models (3) and (4) have lower adjusted R-squared values compared to models (1) and (2).
Source: RogersCasey.

TABLE 11.11 Regression Results: Distressed Securities

	(1)	(2)
Constant	0.892 (8.77)***	0.377 (3.98)***
VIX		
MOVE	−0.030 (−4.18)***	−0.029 (−5.26)***
LBAgg		
TIPS		
Russell 3000		
Russell 2000	0.157 (8.64)***	0.170 (12.07)***
MSCI World		
LagDS		0.478 (9.63)***
Adj R-sq	44.90	67.60
D-W Stat	1.16	2.12

Figures in parentheses are t-statistics.
***Significant at the 1 percent level.
**Significant at the 5 percent level.
*Significant at the 10 percent level.
DS = 0.89 − 0.03 MOVE + 0.16 Russell 2000
1. Regression Equation (1) was obtained by the full model in which all variables are being used.
2. There is a limitation to equation (2) as the series lagged distressed securities is not investable. As such model (2), while producing a higher adjusted R-squared, shall not be used as the best-fit model.
Source: RogersCasey.

TABLE 11.12 Regression Results: Relative Value

	(1)	(2)	(3)	(4)
Constant	0.754 (11.77)***	0.486 (6.10)***	0.747 (11.06)***	0.470 (5.56)***
VIX				
MOVE	−0.019	−0.018	−0.017	−0.016
	(−4.20)***	(−4.43)***	(−3.54)***	(−3.65)***
LBAgg				
TIPS				
Russell 3000			0.088 (5.57)***	0.094 (6.39)***
Russell 2000	0.077 (6.74)***	0.080 (7.57)***		
MSCI World				
LagRV		0.316 (4.94)***		0.328 (4.88)***
Adj R-sq	36.10	45.90	30.40	40.60
D-W Stat	1.36	2.17	1.32	2.10

Figures in parentheses are t-statistics.
***Significant at the 1 percent level.
**Significant at the 5 percent level.
*Significant at the 10 percent level.
$RV = 0.75 - 0.02 \text{ MOVE} + 0.08 \text{ Russell}$
1. Regression Equation (1) was obtained by the full model in which all variables are being used.
2. There is a limitation to equation (2) as the series, since lagged relative value is not investable. As such model (2), while producing a higher adjusted R-squared, shall not be used as the best-fit model.
3. Regressions (3) and (4) are included to illustrate how the corresponding sensitivity varies when Russell 2000 is replaced with Russell 3000. However, these models are not used due to their low adjusted R-squared values.
Source: RogersCasey.

TABLE 11.13   Regression Results: Convertible Arbitrage

	(1)	(2)
Constant	0.791 (9.69)***	0.328 (3.79)***
VIX		
MOVE	−0.013 (−2.27)**	−0.014 (−3.01)***
LBAgg		
TIPS		
Russell 3000		
Russell 2000	0.055 (3.76)***	0.060 (5.06)***
MSCI World		
LagCAI		0.548 (8.39)***
Adj R-sq	13.90	43.70
D-W Stat	0.94	2.00

Figures in parentheses are t-statistics.
***Significant at the 1 percent level.
**Significant at the 5 percent level.
*Significant at the 10 percent level.
CAI = 0.79 − 0.01 MOVE + 0.06 Russell 2000
1. Regression Equation (1) was obtained by the full model in which all variables are being used.
2. Given that lagged convertible arbitrage values are not investable, model (2), while producing a higher adjusted R-squared, shall not be used as the best-fit model.
3. Model (1) has been chosen to best represent returns derived from convertible arbitrage strategy. It has a highest possible adjusted R-squared values and all the independent variables are investable.
Source: RogersCasey.

TABLE 11.14 Regression Results: Macro

	(1)	(2)	(3)	(4)	(5)	(6)
Constant	0.387	0.458	0.450	0.510	0.452	0.495
	(2.39)***	(2.89)***	(2.58)**	(3.00)***	(2.57)**	(2.88)***
VIX						
MOVE						
LBAgg	0.582		0.538		0.493	
	(4.49)***		(3.87)***		(3.54)***	
TIPS		0.426		0.400		0.379
		(4.16)***		(3.65)***		(3.46)***
Russell 3000					0.197	0.206
					(5.60)***	(5.81)***
Russell 2000	0.196	0.198				
	(7.78)***	(7.77)***				
MSCI World			0.220	0.226		
			(5.84)***	(5.94)***		
LagMI						
Adj R-sq	34.60	33.40	24.20	23.40	23.00	22.70
D-W Stat	1.70	1.78	1.68	1.73	1.66	1.71

Figures in parentheses are t-statistics.
***Significant at the 1 percent level.
**Significant at the 5 percent level.
*Significant at the 10 percent level.
MI = 0.39 + 0.58 LBAgg + 0.20 Russell 2000
1. Regression Equation (1) was obtained by the full model in which all variables are being used.
2. Equation (2) is obtained by replacing LB Aggregate with TIPS. This change resulted in a lower adjusted R-squared value, indicating that LB Aggregate describes macro returns better than TIPS.
3. In addition, models (3), (4), (5), and (6) have been included to illustrate the difference in the coefficients when other measures of equity are used, such as the Russell 3000 and the MSCI World Index.
4. Model (1) has been chosen to best represent returns derived from macro strategy. It has a highest possible adjusted R-squared value.
Source: RogersCasey.

TABLE 11.15 Regression Results: Commodities

	(1)	(2)	(3)	(4)
Constant	0.529 (1.43)	0.581 (1.56)	0.319 (0.88)	0.790 (2.15)**
VIX				−0.036 (−1.82)*
MOVE				
LBAgg	−1.082 (−2.23)**	−1.120 (−2.28)**		−1.036 (−2.09)**
TIPS	1.161 (3.05)***	1.162 (3.02)***	0.488 (2.08)**	−1.036 (−2.76)***
Russell 3000				
Russell 2000	0.170 (2.95)***		0.170 (2.91)***	
MSCI World		0.194 (2.39)**		
LagCom				
Adj R-sq	9.10	7.10	6.40	5.50
D-W Stat	1.96	1.95	1.85	1.97

Figures in parentheses are t-statistics.
***Significant at the 1 percent level.
**Significant at the 5 percent level.
*Significant at the 10 percent level.
Com = 0.32 + 0.49 TIPS + 0.17 Russell 2000
1. Regression Equation (3) was obtained by the full model in which all variables are being used.
2. Other possible models also are included in the form of models (1), (2), and (4). Model (2) is obtained by using the MSCI Index instead of the Russell 3000 Index as the independent variable.
3. There is multicollinearity in equation (1), as LB Aggregate and TIPS returns exhibit some positive correlation.
4. Model (1) has not been chosen to represent returns derived from commodities, in spite of the highest adjusted R-squared value. Model (3) is used in an attempt to eliminate the multicollinearity between LB Aggregate and TIPS present in models (1) and (2).
Source: RogersCasey.

TABLE 11.16 Regression Results: NAREIT

	(1)	(2)
Constant	0.597 (1.86)*	0.713 (2.05)**
VIX		
MOVE		
LBAgg		
TIPS	0.531 (2.56)**	0.436 (1.96)*
Russell 3000		0.305 (4.25)***
Russell 2000	0.336 (6.49)***	
MSCI World		
LagDS		
Adj R-sq	24.10	11.90
D-W Stat	2.27	2.18

Figures in parentheses are t-statistics.
***Significant at the 1 percent level.
**Significant at the 5 percent level.
*Significant at the 10 percent level.
NAREIT = 0.60 + 0.53 TIPS + 0.34 Russell 2000
1. Regression Equation (1) was obtained by the full model in which all variables are being used.
2. Equation (2) is included to show how the model would change if the Russell 3000 is used instead of Russell 2000. Equation (1) has a higher adjusted R-squared value and is used as the best-fit model.
Source: RogersCasey.

TABLE 11.17 Regression Results: NCREIF

	(1)	(2)
Constant	0.695 (2.32)**	3.059 (15.56)***
VIX		
MOVE		
LBAgg		
TIPS		−0.118 (−1.72)*
Russell 3000		
Russell 2000		
MSCI World		
LagNCREIF	0.769 (7.72)***	
Adj R-sq	57.10	4.20
D-W Stat	2.59	0.66

Figures in parentheses are t-statistics.
***Significant at the 1 percent level.
**Significant at the 5 percent level.
*Significant at the 10 percent level.
NCREIF = 3.06 − 0.118 TIPS
1. Regression Equation (2) was obtained by the full model in which all variables are being used.
2. From the full model, the only significant independent variable is the TIPS index, although it is not significant at the 5 percent level.
3. Model (1) is included. However, as the lagged values of NCREIF Index is not investable, model (1) is not used.
Source: RogersCasey.

TABLE 11.18 Regression Results: Oil and Gas

	(1)	(2)	(3)	(4)
Constant	0.861 (2.41)**	0.815 (2.22)**	0.877 (2.41)**	0.859 (2.30)**
VIX				
MOVE				
LBAgg		0.801 (2.56)**		0.724 (2.29)**
TIPS	0.629 (2.66)***		0.599 (2.50)**	
Russell 3000			0.250 (3.32)***	0.237 (3.15)***
Russell 2000	0.222 (3.87)***	0.217 (3.79)***		
MSCI World				
LagO&G				
Adj R-sq	12.20	11.80	9.60	8.80
D-W Stat	2.09	2.12	1.96	1.98

Figures in parentheses are t-statistics.
***Significant at the 1 percent level.
**Significant at the 5 percent level.
*Significant at the 10 percent level.
O&G = 0.86 + 0.63 TIPS + 0.22 Russell 2000
1. Regression Equation (1) was obtained by the full model in which all variables are being used, to obtain the higest adjusted R-squared.
2. Model (2) is obtained by replacing TIPS with LB Aggregate. Model (2) has a lower adjusted R-squared value and thus is a poorer model than Model (1).
3. Models (3) and (4) are similar to Models (1) and (2), but use the Russell 3000 instead of the Russell 2000. Models (3) and (4) have lower adjusted R-squareds, indicating that Russell 2000 has more explanatory power than Russell 3000 for oil and gas using this data set.
Source: RogersCasey.

TABLE 11.19   Regression Results: Timber

	(1)	(2)
Constant	1.953 (4.58)***	2.091 (4.89)***
VIX		
MOVE		
LBAgg		
TIPS		
Russell 3000	0.281 (2.54)**	
Russell 2000	−0.196 (−2.17)**	−0.141 (−1.77)*
MSCI World		0.223 (2.20)**
LagTIM		
Adj R-sq	9.40	6.30
D-W Stat	1.81	1.95

Figures in parentheses are t-statistics.
***Significant at the 1 percent level.
**Significant at the 5 percent level.
*Significant at the 10 percent level.
Tim = 1.95 + 0.28 Russell 3000 − 0.20 Russell 2000
1. Regression Equation (1) was obtained by the full model in which all variables are being used.
2. Substituting the Russell 3000 Index in regression (1) with MSCI Index in regression (2) produces a poorer fit for the model. As such, Model (2) is deemed poorer compared to Model (1), since the adjusted R-squared value is smaller in Model (2).
3. Note that even the low adjusted R-squared value in Model (1) implies that the independent variables only explain 9.4 percent of the variation in the returns generated by the timber strategy.
4. Both Model (1) and Model (2) imply that multicollinearity is present by virtue of the conflicting coefficent signs for the independent variables, which have high correlation to each other.
Source: RogersCasey.

TABLE 11.20 Regression Results: Venture Capital

	(1)	(4)
Constant	2.767 (1.41)	0.176 (0.10)
VIX		
MOVE		
LBAgg		
TIPS		
Russell 3000	0.879 (4.12)***	0.830 (4.66)***
Russell 2000		
MSCI World		
LagVen		0.498 (4.60)***
Adj R-sq	27.00	51.10
D-W Stat	0.88	2.13

Figures in parentheses are t-statistics.
***Significant at the 1 percent level.
**Significant at the 5 percent level.
*Significant at the 10 percent level.
Venture = 2.77 + 0.88 Russell 3000
1. Regression Equation (1) was obtained by the full model in which all variables are being used.
2. Given that lagged venture values are not investable, Model (2), while producing a higher adjusted R-squared, shall not be used as the best fit model.
3. Model (1) has been chosen to best represent returns derived from the venture strategy. It has a highest possible adjusted R-squared value, and all the independent variables are investible.
Source: RogersCasey.

TABLE 11.21 Regression Results: Buyout

	(1)	(2)	(3)
Constant	2.709 (4.25)***	2.418 (3.64)***	2.837 (3.88)***
VIX			
MOVE			
LBAgg			
TIPS			
Russell 3000		0.534 (7.39)***	
Russell 2000			0.394 (5.88)***
MSCI World	0.563 (7.65)***		
LagBO			
Adj R-sq	57.20	55.50	43.90
D-W Stat	1.81	1.60	1.38

Figures in parentheses are t-statistics.
***Significant at the 1 percent level.
**Significant at the 5 percent level.
*Significant at the 10 percent level.
Buyout = 2.71 + 0.56 MSCI
1. Regression Equation (1) was obtained by the full model in which all variables are being used.
2. Regression equations for buyouts are not explained by any combination of more than one independent factor.
3. Three independent factors individually explain the buyout return strings, namely: MSCI, Russell 3000, and Russell 2000.
Source: RogersCasey.

TABLE 11.22 Regression Results: All-Private Equity

	(1)	(2)	(3)	(4)
Constant	2.643 (2.94)***	0.748 (0.89)	3.025 (3.4)***	1.063 (1.26)
VIX				
MOVE				
LBAgg				
TIPS				
Russell 3000	0.627 (6.41)***	0.626 (7.81)***		
Russell 2000				
MSCI World			0.645 (6.29)***	0.643 (4.77)***
LagAllPE		0.428 (4.78)***		0.433 (4.77)***
Adj R-sq	48.30	66.40	47.30	65.50
D-W Stat	0.90	1.96	1.08	2.30

Figures in parentheses are t-statistics.
***Significant at the 1 percent level.
**Significant at the 5 percent level.
*Significant at the 10 percent level.
AllPE = 2.64 + 0.63 Russell 3000
1. Regression Equation (1) was obtained by the full model in which all variables are being used.
2. Given that lagged all-private equity values are not investable, Model (2), while producing a higher adjusted R-squared than Model (1), shall not be used as the best fit model.
3. Model (1) has been chosen to best represent returns derived from all-private equity. It has a highest possible adjusted R-squared value, and all the independent variables are investable.
4. Models (3) and (4) are included to show that all-private equity returns can also be explained by the MSCI. However, these models are not selected, since they produce either a smaller adjusted R-squared or incorporate the lagged dependent variable, which is not investable.
Source: RogersCasey.

TABLE 11.23 Monthly Correlations for Dependent and Independent Regression Factors

	ED	EQH	EMN	SS	MA	DS	RV	CAI	MI	Com	REIT	Cur	O&G	VIX	MOVE	LBAgg	TIP	Rus 3000	Rus 2000	MSCI
Event Driven	1.00																			
Equity Hedge	0.82	1.00																		
Equity Market Neutral	0.29	0.36	1.00																	
Short Selling	-0.67	-0.86	-0.13	1.00																
Merger Arbitrage	0.74	0.60	0.41	-0.39	1.00															
Distressed	0.81	0.63	0.20	-0.54	0.52	1.00														
Relative Value	0.73	0.61	0.34	-0.43	0.71	0.71	1.00													
Convertible Arb.	0.54	0.45	0.30	-0.28	0.52	0.57	0.75	1.00												
Macro	0.59	0.62	0.32	-0.45	0.32	0.49	0.41	0.36	1.00											
Commodities	0.19	0.26	0.12	-0.16	0.22	0.14	0.23	0.12	0.31	1.00										
NAREIT	0.42	0.28	0.14	-0.18	0.39	0.36	0.38	0.13	0.27	0.10	1.00									
Currency	0.07	0.04	0.17	0.07	0.09	0.09	0.00	0.11	0.39	0.02	0.15	1.00								
Oil & Gas	0.36	0.17	0.10	-0.13	0.30	0.26	0.40	0.23	0.21	0.21	0.38	0.07	1.00							
Equity Volatility	-0.52	-0.45	-0.02	0.49	-0.43	-0.41	-0.39	-0.18	-024	-0.14	-0.25	-0.01	-0.20	1.00						
Bond Volatility	-0.33	-0.19	-0.07	0.18	-0.32	-0.39	-0.39	-0.25	-0.13	-0.04	-0.09	-0.10	-0.18	0.40	1.00					
LB Agg.	-0.06	0.18	0.11	-0.04	-0.07	0.02	0.02	0.06	0.25	-0.01	0.08	0.13	0.17	0.10	-0.17	1.00				
TIPs	-0.07	0.06	0.13	-0.02	-0.02	0.04	0.04	0.08	0.21	0.13	0.15	0.13	0.17	0.09	-0.22	0.80	1.00			
Russell 3000	0.72	0.75	0.18	-0.75	0.55	0.50	0.50	0.30	0.41	0.13	0.34	0.04	0.25	-0.65	-0.30	-0.05	-0.12	1.00		
Russell 2000	0.83	0.87	0.25	-0.84	0.60	0.62	0.53	0.34	0.51	0.21	0.48	0.05	0.29	-0.59	-0.20	-0.12	-0.16	0.79	1.00	
MSCI	0.69	0.73	0.16	-0.71	0.51	0.51	0.44	0.27	0.41	0.17	0.31	0.04	0.21	-0.60	-0.31	-0.10	-0.15	0.94	0.75	1.00

Notes: Descriptions of factor variables contained in the appendix to this chapter. Data is for 1996 through Q2 2006. Monthly data is not available for NCREIF, venture capital, buyouts, all-private equity, and timber.
Source: RogersCasey.

TABLE 11.24 Quarterly Correlations for Dependent and Independent Regression Factors

	ED	EQH	EMN	SS	MA	DS	RV	CAI	MI	Com	REIT	RE	Cur	O&G	Ven	Buy	PE	TIM	VIX	MOVE	LBAg	TIP	Rus 3000	Rus 2000	MSC
Event Driven	1.00																								
Equity Hedge	0.78	1.00																							
Equity Market Neutral	0.34	0.31	1.00																						
Short Selling	-0.69	-0.85	-0.03	1.00																					
Merger Arbitrage	0.76	0.65	0.65	-0.42	1.00																				
Distressed	0.86	0.60	0.14	-0.60	0.51	1.00																			
Relative Value	0.75	0.59	0.51	-0.38	0.76	0.72	1.00																		
Convertible Arb.	0.57	0.46	0.41	-0.28	0.61	0.53	0.83	1.00																	
Macro	0.59	0.65	0.35	-0.45	0.39	0.49	0.44	0.34	1.00																
Commodities	0.04	0.02	0.04	0.09	0.04	0.12	0.15	0.05	0.13	1.00															
NAREIT	0.50	0.26	0.18	-0.26	0.41	0.52	0.38	0.22	0.31	0.10	1.00														
NCREIF	-0.07	0.02	0.08	0.03	0.12	-0.14	-0.10	-0.33	-0.18	-0.24	0.00	1.00													
Currency	0.07	0.03	0.16	0.09	0.10	0.09	0.03	0.11	0.34	-0.16	0.22	-0.04	1.00												
Oil & Gas	0.27	-0.10	0.15	0.07	0.19	0.30	0.29	0.26	0.00	0.12	0.50	-0.10	0.02	1.00											
Venture	0.51	0.80	0.34	-0.59	0.51	0.31	0.45	0.29	0.41	0.10	0.02	0.10	-0.08	-0.27	1.00										
Buyouts	0.72	0.68	0.19	-0.64	0.62	0.58	0.49	0.27	0.40	-0.01	0.35	0.30	0.07	-0.10	0.57	1.00									
All Private Equity	0.67	0.84	0.32	-0.70	0.59	0.47	0.52	0.31	0.46	0.06	0.18	0.19	-0.02	-0.21	0.92	0.84	1.00								
Timber	0.16	0.18	0.20	-0.10	0.24	0.05	0.13	-0.03	0.15	-0.09	0.10	0.54	0.08	-0.21	0.33	0.55	0.47	1.00							
Equity Volatility	-0.60	-0.46	0.00	0.56	-0.47	-0.59	-0.47	-0.32	-0.14	0.04	-0.36	-0.05	0.10	-0.12	-0.22	-0.48	-0.36	0.01	1.00						
Bond Volatility	-0.33	-0.21	-0.05	0.23	-0.26	-0.41	-0.37	-0.20	-0.20	-0.05	-0.27	-0.08	-0.10	-0.01	-0.19	-0.33	-0.27	-0.18	0.60	1.00					
LB Agg.	-0.33	-0.29	0.24	0.32	-0.16	-0.34	-0.09	0.04	0.02	-0.13	0.06	-0.12	0.28	0.30	-0.23	-0.27	-0.33	0.10	0.33	0.19	1.00				
TIPs	-0.33	-0.27	-0.05	0.23	-0.29	-0.18	-0.18	-0.01	-0.10	0.16	-0.11	-0.26	0.04	0.03	-0.23	-0.27	-0.24	-0.04	0.19	0.06	0.43	1.00			
Russell 3000	0.80	0.83	0.21	-0.85	0.63	0.60	0.47	0.33	0.49	-0.14	0.36	0.08	0.04	0.03	0.54	0.75	0.70	0.19	-0.64	-0.34	-0.29	-0.35	1.00		
Russell 2000	0.85	0.81	0.19	-0.85	0.61	0.70	0.50	0.33	0.54	-0.08	0.57	-0.01	0.07	0.15	0.47	0.67	0.62	0.04	-0.67	-0.30	-0.32	-0.34	0.91	1.00	
MSCI	0.77	0.78	0.17	-0.80	0.57	0.58	0.41	0.25	0.50	-0.08	0.31	0.14	0.07	-0.09	0.52	0.76	0.69	0.20	-0.62	-0.36	-0.38	-0.38	0.96	0.87	1.00

Notes: Descriptions of factor variables contained in the appendix to this chapter. Data is for 1996 through Q1 2006.
Source: RogersCasey.

343

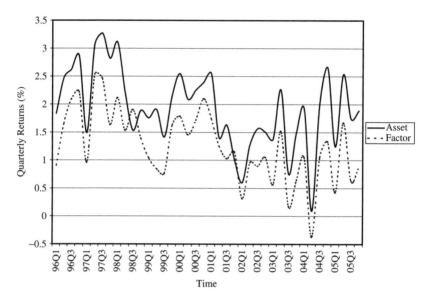

FIGURE 11.12 Quarterly Returns for Efficient Frontier Portfolio (1), Based on Optimized Traditional Assets and Alternative Investments (Constrained at 25 Percent) versus Optimized Factors

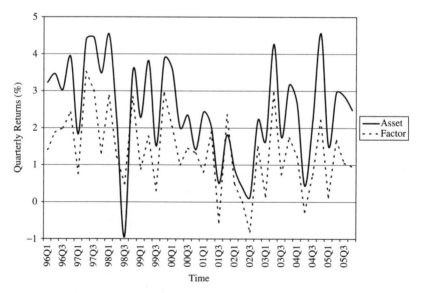

FIGURE 11.13 Quarterly Returns for Efficient Frontier Portfolio (11), Based on Optimized Traditional Assets and Alternative Investments (Constrained at 25 Percent) versus Optimized Factors

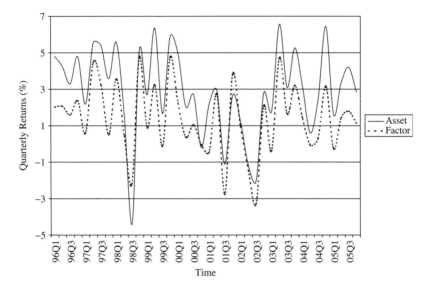

FIGURE 11.14 Quarterly Returns for Efficient Frontier Portfolio (21), Based on Optimized Traditional Assets and Alternative Investments (Constrained at 25 Percent) versus Optimized Factors

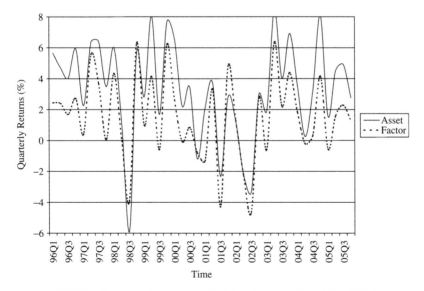

FIGURE 11.15 Quarterly Returns for Efficient Frontier Portfolio (31), Based on Optimized Traditional Assets and Alternative Investments (Constrained at 25 Percent) versus Optimized Factors

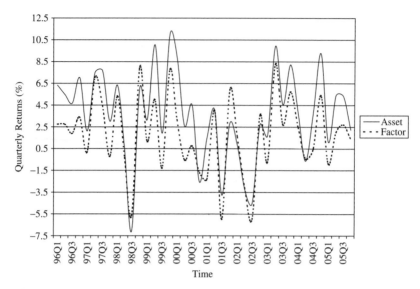

FIGURE 11.16 Quarterly Returns for Efficient Frontier Portfolio (41), Based on Optimized Traditional Assets and Alternative Investments (Constrained at 25 Percent) versus Optimized Factors

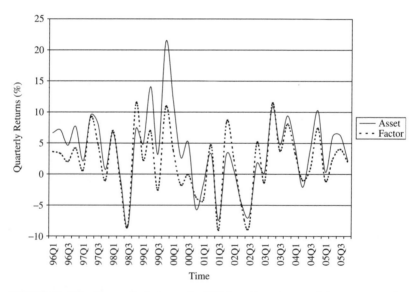

FIGURE 11.17 Quarterly Returns for Efficient Frontier Portfolio (51), Based on Optimized Traditional Assets and Alternative Investments (Constrained at 25 Percent) versus Optimized Factors

Notes

Chapter 2   Investors in Alternative Investments and the Necessary Ingredients for a Successful Program

1. Variations of these concepts have often been referred to by David Swensen of Yale University. See Swensen, D. 2000. *Pioneering Portfolio Management—An Unconventional Approach to Institutional Investment* (New York: The Free Press.)
2. Ibid.
3. The entire concept of rebalancing is a beta-centric notion. Investors wish to maintain strategic allocations to systemic risk factors that are deemed to be desirable over the long term. The manager-specific or alpha-centric element of these factor exposures tends to be ignored during the rebalancing procedure. Often, in this sense, the baby is thrown out with the bathwater. For example, consider an investor who rebalances away from a volatility factor and executes this through the redemption of assets from a hedge fund manager who is closed to new investment. This hedge fund may be able to generate high uncorrelated sources of alpha, but also has a volatility factor expression. Redemption from this manager might eliminate the investor's ability to reinvest with the manager at a later date. Therefore, selection of this vehicle to reduce the factor exposure could be counterproductive from a longer-term perspective.

Chapter 3   Hedge Funds

1. For more information on this concept, see Erb, C. B., and C. R. Harvey. 2005. "The Tactical and Strategic Value of Commodity Futures." Working paper.
2. HFR, Inc.

Chapter 4   Private Equity

1. Nevertheless, private equity remains a less efficient investment area than public equity.
2. However, this potentially could be ameliorated by a large quantity of high-quality start-up companies seeking capital.
3. Mills, K. Gordon. 2000. "LBO Returns in the United States: What Will It Take to Succeed in the New Era of LBOs?" In R. Lake and R. A. Lake (eds.), *Private Equity and Venture Capital: A Practical Guide for Investors and Practitioners.* London: Euromoney Books, pp. 261–273.

4. Atkins, B., and M. Giannini. 2003. "Risk Management for Private Equity Funds of Funds." In L. Jaeger (ed.), *The New Generation of Risk Management for Hedge Funds and Private Equity Investments*. London: Euromoney Books, pp. 215–227.

Chapter 5   Real Estate

1. Kaiser, R. 2005. "Investment Styles and Style Boxes in Equity Real Estate: Can the Emerging Model Succeed in Classifying Real Estate Alternatives?" *Journal of Real Estate Portfolio Management*, Vol. 11, No. 1: 5–18.
2. McDonald, L., and B. Stiver. 2004. "Institutional Real Estate—Investment Style Categories." RogersCasey, LLC.
3. Ibid.
4. Hahn, T., D. Geltner, and N. Gerardo-Lietz. 2005. "Real Estate Opportunity Funds." *Journal of Portfolio Management* (Special Real Estate Issue), September: 143–153.
5. Lee, S., and S. Stevenson. 2005. "The Case for REITs in the Mixed-Asset Portfolio in the Short and Long Run." *Journal of Real Estate Portfolio Management*, Vol. 11, No. 1: 55–67.
6. Fisher, J., and W. Goetzmann. 2005. "Performance of Real Estate Portfolios." *Journal of Portfolio Management* (Special Real Estate Issue, September): 32–45.
7. Kaiser, R. 2005. "Analyzing Real Estate Portfolio Returns." *Journal of Portfolio Management* (Special Real Estate Issue, September): 134–142.

Chapter 6   Currency, Commodities, Timber, and Oil and Gas

1. Lindsay, I., and S. Arnott. 2005. "Currency: An Untapped Alpha Source." Goldman Sachs Asset Management Perspectives.
2. For more information on this concept, see Dalio, R. 1998. "Inefficiencies and Opportunities in the Currency Markets." Bridgewater.
3. Erb, C. B., and C. R. Harvey. 2005. "The Tactical and Strategic Value of Commodity Futures." Working paper.
4. Caufield, J. 1998. "Timberland Return Drivers and Investing Styles for an Asset that Has Come of Age." *Real Estate Finance*, Winter: 65–78.
5. Figures supplied by Molpus Woodlands Advisors.

Chapter 8   Cash Flow Forecasting and Its Implications for Rebalancing

1. Throughout this discussion, the term *partnership* is used, but it denotes other variations of private funds, such as limited liability companies (LLCs) and private trusts.
2. Cardie, H., K. Cattanach, and M. Kelly. 2000. "How Large Should Your Commitment to Private Equity Really Be?" *Journal of Wealth Management*, Fall: 39–45.

3. Nevins, D., A. Conner, and G. McIntire. 2004. "A Portfolio Management Approach to Determining Private Equity Commitments." *Journal of Alternative Investments*, Spring: 32–46.
4. Takahashi, D., and S. Alexander. 2002. "Illiquid Alternative Asset Fund Modeling." *Journal of Portfolio Management*, Winter: 90–100.

Chapter 9   Leverage and Portable Alpha

1. Jaeger, L. 2002. *Managing Risk in Alternative Investment Strategies: Successful Investing in Hedge Funds and Managed Futures*. Harlow, U.K.: FT Prentice Hall.

Chapter 10   Factor Analysis

1. Dorsey, A., et al. 2003. "Are Hedge Funds or Hedge Fund of Funds an Asset Class or a Strategy Among Asset Classes?" RogersCasey white paper. Darien, Connecticut.
2. An asset with a beta of 1.0 has systemic risk equal to its market. However, it may have additional idiosyncratic risk in addition to its systemic risk.
3. This also assumes that an investor's equity allocation is equal to the market and that additional idiosyncratic risk provides no additional compensation.
4. Alpha can be viewed as the average of the residuals in the model. It is the residuals themselves that are uncorrelated to other factors in the model.
5. The use of macroeconomic models to determine asset class performance can be challenging. Typically, these models also require estimates of economic surprises to predict asset-class returns.
6. PCA also is helpful in identifying the presence of new unidentified factor exposures in a model over time. The challenge then is to identify these new factors.
7. Lehman Brothers. 1999. "Global Relative Value." Fixed Income Research.

Chapter 11   Factor Analysis: The Findings and Discovering Active Alpha

1. Peterson, S., and J. Grier. 2006. "Covariance Misspecification in Asset Allocation." *Financial Analysts Journal*, Vol. 62, No. 4: 76–85.
2. Singer, B., R. Staub, and K. Terhaar. 2003. "Appropriate Policy Allocation for Alternative Investments." *Journal of Portfolio Management*, No. 8278, Spring: 101–110.
3. Dorsey, A. 2005. "Implementation Considerations when Using Absolute-Return Strategies for Traditional Portfolio Risk Reduction." In V. R. Parker (ed.), *Managing Hedge Fund Risk, 2nd ed.* London: Risk Books, pp. 43–64.
4. The use of the Sharpe ratio in considering alternative investments typically understates the risk-adjusted return potential of these assets. The standard deviation denominator of this calculation presumes a normal distribution of returns from an investment and ignores the potential skewness of returns that actually may occur.

5. Markowitz, H. 1991. *Portfolio Selection: Efficient Diversification of Investments, 2nd ed*. Malden, Mass.: Blackwell Publishing.
6. Dorsey, "Implementation Considerations."
7. When attempting factor overlays, it is important to test the momentum of factors in terms of their effect on dependent variables. These sensitivities change over time. If the investments in a portfolio experience a sudden change in their betas to factors, then the amount of factor overlay may be under- or overestimated.
8. The appendix section on the methodology for regression analysis was initially drafted by Srivatsa Kilambi. Srivatsa Kilambi and Kenneth Voon Keat Sui conducted the mean variance optimizations and regressions for this chapter. Gujarati, D. 1995. *Basic Econometrics, 3rd ed*. New York: McGraw-Hill. Shim, J. 2000. *Strategic Business Forecasting*. New York: St. Lucie Press. Hanke, J., D. Wichern, and A. Reitsch. 2000. *Business Forecasting, 7th ed*. Upper Saddle River, N.J.: Prentice Hall.
9. Using lagged independent variables can help improve regression fits.

Glossary

Active Management   Active management reflects an investment manager or strategy that attempts to exceed the performance of a relevant benchmark or asset class. Active management is in contrast to passive management, which attempts to only match the performance of a benchmark or asset class. Active management fees are higher than passive management fees.

Adjusted R-Squared   A more appropriate measure for explaining the variation in a dependent variable based on a regression equation. A goodness-of-fit measure (proportion of the total sample variation in the dependent variable that is explained by the independent variables) in multiple regression analysis that penalizes additional explanatory variables by using a degrees of freedom adjustment in estimating the error variance.

Alpha   Alpha is a measure of a fund's return that is generated independently from the beta returns that are influenced by the fund's benchmark. Many investors in non-directional, or low beta, and low correlation funds are seeking an independent alpha return that these investments are capable of generating. These uncorrelated returns when added to a diversified portfolio may improve the portfolio's overall returns and reduce its volatility.

Autocorrelation   In a time-series model, correlation between the errors in different time periods. A series that exhibits positive serial correlation, a positive (negative) error in one period increases the likelihood for a positive (negative) error in the next period. The converse is true for negative serial correlation, whereby if there is a positive (negative) error in one period, it is more likely to be followed by a negative (positive) error in the next period. The presence of autocorrelation indicates that shocks to a given series are persistent.

Autoregressive Conditional Heteroscedasticity (ARCH)   ARCH is used in a scenario where the variance of an error term fails the assumption of being homoscedastic. ARCH identifies a relationship between past observations and future observations.

Backfill Bias   Backfill bias in indexes is the instance where funds that report to an index provide historical performance that theretofore had not been included in the index. The concept is that a reporting fund would not report this data unless it was favorable, thus biasing the index upward.

Backwardation   A relationship between a futures price that in the current market is lower than the expected future cash or spot price. Simply put, the spot price is greater than the futures price.

Basis Points   A basis point is one one-hundredth of a percentage point.

Benchmark   A benchmark typically represents a standard investment index against which an investment fund can be measured in terms of performance, volatility, beta, and correlation. Examples include the S&P 500, 90-day U.S. Treasury bills, and three-month LIBOR rates.

Beta   Beta is the amount of return for a security or fund that is explained by its benchmark. A high beta for a fund is a measure of its directional movement with its benchmark. Nondirectional funds have betas near zero and generate returns that are unrelated to the returns of market benchmarks.

Cap Rates   Cap rates pertain to real estate and represent the ratio of net funds from operations for a property divided by the appraised value or purchase price of the property.

Capital Call   Once an investor has made a capital commitment to a private fund, whether invested in private equity, real estate, or hard assets, periodically the general partner will make capital calls. A capital call is a request by the general partner to each of the limited partners, on the basis of their prior commitments of capital, to fund an identified investment to be contained in the partnership.

Carried Interest   For private equity funds, the carried interest is the performance fee paid to the general partner. Unlike in the case for hedge funds, however, the carried interest is paid to a private equity general partner only at the conclusion of profitable transactions, proceeds from which are distributed to limited partners. In contrast, performance fees are paid to the general partners of hedge funds on an annual basis and based on the mark-to-market profits for the fund each year.

Clawback   A clawback feature, usually for a private equity fund, enables the limited partners of a fund to demand a return of prior period performance fees paid to the general partner, in the event that the fund ultimately exhibits no net profit above a predescribed preferred rate to the limited partners at the end of the life of the fund.

"Closed" Hedge Funds   The term *closed*, as it pertains to hedge funds, represents a situation when a fund no longer accepts new assets from investors. A related term is "soft closed," which indicates that a fund may be closed to new investors but open to new capital from existing investors. The term "hard closed" refers to a fund that is closed to capital both from new and from existing investors.

Committed Capital   Committed capital, as opposed to invested capital, relates to the total amount that an investor commits usually to a private equity or real estate fund. This amount will be "called" by the general partner over time as capital is required to complete transactions and make follow-on investments.

Commodity Trading Advisers (CTAs)   CTAs are funds that specialize in trading commodities in cash markets or through futures contracts. Systematic trading and discretionary trading are examples of substyles of this strategy.

Contango   A relationship between a futures price that in the current market is higher than the expected future cash or spot price. Simply put, the spot price is less than the futures price.

Convertible Bond Arbitrage   Convertible arbitrage typically entails holding a long position in a convertible bond and a short position in the same issuer's common stock. Assuming the potential conversion of the bond, the combined position is hedged although it is net long.

Core Real Estate Core properties tend to be described as the most conservative type of real estate investment, since they typically have low or zero levels of debt associated with their capital structure, are fully occupied with strong credit-rated tenants located in major markets, and have leases with long lives.

Correlation Correlation for a fund measures the degree of similar movement in performance that the fund generates relative to the performance of another fund or benchmark.

Directional Strategies These strategies have a relatively high systemic exposure, beta, and correlation with traditional capital markets. These funds tend to have relatively high volatility and return targets. Examples of directional strategies include global macro and long/short equity.

Distressed Securities Distressed investing involves the purchase of securities that are impaired from a credit quality perspective. These securities may carry low ratings from credit rating agencies. They also may be near or in default. A benefit of investing in distressed securities is their prospect of enhanced value through corporate reorganization.

Duration Duration is a measure of volatility for a fixed income investment. Short-duration securities are less sensitive to movements in interest rates than long-duration securities. Short-duration instruments also typically have shorter time periods to maturity than long-duration investments.

Durbin-Watson (D-W) Statistic A statistic used to test for first order serial correlation in the errors of a time series regression model under the classical linear model assumptions. A statistic lower than 1.5 generally indicates that there is positive serial correlation, while a statistic of greater than 2.5 generally indicates that there is negative serial correlation. As a rule of thumb, if D-W statistic is between 1.7 and 2.3, it indicates the absence of autocorrelation.

Emerging Hedge Fund Managers Generally, the term *emerging hedge fund manager* implies a hedge fund with a short track record or few assets under management. The term can also refer to minority-owned firms.

Emerging Markets Emerging markets generally are considered those located outside of developed nations. Funds that invest in securities and issuers that are domiciled in emerging markets are considered emerging market funds. Securities can include those issued by corporate and sovereign entities.

Equity Market Neutral Equity market neutral funds are those that employ a long/short equity strategy, but do so while maintaining an approximate zero net exposure. In other words, the gross long positions and gross short positions for these funds roughly offset each other from a dollar perspective. Equity market neutral funds may execute their strategy through discretionary or systematic approaches, and they may seek to maintain a neutral position in beta exposure and style exposure.

ERISA Plans An ERISA plan is a corporate defined-benefit pension plan that is governed under the rules and regulations of the Employee Retirement Income Security Act of 1974.

Event Driven Event-driven hedge funds seek to invest in securities of issuers that prospectively will undergo certain events that will change the value of the companies or their securities. Examples of these types of situations are corporate reorganizations, spinoffs, stock buybacks, and other recapitalizations. This strategy may be executed in a long only or in a hedged fashion. Securities used may emanate from any section of an issuer's capital structure.

Exchange-Traded Funds (ETFs) Exchange-traded funds are publicly traded closed-end funds that are invested in such a fashion so as to emulate industry sectors, market capitalization, or market indexes.

Exotic Betas A beta for an alternative investment factor, such as volatility, is considered to be an exotic beta. A nuance in the consideration of exotic betas is that they can be isolated and in some cases passively replicated, in which case true alpha for an investment strategy becomes smaller.

F-Test Serves as a tool in evaluating the significance of an overall regression model.

Fixed-Income Arbitrage Fixed-income arbitrage is a hedge fund strategy that uses long and short positions in debt securities. A wide range of geographic, issuer, and seniority of securities may be used. Typically, fixed-income arbitrage hedge funds utilize significant amounts of leverage. Often, this strategy is focused on relative-value trades among different types or duration securities.

Fund of Funds Fund of funds are entities that invest often in numerous underlying funds. For instance, a hedge fund of funds may have an investment as a limited partner in various unaffiliated hedge funds. The same can be said for private equity, real estate, or diversified asset-class funds of funds. A benefit from the fund of funds approach is attaining diversification among underlying fund investments. An investor can gain this benefit through a fund of funds, rather than making the individual underlying fund investments themselves.

Gating Provisions Gating provisions refer to the ability for an investment fund to limit redemptions by investors in the event that a large proportion of investors or assets invested in the fund seek to redeem simultaneously. The occurrence of this instance often is in conjunction with a problem that has developed at a fund, such as poor performance, an unexpected change in the style or status of the fund, the departure of a key employee, or loss of investor confidence in the fund or its management.

General Partner A general partner of a private investment fund, a limited liability company, or a limited partnership is the controlling partner who makes decisions for all limited partners. The general partner is paid a management fee and often a performance fee that is calculated as a percentage of profits earned by the fund.

Global Macro Global macro hedge funds are those that invest in global securities in an effort to capture relative value or directional opportunities. Investments are based on macroeconomic themes across worldwide markets. This approach is multifaceted in the types of securities, national issuers, and currencies that are used. Investments are both long and short. Generally, significant amounts of leverage and derivatives are utilized to express positions.

High-Water Mark A high-water mark is the high NAV price that a fund has achieved. High-water marks often are used in performance fee calculations. Typically, for a hedge fund to be able to charge a performance fee, its NAV must be higher than the level it attained at the end of the prior year. For example, if a fund with a NAV of $100 at the end of year one see its NAV decline to $50 in year two, it would have no profit and no ability to charge a performance fee. At the end of year three, if the fund's NAV amounted to $75, even though the fund was up 50 percent for the year, it would not have the right to charge a performance fee, because its NAV did not exceed its high watermark of $100.

Homoscedastic The variance of the error term in a regression is a constant.

Hurdle Rate Some performance fees are subject to a hurdle rate, which is the rate above which a fund is required to earn before it can charge a performance fee. Often hurdle rates are set at a risk-free rate, such as 90-day U.S. Treasury bills or short-term LIBOR rates.

Indenture An indenture is the document that contains covenants that govern an issue of debt. Covenants are certain tests and restrictions that measure limits, timing, or amounts of leverage, assets, cash flow, and interest payments such that triggering any of these thresholds leads to an event of default on debt.

Index Fund Index funds are investable funds that seek to replicate a passive index.

Information Ratio The information ratio often is referred to as the performance of an investment manager or fund divided by the standard deviation of that performance string.

Investable Indexes Investable indexes are indexes that are not solely provided in a published nominal form, but also are available in a commingled fund that is accessible to investors. The importance of indexes being investable is that they then provide a passive alternative against which investors may measure the performance of their active fund managers. In this way, investable indexes may be an effective benchmark for investors.

J Curve The J curve represents an initial period of time during which a private investment fund experiences flat or negative performance. Typically, this occurs in the very early stages of a private fund, and it may be more pronounced for venture capital than other types of private investment funds.

Kurtosis Kurtosis, also referred to as a "fat-tailed" distribution, indicates a distribution of returns that may be normal or symmetrical in shape around its mean, but has more frequent than expected observations in the tails of the distribution. High kurtosis is not desired, but it can be more acceptable when it occurs with a positive skew.

Leverage There are several types of leverage, including cash leverage, notional leverage, and structural leverage. Cash leverage simply relates to funds that are borrowed from a bank or through the sale of promissory securities. Notional leverage relates to embedded leverage in a type of security, such as a derivative. Structural leverage relates to the nature of a trading strategy, such as a leveraged buyout, or other qualitative factors in play that may cause an investor to have concentration risk across a series of investments, such as basing them all on a certain type of assumption, research, or relationship.

Leveraged Buyouts (LBOs) An LBO is a transaction based on borrowed capital in order to purchase the equity control of a company.

Limited Partner A limited partner is a passive partner of a private investment fund, limited liability company, or limited partnership. A limited partner has no control over the affairs of a fund. In addition to this passive role, the limited partner has limited liability as it pertains to the liabilities of the fund.

Lockup Period   Lockups often are used in conjunction with a period of initial investment in a fund. For hedge funds, lockup periods usually range from one to three years. During this initial time frame, an investor is restricted from withdrawing or redeeming money from the fund. Often, financial penalties are applied in the event of early redemption. Reasons for having lockup periods include: (1) to dissuade short-term investors from investing in a fund; (2) to enable an investment manager to plan its business more strategically, knowing that its investor base and management fee will be stable; and (3) to enable an investment manager greater freedom to invest in a concentrated or illiquid fashion.

Long/Short Equity Hedge Funds   Long/short equity funds are those that invest in both long positions and short positions in corporate equities. These funds may have a greater dollar amount of gross long exposure than gross short exposure, in which case they are net long. The alternative may exist as well, in which case a fund is net short.

Management Fee   A management fee is usually paid quarterly to an investment manager. Typical management fees for hedge funds range from 1 percent to 3 percent per year. Typical private equity management fees decline in later years of a fund's existence.

Margin Call   A margin call is a request for additional capital by a broker from an investor. The request usually is triggered in the event that the equity capital in an investor's account falls below acceptable, prearranged, or regulated levels relative to the amount of leverage or borrowings that the investor has accumulated in the account.

Market Neutral   See **Equity Market Neutral.**

Mean-Variance Optimization (MVO)   Mean-variance optimization is a technique used in portfolio construction based on trade-offs between return (i.e., the mean return) and risk (i.e., the standard deviation, or square root of its variance). Resampling is the generation of a series of portfolios that are statistically equivalent to the MVO portfolio.

Merger Arbitrage   Merger arbitrage involves investment in the securities of issuers that are engaged in merging or the acquisition of one another. Typically, for deals that require the exchange of securities, a merger arbitrage hedge fund is long the securities of companies being acquired and short a smaller amount of the securities of the acquirers. This hedged position represents a spread trade that closes over the period of time required for the acquisition to be consummated. For all-cash transactions, a merger arbitrage fund may be long the securities of the company to be acquired with no corresponding short position or perhaps a short position in similar types of securities from other issuers as a hedge. Typically, leverage is used to express positions.

Mezzanine Debt   Mezzanine debt is typically either unsecured or second-lien secured debt, often placed in private companies. Frequently, this debt has current coupon benefits as well as warrants exercisable into equity. Thus, the total return to a mezzanine investor usually has a combination of debt and equity characteristics. Mezzanine debt investing from a return and risk perspective lies in between secured lending and equity investing.

Middle Market Middle market investing is focused on corporations that have revenue and enterprise values that are in between large and small-sized companies. The precise demarcation of these boundaries changes over market cycles.

Monte Carlo Simulations Monte Carlo simulations can be used as a tool to create probabilistic outcomes for portfolio allocations, based on assumptions for asset classes and portfolio cash flows.

Multicollinearity Multicollinearity describes linear dependence among variables. It often is referred to as intercorrelation among the independent variables. Multicollinearity occurs when independent variables interfere with each other and render regression results meaningless.

Multistrategy Hedge Funds Multistrategy hedge funds are those that invest across more than one hedge strategy. Multistrategy hedge funds typically invest in a broad enough number of strategies such that they are able to take advantage of opportunities in specific strategies as they occur. Effective multistrategy hedge funds tend to be larger organizations with expert groups that specialize in separate hedge strategies.

Negative Selection Bias Negative selection bias reflects a precondition that may cause the selection of potentially poor performing funds. An investor with overly demanding requirements may narrow its universe of available funds. Highly sought-after funds have their pick of investors, such that they may choose not to take money from investors that have too many requirements, such as real-time transparency or overly liberal redemption terms. Funds that are in less demand by investors (perhaps because they are less skillful or less tested) may be more amenable to accepting demanding requirements from an investor.

Net Asset Value (NAV) Net asset value is the calculation of the assets minus the liabilities of a fund, which then is represented on the basis of per membership units outstanding. Usually NAVs are calculated only once per month or once per quarter and represent estimates of a fund's value. Often NAVs are adjusted slightly for inaccuracies in the subsequent periods.

Nondirectional Strategies These strategies have relatively low systemic exposure, beta, and correlation with traditional capital markets. They also tend to have relatively low volatility and return targets. Examples of nondirectional strategies include equity market neutral and convertible bond arbitrage.

Opportunistic Real Estate Opportunistic real estate is the most aggressive type of real estate investment and therefore is perhaps one of the most difficult to characterize through generalizations. Some unifying themes are that properties tend to be existing real estate that is either distressed or highly leveraged, or they are new developments of speculative buildings.

Optionality Optionality characterizes a situation where an investor possesses the ability to potentially benefit or profit from an investment under certain circumstances. Optional gain may be in addition to or separate from an investment's primary or initial investment purpose or merit.

Passive Management Passive management reflects an investment manager, index, or strategy that attempts only to match the performance of a relevant benchmark or asset class. Passive management is in contrast to active management, which attempts to exceed the performance of a benchmark or asset class. Passive management fees are lower than active management fees.

Performance Fee A performance fee is an incentive award paid to an investment manager in the event that the fund is profitable. Some performance fees have hurdle rates, above which the fund must generate a profit prior to the performance fee taking effect. When a performance fee is charged by a fund, it is based on profits after a management fee is paid.

PIPEs PIPEs are private investment in public entities. PIPEs, also known as Reg D or Regulation D investments, are exempt from initial registration with the Securities and Exchange Commission in the United States.

Portable Alpha Portable alpha refers to the creation of a market-neutral or zero-beta actively managed portfolio, which is used in conjunction with derivatives that generate a passive index return.

R-Squared R-squared indicates the percentage of variation in a dependent variable that can be explained by a regression equation. See **Adjusted R-Squared.**

Reg D Regulation D, or Reg D, investments are private placements in private or public companies that are exempt from initial registration with the Securities and Exchange Commission. Reg D investments in public companies are also known as PIPEs, or private investment in public entities.

Registered Investment Adviser (RIA) RIAs are investment advisers that have registered either with the Securities and Exchange Commission or with the securities regulatory authority of the state of their incorporation.

Relative Value Arbitrage Relative value arbitrage generally relates to non-directional strategies that attempt to capture a pending convergence in valuation between securities. As such, the positions typically are paired and therefore have a natural hedge in place. Relative value hedge strategies include convertible bond arbitrage, pairs trading, fixed-income arbitrage, and market-neutral equity.

Reporting Bias Reporting bias is the notion that not all funds report to an index. The funds that report may be the ones with positive performance, rather than those with negative performance. Another aspect of reporting bias is that not all funds in a strategy report to indexes. Some of the largest best-performing hedge funds do not report to indexes, because they do not seek publicity and often are no longer accepting capital from new investors.

Risk Premium The expected return of an asset(s) minus the risk-free rate of return.

Roll Return Inherent opportunity for return in rolling from short-dated to long-dated futures contracts, either as a long buyer of backwardated futures contracts or a short seller of contangoed futures contracts.

Securities and Exchange Commission (SEC) The U.S. Securities and Exchange Commission is the government agency that is mandated by the United States Congress with regulating and policing the securities markets in the United States. Registered investment advisers are subject to regular audit and review by the SEC. Although unregistered funds are not subject to regular inspection by the SEC, the SEC still has enforcement power over unregulated investment entities domiciled in the United States, particularly in the case of fraud.

Serial Correlation See **Autocorrelation.**

Sharpe Ratio The Sharpe ratio is the ratio of a fund's performance to its standard deviation. Typically, a risk-free rate is deducted from a fund's performance in the calculation of Sharpe. A comparison of the Sharpe ratios for a number of funds enables an investor to compare risk-adjusted returns, or the amount of return generated by each fund relative to the amount of risk or volatility that is sustained.

Short Selling Short selling entails borrowing securities that are not owned and their subsequent sale. An open short position requires the eventual repurchase of the securities to return them to the investor who lent them. An open short position creates an open-end liability for the short seller.

Side Letters A side letter is an agreement between a fund manager and an investor, whereby the investor secures terms or conditions that are improved from those stated in the fund's governing documents.

Side Pocket A *side pocket* is a term often used with hedge funds to refer to a separate investment vehicle that holds investments in less liquid assets. Side pockets typically have liquidity rights that are much longer than the terms of the hedge fund in which they reside. Also, the calculations of performance fees on side pocket investments usually coincide with their fair market markups, markdowns, or liquidations. Often investors have the ability to opt into or out of side pocket investments.

Skewness Skewness indicates an asymmetrical shape to a distribution of historical returns. Negative skewness indicates a bias to underperformance relative to the mean, while positive skewness indicates a bias toward outperformance relative to the mean.

Socially Responsible Investing (SRI) SRI is the act of creating constraints on an investment manager's portfolio, such that it will not hold investments in securities issued by companies deemed to be socially irresponsible. Examples include companies engaged in social "evils" such as the production or sale of tobacco, alcohol, or firearms. SRI also may extend to restricting investment managers from using certain third-party service providers that may also be engaged in behavior deemed to be reprehensible by the investor.

Standard Deviation Standard deviation is the measure variability of a distribution of data around its mean. Standard deviation is considered to be a measure of risk. The larger the standard deviation for an investment fund's historical monthly returns, the more volatile that fund's returns have been.

Statistical Arbitrage The statistical arbitrage hedge strategy is a catch-all phase that describes hedge funds engaged in computer-driven trading programs, trading pairs of securities based on statistical valuation spreads, or other quantitatively driven methods that seek to capture discrepancies between the valuation of securities.

Style Analysis Style analysis refers to a description of investment styles in asset classes. Examples in equity include large capitalization versus small capitalization and value versus growth.

Survivor Bias There can be a propensity for failed funds to be excluded from historical index return strings. Typically, these failed funds do not report the last periods of performance as they are failing. Furthermore, their historical returns may be eliminated as well. A representation of only surviving funds can artificially inflate historical index returns.

t-Statistic   Indicates the significance of each explanatory variable in predicting the dependent variable. Generally, a t-value greater than $+2$ and less than -2 is considered to be significant.

Tracking Error   Tracking error is the standard deviation of the difference in returns between a fund and its benchmark.

Transparency   Transparency for any investment fund relates to the degree of information that the fund provides to its limited partners, service providers, or third parties. Certain related terms include the following: "security-level transparency," which is sharing the specific types and amounts of securities held in an investment fund; "risk-level transparency," which is sharing the aggregate risk factors and vulnerabilities that may negatively affect the performance of a fund; "sector-level transparency," which is sharing the allocation of investments in a fund by industry sectors; "strategy-level transparency," which is sharing the allocations to various strategies used by a fund; and "factor-level transparency," which is sharing the various investment factors to which a fund is sensitive.

Unrelated Business Taxable Income (UBTI)   Tax-exempt investors in U.S. investment partnerships are subject to UBTI tax liabilities. Unrelated business taxable income is income generated through debt-financed activities. Capital gains or income generated from securities or property that is acquired with debt by a partnership is subject to the UBTI tax.

Value-Added Real Estate   Value-added real estate results in an expected risk and return profile that is more aggressive than either the core or core plus strategies. Properties in this category of real estate usually are not fully leased and may require renovation or redevelopment.

Value at Risk   Value-at-risk calculations seek to identify the percentage of a portfolio that is at risk of loss with a 95 percent or 99 percent confidence level.

Variance Inflation Factor (VIF)   The strength of multicollinearity is measured by VIF. A VIF near 1 suggests that multicollinearity is not a serious problem for an independent variable and its estimated coefficient and that the t-value will not change much as other independent variables are added to and deleted from the regression equation.

Venture Capital (VC)   Venture capital is an area of private equity that is focused on early-stage companies. This area of investment is considered to be high in risk for loss but also holds high return potential. As a result, long-term performance from venture capital can be among the highest in volatility for alternative investments.

Volatility Index (VIX)   The VIX is an acronym for the Chicago Board Options Exchange's (CBOE) Volatility Index. VIX was introduced in 1993. It is an implied volatility index that measures the expected 30-day forward-looking volatility in the S&P 500 Index, based on the prices of short-dated options on the S&P 500 Index. The VIX often moves in the opposite direction to the S&P

500, and therefore tends to be a signal of negative sentiment for the overall equity market.

Waterfall   A waterfall in private equity usually relates to the prioritization of cash returns on investment. The participants in these cash returns, depending on certain prioritization or fee catch-up features, are the general partner and limited partners in private equity funds.

References

Amenc, N., S. El Bied, and L. Martellini. 2003. "Predictability in Hedge Fund Returns." *Financial Analysts Journal*, Vol. 59, No. 5, Sept./Oct.: 32–46.

Amenc, N., and L. Martellini. 2002. "Portfolio Optimization and Hedge Fund Style Allocation Decisions." *Journal of Alternative Investments*, Fall: 7–20.

Anson, M. 2002. *Handbook of Alternative Assets*. Hoboken, N.J., The Frank J. Fabozzi Series, John Wiley & Sons, Inc.

Anson, M. 2004. "Strategic versus Tactical Asset Allocation: Beta versus Alpha Drivers." *Journal of Portfolio Management*, Winter: 8–22.

Anson, M., S. Hudson-Wilson, and F. Fabozzi. 2005. "Privately Traded Real Estate Equity." *Journal of Portfolio Management* (Special Real Estate Issue), September: 109–113.

Arshanapalli, B., T. Goggin, and W. Nelson. 2001. "Is Fixed-Weight Asset Allocation Really Better?" *Journal of Portfolio Management*, Spring: 27–38.

Asness, C. 2002. "Do Hedge Funds Add Value?" *AIMR Conference Proceedings on Hedge Fund Management*, April: 16–26.

Atkins, B, and M. Giannini. 2003. "Risk Management for Private Equity Funds of Funds." In L. Jaeger (ed.), *The New Generation of Risk Management for Hedge Funds and Private Equity Investments*. London: Euromoney Books, pp. 215–227.

Bacmann, J.-F., G. Gawron. 2004. "Fat Tail Risk in Portfolios of Hedge Funds and Traditional Investments." RMF Investment Management, white paper. Pfaffikon, Switzerland.

Bank for International Settlements. 2005. "Triennial Central Bank Survey: Foreign Exchange and Derivatives Market Activity in 2004." Basel, Switzerland.

Banz, R. 2004. "Where Have They Hidden My Alpha?" Pictet Asset Management. Geneva, Switzerland.

Barra, Inc. 1998. "Forecasting Risk with Multiple-Factor Models." *Barra Risk Model Handbook*. Berkeley, California.

Blaschka, F. 2003. "Benchmarking Real Estate Performance—Considerations and Implications." The Townsend Group.

Blaschka, F. 2005. "Underappreciated Risks in Today's Institutional Investing Environment." *PREA Quarterly*, Fall: 41–47.

Brown, W. 2000. "Convertible Arbitrage: Opportunity & Risk." Tremont Capital Management. Rye, New York.

Cardie, H., K. Cattanach, and M. Kelly. 2000. "How Large Should Your Commitment to Private Equity Really Be?" *Journal of Wealth Management*, Fall: 39–45.

Caufield, J. 1998. "Timberland Return Drivers and Investing Styles for an Asset that Has Come of Age." *Real Estate Finance*, Winter: 65–78.

Chen, H., K. Ho, C. Lu, and C. Wu. 2005. "Real Estate Investment Trusts." *Journal of Portfolio Management* (Special Real Estate Issue), September 2005: 46–54.

Clark, K., and K. Winkelmann. 2004. "Active Risk Budgeting in Action: Understanding Hedge Fund Performance." Strategic Research Paper, Goldman Sachs Asset Management, New York.

Crerend, W. 1998. *Fundamentals of Hedge Fund Investing: A Professional Investor's Guide*. New York: McGraw-Hill.

Crichton, M. 1969. *The Andromeda Strain*, New York: Dell, p. 247.

Cross, S. 1998. "All About the Foreign Exchange Market in the United States." Federal Reserve Bank of New York, New York.

Dalio, R. 1998. "Inefficiencies and Opportunities in the Currency Markets." Bridgewater Associates, Inc., Westport, Connecticut.

Darnell, M., and D. Levanoni. 2004. "What Really Differentiates Currency Managers?" First Quadrant, Partners Message, Vol. 1, No. 6.

DeFusco, R., D. McLeavey, J. Pinot, and D. Runkle. 2001. *Quantitative Methods for Investment Analysis*. Charlottesville, Va.: Association for Investment Management and Research.

Doherty, N., and H. Singer. 2002. "The Benefits of a Secondary Market for Life Insurance Policies." Wharton—Financial Institutions Center, working paper.

Dorsey, A. 2003. "The Perspective of Consultants on Hedge Fund and Private Equity Risk." In L. Jaeger (ed.), *The New Generation of Risk Management for Hedge Funds and Private Equity Investments*. London: Euromoney Books, pp. 291–308.

Dorsey, A. 2004. *How to Select a Hedge Fund of Funds—Pick the Winners and Avoid the Losers*. New York: Institutional Investor Books.

Dorsey, A. 2005. "Implementation Considerations when Using Absolute-Return Strategies for Traditional Portfolio Risk Reduction." In V. R. Parker (ed.), *Managing Hedge Fund Risk, 2nd ed*. London: Risk Books, pp. 43–64.

Dorsey, A. 2006. "Examining the Increasing Institutionalisation of an Industry: What Are Institutional Investors' Expectations of Hedge Funds?" In S. Jaffer (ed.), *Hedge Funds: Crossing the Institutional Frontier*. London: Euromoney Books, pp. 45–53.

Dorsey, A., et al. 2003. "Are Hedge Funds or Hedge Fund of Funds an Asset Class or a Strategy among Asset Classes?" RogersCasey. Darien, Connecticut.

Elton, E., M. Gruber, S. Brown, and W. Goetzmann. 2003. *Modern Portfolio Theory and Investment Analysis, 6th ed*. Hoboken, N.J.: John Wiley & Sons, Inc.

Ennis, R., and M. Sebastian. 2005. "Asset Allocation with Private Equity." *Journal of Private Equity*, No. 15872, Summer: 81–87.

Erb, C. B., and C. R. Harvey. 2005. "The Tactical and Strategic Value of Commodity Futures." Working paper.

Fabozzi, F. J. 2000. *Fixed Income Analysis*. New Hope, Penn. Frank J. Fabozzi Associates.

Foerster, S. 2006. "What Drives Hedge Fund Returns?" *Canadian Investment Review*, Summer: 16–21.

Fung, W., and D. Hsieh. 2003. "The Risk in Hedge Fund Strategies: Alternative Alphas and Alternative Betas." In L. Jaeger (ed.), *The New Generation of Risk Management for Hedge Funds and Private Equity Investments*. London: Euromoney Books, pp. 72–87.

Galati, G., and M. Melvin. 2004. "Why Has FX Trading Surged? Explaining the 2004 Triennial Survey." *BIS Quarterly Review*, December: 67–74.

Gompers, P., and J. Lerner. 2000. *The Venture Capital Cycle*. Cambridge, Mass.: MIT Press.

Gujarati, D. 1995. *Basic Econometrics, 3rd ed*. New York: McGraw-Hill.

Hahn, T, D. Geltner, and N. Gerardo-Lietz. 2005. "Real Estate Opportunity Funds." *Journal of Portfolio Management* (Special Real Estate Issue), September 2005: 143–153.

Hanke, J., D. Wichern, and A. Reitsch. 2001. *Business Forecasting, 7th ed*. Upper Saddle River, N.J.: Prentice Hall.

Healy, T., T. Corriero, and R. Rozenov. 2003. "Timber as an Institutional Investment." White paper subsequently published in *The Journal of Alternative Investments*, Winter 2005.

Hudson-Wilson, S., F. Fabozzi, and J. Gordon. 2003. "Why Real Estate." *Journal of Portfolio Management* (Special Real Estate Issue): 12–25.

Hudson-Wilson, S., J. Gordon, F. Fabozzi, M. Anson, and M. Giliberto. 2005. "Why Real Estate." *Journal of Portfolio Management* (Special Real Estate Issue), September: 12-22.

Infometrix, Inc. 1991. "Comparison of Factor Based PLS and PCR to Traditional Calibration Methods." Chemometrics Technical Note. Woodinville, Washington.

Jaeger, L. 2002. *Managing Risk in Alternative Investment Strategies: Successful Investing in Hedge Funds and Managed Futures*. Harlow, U.K.: FT Prentice Hall.

Jaeger, L. 2003. *The New Generation of Risk Management for Hedge Funds and Private Equity Investments*. London: Euromoney Books.

Jaeger, L. 2005. *A Guide to Hedge Fund Return Sources*. New York: Institutional Investor Books.

Jaeger, L., and S. Higbee. 2003. "Sources of Systematic Return in Hedge Funds." Partners Group. Zug, Switzerland.

Kaiser, R. 2005. "Analyzing Real Estate Portfolio Returns." *Journal of Portfolio Management* (Special Real Estate Issue), September: 134–142.

Kaiser, R. 2005. "Investment Styles and Style Boxes in Equity Real Estate: Can the Emerging Model Succeed in Classifying Real Estate Alternatives?" *Journal of Real Estate Portfolio Management*, Vol. 11, No. 1: 5–18.

Knight, J., and S. Satchell. 2005. *Linear Factor Models in Finance*. Oxford, U.K.: Elsevier Finance.

Kooli, M. 2005. "Do Hedge Funds Outperform the Market?" *Canadian Investment Review*, Winter: 18–25.

Kooli, M., P. Klein, R. Cultraro, T. Lett, and W. Brodkin. 2005. "Finding a Home for Hedge Funds." *Canadian Investment Review*, Summer: 20–21.

Lake, R., and R. A. Lake. 2000. *Private Equity and Venture Capital: A Practical Guide for Investors and Practitioners.* London: Euromoney Books.

Lederman, J., and R. Klein. 1995. *Hedge Funds: Investment and Portfolio Strategies for the Institutional Investor.* New York: McGraw-Hill.

Lee, S., and S. Stevenson. 2005. "The Case for REITs in the Mixed-Asset Portfolio in the Short and Long Run." *Journal of Real Estate Portfolio Management*, Vol. 11, No. 1: 55–67.

Lehman Brothers. 1999. "Global Relative Value." Fixed Income Research. New York.

Leibowitz, M., and A. Bova. 2005. "Allocation Betas." *Financial Analysts Journal*, Vol. 61, No. 4: 70–82.

Lett, T. 2005. "All Things in Good Measure." *Canadian Investment Review*, Summer: 22–24.

Lhabitant, F.-S. 2002. *Hedge Funds: Myths and Limits.* West Sussex, U.K.: John Wiley & Sons, Ltd.

Lhabitant, F.-S., and M. Learned. 2002. "Hedge Fund Diversification: How Much Is Enough?" *Journal of Alternative Investments*, Winter: 23–49.

Lindsay, I., and S. Arnott. 2005. "Currency: An Untapped Alpha Source." Goldman Sachs Asset Management Perspectives.

Linneman, P., and D. Moy. 2003. "Understanding the Return Profiles of Real Estate Investment Vehicles." *Wharton Real Estate Review*, Vol. 7, No. 2: 13–29.

Litterman, R. 2003. *Modern Investment Management: An Equilibrium Approach.* Hoboken, N.J.: John Wiley & Sons, Inc.

Marcato, G. 2004. "Style Analysis in Real Estate Markets and the Construction of Value and Growth Indexes." *Journal of Real Estate Portfolio Management*, Vol. 10, No. 3: 203–215.

Markowitz, H. 1991. *Portfolio Selection: Efficient Diversification of Investments,* 2nd ed. Malden, Mass.: Blackwell Publishing.

Matos, E. 2000. "Distressed Securities Investing." Tremont Capital Management. Rye, New York.

McDonald, L., and B. Stiver. 2004. "Institutional Real Estate—Investment Style Categories." RogersCasey.

Mills, K. Gordon. 2000. "LBO Returns in the United States: What Will It Take to Succeed in the New Era of LBOs?" In R. Lake and R. A. Lake (eds.), *Private Equity and Venture Capital: A Practical Guide for Investors and Practitioners.* London: Euromoney Books, pp. 261–273.

Montgomery, D., E. Peck, and G. Vining. 2001. *Introduction to Linear Regression Analysis, 3rd ed.* New York: John Wiley & Sons, Inc.

NAREIT. 2003. "The Investor's Guide to Real Estate Investment Trusts (REITs)." National Association of Real Estate Investment Trusts, Inc.

Nevins, D., A. Conner, and G. McIntire. 2004. "A Portfolio Management Approach to Determining Private Equity Commitments." *Journal of Alternative Investments*, Spring: 32–46.

Nicholas, J. 1999. *Investing in Hedge Funds—Strategies for the New Marketplace.* Princeton, N.J.: Bloomberg Press.

367

Parker Feld, K., D. R. Rich, and C. B. Steward. 2005. "Affordable Alpha: Active Currency Management in International Equity Portfolios." Wellington Management. Boston, Massachusetts.

Parker Reynolds, V. 2005. *Managing Hedge Fund Risk, 2nd ed.* London: Risk Books.

Peterson, S., and J. Grier. 2006. "Covariance Misspecification in Asset Allocation." *Financial Analysts Journal*, Vol. 62, No. 4: 76–85.

Private Equity Analyst. 2004. "Guide to the Secondary Market." Wellesley, Massachusetts.

Private Equity Analyst. 2004. *Private Equity Funds of Funds: State of the Market,* 3rd ed. Wellesley, Massachusetts.

Rasmussen, M. 2003. *Quantitative Portfolio Optimisation, Asset Allocation and Risk Management.* Hampshire, U.K.: Palgrave Macmillan.

The Rock Creek Group. 2004. "What Is the Appropriate Benchmark for Hedge Fund of Funds?" Washington, D.C.

Scherer, B. 2004. *Portfolio Construction and Risk Budgeting, 2nd ed.* London: Risk Books.

Schneeweis, T., H. Kazemi, and G. Martin. 2001. "Understanding Hedge Fund Performance: Research Results and Rules of Thumb for the Institutional Investor." Lehman Brothers. New York.

Schneeweis, T., and R. Spurgin. 1996. "Multi-Factor Models in Managed Futures: Hedge Fund and Mutual Fund Return Estimation." Draft paper. Amherst, Massachusetts.

Seitel, C. 2006. "Inside the Life Settlement Industry: An Institutional Investor's Perspective." *Journal of Structured Finance*, Summer: 38–40.

Sharpe, W. 1994. "Factor-Based Expected Returns, Risk and Correlations." In *Macro-Investment Analysis.* Electronic work in progress. Stanford University.

Shim, J. 2000. *Strategic Business Forecasting.* New York: St. Lucie Press.

Swensen, D. 2000. *Pioneering Portfolio Management: An Unconventional Approach to Institutional Investment.* New York: The Free Press.

Takahashi, D., and S. Alexander. 2002. "Illiquid Alternative Asset Fund Modeling." *Journal of Portfolio Management*, Winter: 90–100.

Terhaar, K., R. Staub, and B. Singer. 2003. "Appropriate Policy Allocation for Alternative Investments." *Journal of Portfolio Management*, Spring: 101–110.

Todd, P. 2002. "Asset Allocation: From the Perspective of an Institutional Investor." Gartmore Riverview, LLC. Rumson, New Jersey.

Urban Land Institute, and PricewaterhouseCoopers LLP. 2006. *Emerging Trends in Real Estate 2006.* Washington, D.C.: Urban Land Institute.

Wander, B., and D. Bein. 2002. "How to Incorporate Hedge Funds and Active Portfolio Management into an Asset Allocation Framework." Risk Management Perspectives. Analytic Investors, Inc. Los Angeles, California.

Waring, B., and L. Siegel. 2006. "The Myth of the Absolute-Return Investor." *Financial Analysts Journal*, Vol. 62, No. 2, March/April: 14–21.

Whipple, W. 2002. "The Real Estate Benchmarking and Liquidity Dilema." *PREA Quarterly*, Spring: 53–55.

Whipple, W. 2005. "Strategies for Pension Planners." *PREA Quarterly*, Fall: 48–54.

Winkelmann, K. 2004. "Improving Portfolio Efficiency." *Journal of Portfolio Management*, Winter: 23–38.

Wooldridge, J. 2006. *Introductory Econometrics: A Modern Approach*. Madison, Ohio: Thomson South-Western.

Zimmermann, H., W. Drobetz, and P. Oetmann. 2003. *Global Asset Allocation: New Methods and Applications*. Hoboken, N.J.: John Wiley & Sons, Inc.

Index